Professional Development for School Improvement

Empowering Learning Communities

Stephen P. Gordon

Texas State University-San Marcos

Boston • New York • San Francisco • Mexico City
Montreal • Toronto • London • Madrid • Munich • Paris
Hong Kong • Singapore • Tokyo • Cape Town • Sydney

This book is dedicated to my most valued colleague, my best friend, and my wife—Jovita

---

Senior Editor: *Arnis E. Burvikovs*
Series Editorial Assistant: *Christine Lyons*
Manufacturing Buyer: *Andrew Turso*
Senior Marketing Manager: *Tara Whorf*
Production Coordinator: *Pat Torelli Publishing Services*
Cover Designer: *Suzanne Harbison*
Editorial-Production Services: *TKM Productions*
Electronic Composition: *TKM Productions*

For related titles and support materials, visit our online catalog at www.ablongman.com.

Library of Congress Cataloging-in-Publication Data

Gordon, Stephen P.
Professional development for school improvement : empowering learning communities / Stephen P. Gordon.
p. cm.
Includes bibliographical references and index.
ISBN 0-205-26831-5
1. Teachers--In-service training. I. Title.

LB1731.G62 2004
370'.71'55—dc21 2003051822

Printed in the United States of America

10 9 8 7 6 5 4 3 2 07 06 05

Contents

PART II • *Frameworks for Professional Development* 29

First Foreword

Historical Context

This book on professional development as the essential vehicle for school improvement will, I believe, become a classic in the literature on instructional leadership. It is being published as a graduate-level text, but it should be on the desk of every educator aspiring to lead school improvement efforts in the next decade.

Those who know Steve Gordon's contribution to the *Handbook of Research on School Supervision* (Gordon & Nicely, 1998) will recognize his unusual ability to bring research, theory, and practice into alignment with each other, while avoiding narrow preconceptions, abstract meandering, and fad. From a historical perspective, this work fills an urgent need.

Professional staff development, known as in-service education until recent times, has had a hectic existence as a specialized professional discipline beginning in the early 1940s. The extensive period of teacher shortages, beginning with World War II and exacerbated by the baby boom, has continued into this new century. The perpetual use of unqualified or uncertified teachers has been both a stimulus to staff development and a source of confusion and conflict. The use of staff development for upgrading the least well-prepared teachers supported the misconception that it was only for those in trouble.

Despite the confusion and conflict, professional staff development still emerges as a major function of leadership for improving performance of all school personnel. Gordon's book emphasizes this perspective, building on the deep roots of the last half century.

One of the earliest works espousing staff development of administrators and supervisors as well as for teachers was the *1957 Yearbook of the National Society for the Study of Education* edited by Nelson B. Henry. The turbulent years of the 1960s continued to foment the importance and character of in-service professional development. During this decade, the National Science Foundation and the National Defense Education Act (1964) funded teacher institutes, while a rash of innovative new teaching programs— individuation, team teaching, programmed instruction, and so on—gave new status to staff development that could effectively impact teaching

In the 1970s, a broad array of staff-development delivery systems—from local to regional, from state to federal and associational—were formed. In addition, Gordon Lawrence and his colleagues (1974) in Florida completed the first really rigorous national study of the patterns of effective staff development. Out of these events emerged some unifying concepts, theoretical perspectives, and even some principles of good practice.

In the 1980s, research and evaluation studies became more numerous and systematic, producing a substantial knowledge base, reflected in publications by Harris (1980, 1989) stressing program design and applications. The *NSSE Yearbook on Staff Development* (1983) reported on numerous development and research projects from the Research and Development Center in Austin, Texas, the Far West Laboratory of Educational Development, and research centers at various universities. This expanding body of well-documented practice is updated and extended in this current work by Steve Gordon.

Despite the distractions in policy and practice related to teacher evaluation, site-based management, high-stakes testing, and accountability throughout the 1980s and 1990s, staff development continues to grow in public and in professional acceptance, and in sophistication of program design. Gordon's work is a synthesis of much that specialists in this field have come to know and practice. Despite countervailing trends, fads, and growing commercialization, staff development as conceptualized in this book is here to stay for one major reason: *It is the only known, reliable way of improving practice for all professionals in our schools to enhance learning.*

Ben M. Harris
M. K. Hage Centennial Professor
of Education, Emeritus
The University of Texas at Austin
The University of Texas–Pan American

References

Gordon, S. P., & Nicely, Jr., R. F. (1998). Supervision and staff development. In G. R. Firth & E. F. Pajak (Eds.), *Handbook of research on school supervision* (pp. 801–841). New York: Simon & Shuster Macmillan.

Griffin, G. A. (1983). Staff development. *82nd Yearbook, Part II. National Society for the Study of Education.* Chicago: The University of Chicago Press.

Harris, B. M. (1980). *Improving staff performance through in-service education.* Boston: Allyn and Bacon.

Harris, B. M. (1989). *In-service education for staff development.* Boston: Allyn and Bacon.

Henry, N. B. (Ed.). (1957). In-service education for teachers, supervisors, and administrators. *56th Yearbook, National Society for the Study of Education.* Chicago: The University of Chicago Press.

Lawrence, G., Baker, D., Elzie, P., & Hanson, B. (1974). *Patterns of effective in-service education.* Gainesville: University of Florida, College of Education.

Second Foreword

Professional Development and School Improvement

After reading *Professional Development for School Improvement*, one would be hard-pressed to find a single work on professional development that provides such a vast array of strategies, plans, methods, and inventories combined with specific case studies and challenging student assignments.

The nub of the book is the unshakable premise that staff-development programs such as reflective inquiry, action research, teacher leadership, and peer coaching are all vehicles to promote the intellectual and self-reflective development of teachers as they strive to achieve learning goals for students. In essence, a smart, respectful, and intellectually stimulating place for teachers creates the same type of teaching and learning environment for students.

Stephen Gordon has the focus right: Good professional development *is* school improvement. You can't get one without the other. Any use of staff development that doesn't aim at the collective educational priorities of the school robs students of all that they might achieve. Great schools that educate students well, with equity and excellence in mind, are the places where professionals work together in goal setting, study each other's classrooms, and assess student progress together. Professional development provides the ongoing learning opportunities to make a school's vision the reality of practice.

I know Steve Gordon well. He has been coauthor with me on another Allyn and Bacon text focused on instructional leadership, supervision, and school improvement. I have observed his career from school teacher, to state department leader of staff-development programs, to university faculty member. The growth, practicality, and focus of his work have evolved into this most comprehensive and practical treatment. *Professional Development for School Improvement* is highly readable, chock-full of excellent examples, with formats and surveys that can be used immediately in the real world of schools. This book will be the reader's friend for life, very useful upon the first reading and then a constant reference to the real life of school planning and implementation.

Carl D. Glickman
Roy F. and Joann Cole Mitte Endowed Chair in School Improvement
Southwest Texas State University-San Marcos

Preface

During the first class in a graduate course on professional development that I teach, I ask the students to do a two-part exercise. In the first part of the activity, small groups of students label sheets of newsprint "What Is." The students are asked to list under that heading words or short phrases that describe professional development programs in which they recently have participated. Nearly all of my students are either teachers or school administrators, and they have little difficulty in reaching consensus on characteristics of professional development as currently practiced. Invariably, the newsprint the students tape on the classroom walls has words and phrases like *boring*, *useless*, *irrelevant*, *one-size-fits-all*, and *top-down*. Sadly, the research on traditional professional development programs mirrors the negative terms of my students. Whether we have used the term *in-service training*, *in-service education*, *staff development*, or *professional development*, historically the process has not been popular with educators, nor has it been successful in improving schools.

In the second part of the activity, I ask the students to label new sheets of newsprint "What Should Be," and to list terms that describe their conception of an ideal professional development program. Although the precise language students use to describe their ideal program varies somewhat from group to group, again there is remarkable consistency across the groups. Phrases like *teachers involved in planning*, *relevant to classroom practice*, and *active learning* can be found on most or all students' lists. As with the students' descriptions of traditional professional development, their ideas on what makes for effective professional development are consistent with the research on effective programs. I tell the students toward the end of our first class that they already understand what makes up conventional, ineffective professional development programs, as well as characteristics of effective programs, and that our task for the rest of the semester is to explore ways to bridge the gap between what is and what should be.

One purpose of this book, like the course on professional development referred to above, is to consider ways to bridge the gap between the current and desired state of professional development in PK–12 schools. Another purpose is to link professional development to school improvement, and in particular to the improvement of teaching and learning. In order for *effective* professional development to be *successful* professional development, it must become a vehicle for school improvement, a means to the ultimate goal of student growth and development.

Part I of the book (Chapter 1) introduces a comprehensive model for professional development and school improvement, and discusses three themes that permeate that model and the text: the need to empower all members of the school community, the need to provide professional development consistent with the research on effective development programs, and the need to adhere to the principles of adult learning when facilitating the professional growth of educators. Part II of the book (Chapters 2 through 6) describes a variety of frameworks for professional development under the broad categories of training, collegial support, reflective inquiry, teacher leadership, and external support. Part III (Chapters 7 through 10) addresses capacity-building functions of professional development—functions that increase the ability of individuals, groups, and schools to affect student learning. Capacity-building functions include professional development for school leaders, improvement of school culture, team development, and individual teacher development. Part IV (Chapters 11 and 12) includes a discussion of the core function of professional development, the improvement of teaching and learning, as well as a model for program development.

An important point to be made at the outset is that this book provides only one of many frames for viewing professional development and school improvement. None of the frames presented in the literature—including the one presented on the following pages—is *the* correct frame for conceptualizing professional and school development. Readers are encouraged to seek a variety of views within the field, and to construct their own knowledge base, theory, and vision.

Acknowledgments

I first wish to thank the graduate students and school practitioners I have worked with over the last several years. Many of the ideas presented in this book result from collaborative inquiry and reflective dialogue with these colleagues. I am grateful for the camaraderie and support of the faculty in the Educational Administration Program at Texas State University-San Marcos: Dean John Beck, Acting Department Chair Mike Boone, Brenda Beatty, Carl Glickman, Marla McGhee, Larry Price, Marianne Reese, Charles Slater, and Duncan Waite. Many thanks to graduate assistants Jason Fink and Susan Maxey for their assistance in researching the literature and reviewing manuscript drafts. In particular, I am grateful to graduate assistant Jane Butters for her varied contributions during the development of the book. Jane's many hours of work on the project were above and beyond the call of duty, and her assistance has made this a better book. I also thank the following reviewers for their helpful comments on the manuscript: Mike Cunningham (Marshall University), Larry Hughes (University of Houston), Joyce E. Killian (Southern Illinois University), Sandra Lowery (Stephen F. Austin State University), David J. Parks (Virginia Tech), C. John Tartar (St. John's University), and Kathryn S. Whitaker (University of Northern Colorado).

To the Instructor

A typical semester calendar will allow the instructor to assign one chapter a week, with additional weeks available for introducing the course and for student presentations or exams. The instructor teaching on the semester system who wishes to divide the reading and discussion of some chapters across two weeks will find Chapters 10 and 11, the two longest chapters, most appropriate for such extensions. If the class meets on the quarter system, it is recommended that Chapters 2 and 3 as well as 6 and 7 be assigned during the same weeks. Assignments at the end of each chapter are intended as outside exercises, with final products in the form of short papers. A typical pattern of assignments would be to have students choose one assignment every few weeks, with three to five assignments across the entire term. A complete instructor's guide that includes discussion questions, group activities, and Powerpoint slides for this book is available on Allyn and Bacon's Supplements Central. This protected website can be accessed by contacting your sales representative.

Part I

Introduction

1 The Emerging Field of Professional Development

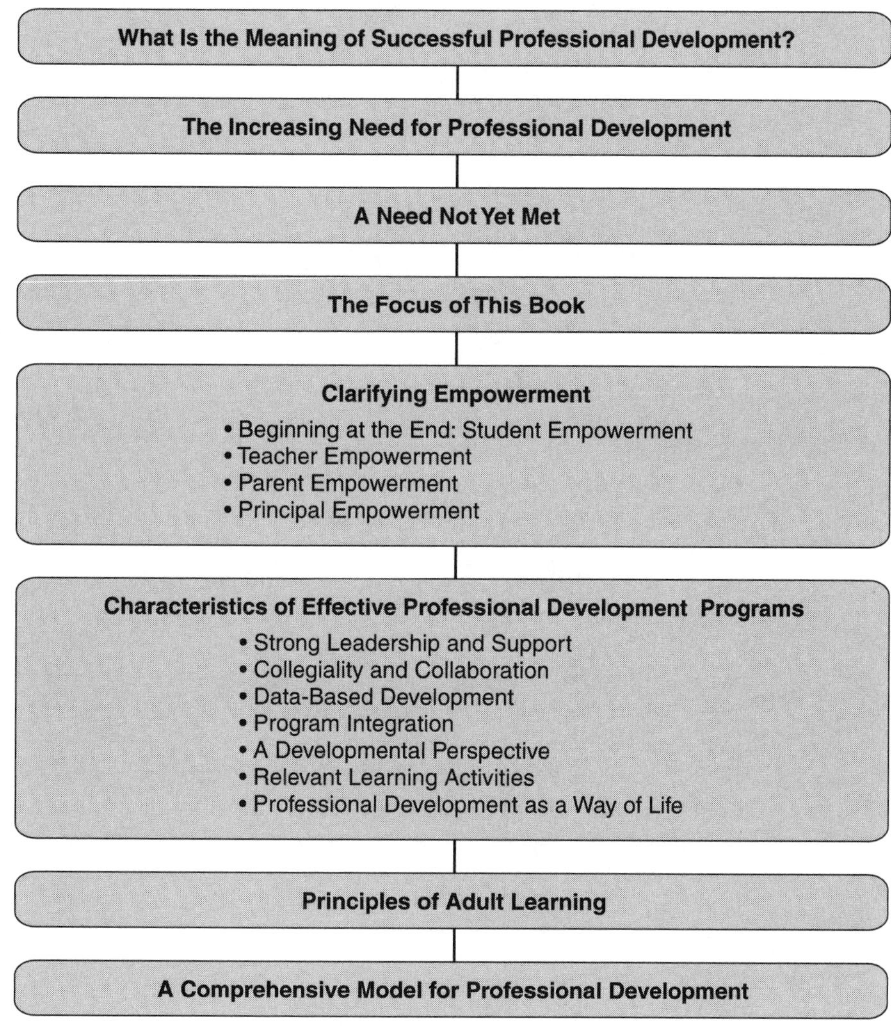

What Is the Meaning of Successful Professional Development?
The Increasing Need for Professional Development
A Need Not Yet Met
The Focus of This Book
Clarifying Empowerment
• Beginning at the End: Student Empowerment
• Teacher Empowerment
• Parent Empowerment
• Principal Empowerment
Characteristics of Effective Professional Development Programs
• Strong Leadership and Support
• Collegiality and Collaboration
• Data-Based Development
• Program Integration
• A Developmental Perspective
• Relevant Learning Activities
• Professional Development as a Way of Life
Principles of Adult Learning
A Comprehensive Model for Professional Development

Which of the following scenarios are examples of successful professional development?

Scenario A
Jill Evans, central office staff developer, is finishing up a morning lecture on effective teaching to the staff of Simpson High School. During her lecture, Evans has used the same outline of topics, handouts, and transparencies that were used by the presenters at a recent state department of education conference on effective teaching. She is surprised that 20 percent of the high school teaching staff have elected to take a personal day rather than attend the required in-service, since the research she is reviewing is the basis for the district's new teacher evaluation instrument. She is more than a little miffed at the fact that 10 percent or so of those present have been reading newspapers, correcting student papers, or doing needlepoint rather than paying attention to her presentation. However, the remaining teachers have been attentive and most of them have been taking notes and asking relevant questions throughout the session. This afternoon, George Jackson, assistant superintendent, will discuss the new evaluation instrument with the staff. Jill Evans is confident that the links between the effective teaching research that she has discussed and the new evaluation instrument will be clear to everyone by the end of the day.

Scenario B
Marty Osborne, superintendent of Boone School District, is beaming. For the first time in his five years as superintendent, teachers are leaving a districtwide in-service meeting with smiles on their faces. Thanks to a great deal of effort, not to mention a substantial speaker's fee, Osborne had been able to secure Jack Ramsey as the day's speaker. Ramsey had been an All-American football star in college and had gone on to become one of the winningest football coaches in collegiate history. Now retired from coaching, he has become a popular motivational speaker. Ramsey's forte is humor laced with the message of the need to maintain a positive attitude. He had been in rare form that morning. The teachers and administrators in the audience laughed so hard they barely could stay in their seats. Yet, at two different points in his speech, Jack Ramsey's stories of individuals who had overcome adversity brought many of those in the auditorium to tears. At the conclusion of his speech, Ramsey was given a five-minute standing ovation. The ratings of the in-service session would be the highest that Osborne had seen since he assumed the superintendency.

Scenario C
The teachers at Seifert Middle School brought a new idea to Principal Kurtz. During the upcoming staff-development day, why not let the teachers select their own professional-development experience, provided that they were engaged in productive activity for the school day? Kurtz agreed to the idea, with the stipulation that each teacher submit a one-page report

on what they did during the staff-development day and how they benefited professionally from the experience. On the day in question, teachers engaged in a variety of activities. The coaching staff met in a day-long planning session. Three teachers went to the district's media center to preview and borrow instructional materials for use over the next several weeks. Most of the teachers spent the day either at their homes or in their classrooms, grading papers, writing lesson plans, organizing materials, or creating bulletin boards. At the next faculty meeting, nearly every teacher in the school agreed that the day in question had been more worthwhile than any staff-development activity in memory.

The answer to the question, Which of the scenarios are examples of successful professional development? is None of the above! Each of the professional development efforts described in the scenarios falls far short of this chapter's definition of successful professional development. We'll return to our three scenarios in a moment. For now, let's take a look at the meaning of *successful professional development.*

What Is the Meaning of Successful Professional Development?

There are nearly as many definitions of *professional development* as there are authors who have written about the topic. I'll take a slightly different path by offering a definition of *successful* professional development, which includes a combination of experiences that empower (1) individual educators, (2) educational teams, and (3) the educational organization to improve (4) curriculum, (5) instruction, and (6) student assessment in order to (7) facilitate student growth and development. The first three elements in this definition (empowerment of individual educators, teams, and the organization) are concerned with *capacity building.* Capacity building does not directly affect student learning, but increases the ability of individuals, groups, and schools to affect student learning. The next three elements (improvement of curriculum, instruction, and student assessment) are *core elements* of professional development—they affect student learning directly. The seventh element, facilitating student growth and development, is the ultimate purpose of professional development.

We can begin to see now that none of the scenarios at the beginning of the chapter contain all elements of successful professional development. In Scenario A, Jill Evans attempted to transmit the state's model of effective teaching to a group of mostly passive (and some passively aggressive) teachers, a model that was going to be enforced by the new evaluation system. This is hardly the way to go about empowering teachers. Although the in-service may result in behavioral change once or twice a year when teachers are being observed by administrators using the new evaluation system, it will not result in any meaningful, lasting improvement in curriculum, teaching, or student assessment. The humorous, rousing speech of Jack Ramsey in Scenario B made everyone feel good, and may even raise the level of faculty motivation for a few days, but it does not address the real issues of empowerment or the difficult, unglamorous work of authentic professional development. As evidenced by the faculty in Scenario C, teachers need time to plan, gather resources, organize materials and classrooms, and grade student work; however, the provision of more unstructured time by itself will neither empower teachers nor improve curriculum, instruction, and student assessment.

It is an unfortunate state of affairs that much of what currently is practiced in schools under the guise of professional development can be placed in the same general category as the three scenarios: well meaning, of some short-term benefit to some teachers, but ultimately unsuccessful. However, there *are* professional development programs that can empower individual educators, teams, and organizations as well as improve curriculum, teaching, and assessment, and that can lead to student growth and development. The remainder of this text is dedicated to discussing possibilities for making authentic professional development a reality.

The Increasing Need for Professional Development

In this age of school reform, there is a growing consensus on what practices are needed to improve schools, teaching, and learning, yet attempts to implement these practices in schools often have failed. Consider the following examples:

- There is increasing agreement that teachers need to be involved in school governance (Glickman, Gordon, & Ross-Gordon, 2001). Yet, shared governance can lead to disjointed decisions (Meadows & Saltzman, 2002; Midgley & Wood, 1993), increased conflict, reinforcement of the status quo, pressure for short-term success at the expense of long-term improvement, discourse and debate rather than action (Glickman, Hayes, & Hensley, 1992; Meadows & Saltzman, 2002), teacher and principal disappointment and frustration, and, eventually, teacher withdrawal from participation in school governance. *Professional development is necessary to avoid such negative consequences and facilitate shared governance by helping stakeholders to develop a common vision as well as skills for shared decision making, planning, conflict management, data-based inquiry, and critical reflection.*
- Experts on school restructuring call for transformational leadership, in which school leaders foster a collaborative, professional culture, facilitate teacher development, and help teachers solve problems (Green & Etheridge, 2001; Leithwood, 1992; Sweetland, 2001; Wilmore & Thomas, 2001). Yet, in their preparation programs and careers, school leaders traditionally have focused on transactional leadership based on power, top-down decision making, and rewards controlled by the leader (Leithwood, 1992). *Professional development for school leaders is necessary to help them develop the communication, trust-building, collaborative, problem-solving, and facilitative skills needed for transformational leadership.*
- Knowledge of how students learn indicates the need for learning that is based on students' experiences and interests, is thematic and integrated, involves active participation, is collaborative, and allows students to construct their own meaning (Caine &

Caine, 1994, 1997; Citino, 2001; Kovalik & Olsen, 1994; Plucker & Slavkin, 2000). Yet, the typical classroom is teacher centered, with lessons dominated by teacher lectures, teacher questions requiring straight recall, and student seatwork. Student learning primarily is focused on repetition and memorization. All too often, teaching and learning in conventional classrooms is characterized by routine and boredom (Caine & Caine, 1997; de Souza Fleith, 2000; Sarason, 1996). *Professional development is needed to help teachers better understand how students learn, engage in critical analysis of their teaching, and make their teaching more student centered and meaningful so that they can enable students to become active participants, critical thinkers, and life-long learners.*

- We know that teachers in successful schools have developed a shared technical culture including common purpose, expertise, and methods for analyzing and solving curriculum and instructional problems. They are engaged in continuous dialogue about their teaching practice. They collaboratively research, design, experiment with, and improve curriculum and teaching (Glickman, Gordon, & Ross-Gordon, 2001; Rosenholtz, 1989). Yet, conventional schools are characterized by teacher isolation, a lack of teacher dialogue, little teacher involvement in schoolwide curriculum and instructional decisions, and the absence of a shared technical culture (Glickman, Gordon, & Ross-Gordon, 2001). *Professional development is needed to foster collegiality and professional dialogue, to help teachers develop a common educational purpose, and to facilitate collaborative planning, experimentation, and critique of teaching practice.*

- Although not all change leads to school improvement, school improvement does not take place without change. Yet, the conventional school culture tends to be resistant to *any* meaningful change, because significant change by its very nature threatens assumptions, values, norms, roles, and relationships that are part of the culture. *Professional development can assist educators to identify and critically examine aspects of a school's culture that are inconsistent with the empowerment of students as life-long learners, and can lead to both cultural change and changes in curriculum, instruction, and student assessment. Professional development can help transform schools into what Roland Barth (2000) describes as a "community of learners, a culture of adaptability, and a place of continous experimentation and invention" (p. 69).*

These five areas—shared governance, transformational leadership, student-centered teaching, teacher collegiality, and cultural change—are a few critical aspects of school improvement that call for professional development. But we can go beyond these examples; it can be argued that *any* significant attempt at school improvement will have a greater chance of success if it is integrated with effective professional development. Hopkins, Ainscow, and West (1994) assert that "staff development is inextricably linked to school development" (p. 113). Fullan (1991) states, "There is no single strategy that can contribute more to meaning and improvement than ongoing professional development" (p. 318). In an era when leaders at the national and state levels as well as the general public are insisting that schools improve—in the face of repeated failures to bring that improvement about through bureaucratic control—policymakers and educational leaders are recognizing the need for professional development as the cornerstone of future reform efforts.

A Need Not Yet Met

Although the need for professional development is apparent to those who study school improvement, effective professional development is *not* taking place in most schools. The current state of professional development is aptly described by Miles (1995):

> A good deal of what passes for "professional development" in schools is a joke—one that we'd laugh at if we weren't trying to keep from crying. It's everything that a learning environment shouldn't be: radically undersourced, brief, not sustained, designed for "one size fits all," imposed rather than owned, lacking any intellectual coherence, treated as a special add-on event rather than as part of a natural process, and trapped in the constraints of the bureaucratic system we have come to call "school." In short, it's pedagogically naive, a demeaning exercise that often leaves its participants more cynical and no more knowledgeable, skilled, or committed than before. (p. vii)

Fullan's (1991) review of research supports Miles's dismal picture of typical efforts at professional development. He found that such efforts fail for the following reasons:

- The extensive use of one-shot workshops, which are ineffective
- Topics that are selected by nonparticipants
- A lack of follow-up following the introduction of new concepts and practices
- Failure to evaluate programs
- Failure to address individual needs and concerns
- District and multidistrict programs that do not address factors within individual schools
- Absence of a conceptual basis for program planning and implementation

My own observations support the conclusions of Miles and Fullan. I would add to their program factors the following contextual factors in the failure of traditional professional development efforts:

- A failure of university preparation programs to expose either preservice teachers or preservice school administrators to the knowledge base on professional development

- A failure of the general public to recognize the value of professional development in PK–12 education, and thus a lack of public support for providing the resources necessary for quality professional development

- Conventional school cultures that are resistant to professional development because of the threat of change inherent in authentic development, resulting in superficial activities with no potential for bringing about meaningful change

Although the track record of professional development in schools has not been a good one, there is hope for the future. This hope is based on two premises. First, one can predict with a reasonable degree of confidence that the pressure for school improvement being experienced by policymakers and educational leaders will cause them to move beyond rhetoric and to commit the resources necessary to make quality professional development an essential aspect of school improvement. Second, despite the historical failure of professional development in PK–12 schools, there now exists a variety of successful professional development programs that not only share common characteristics but also reveal clearly the connection between professional development and school improvement. We'll discuss characteristics of effective programs later in this chapter, and examine specific examples of effective programs throughout the text.

The Focus of This Book

Because the term *professional development* means different things to different people, it's necessary to let you know what aspects of professional development will be addressed in this book. I'll do this by setting up some parameters, with content inside those parameters the focus of the text, and content outside of the parameters considered to be beyond its scope. Parameter 1 relates to the *professional development continuum*. This continuum begins with the recruitment of promising individuals into professional preparation programs. It continues with preservice preparation. Next comes hiring and placement, followed by an induction phase. The final phase of the continuum is continuing professional development, which should last for the remainder of the educator's career. An illustration of the professional development continuum follows:

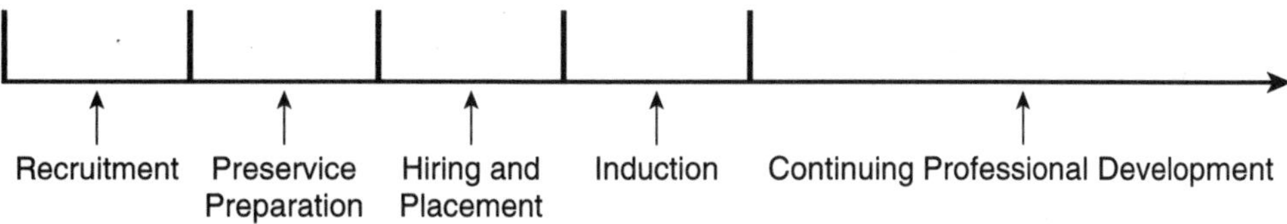

I am a strong proponent of the proposition that each phase of the continuum is critical. However, this book will focus only on the last two phases of the continuum. Parameter 1, then, is that this text is concerned with the professional development of *in-service educators*.

Parameter 2 is that professional development always will be discussed in this book with an eye toward *school improvement*. As you may already have inferred, my position is that professional development and school improvement are two sides of the same coin; professional development is the most critical dimension of school improvement!

Parameter 3 is that this text is concerned with *school-focused* professional development. Traditionally, staff development has been led, planned, and delivered at the district level, but focused on the individual. With the trend toward school-based management has come a corresponding trend toward school-based professional development. Both trends are based on the increasingly accepted belief that the school, rather than the district (too large a unit) or the individual (too small a unit), is the most appropriate unit of change. I agree with this proposition but prefer the term *school-focused* rather than *school-based* professional development. School-focused development can be delivered at any level (individual, school, district) provided that its purpose is improvement at the school level (Georgia State Department of Education, 1990).

Parameter 4 is that this book is concerned with professional development that facilitates *empowerment*. The word has been overused, but if it is properly conceptualized, it remains the best word for conveying the spirit of this text. It will, however, be necessary to clarify the meaning of empowerment, a task that we will take on later in this chapter.

Parameter 5 is that this book primarily is concerned with *intentional professional development* as opposed to serendipitous development. It is possible for an educator to grow professionally through unplanned trial and error in the classroom, casual conversations with other teachers at the copy machine, or reflection during one's morning shower! We should acknowledge and celebrate such serendipitous growth. The focus of this text, however, is on intentional efforts to facilitate the empowerment of individual educators, teams, and organizations and the improvement of curriculum, instruction, and student assessment with the ultimate purpose of improved student learning. Figure 1.1 illustrates the five parameters, with the area inside those parameters representing the focus of the text. There are many aspects of professional development outside of the parameters depicted in Figure 1.1. I am not saying that those areas are unimportant, but only that they are beyond the scope of this book.

The next three sections of this chapter will discuss themes that will permeate the text: empowerment, characteristics of effective professional development programs, and principles of adult learning.

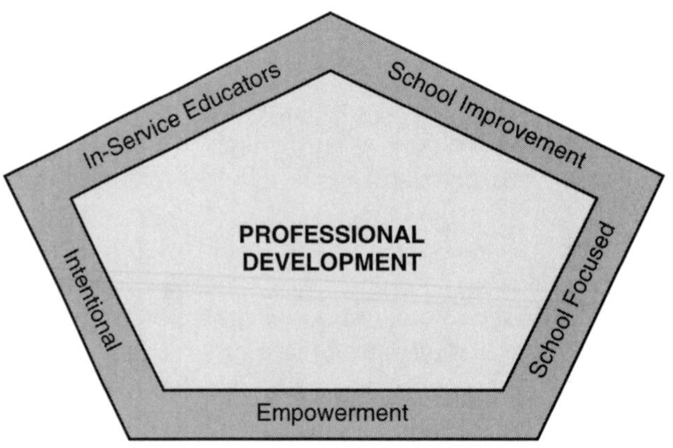

FIGURE 1.1 Focus of the Text

Clarifying Empowerment

The word *empowerment* has been claimed by both liberals and conservatives. It has been misused, abused, and overused. Yet, it remains a powerful concept in education and professional development. Because empowerment is a theme throughout this text, I need to clarify its meaning before proceeding further. Empowerment has been assigned myriad definitions. To name a few, it has been defined as "the ability to confront oppression," "a sense of efficacy," "a positive identity," "autonomy," "participation in decision making," "motivation," and "recognizing and maximizing inherent strengths." The general meaning of *empowerment* in this text is enablement for life-long learning, teaching, and leadership, although more detailed explanations are required for different groups of stakeholders within the school community. Let's further consider empowerment as it is used in this book by asking and answering a series of questions:

Q: Who should become empowered?

A: *All members of the school community!* This population includes, but is not limited to, principals, teachers, parents, and students. Although the ultimate purpose is student empowerment, this is most likely to be realized if the other members of the school community are themselves empowered.

Q: How does empowerment take place?

A: It will take the rest of this book to answer this question, but for now, let's say that it is not possible for you or me to empower another. Rather, we can only foster conditions that will facilitate others to empower themselves (Rallis & Goldring, 2000). Sandra Stone (1995) talks about building foundations for empowerment by respecting, validating the worth of, and focusing on the success of those we wish to become empowered. Stone proposes that members of the school community can further be empowered by a sense of ownership of their environment, the freedom to make choices, autonomy in setting and meeting goals, and making meaningful decisions.

Q: What happens to those who become empowered?

A: Stone (1995) notes that those who become empowered exhibit more intrinsic motivation, responsibility, independence, risk taking, collaboration, and self-evaluation. All of these behaviors in turn allow individuals and communities to grow and develop. Moreover, they are all consistent with the values of a democratic society.

Now that a general overview of empowerment has been provided, we can discuss the empowerment of specific groups within the school community: students, teachers, parents, and principals.

Beginning at the End: Student Empowerment

Why student empowerment? Lincoln (1995) presents three reasons for empowering students: the social-legal, the scientific, and the political. The social-legal view of children, increasingly reflected in civil rights mandates, has evolved to a point where the empowerment of children is becoming a societal norm. Children are now viewed "as both the inheritors and the inheritance of the future... as repositories of hope and change" (p. 88). Within the scientific context, medical and social science research has discovered that children learn best through actively participating in and constructing their own views of their social world. Enabling students to engage in participatory, constructive learning leads to their personal and social empowerment. Regarding the political context, if one purpose of education is to prepare citizens to participate in the democratic process, then it is necessary to empower students for such participation. Lincoln (1995) notes that traditional schooling in the United States has not been consistent with its avowed purpose:

> We have retrofitted children to the presumed roles they would occupy as adults, including fueling the Industrial Revolution and the management revolution. We have assigned them to social statuses that relate only to race, economic status, or gender, rather than to explored "intelligences." In the case of some children, we have simply written them off. In an emerging political context, we are beginning to understand that the support of a democratic, just, and economically viable and prosperous society requires active participation and critical thinking skills far beyond what many of our students experience in school. (p. 89)*

To Lincoln's three arguments, I would add a fourth: *the moral argument*. If society truly believes that all persons are created equal and are entitled to life, liberty, and the pursuit of happiness, then it becomes the moral responsibility of educators to facilitate student empowerment toward those ends. Moreover, educators have a moral responsibility to go the extra mile to enable those who are currently disempowered because of race, ethniticity, social status, gender, disability, or personal circumstances.

Empowerment was defined as enabling life-long learning, teaching, and leadership. How does this definition apply to student empowerment? Student *empowerment for life-long learning* includes enablement for emotional, cognitive, physical, social, and moral development. These different types of student growth are so interrelated that one cannot be separated from the others. Thus, true empowerment to learn enables the growth and development of the whole student.

Empowerment to teach means enabling students to facilitate each other's development. This aspect of student empowerment is based on the fact that humans are social beings and often experience their most significant growth through collaborative learning. Also, empowering students to teach each other is congruent with the moral imperative that humans assist one another to learn and grow.

Finally, *empowerment to lead* includes enabling students to engage in individual and collaborative leadership at the classroom, school, and eventually community and societal levels. Not all students of all ages can be leaders in all situations, but each student can be a leader in *some* situations, and all students should be empowered to participate in the collective leadership that democracy entails.

*Yvonna S. Lincoln, "In Search of Student Voices," *Theory Into Practice, 34*(2), 88–93. From a theme issue on Learning from Student Voices. Reprinted by permission of Yvonna S. Lincoln.

What conditions are present in schools where students are provided opportunities for empowerment? Short and Greer (1993) have studied schools that were successful in fostering student empowerment. They found that these schools were student centered and created opportunities for student personal control and the development of self-efficacy. The empowering schools also displayed flexibility and resourcefulness in meeting student needs, and created environments that suported student risk taking and experimentation.

Empowering schools ultimately are concerned with student empowerment. As a means to that end, however, such schools are concerned with empowering *all* members of the school community, including teachers, parents, and principals.

Teacher Empowerment

Teacher empowerment has been defined in various ways. Browder (1994) defines it as "any activity or means that enhances the professional status of teachers" (p. 137). Teacher empowerment has also been defined by various authors as teacher enablement, liberation, autonomy, impact, leadership, power, authority, responsibility, self-esteem, self-efficacy, professional growth, and teacher participation in school governance, site-based management, and school restructuring (see Gideon & Erlandson, 2001; Shen, 2001; Speck & Knipe, 2001). Short and Rinehart (1992) asked over 200 teachers what made them feel empowered. The study identified six dimensions of empowerment: decision making, professional growth, status, self-efficacy, autonomy, and impact.

My conception of teacher empowerment is tied directly to the definition of student empowerment proposed earlier—it involves enabling teachers for life-long learning, teaching, and leadership. Teachers need to be *empowered learners*. If teachers are expected to facilitate holistic student learning, then the school needs to be a place that enables continued emotional, cognitive, social, and moral development of teachers themselves.

Empowerment to teach certainly includes teachers' pedagogical development, but it also means enabling teachers to facilitate the development of other adults within the school community. Teachers in successful schools foster each other's growth by engaging in professional dialogue, helping each other to develop and test curriculum materials, teaching each other new teaching methods, and critiquing each other's teaching (Lambert, 2002; Little, 1982; Pajak & Glickman, 1989).

Empowerment to lead includes developing skills for both classroom and school leadership. There are a variety of specific leadership roles consistent with individual interests and abilities that teachers can assume. Additionally, all teachers ought to be prepared and encouraged to participate in school governance, including schoolwide decisions about curriculum, instruction, and student assessment.

How is teacher empowerment actualized? Wilson and Coolican (1996) maintain that empowerment can be fostered through changes in the school culture that "enhance meaningfulness, a sense of competence, and self-determination" (p. 113). Based on her ethnographic study of 40 elementary and middle school teachers and their administrators, Melenyzer (1991) concludes that cultural norms, social practices and knowledge, and enabling leadership all work together to promote and sustain teacher empowerment. Other authors have proposed specific skills that teachers need to develop as part of the empowerment process. After studying teacher empowerment in over 180 restructuring schools, Klecker and Loadman (1996) conclude that teachers need to be provided with experience and skill development in information gathering, information synthesis, group process, consensus building, and communication. My own belief is that transformational leadership, cultural norms, and skill development *all* contribute to teacher empowerment. When all three of these factors are present, optimal conditions exist for empowerment to become a reality.

Parent Empowerment

One view of empowerment holds that teacher enablement and parent enablement are conflicting goals; empowering one of those two groups tends to further disempower the other. Since I don't accept the concept of empowerment as a "zero-sum game," I generally disagree with this view. However, I do believe that *if a school works to enable only one of those two groups, then further disempowering of the other group becomes a real possibility.* It is parents who most often are left out of school empowerment efforts. Enabling teachers without also enabling parents can lead to conflict between the two groups and lessen overall school effectiveness (Goldring & Bauch, 1994; Hargreaves, 2001; Million, 2001; Sparks, 2001). Disempowered parents make poor educational partners! Conversely, empowered parents can contribute to school improvement and increased academic achievement (Dodd & Konzal, 2000; Riley, 1994).

Parent empowerment, like student and teacher empowerment, includes empowerment to learn, teach, and lead. To become *empowered learners*, parents need to develop or enhance knowledge of child development in general and their children's learning needs, interests, abilities, and learning styles. They also need to become familiar with the school's curriculum as well as teaching and assessment strategies used in their children's classroom. This type of learning is only possible through ongoing communication among parents, teachers, and students.

Empowerment to teach takes place when parents become full partners in the education of their children. This mean that parents are involved in the diagnosis of their children's learning needs, preparation for and extension of classroom learning, and assessment of their children's growth.

Empowerment to lead means that parents are prepared and encouraged to participate in decision making regarding the school's curriculum, instruction, and student assessment. Riley (1994) calls this type of enablement *parent as advocate* and maintains that schools are less comfortable with this than with more traditional types of involvement such as assisting with homework, monitoring their child's achievement, and volunteering at school. Riley recommends three dimensions of successful movement toward a more balanced home-school partnership. First, school leadership shifts from a position of power over people to a position where power is shared. Second, parents, teachers, and administrators must be reeducated concerning their educational roles. Parents must be provided the information necessary to effectively participate in school decision making. Teachers must learn to listen to parents and to use the information provided by parents to respond to students' needs. Administrators need to be enabled to challenge traditional power relationships and to become transformational leaders. Third, parents and educators need to examine issues of equity and conditions of bias, acknowledging early on that equal treatment of students is not necessarily the same as equitable treatment.

My own experiences are consistent with Riley's view. Many teachers I have worked with have been very excited about the concept of teacher empowerment but less than enthusiastic about the notion of parent empowerment. Teacher professional development on the need to empower parents thus may be a prerequisite for parent empowerment. What was said earlier about students who are disempowered by race, ethnicity, social status, and so on, applies equally to parents and guardians: Schools have a moral responsibility to make special efforts to empower those who traditionally have been marginalized.

Principal Empowerment

Discussions of empowerment among educators seldom have focused on principal empowerment (McCay, 2001). After all, isn't it the principal who has the power of which students, teachers, and parents are trying to get a piece? My own work with principals indicates that many principals are, in fact, *disempowered.* Most principals spend a great deal of each workday dealing with student discipline, parental complaints, personnel issues, and bureaucratic paperwork. This is hardly the agenda of a transformational leader! Additionally, many principals continuously are caught between several rocks and a hard place, constantly being buffeted by conflicting expectations of students, teachers, parents, and central office administrators. One principal in a school district that I visit regularly stated that, for him, the biggest difference between being a teacher and being a principal was the loss of control over his work-life. This sense of being rudderless, of moving from crisis to crisis, of being overwhelmed by a sea of external expectations and administrivia, is quite common among administrators, and quite the opposite of the sense of empowerment that principals need to possess if they are to facilitate the empowerment of other members of the school community. If student empowerment is the end point, then in many schools principal empowerment needs to become the entry point in the empowerment process. Like students, teachers, and parents, principals can be empowered as learners, teachers, and leaders.

Principal *empowerment to learn* means enabling the principal's emotional, cognitive, social, and moral development. Part of this empowerment involves breaking down false assumptions that school leaders have finished needed growth and development, or that principals cannot afford to take the time to engage in new learning. Indeed, an empowered principal realizes that he or she cannot afford *not* to engage in continuous learning. To empower principals as learners means shifting the principalship from a management mode to an inquiry mode.

Principal *empowerment to teach* means returning to the concept of the principal as the *principal teacher.* Empowering principals as teachers means enabling them to create what Silins (1994) calls *intellectual stimulation*, defined as "the degree to which the leader provides intellectual and problem-oriented guidance. The leader arouses followers to think in new ways.... Followers are encouraged to question their own and other's assumptions, beliefs and values, and develop independent problem-solving capabilities" (p. 268).

Principal *empowerment to lead* means enablement for transformational leadership. This involves developing or enhancing a wide range of leadership skills not emphasized in conventional preservice or in-service principal development programs. These include communication, trust-building, entrepreneurial, collaborative, problem-solving, group process, and facilitative skills. Empowerment to lead also means developing or enhancing personal characteristics like those described by Blase and Blase (1994): optimism, caring, honesty, friendliness, and enthusiasm. Finally, empowerment for transformational leadership means developing particular values, including collegiality, democracy, innovation, experimentation, risk taking, critical reflection, and teacher autonomy (Blase & Blase, 1994; Conzemius, 2000; DuFour, 2001).

Empowerment of principals as learners, teachers, and transformational leaders will require a major paradigm shift for all members of the educational community. It also will require a great deal of professional development for principals—not a high priority in most school systems. Finally, it will require a restructuring of the principalship so that principals are provided incentives, support, and rewards for engaging in career-long learning, teaching, and transformational leadership.

This section has provided only a brief overview of the meaning of empowerment. Subsequent chapters will paint an increasingly detailed picture of empowering schools and the role of professional development in such schools. For now, let's turn our attention to the characteristics of effective professional development programs, which can be the primary vehicle for empowerment.

Characteristics of Effective Professional Development Programs

Over the last several years I have carried out a national study on outstanding school-focused professional development programs. The methodology and detailed results of this study are reported elsewhere (Gordon, 2000). All of the "exemplars" of effective professional development presented in this text are programs in schools that participated in the national study. In the study, I found that, even though each of the professional development programs had a different focus, the programs had several common characteristics. These characteristics are similar to those identified in a long line of research and literature on effective professional development (Birman, Desimone, Porter, & Garet, 2000; Boyer, Crowther, Fast, Kasselman, Nolte, & Wilson, 1993; Gordon & Nicely, 1998; Guskey, 1995; Norton, 2001; Richardson, 2000; Sparks & Hirsh, 2000; Wood & Thompson, 1993). The characteristics are strong leadership and support, collegiality and collaboration, data-based development, program integration, a developmental perspective, relevant learning activities, and professional development as "a way of life."

Strong Leadership and Support

Professional development requires strong leadership. This leadership usually comes from the principal, but it is sometimes provided by an assistant principal, a teacher or group of teachers, or a staff developer from the district's central office. If the leadership begins with an administrator or staff developer, efforts are made to involve teachers in leadership early on and to increase teacher leadership over time. Leaders establish an atmosphere of support and trust, offer incentives and rewards for participation, and provide sustained moral and material support. Leaders also encourage and reward teacher experimentation and risk taking. Finally, leaders serve as role models by participating fully in professional development activities

Collegiality and Collaboration

In effective professional development, teachers, staff developers, and administrators are considered equals, and they collaborate on all phases of program development. Teachers are involved in program planning and delivery. Schools form collaborative partnerships with other schools, universities, businesses, and critical friends. Also, there is cooperation and coordination between the school and the central office. Ordinarily, a central office administrator or staff developer is assigned the task of supporting the school's professional development program.

Data-Based Development

Effective professional development programs begin with gathering and analyzing a variety of needs assessment data. As programs are planned and implemented, participants continue to gather data as a basis for continuous program improvement. Many data are gathered at the classroom level, then shared and analyzed at the team and school levels. Comprehensive program evaluations are conducted periodically and serve as the basis for program improvement. Teachers are involved in planning program evaluations, gathering and analyzing evaluation data, and making necessary program revisions.

Program Integration

Integration in effective professional development programs occurs on several levels. Schoolwide professional development goals and school improvement goals are integrated. Individual, team, school, and district goals are integrated. Also, new professional development programs are integrated with existing programs.

A Developmental Perspective

Effective professional development programs are characterized by long-range planning and development. Participants take an incremental approach. The most essential and attainable goals are addressed first, with the program evolving over time toward increasing complexity. Continuous improvement is the aim of even the most comprehensive programs. The principles of change theory are taken seriously. Like Fullan (1991), participants see professional development as a process, not an event; professional development is ongoing. There is a realization that within the change process particular teachers have different levels of concern and expertise, and hence require different types of information and assistance. As teachers develop new skills and strategies, a variety of follow-up activities are provided to implement and sustain desired change.

Relevant Learning Activities

In effective programs, many or most learning activities take place at the school site. Activities that take place at other sites are focused on the school's improvement goals. Differentiated learning activities meet individual or small-group needs. Learning activities are participatory and experiential. Usually, learning can be applied immediately at the classroom or school level. Learning activities are consistent with the principles of adult learning (these principles will be discussed in the next section).

Professional Development as a Way of Life

It is interesting that most of the professional development activities in the programs that I have examined are voluntary. Yet, attendance at professional development in all of these schools is exceedingly high. One reason for this high rate of participation is what can be called *peer norms of participation*, norms among teachers that they have an obligation to attend professional development activities that have a strong potential to improve teaching and learning. Since the teachers in these schools participate in the planning and delivery of professional development programs, it's only natural that they would consider the programs to be worthwhile! Indeed, teachers in these schools consider continuous professional development to be absolutely essential to their professional growth and the improvement of teaching. They describe professional development as a "way of life" in their schools—a way of life that they never want to give up.

The characteristics of effective professional development programs will be addressed more fully at various points throughout the text. For now, let's examine in detail one characteristic that, despite its powerful potential, staff developers have paid little attention to over the years: accommodation to the principles of adult learning.

Principles of Adult Learning

Since professional development is a form of adult learning, it makes sense to examine principles of adult learning as part of our discussion of effective professional development programs. Despite their obvious relationship, research on professional development in schools and studies on adult learning have for the most part been carried out by different researchers and reported in separate bodies of literature (a notable exception is the 1989 book *Promoting Adult Growth in Schools* by Sara Levine). Different researchers and writers have proposed principles of adult learning (Caffarella & Barnett, 1994; Guglielmino, 1993; Knowles, 1980; Kroth & Boverie, 2000; Merriam, 2001; Merriam & Caffarella, 1999; Zemke & Zemke, 1995). Although the specific principles listed by various experts are not identical, there is substantial support in the literature for all of the principles discussed below. In addition to reviewing these general principles, we'll also discuss how each principle can be applied to professional development in schools.

- *Adults are motivated to learn when the learning will meet a need or interest they are experiencing in their personal or work lives.* For professional development, this principle supports conducting formal and informal needs assessments and designing professional development programs around identified needs. It also calls for relating learning activities to educators' experiences, problems, or concerns. Finally, it means providing opportunities and support for immediate application of learning at the classroom or school level.
- *Adults bring considerable life experience and prior knowledge to the learning situation.* This principle has numerous implications for professional development in schools. First, schools should take advantage of educators' life experiences and prior knowledge by inviting them to participate in the design, implementation, and assessment of professional development programs. Second, educators should be encouraged to reflect on their experiences and knowledge. Third, during learning activities, educators should be invited to share their experiences and knowledge, in order to have that knowledge and experience affirmed as well as to facilitate others' learning. Fourth, opportunities should be provided for educators to assimilate new learning by integrating it with past experiences and prior knowledge.
- *Adults learn best when they are actively involved in the learning process.* As noted by Zemke and Zemke (1995), "Most adults aren't used to sitting passively for long stretches. Without activity, they turn into mushrooms before your eyes" (p. 40). For professional development, this means that lectures and other methods associated with passive learning must be kept to a minimum. Training programs need to include active learning strategies such as discussion groups, collaborative projects, brainstorming, role playing, case studies, micro-teaching, problem-based learning, and simulations. Moreover, professional development needs to move beyond training sessions to field-based activities such as curriculum development, instructional design, team teaching, improvement of student assessment, action research, peer coaching, and reflective writing.
- *Adults have widely varying learning styles.* Various learning style models emphasize differences in adults' cognitive structure, motivational needs, sociological needs, perceptual modes, and thought processing. Chapter 10 includes a discussion of adult learning styles and implications for teacher development. For now, let's focus on some broad implications for professional development. One implication is that staff developers need to offer educators a variety of learning activities so that different learning styles are accommodated on a regular basis. A second implication is that professional development programs need to provide opportunities for participants to "stretch themselves" and broaden their learning styles by becoming comfortable and successful with new ways of learning.

- *As adults develop personally and professionally, they have an increasing need to be self-directed.* Guglielmino (1993) notes that programs that have provided teachers with opportunities to direct their own professional development have had mixed results, with some teachers experiencing high levels of enthusiasm and success, and others unable to participate effectively in self-directed learning. She goes on to discuss how these apparently contradictory results are actually quite understandable:

  > For years, formalized programs of teacher development have been primarily other-directed. Teachers have been told what the topics will be, when they will report, what they will do, and how long they will stay. When we suddenly change the rules and ask them to prepare a goal statement and plan their own self-development, some will seize the opportunity immediately, but many others will need some transition to adjust their thinking and begin to see their role in a new light. As they hone their skills of analysis and planning for their own learning and begin to realize some of the benefits, their enthusiasm and expertise grow. (p. 232)

  Teachers thus have different *entry points* on the path to empowerment. Some may initially need more structure, more direction, or more assistance than others. But the directionality of professional development ought to be toward increasing teacher autonomy, with the staff developer gradually shifting to a role of facilitator and resource provider.
- *Adult learners have affiliation needs.* Caffarella and Barnett (1994) define *affiliation needs* as "the desire for learners to be connected and supportive of each other's learning" (p. 32). They note that this aspect of adult learning has received increasing attention in recent years. This principle should not be viewed as conflicting with adults' increasing need to be self-directive. Mature adult learners are both autonomous *and* collaborative. Applied to professional development, this principle supports such concepts as collective goals, cooperative learning, collaborative inquiry, collegial support groups, and peer coaching.

One observation that many PK–12 educators make when reviewing principles of adult learning is that these principles apply to children as well, hence they should be called principles of *learning* rather than *adult learning*. Indeed, it may be more accurate to view the difference between adult learning and children's learning as a matter of degree rather than a dichotomy (Knowles, 1980). For example, like adults, children bring life experiences and prior knowledge to the learning situation. However, adults have *more* life experiences and *more* prior knowledge than do children, hence they have more to contribute to the learning process and a more complex task of assimilating new learning with old learning than do children. For another example, both children and adults have different learning styles, but because adults have had more roles and experiences than children, their learning styles are even more varied from one another than are children's learning styles. For a final example, although children move toward an increasing need for self-direction as they mature, most adults, who have had more time and opportunity to mature, have moved much further along the continuum from other-directed toward self-directed.

Regardless of the extent to which the principles of adult learning also apply to children, one must admit that conventional schools have not applied these principles to their own professional development programs! It seems that one thing that may be said with confidence is that it is time for educators to take the principles of adult learning seriously and to design professional development programs consistent with those principles.

A Comprehensive Model for Professional Development

As we review the various aspects of empowerment, the characteristics of effective professional development, and the principles of adult learning discussed in this chapter, a remarkable consistency among these three areas becomes apparent. All three areas support a dual emphasis on individual and collective development, shared decision making, active involvement in the growth process, collaborative inquiry, movement toward autonomy, and facilitative rather than controlling leadership. Empowerment, characteristics of effective professional development, and principles of adult learning are three themes that recur throughout this text. They form the outer band of a comprehensive model for professional development. Let's take a look at the other components of this model, shown in Figure 1.2.

Part II of this book, *Frameworks for Professional Development* (listed in the second band from the outside in Figure 1.2), consists of the following:

- *Training* (Chapter 2)
- *Collegial Support Frameworks*, including peer coaching, collaborative work teams, and co-teaching (Chapter 3)
- *Reflective Inquiry Frameworks*, including study groups, action research, and reflective writing (Chapter 4)
- *Teacher Leadership* (Chapter 5)
- *External Support Frameworks*, including partnerships, networks, and teacher centers (Chapter 6)

Part III is entitled *Capacity-Building Functions of Professional Development*. These functions (listed in the third band from the outside in Figure 1.2) are:

- *School Leader Development* (Chapter 7)
- *Improvement of School Culture* (Chapter 8)
- *Team Development* (Chapter 9)
- *Individual Teacher Development* (Chapter 10)

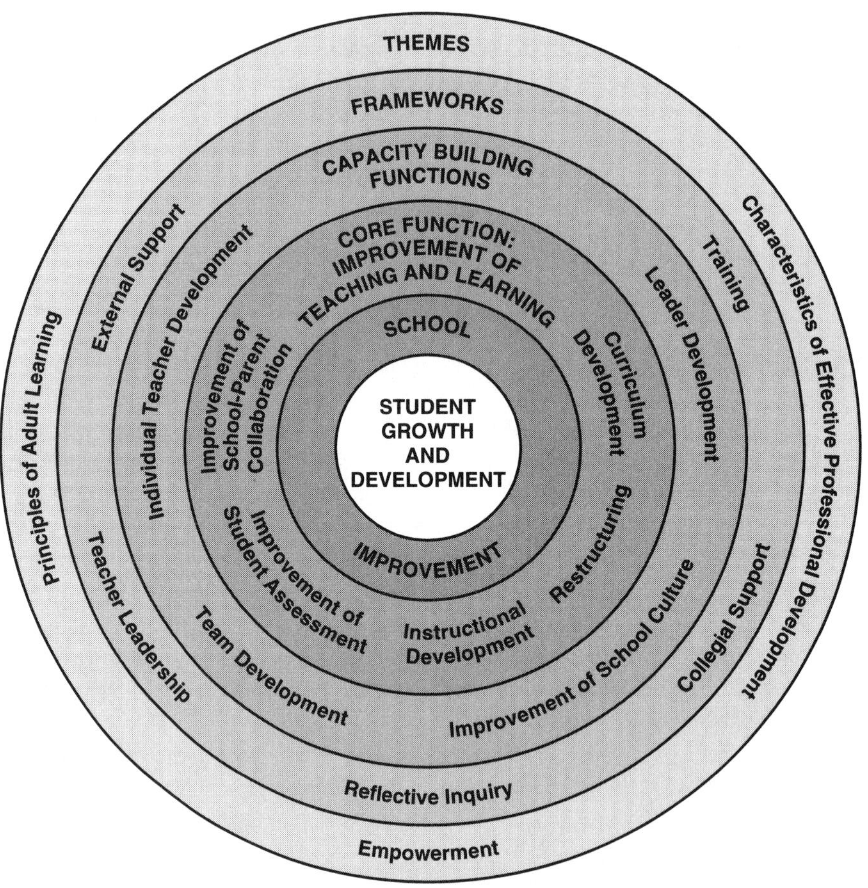

FIGURE 1.2 Comprehensive Model: Professional Development for School Improvement

Part IV, *Conclusion*, includes two chapters:

- *Core Function of Professional Development: Improvement of Teaching and Learning* (Chapter 11), including curriculum development, restructuring, instructional development, improvement of student assessment, and improvement of school-parent collaboration (listed in the fourth band from the outside in Figure 1.2)
- *Program Development* (Chapter 12)

Components listed in the first four bands of Figure 1.2 lead to school improvement (fifth band from the outside) and, ultimately, student growth and development (center of Figure 1.2).

This chapter has introduced the emerging field of professional development and provided an overview of a professional development model to be used as the primary vehicle for school improvement. The remainder of this book will consist of a journey through the various dimensions of that model. Let the journey begin!

Summary

Chapter 1 defined *successful professional development* as "a combination of experiences that empower individual educators, educational teams, and the educational organization to improve curriculum, instruction, and student assessment in order to facilitate student growth and development." The need for professional development as a vehicle for school improvement was discussed. Although the track record of professional development in schools was judged to be a poor one, the pressure for school reform and the emergence of a variety of successful programs were cited as reasons for optimism concerning the future of professional development.

The focus of the book was described as including in-service educators, school improvement, campus-focused professional development, empowerment, and intentional (as opposed to serendipitous) development. Major themes of the book were previewed, including empowerment of all members of the school community, characteristics for effective professional development programs, and principles of adult learning. Finally, a comprehensive model of professional development for school improvement, to be explored further throughout the text, was presented.

Assignments

1. Locate two articles, papers, or chapters by different authors on student, teacher, parent, or principal empowerment. Compare and contrast the authors' views on empowerment with each other and with the view of empowerment discussed in Chapter 1.
2. Read two articles, papers, or chapters from the literature on adult education and/or adult learning that are relevant to the professional development of teachers. Write a paper summarizing the knowledge about adult learning that you gained from your reading as well as implications for professional development in PK–12 schools.
3. Write a paper describing a professional development program in which you have participated. Include in your paper a discussion of whether or not the characteristics of effective professional development presented in Chapter 1 were present in the program. Also, include your conclusions concerning the program's overall level of success.
4. Interview a staff developer on his or her perceptions of the characteristics of effective professional development programs. Write a paper in which you discuss the staff developer's perceptions as well as the extent to which his or her perceptions agree with Chapter 1's list of characteristics of effective development.
5. Interview (a) a school superintendent, principal, or assistant principal, (b) a teacher, and (c) a parent on their definitions and perceptions of the term *empowerment.* Write a paper comparing and contrasting the interviewees' responses.

References

Barth, R. S. (2000). Building a community of learners. *Principal, 79*(4), 68–69.

Birman, B. F., Desimone, L., Porter, A. C., & Garet, M. S. (2000). Designing professionsal development that works. *Educational Leadership, 57*(8), 28–33.

Blase, J., & Blase, J. R. (1994). *Empowering teachers: What successful principals do.* Thousand Oaks, CA: Corwin Press.

Boyer, K., Crowther, S., Fast, D., Kasselman, J., Nolte, S., & Wilson, D. (1993). *Outcome based staff development.* Topeka: Kansas State Board for Education. (ERIC ED 368 696).

Browder, L. H. (1994). Exploring the meanings of teacher empowerment. *International Journal of Educational Reform, 3*(2), 137–153.

Caffarella, R. S., & Barnett, B. G. (1994). Characteristics of adult learners and foundations of experiential learning. *New Directions for Adult and Continuing Education, 62,* 29–42.

Caine, R. N., & Caine, G. (1994). *Making connections: Teaching and the human brain* (rev. ed.). Menlo Park, CA: Addison-Wesley.

Caine, R. N., & Caine, G. (1997). *Education on the edge of possibility.* Alexandria, VA: Association for Supervision and Curriculum Development.

Citino, L. C. (2001). Using student-driven themes and international relations. *Middle Ground, 4*(5), 38–39.

Conzemius, A. (2000). Framework. *Journal of Staff Development, 21*(1), 38–41.

de Souza Fleith, D. (2000). Teacher and student perceptions of creativity in the classroom environment. *Roeper Review, 22*(3), 148–153.

Citino, L. C. (2001). Using student-driven themes and international relations. *Middle Ground, 4*(5), 38–39.

Dodd, A. W., & Konzal, J. L. (2000). Parents and educators as partners. *The High School Magazine*, 7(5), 8-13.

DuFour, R. (2001). In the right context. *Journal of Staff Development, 22*(1), 14-17.

Fullan, M. G., with Stiegelbauer, S. (1991). *The new meaning of educational change* (2nd ed.). New York: Teachers College Press.

Georgia State Department of Education. (1990). *School-focused staff development guide*. Atlanta: Author. (ERIC ED 340 090).

Gideon, B. H., & Erlandson, D. A. (2001). I want you to come up with the ideas. *Journal of Staff Development, 22*(4), 14–17.

Glickman, C. D., Gordon, S. P., & Ross-Gordon, J. M. (2001). *Supervision and instructional leadership: A developmental approach* (5th ed). Boston: Allyn and Bacon.

Glickman, C. D., Hayes, R., & Hensley, F. (1992). Site-based facilitation of empowered schools: Complexities and issues for staff developers. *Journal of Staff Development, 13*(2), 22–26.

Goldring, E. B., & Bauch, P. A. (1994, April). *Teacher empowerment and parent participation in urban high schools of choice: Consumerism or partnership?* Paper presented at the annual meeting of the American Educational Research Association, New Orleans. (ERIC ED 379 366).

Gordon, S. P. (2000, November). *Professional development for teacher and school renewal: Alternative pathways, common characteristics.* Paper presented at the University Council for Educationl Administration Annual Convention, Albuquerque.

Gordon, S. P., & Nicely, R. F. (1998). Supervision and staff development. In G. R. Firth & E. Pajak (Eds.), *Handbook of research on school supervision* (pp. 801–841). New York: Macmillan.

Green, R. L., & Etheridge, C. P. (2001). Collaboration to establish standards about accountability: Lessons learned about systemic change. *Education, 121*(4), 821–829.

Griffin, G. A. (1983). *Staff development, part II: 82nd Yearbook of the National Society for the Study of Education.* Chicago: University of Chicago Press.

Guglielmino, L. M. (1993). Staff development programs based on teacher choice: Insights from adult education research. *Journal of Personnel Evaluation in Education, 71,* 231–233.

Guskey, T. R. (1995). Professional development in education: In search of the optimal mix. In T. R. Guskey & M. Huberman (Eds.), *Professional development in education* (pp. 114–131). New York: Teachers College Press.

Hargreaves, A. (2001). Beyond anxiety and nostalgia: Building a social movement for educational change. *Phi Delta Kappan, 82*(5), 373–377.

Hopkins, D., Ainscow, M., & West, M. (1994). *School improvement in an era of change*. New York: Teachers College Press.

Klecker, B., & Loadman, W. E. (1996, February). *A study of teacher empowerment in 180 restructuring schools: Leadership implications*. Paper presented at the annual meeting of the American Association of Colleges for Teacher Education, Chicago. (ERIC ED 393 823).

Knowles, M. S. (1980). *The modern practice of adult education: From pedagogy to andragogy*. New York: Cambridge University Press.

Kovalik, S., & Olsen, K. (1994). *ITI: The model. Integrated thematic instruction* (3rd ed.). Kent, WA: Books for Educators.

Kroth, M., & Boverie, P. (2000). Life mission and adult learning. *Adult Education Quarterly, 50*(2), 134–149.

Lambert, L. (2002). A framework for shared leadership. *Educational Leadership, 59*(8), 37–40.

Leithwood, K. A. (1992). The move toward transformational leadership. *Educational Leadership, 49*(5), 8–12.

Levine, S. L. (1989). *Promoting adult growth in schools: The promise of professional development*. Boston: Allyn and Bacon.

Lincoln, Y. S. (1995). In search of students' voices. *Theory into Practice, 34*(2), 88–93.

Little, J. W. (1982). Norms of collegiality and experimentation: Workplace conditions of school success. *American Educational Research Journal, 19*(3), 325–340.

McCay, E. (2001). The learning needs of principals. *Educational Leadership, 58*(8), 75–77.

Meadows, B. J., & Saltzman, M. (2002). Shared decision-making: An uneasy collaboration. *Principal, 81*(4), 41–48.

Melenyzer, B. J. (1991, November). *Empowering the school community: Meeting the challenge through intra-university and university-school district collaboratives*. Paper presented at the annual conference of the National Council of States of Inservice Education, Houston. (ERIC ED 343 846).

Merriam, S. B. (2001). Andragogy and self-directed learning: Pillars of adult learning theory. *New Directions for Adult and Continuing Education, 89*, 3–13.

Merriam, S. B., & Caffarella, R. S. (1999). *Learning in adulthood* (2nd ed.). San Francisco: Jossey-Bass.

Midgley, C., & Wood, S. (1993). Beyond site-based management: Empowering teachers to reform schools. *Phi Delta Kappan, 75*, 245–252.

Miles, M. B. (1995). Foreword. In T. R. Guskey & M. Huberman (Eds.), *Professional development in education: New paradigms and practices* (pp. vii–ix). New York: Teachers College Press.

Million, J. (2001). Treat all parents right. *The Education Digest, 67*(4), 37–38.

Norton, J. (2001). Grounded in research. *Journal of Staff Development, 22*(3), 30–32.

Pajak, E. F., & Glickman, C. D. (1989). Dimensions of school district improvement. *Educational Leadership, 46*(8), 61–64.

Plucker, J. A., & Slavkin, M. L. (2000). Unify curriculum around the needs of students, teachers, and community alike. *Principal Leadership, 66(3)*, 55–60.

Rallis, S. F., & Goldring, E. B. (2000). *Principals of dynamic schools: Taking charge of change*. Thousand Oaks, CA: Corwin Press.

Richardson, J. (2000). Learning benefits everyone. *Journal of Staff Development, 21*(1), 54–59.

Riley, A. (1994). Parent empowerment: An idea for the nineties? *Education Canada, 34*(3), 14–20.

Rosenholtz, S. V. (1989). *Teachers' workplace: The social organization of schools*. New York: Longman.

Sarason, S. B. (1996). *Revisiting "The culture of the school and the problem of change*." New York: Teachers College Press.

Shen, J. (2001). Teachers and principal empowerment: National, longitudinal and comparative perspectives. *Educational Horizons, 79*(3), 124–129.

Short, P. M., & Greer, J. T. (1993, October). *Empowering students: Variables impacting the effort*. Paper presented at the annual meeting of the University Council for Education Administration, Houston, TX.

Short, P. M., & Rinehart, J. S. (1992). School participant empowerment scale: Assessment of level of empowerment within the school environment. *Educational and Psychological Measurement, 52*, 951-960.

Silins, H. C. (1994). Leadership characteristics and school improvement. *Australian Journal of Education, 38*(93), 266-281.

Sparks, D. (2001). Why change is so challenging for schools. *Journal of Staff Development, 22*(3), 42–47.

Sparks, D., & Hirsh, S. (2000). *A national plan for improving professional development*. Oxford, OH: National Staff Development Council.

Speck, M., & Knipe, C. (2001). *Why can't we get it right? Professional development in our schools*. Thousand Oaks, CA: Corwin Press.

Stone, S. J. (1995). Empowering teachers: Empowering children. *Childhood Education, 71*(5), 294–295.

Sweetland, S. R. (2001). Authenticity and sense of power in enabling school structures: An empirical analysis. *Education, 121*(3), 581–588.

Tirozzi, G. N. (2001). The artistry of leadership: The evolving role of the secondary school principal. *Phi Delta Kappan, 82*(6), 434–439.

Wilmore, E., & Thomas, C. (2001). The new century: Is it too late for transformational leadership? *Educational Horizons, 79*(3), 115–123.

Wilson, S. M., & Coolican, M. J. (1996). How high and low self-empowered teachers work with colleagues and school principals. *Journal of Educational Thought, 30*(2), 99–117.

Wood, F. W., & Thompson, S. R. (1993). Assumptions about staff development based on research and best practice. *Journal of Staff Development, 14*(4), 52–57.

Zemke, R., & Zemke, S. (1995). Adult learning: What do we know for sure? *Training, 32*(6), 31–34, 36, 38, 40.

Resources

Blase, J., & Blase, J. R. (1994). *Empowering teachers: What successful principals do*. Thousand Oaks, CA: Corwin Press.

Guskey, T. R., & Huberman, M. (Eds.). (1995). *Professional development in education: New paradigms and practices*. New York: Teachers College Press.

Merriam, S. B. (2001). Andragogy and self-directed learning: Pillars of adult learning theory. *New Directions for Adult and Continuing Education, 89*, 3–13.

Merriam, S. B., & Caffarella, R. S. (1999). *Learning in adulthood* (2nd ed.). San Francisco: Jossey-Bass.

Short, P. M., & Greer, J. T. (1997). *Leadership in empowered schools: Themes from innovative efforts*. Upper Saddle River, NJ: Prentice-Hall.

Sparks, D., & Hirsh, S. (1997). *A new vision for staff development*. Alexandria, VA: Association for Supervision and Curriculum Development, and Oxford, OH: National Staff Development Council.

Sparks, D., & Hirsh, S. (2000). *A national plan for improving professional development*. Oxford, OH: National Staff Development Council.

Speck, M., & Knipe, C. (2001). *Why can't we get it right? Professional development in our schools*. Thousand Oaks, CA: Corwin Press.

Review of Professional Development Model, Part I

Part I provided initial discussions of three themes for the text: empowerment, characteristics of effective professional development, and principles of adult learning. These three themes encompass the professional development model presented in this text and thus are listed in the outer band of Figure I.1 below. In Part II, we will discuss the next component of the model: frameworks for professional development. These frameworks include training, collegial support, reflective inquiry, teacher leadership, and external support.

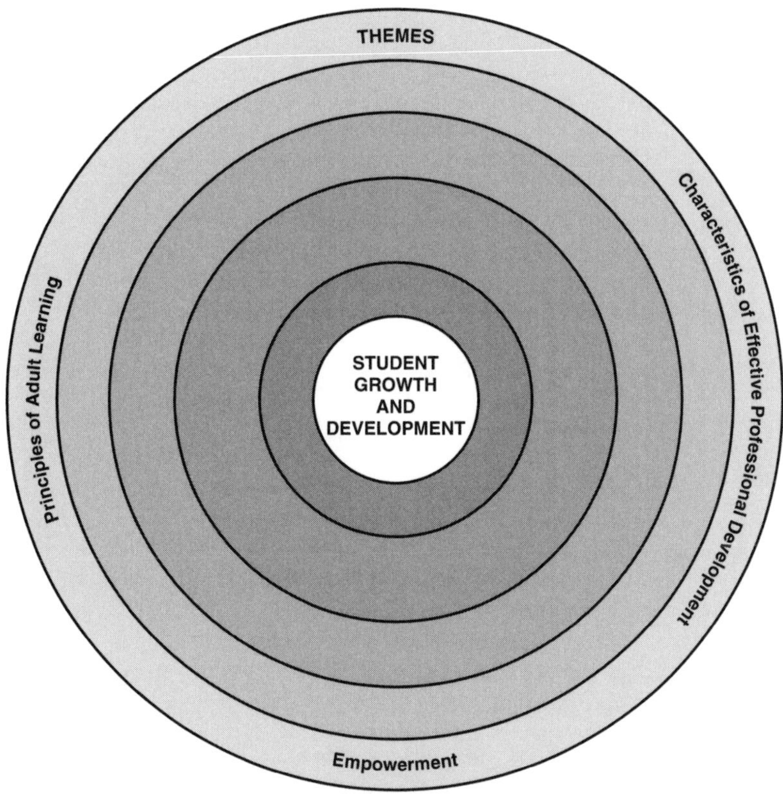

FIGURE I.1 Comprehensive Model: Professional Development for School Improvement

Part II

Frameworks for Professional Development

2 Training

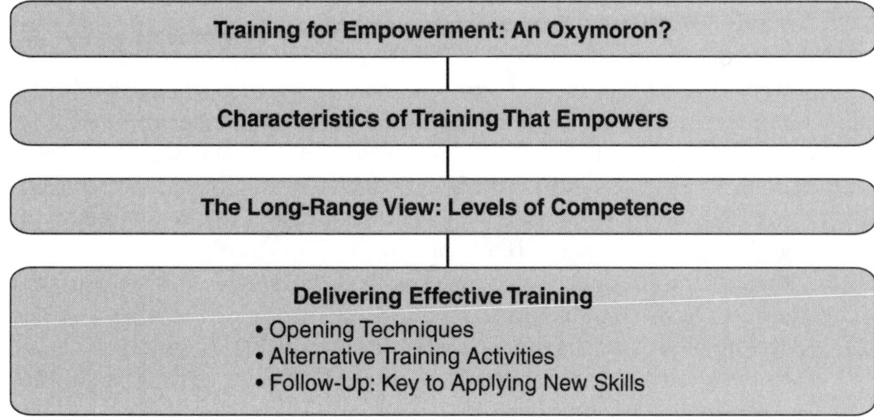
Training for Empowerment: An Oxymoron?
Characteristics of Training That Empowers
The Long-Range View: Levels of Competence
Delivering Effective Training
• Opening Techniques
• Alternative Training Activities
• Follow-Up: Key to Applying New Skills

Historically, the primary framework for the professional development of in-service educators has been training. The first systematic form of in-service training in the United States was the teacher institutes of the mid-eighteenth century, which had as their purpose the transmission to teachers of subject area knowledge and "moral character" (Spring, 1994). Eventually, the institutes changed their focus to training in the methods of teaching (DeLuca, 1991; Magestro & Stanford-Blair, 2000). Throughout most of the twentieth century, training remained the cornerstone of professional development.

A variety of training formats have been used over the years, including institutes, clinics, seminars, workshops, courses, academies, and individualized training. Theoretically, each of these formats is defined differently. *Institutes* are intensive learning experiences in a specific area of study. They often take place for a period of one to three weeks. *Clinics* focus on analyzing and solving specific problems or learning specific techniques through expert demonstration or coaching under authentic or simulated conditions. *Seminars* are small groups working closely with acknowledged experts in their field. Participants meet regularly to receive training, hold discussions, and share information, and they may be involved in individual projects assisted by the seminar leader and other participants. *Workshops* are flexible structures that focus on the discussion, demonstration, and application of skills and strategies. Training programs often involve a series of workshops spaced several weeks apart, with application of skills in the work setting between workshops. *Courses* are usually highly systematized, with standardized learning outcomes, a required amount of instructional time, the completion of outside assignments, and a minimum standard of performance, usually in exchange for credit hours from a college or university or approved continuing education units. *Academies* are continuing or recurring programs, usually receiving long-term support from government agencies, professional associations, school districts, higher education, or other institutions. They tend to focus on a particular area of study, and may serve as an organizational umbrella, offering training in the focus area through a variety of other formats. For example, an academy might periodically offer institutes, seminars, workshops, courses, and so on. Finally, *individualized training* allows the participant to complete a program that assesses individual learning needs, allows the participant to complete learning activities at his or her own pace, and provides for individual assessment of the participant's progress. Figure 2.1 provides an example of each of these training formats.

The distinctions among these various training formats have always been less than crystal clear in the professional literature, and they often break down completely in the real world of PK–12 professional development. It is not uncommon for what is essentially the same training program to be called a seminar in one school district, a workshop in a second district, and an institute in a third district. (Thus, based on the widespread variation in how practitioners label training programs, it would probably not be especially appreciated if you were to inform the staff-development director in your local school district that what she is calling an academy is actually an institute.) Another problem with attempting to define various group training formats is that in PK-12 education most of the structures associated with group training also are used for other purposes. For example, besides serving as a training format, the "workshop" is often used to develop curriculum, discuss or create instructional materials, analyze student assessment data, and so on.

FIGURE 2.1 Examples of Different Training Formats

Format	*Example*
Institute	In a three-week summer science institute, teachers learn how to implement an experiential science curriculum.
Clinic	In a Saturday computer clinic, teachers are partnered with technology specialists who demonstrate use of new instructional software, and coach teachers as they try out the new software.
Seminar	A group of beginning teachers and their mentors attend monthly seminars on how new teachers can have a successful first year. The seminar is facilitated by a professor from a nearby university. Participants select seminar topics, and numerous guests are invited to engage in dialogue with participants on chosen topics.
Workshop	Teachers participate in a series of five-day-long workshops on cooperative learning. The workshops include presentation of theory, demonstrations, and practice with feedback.
Course	The district's professional development center collaborates with a local university to offer a semester-long course on constructivist teaching. The course meets one evening a week for three hours. Outside work, including classroom applications, is required. Teachers may enroll in the course either for university graduate credit or district continuing education units.
Academy	The regional educational service agency hosts an ongoing leadership academy that offers leadership institutes, seminars, workshops, and courses for school administrators, staff developers, teachers, and parents.
Individualized Training	A teacher sets an individual goal of improving classroom interaction, and designs a year-long plan to meet that goal. The plan includes attending workshops, reading, visiting other classrooms, and having a colleague observe new strategies and provide feedback. The teacher gathers data on his or her progress, and documents learning through the development of a teacher portfolio.

Now that we've overviewed the various training formats, it's time to address a critical issue: Can training be consistent with the principles of empowerment, effective professional development, and adult learning that we discussed in Chapter 1?

Training for Empowerment: An Oxymoron?

Although still widely used in practice, when training is addressed in the PK–12 professional development literature it often is discussed with a negative connotation, even being portrayed as antithetical to authentic professional development. This is in sharp contrast to other professions, in which training is considered an integral component of professional development (Tillema & Imants, 1995).

Why has training received such a negative image among many scholars in the field? One reason is that training has been long associated with behavioral psychology, including concepts such as stimulus and response, positive and negative reinforcement, and so on. Such concepts often are accompanied by images of salivating dogs, rats running through mazes, and dolphins being thrown fish as a reward for performing on command. Hence, a common reaction is: "You train animals, not people."

A second reason for training's negative image is that much of PK–12 professional development training has been so poor. It often has been based on an administrator's whim, a current fad, or the availability of a particular program or presenter, rather than on teacher and student needs. Traditionally, teachers have had little, if any, participation in program development. Training often has taken the form of one-shot lectures and demonstrations unrelated to teachers' experience, knowledge base, responsibilities, or problems. Seldom has there been adequate follow-up to help teachers to transfer training to their schools and classrooms.

A third reason why training has lost popularity in the literature is that teaching has increasingly become viewed as a complex craft, requiring reflective practitioners rather than teachers possessing only the technical skills associated with training (Tillema & Imants, 1995). This view is accompanied by a belief that reflective practice is fostered through professional development activities other than training, such as action research, study groups, and self-directed learning.

My own belief is that the scholar who considers training and empowerment to be polar opposites, as well as the practitioner who continues to rely on the poorly designed training programs that many scholars decry, both have taken too narrow a view of training. Training *can* be part of a professional development program that facilitates empowerment and reflective practice. Numerous training programs that I have attended as a trainee have contributed to my own sense of empowerment. Many of my students as well as practitioners with whom I have worked have credited training programs with facilitating their empowerment. Training that empowers, however, includes a number of characteristics not present in traditional training programs. The next section describes those characteristics.

Characteristics of Training That Empowers

Based on my experience as a trainee, trainer, and observer of training, nearly all training programs that foster empowerment—regardless of content—possess the following characteristics:

- The training is based on participants' perceptions of student, educator, or school needs. The training content is not offered as an end in itself, but rather to help participants meet the perceived needs.
- Participants are involved in planning, delivering, and evaluating the training.
- School administrators participate fully in all phases of training.
- Participants are provided full information about the program in advance, including the purpose of the training, an overview of program content, and activities the

participants are expected to engage in between training sessions or after the training is complete (for example, outside readings, trying out new skills and strategies in the classroom, participating in peer coaching between sessions, and so on).

- Participation is voluntary. However, once a fully informed participant makes a formal commitment to participate in the program, it is appropriate to expect the participant to fulfill his or her commitment.
- Training is long term, allowing incremental skill development over several sessions.
- The trainer or training team acknowledges and makes use of participants' experience, prior knowledge, beliefs, and professional roles and responsibilities.
- Participants are actively engaged in a variety of learning activities.
- Activities include demonstration of new skills, and feedback on performance.
- Learning is differentiated in at least some training sessions; different participants are involved in different learning activities based on their concerns, intrests, and needs.
- The training has sufficient flexibility to accommodate participants' evolving perceptions, concerns, and requests.
- The training is part of a larger program that includes other professional development frameworks intended to assist the participants to transfer new skills and strategies to the classroom or school. Other aspects of the program might include peer coaching, team teaching, collegial support groups, action research, reflective writing, follow-up sessions, and so on.
- Although part of the participants' commitment to the training includes experimenting with transfer of new skills and strategies to the classroom or school, no attempt is made to force the participant to permanently adopt the new skills and strategies.

The obsevations that I have made concerning training that empowers are not new. They are consistent with a long line of research (Joyce, Murphy, Showers, & Murphy, 1989; Lawrence, 1974; Richardson, 2000; Sparks & Hirsh, 2000; Stallings, 1989). The challange is to convince districts and schools to incorporate those characteristics into their training programs.

The Long-Range View: Levels of Competence

Effective training takes time, because skill development occurs in stages. As participants move through these stages, they increase their level of competence. A model identifying levels of competence in skill development was origionally developed by Howell (1982) and later extended by Pike (1994). Pike's version of the model is shown in Figure 2.2.

The first four levels of competence were identified by Howell (1982). Individuals at the lowest skill level, *unconscious incompetence*, are unaware that they lack skills in a particular area. For example, teachers who have little or no training in cooperative

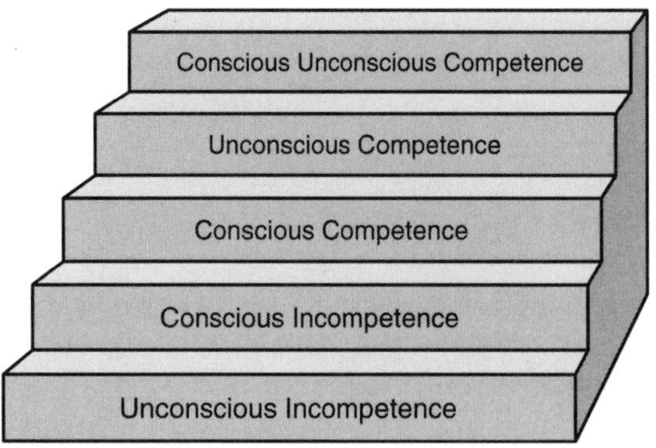

FIGURE 2.2 Levels of Competence

Source: Robert W. Pike, *Creative Techniques Handbook* (2nd ed., p. 6). Copyright 1989, 1994 by Robert W. Pike, Creative Techniques International, Inc., 7620 W. 78th St., Edina, MN 55439, 800-383-9210. Used by permission. All rights reserved.

learning may believe that some small-group activities they use in their classrooms constitute cooperative learning, when they actually are failing to include several essential elements of a cooperative lesson. The purpose of training at this stage is to make participants aware of their need for skill development.

The next level is *conscious incompetence*. At this level, individuals realize that something they are attempting to do is not working, but they don't realize why they are stuggling. In the example of teachers attempting to introduce cooperative learning, they may realize that their group work is not resulting in student learning, but they don't understand that things aren't working out because they are not properly structuring cooperative lessons. They may conclude that "cooperative learning" doesn't work for them, abandon their efforts, and return to their traditional teaching methods. Individuals at this stage have become conscious of their incompetence through trial and error, but have not consciously analyzed their poor performance (Howell, 1982). Training at this stage could consist of skill demonstration, skill practice, feedback, and reflection on skill development efforts.

Level 3 is *conscious competence*, in which the trainees begin to really understand the skill or strategy. They begin to implement the skill or strategy one step at a time, reflecting on whether they are effectively or ineffectively implementing each step. They are able to analyze a problem, examine alternative ways of addressing the problem, and select the best alternative to be applied when a similar problem occurs in the future. In the cooperative learning example, this stage might involve teachers experimenting with cooperative learning in their classrooms, mechanically implementing each essential element in a cooperative lesson, receiving feedback and reflecting on their efforts, and making changes in future lessons to address problems with teacher or student performance. Training at this stage might consist of analyzing videotaped lessons, coaching, participation in collegial support groups, and so on.

The fourth level is *unconscious competence*, in which individuals continuously and unconsciously collect data from the external environment, and spontaneously (and appropriately) respond to that data. They adjust their behavior in the present situation rather than only in future, similar situations. The teacher who has reached this stage has become adept not only at planning effective cooperative lessons but also at "thinking on his or her feet" during those lessons, responding effectively to the many unanticipated problems that arise in any lesson. However, if asked by an observer why he or she took a particular action or responded to a student in a certain manner, the teacher might not be able to explain his or her behavior, or even remember the behavior in question. At this stage, it is difficult for a teacher to help other teachers develop the skills that he or she has mastered. Training at Level 4 could consist of teachers learning to better analyze and articulate their own teaching, and to develop leadership skills for assisting others to develop the skills that they have mastered.

Pike (1994) has proposed *conscious unconscious competence* as the fifth level of skill development. Individuals who have reached this level can not only spontaneously assess and respond to dynamic situations but also can explain why and how they behaved as they did. Reaching this level may not be critical in some training programs but it is critical in training educators. To begin with, experts know that many teachers respond more positively to training when other teachers are the trainers or at least part of a training team (Gordon, 1997). If teachers who have mastered skills or strategies are to become effective trainers of other teachers, they must reach the fifth level of competence. Moreover, teachers are better able to transfer new skills to their classrooms if provided with assistance from mentors, peer coaches, collegial support groups, and so on. Colleagues attempting to help teachers transfer skills from training to practice are more likely to be successful in their assistance efforts if they have reached Pike's conscious unconscious competence.

Effective training, then, must include strategies for helping trainees to discover their need for skill development, then develop mechanical competence, then spontaneous competence, and finally the ability to articulate and teach their skills to other educators. The incremental nature of effective training means that one-shot training sessions are of little use. Educators need to take a long-term view of skill development, gradually facilitating teachers toward higher levels of competence.

Our general discussion of competence levels needs to be accompanied by comments about individual competencies needed, and individual growth through levels of competence. Needed competencies vary according to the context of teaching and the teaching assignment. For example, the competencies needed by a teacher in an urban school with a primarily minority, low SES student population are significantly different from competencies needed by a teacher in a suburban school with a primarily Caucasian, upper-middle-class student population. Moreover, a teacher's background and experience influence needed competencies. An experienced, middle-aged African American teacher who was born and raised within a few blocks of the urban, primarily African American school where she teaches will very likely have different competency needs than a beginning Caucasion teacher at the same school who is from a small town with little diversity. Finally, even teachers who need to develop the same competency will likely move through the five levels of competence at different rates, and may need to engage in different learning experiences to reach higher levels of competence. This discussion supports moving away from one-size-fits-all training to training with a variety of learning options and individualized pacing of skill development.

Delivering Effective Training

This section begins with a review of techniques for opening a training session. Next, alternative training activities are described, with an emphasis on experiential learning. Finally, the need for follow-up is discussed, and an exemplar of follow-up is provided.

Opening Techniques

Corbett (1992) has proposed a variety of techniques for opening a training session. Icebreakers can introduce participants and content, reduce anxiety, establish climate, motivate participants, promote creativity, set norms, and establish the trainer as facilitator rather than controller of learning. When selecting icebreakers, the trainer needs to consider training content, the culture of the group, and individual learning styles. To address different learning styles, Corbett suggests varied activities within the same icebreaker: In a training program on leadership, for example, participants could be asked to write out their conceptions of leadership (abstract learning), construct physical models that symbolize those conceptions (concrete learning), and list leadership characteristics represented in the physical models (sequential learning).

Beyond icebreakers, Corbett (1992) suggests several other opening techniques, including providing logistical information (restroom locations, session schedule, and so on), encouraging participation, dealing with distorters and attitudes, clarifying and integrating trainee and trainer goals, and providing structures for trainees to connect training to their professional responsibilities. One opening technique recommended by Corbett for connecting training to one's job responsibilities is to introduce the reflective log, which the trainee then uses throughout the training program. The trainee might write about concepts learned, feelings concerning those concepts, and ideas for applying learning.

Alternative Training Activities

Dale (1969) has presented the "cone of experience" (Figure 2.3) as a way of illustrating the relative value of alternative training activities. As we move from the top (involvement level 11) to the bottom (involvement level 1) of the cone, activities are more likely to result in retention of learning. The more experiential or active the learning, the higher the retention.

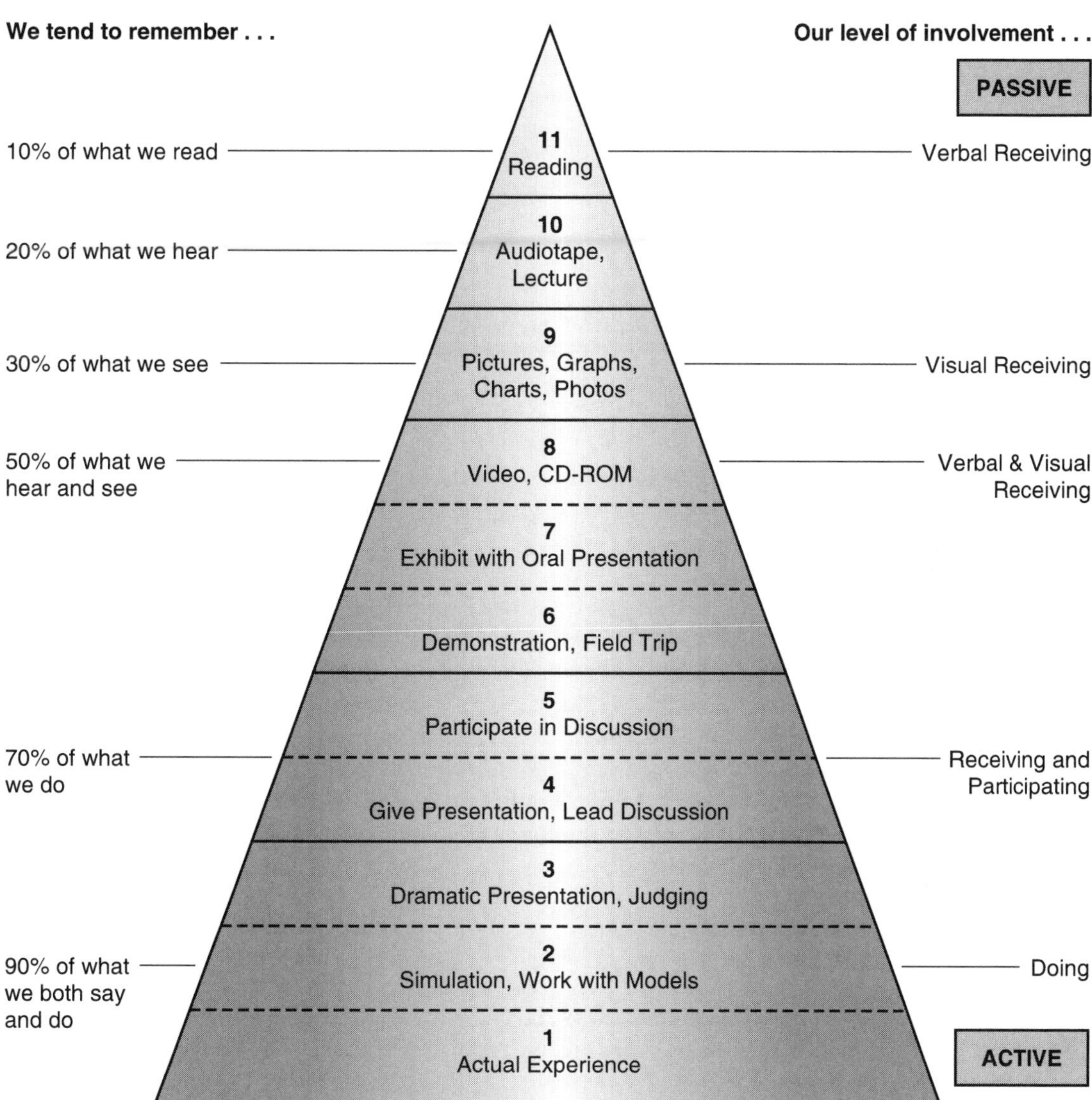

FIGURE 2.3 Cone of Experience

Source: Adapted from *Audio-Visual Methods in Teaching* (1st ed.) by E. Dale. © 1969. Reprinted with permission of Wadsworth, a division of Thomson Learning: www.thomsonrights.com. Fax 800-730-2215.

Traditional training of in-service teachers—consisting of talks, lectures, and readings—nests at the top of the cone. Is it any wonder why so little retention and application has resulted from conventional in-service training? Although talks, lectures, and readings have their place in training programs, they should be used selectively. Effective training emphasizes activities at the bottom of the cone (involvement levels 6 through 1). With this in mind, let's list examples of specific training activities for each of the bottom 6 levels of the cone of experience:

Level 6: Demonstration, Field Trip

- Trainer demonstrates skill or strategy in workshop setting or in participants' classrooms.
- Participants view videotapes of expert teachers using skills or strategies in their classrooms.
- Participants go on field trips to other schools to observe use of skills or strategies.
- Participants demonstrate skills or strategies to other trainees, through workshop demonstration, video, or live classroom demonstration, followed by feedback and discussion.
- During field trips or tours, participants take field notes, conduct interviews, or videotape subjects using strategies or skills.

Level 5: Participate in Discussion

- *Open whole-group discussion.* This consists of a general discussion of a broad topic. The most effective whole-group discussions involve interaction between trainer and participants as well as among participants (with emphasis on the latter).
- *Focused whole-group discussion.* Discussion focuses on a specific topic, structured by asking participants to respond to preplanned discussion questions or a particular problem, issue, trend, vignette, scenario, case, video, article, book, demonstration, or model.
- *Buzz session.* The participants are split into small groups for open or focused discussion, followed by small-group reports to the whole group and whole-group discussion.
- *Brainstorming.* The whole group or small groups generate a list of alternatives for addressing a stated problem or goal.
- *Panel-based discussion.* Several panel members engage in an informal discussion of an issue, followed by questions and answers or whole-group discussion.

Level 4: Give Presentation, Lead Discussion

- Participants make oral presentations on training concepts, readings, or completed projects.
- Participants lead whole-group discussions, buzz sessions, or brainstorming.

- Participants assume roles of debaters, symposium speakers, or panel members.

Level 3: Dramatic Presentation, Judging

- Participants participate in role play.
- Participants present a skit.
- Participants present a self-created video, slide show, photography exhibit, drawings, poetry, or multimedia program.
- Participants participate in a mock trial to decide on an educational issue or to judge the value of an educational model or program.

Level 2: Simulation, Work with Models

- Participants complete a simulation or problem-based learning project.
- Participants use the case-study method.
- Participants participate in an educational game requiring skills and decisions similar to those required in real-world situations.
- Participants micro teach, micro coach, and so on.
- Participants design a model or strategy for addressing a need or problem typically present in actual practice. At this level, the designers may present their model or strategy to the trainer and other trainees for feedback, but the design is not implemented in actual practice.
- Participants practice technical or interpersonal skills under conditions approximating actual practice.

Level 1: Actual Experience

- Participants design, administer, and analyze their own training needs assessment.
- Participants brainstorm ways to apply new strategies or skills during actual practice.
- Participants design a program, project, unit, lesson, student assessment strategy, and so on, which they will implement in actual practice.
- Participants develop resources and materials that they will use in actual practice.
- Participants try out new strategies or skills in actual practice.
- Participants receive feedback or analyze data on application of new strategies or skills in actual practice.
- Participants participate in designing or implementing an action plan for skill improvement in actual practice.
- Participants present to others on real-world application, results, and improvement plans.

Although experiential learning has far greater potential than conventional training, to be effective it must be properly structured. Robert Pike (1994) has proposed a model for structuring experiential activities such as role plays, simulations, and case studies. Pike's model includes the following seven steps:

1. Select a focus issue (examples are effective classroom communication, conflict management, an instructional problem, ethical behavior, and so on).
2. Select an incident or situation that will serve as a context for trainee decision making. For example, if the focus issue was ethical behavior, the trainees might be asked to step into a fictional dilemma in which they were forced to make an ethical decision and justify that decision.
3. Provide sufficient details for trainees to be able to understand the situation and make informed decisions.
4. Identify a product or products that should result from the activity (a rationale for a choice from competing alternatives, an action plan, a rank-ordering, and so on).
5. Decide on group size (Pairs? Groups of three? Groups of four?).
6. Decide on group composition. Will groups be based on years of experience? Grade-level taught? Content area? Gender? Type of position (administrator, classroom teacher, specialist)? Will group composition be heterogeneous or homogeneous?
7. Set a time limit for completion of the task.*

Pike (1994) notes that sometimes it is more appropriate for the trainer to create the situation, and at other times the trainees themselves can create situations based on their past experiences. When trainees are asked to create their own situations, the trainer needs to provide guidelines so that trainee-designed situations provide sufficient information for use in a subsequent role play, simulation, or case study.

Effective training for teachers connects experiential learning in training sessions with classroom practice (Sparks, 2000). For example, a training process described by Stallings (1989) begins with participants analyzing observation data on their classroom teaching and, through that analysis, becoming aware of their need to improve their instuction. Training sessions use a variety of experiential activities to help teachers develop new skills, but also provide opportunities for teachers to modify learning so it is useable in their own classrooms. Teachers try out new teaching strategies in their classrooms and then assess effects. Participants observe each other's classrooms and analyze data on their use of new skills. During training sessions, teachers share problems they are experiencing with classroom application and discuss solutions. The train-

*Robert W. Pike, *Creative Techniques Handbooks* (2nd ed., pp. 101–102). Copyright 1989, 1994 by Robert W. Pike, Creative Techniques International, Inc., 7620 W. 78th St., Edina, MN 55439, 800-383-9210. Used by permission. All rights reserved.

ing cycle of classroom application, assessment, and reflection allows for continuous improvement. Similarly, training models developed by Joyce and Showers (1988) combine workshop skill development with peer coaching and peer study groups that support classroom application of new skills. (Chapter 3 describes the Joyce and Shower's coaching models in detail.)

Throughout this text, I argue that professional development should be school focused. One problem with attempting to provide school-based training is that districts often cannot afford to hire expert trainers to provide separate training sessions at individual schools. One solution to this problem is a trainer of trainers model, in which experts train a cadre of educators from across the district who then provide the same training (with adaptions for the local site) at their home schools. This solution has the advantage of an on-site trainer who is present on a daily basis to help teachers apply new skills.

Still, sometimes many schools in a district wish to receive district training from outside experts whose services are too costly to hire on a school by school basis. One way to make this possible is to integrate video teleconferencing led by experts at a central location with on-site activities at individual schools. Warger and Zorfass (1994) suggest a number of teleconference activities that promote active participation by participants at local sites. *Panel discussions* can involve two or three experts responding to questions or comments by the host, studio guests, and site participants. *Site activities* are group activities to be completed at participating sites, with directions and time for completing an activity on site screens. *Site discussions* are led by site discussion leaders and involve participants sharing experiences and brainstorming ways to apply new learning. Discussions can take place within or across sites and are followed by debriefing, in which sites share responses and ideas by calling in live to the studio. *Call-ins* from sites to the studio take place during allotted time periods and allow site participants to report on-site discussions and activities; share their own thinking, expertise, and resources; and request additional information from studio experts. *Workshop corners* are live studio demonstrations followed by site participants trying out the demonstrated skill or explaining how they will apply the skill to their own situations. *Video roll-ins* are videos of actual classrooms or schools, often periodically stopped for discussions by participants and followed by site responses to the video. *School-based assignments* can foster site participants' interactions between general sessions, or classroom application of workshop learning. Reflections on school-based assignments can be submitted electronically prior to the next program and shared with other sites at the beginning of the next general session (Warger & Zorfass, 1994). As we review these possibilities, it becomes clear that video teleconferencing can promote active learning and can be integrated with school-based training.

Thus far in this chapter we have focused on what to include in training programs. Another approach is to discuss what trainers should *avoid*. Inset 2.1 provides a list of things that a trainer should never do.

INSET 2.1 • *Sharp's "Never-Evers" of Workshop Facilitation*

Peggy Sharp (1992) has proposed the following "never-evers" of workshop facilitation, which seem applicable to other training formats as well.

1. Never ever forget that individuals at the workshop are unique, with needs, interests, and experiences particular to them. . . .
2. Never ever require individuals to participate in an activity. . . .
3. Never ever talk to participants as if they are children. . . .
4. Never ever ridicule participants or their experiences. . . .
5. Never ever neglect the participants' personal needs. . . .
6. Never ever say that you are going to rush through and compress material in order to complete what is usually a longer workshop in a shorter length of time. . . .
7. Never ever say that you would be able to do something else if you had more time in the workshop. . . .
8. Never ever say that you would have brought more materials if it had been possible. . . .
9. Never ever tell participants what you've forgotten. . . .
10. Never ever give excuses. . . .
11. Never ever read from a lengthy prepared text. . . .
12. Never ever share illegible handouts. . . .
13. Never ever share a disorganized "mishmash" for a handout. . . .
14. Never ever give participants something to read and then read it with them. . . .
15. Never ever share overhead transparencies that participants cannot see or read. . . .
16. Never ever share with participants a workshop schedule that is impossible to follow. . . .
17. Never ever go past the scheduled time. . . .
18. Never ever forget that you have an audience. . . .
19. Never ever take the workshop so seriously that everyone (including the facilitator) cannot have fun. . . .
20. Never ever plan a workshop without considering this list of never-evers. (pp. 38–40)

Source: P. A. Sharp, "The 'Never-Evers' of Workshop Facilitation," *Journal of Staff Development, 13* (2) (1992): 38–40. Reprinted with permission of the National Staff Development Council, 1999.

Follow-Up: Key to Applying New Skills

Killion and Kaylor (1991) define *follow-up* as activities that "provide participants with feedback about their efforts and address their special concerns regarding the implementation of transfer of new learning into their work settings" (p. 64). These authors report that using follow-up activities such as help groups, problem-solving groups, and support groups have a number of positive impacts on transfer. With follow-up, trainees are more comfortable with new skills, more willing to take risks in trying them out, more willing to persist in the face of problems with applying new skills, more flexible in their application of new skills, and more likely to integrate new skills into their teaching repertoire (Bradshaw, 2002; Killion & Kaylor, 1991). Exemplar 2.1 describes a wide range of effective follow-up activities at Kutz Elementary School in Central Bucks County (PA) School District.

EXEMPLAR 2.1 • *Follow-Up at Kutz Elementery*

Central Bucks (PA) School District offers a wide variety of professional development training. Initial training takes place at the district level, with extensive school-based follow-up. This study examines follow-up at Kutz Elementary School.

Collegiality is a trademark of follow-up at Kutz. Teachers attend workshops as partners or teams, and after initial training, they are given time to plan together how they will apply workshop learning at the school, grade, or classroom level. They also are given opportunities to observe and coach each other during application of workshop skills. School-based follow-up is also provided by district experts. One teacher described this type of support: "The staff developers will come in and they will do a lesson for you to observe. They'll do anything you want them to. They'll team teach with you. They'll come in to help you plan. The key is, the support is there."

Follow-up also takes place at the group level. Group follow-up may take the form of a refresher course or workshop, a study group for in-depth exploration of a new strategy, or a meeting to share experiences and ideas. One teacher summarized the latter: "In these follow-up sessions, people bring ideas—'This is what went really well,' 'This is what really flopped,'—and they'll bring examples." Group follow-up also occurs during schoolwide faculty meetings: "We've even put the agenda for the faculty meeting aside and said, 'We're going to do staff development' because it's so valued in the building."

Each year teachers write professional appraisal plans that tend to dovetail with training and follow-up. Professional development goals in these plans often involve application and integration of new strategies and skills learned in previous training. Implementation plans might include attending follow-up workshops; extending knowledge through additional reading; observing other teachers; brainstorming with colleagues; or inviting district staff developers to share materials, teach demonstration lessons, co-plan, or observe lessons and provide feedback. Implementation of the plan is assessed in a mid-year and a final review. Professional appraisal plans can be individualized or collaborative. One teacher described a plan being implemented with a partner after they attended initial training on performance-based assessment:

> This year I'm collaborating with a great partner in developing assessments in different content areas. In addition, the principal has given us articles on assessment and we have attended sessions on assessment. . . . For me, there is a daily follow-up, because we're working together to get to that goal.

(continued)

EXEMPLAR 2.1 • *Continued*

Structured follow-up at Kutz has led to an informal schoolwide support network. Two teachers discussed this network as follows:

> ***Teacher 1:*** I've found an established network with my colleagues after attending the staff development sessions. For example, I went to a development session on spelling, and afterwards I got memos from other teachers... and now, instead of just my grade-level partner, I have 25 other teachers that I can tap for resources.
>
> ***Teacher 2:*** Even though we have four walls and a door, I feel like every classroom is connected. I go down to fourth grade and say, "Do you have this kind of book?" I can go to any classroom teacher, the library, the computer technician, and if they don't have [what you need] they will tell you somebody to check with.

This schoolwide support includes teachers inviting colleagues to observe their classes: "Possibly you hit a trouble area, and there is a similar problem that's been solved in another class, so you go there to see how it was solved."

To summarize, ongoing training and follow-up at Kutz Elementary have become part of the school culture. As one teacher expressed, "I'd use the term 'systematized'; it is part of the way we do business day in and day out." Another teacher summed up the way the staff at Kutz Elementary feels about district and school support for professional development: "For personal growth, to keep education on the cutting edge, I think it's an absolute necessity... I just can't imagine teaching without the staff development that we have."

At the beginning of this chapter a variety of training formats were described. One decision a school needs to make is which format or combination of formats will be used. Other basic decisions to be made are who will deliver the training and when the training will be provided. Inset 2.2 provides a needs assessment allowing teacher input for those decisions.

INSET 2.2 • *Training Needs Assessment*

Note: This needs assessment is concerned with training formats, who delivers training, and when training takes place. Needs assessments that relate to program content can be found in future chapters.

Directions: For each item, choose the single response with which you most agree. Possible responses for each item are:

A. I definitely would not choose this option.

B. This option would be acceptable, but it's not one of my favorites.

C. This would be an excellent option.

Possible Training Formats

1. *Summer institutes:* Two to three weeks of intensive training in a specific area of study
2. *Clinics:* Focused on analyzing and solving specific problems or learning specific techniques under authentic or simulated conditions
3. *Seminars:* Small groups working closely with experts, holding discussions, sharing information, completing individual projects
4. *Workshops:* Discussion, demonstration, and application of skills and strategies
5. *Courses:* Standardized outcomes, required instructional time, outside assignments, university or continuing education credits
6. *Academies:* Long-term programs focused on a particular area of study, may include a variety of formats like those described in the first five items
7. *Individualized learning packets:* Pretests, learning materials, posttests
8. *Individualized computer-assisted instruction:* Multimedia, interactive, includes simulations
9. *Individualized classroom-based training:* Gather and analyze classroom data, identify learning goals, design action plan, implement plan, consult with staff developer throughout process
10. *Video teleconferencing:* Presentations and demonstrations from a central location combined with interactive discussion and school-based activities

(continued)

INSET 2.2 • Continued

Who Should Deliver Training?

11. University professors
12. Private consultants
13. District staff developers
14. Campus administrators
15. Teachers from other schools
16. I could deliver training
17. Other teachers from my school

Possible Times for Training

18. Morning sessions (released time)
19. Afternoon sessions (released time)
20. Alternating morning and afternoon sessions (released time)
21. All-day sessions (released time)
22. Evenings
23. Saturdays
24. Intersessions
25. Summer

Summary

This chapter described various training formats. Characteristics of training that empowers were discussed. A long-range view of training consistent with participants incrementally moving through five levels of competence was proposed. Strategies for delivering effective training were presented with a focus on experiential learning and the value of follow-up.

Assignments

1. Locate articles or chapters describing the implementation of three different training models not described in this chapter. Write a paper summarizing, comparing, and contrasting the training models. Include in your paper a discussion of any research or evaluation on the effectiveness of the models.
2. Interview a staff developer on his or her perceptions of the characteristics of effective training. Write a paper summarizing the staff developer's responses and comparing the responses to the characteristics of effective training discussed in this chapter.

3. Write a paper describing a training program that you have participated in or examined, and assess the extent to which the program included the characteristics of effective training reported in this chapter.

4. Write a paper including a short case study that could be used as a basis for practicing a skill or strategy during a training program. Also include in your paper (a) learning objectives, (b) a focus issue, (c) a task that participants would be asked to complete after reading the case study, (d) a product that should result from the task , and (e) a time limit for completing the task. Include in your paper any additional information necessary for participants to make effective use of the case study.

References

Bradshaw, L. K. (2002). Technology for teaching and learning: Strategies for staff development and follow-up support. *Journal of Technology and Teacher Education, 10*(1), 131–150.

Corbett, A. H. (1992). Give participants responsibility for learning: Techniques for opening a workshop. *Journal of Staff Development, 13*(1), 40–42.

Dale, E. (1969). *Audiovisual methods in teaching.* Hinsdale, IL: Dryden Press.

DeLuca, J. R. (1991). The evolution of staff development for teachers. *Journal of Staff Development, 12*(3), 42–46.

Gordon, S. P . (1997, March). *The good, the bad, and the ordinary: Examining more and less effective staff development programs.* Paper presented at the Annual Meeting of the American Educational Research Association, Chicago.

Howell, W. S. (1982). *The empathic communicator.* Belmont, CA: Wadsworth.

Joyce, B., Murphy, C., Showers, B., & Murphy, J. (1989). School renewal as cultural change. *Educational Leadership, 47*(3), 70–77.

Joyce, B., & Showers, B. (1988). *Student achievement through staff development.* New York: Longman.

Killion, J. P., & Kaylor, B. (1991). Follow-up: The key to training for transfer. *Journal of Staff Development, 12*(1), 64–66.

Lawrence, G. (1974). *Patterns of effective inservice education. A state of the art summary of research on materials and procedures for changing teacher behaviors in inservice education.* Tallahassee, FL: Florida State Department of Education.

Magestro, P. V., & Stanford-Blair, N. (2000). A tool for meaningful staff development. *Educational Leadership, 57*(8), 34–35.

Pike, R. W. (1994). *Creative training techniques handbook* (2nd ed.). Minneapolis, MN: Lakewood Books.

Richardson, J. (2000). Learning benefits everyone: Award-winning schools point to the best in professional development. *Journal of Staff Development, 21*(1) 54–59.

Sharp, P. A. (1992). The "never-evers" of workshop facilitation. *Journal of Staff Development, 13*(2), 38–40.

Sparks, D. (2000). It all comes down to the teacher. *Journal of Staff Development, 21*(4) 30–33.

Sparks, D., & Hirsh, S. (2000). *A national plan for improving professional development.* Oxford, OH: National Development Staff Council.

Spring, J. (1994). *The American school, 1642–1993* (3rd ed.). New York: McGraw-Hill.

Stallings, J. (1989, March). *School achievement effects and staff development: What are some critical factors?* Paper presented at the annual meeting of the American Educational Research Association, San Francisco.

Tillema, H. H., & Imants, J. G. M. (1995). Training for the professional development of teachers. In T. R. Guskey & M. Huberman (Eds.), *Professional development in education: New paradigms and practices* (pp. 135–150). New York: Teachers College Press.

Warger, C. L., & Zorfass, J. M. (1994). Successful practices when using satellite technology to enhance districtwide staff development. *Journal of Staff Development, 15*(2), 42–47.

Resources

Birman, B. F., Desimone, L., Porter, A. C., & Garet, M. S. (2000). Designing professional development that works. *Educational Leadership, 57*(8), 28–32.

Champion, R. (2000). *Learning the craft of training*. Oxford, OH: National Staff Development Council.

Killion, J. P., & Kaylor, B. (1991). Follow-up: The key to training for transfer. *Journal of Staff Development, 12*(1), 64–66.

Magestro, P. V., & Stanford-Blair, N. (2000). A tool for meaningful staff development. *Educational Leadership, 57*(8), 34–35.

Richardson, J. (2000). Learning benefits everyone: Award-winning schools point to the best in professional development. *Journal of Staff Development, 21*(1), 54–59.

Tillema, H. H., & Imants, J. G. M. (1995). Training for the professional development of teachers. In T. R. Guskey & M. Huberman (Eds.), *Professional development in education: New paradigms and practices* (pp. 135–150). New York: Teachers College Press.

3 Collegial Support Frameworks

Peer Coaching

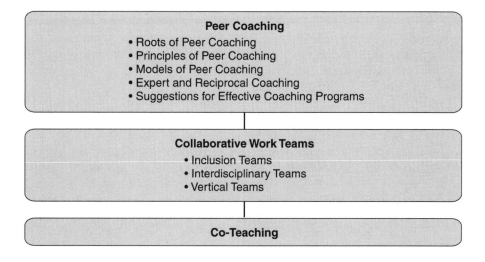

- Roots of Peer Coaching
- Principles of Peer Coaching
- Models of Peer Coaching
- Expert and Reciprocal Coaching
- Suggestions for Effective Coaching Programs

Collaborative Work Teams

- Inclusion Teams
- Interdisciplinary Teams
- Vertical Teams

Co-Teaching

Teachers in successful schools provide support to one another through collaborative planning, observation, and analysis of each other's teaching, and ongoing professional dialogue (Casalegno, 2000; Elliott & Schiff, 2001; Little, 1982; Slater & Simmons, 2001). Improvement means change, which in turn means risk. If educators are asked to be risk-takers, then they should be provided the means for supporting one another as they journey through risky waters. Peer coaching, collaborative work teams, and co-teaching are three frameworks for collegial support discussed in this chapter.

Peer Coaching

Peer coaching involves teachers observing each other's instruction, collecting and analyzing data, and problem solving for the purpose of improving teaching and learning. Here, we'll discuss the historical roots, principles, and types of peer coaching, as well as suggestions for effective peer coaching programs.

Roots of Peer Coaching

Peer coaching has roots both in clinical supervision and in the Joyce and Showers training model briefly introduced in Chapter 2. *Clinical supervision* (Cogan, 1973; Goldhammer, 1969) is a nonevaluative assistance model calling for (1) a supervisor-teacher preconference, (2) a classroom observation of the teacher by the supervisor, (3) a supervisor analysis of observation data and planning for the postconference, (4) a supervisor-teacher postconference, and (5) a critique of the previous four steps. The extensive time commitment required for clinical supervision, along with many teachers' preference for receiving instructional assistance from other teachers, eventually led to *peer clinical supervision*, which followed the same steps as traditional clinical supervision but consisted of teachers observing and conferencing with one another.

Joyce and Showers (1980) introduced *coaching* as a way of transferring skills and strategies learned during a training program into the teacher's active instructional repertoire. Training in a new skill consisted of an explanation of the theory underlying the skill, demonstration or modeling of the skill, and skill practice with feedback. Teachers were then provided coaching as they applied the new skills in their classrooms. In their early writings on coaching, Joyce and Showers (1982) stated that they were not sure who should provide coaching. Based on success with teachers coaching other teachers, peer coaching eventually became the norm (Showers, 1985; Speck & Knipe, 2001). Due partly to the popularity of the Joyce and Showers model, and partly to the negative connotations many teachers associate with the word *supervision*, the term *peer clinical supervision* seldom is used today. *Peer coaching* is now the term usually associated with teachers observing and conferencing with each other.

Principles of Peer Coaching

Although several models of peer coaching have been developed over the last two decades, nearly all of these models subscribe to the following key principles:

- *Peer coaching is nonevaluative.* It has nothing to do with a school's formal system for judging teacher competence or effectiveness.
- *Peer coaching is collegial in nature.* All participants are treated as professionals and equals. A coach never attempts to force another teacher to accept a particular interpretation. The teacher being coached always makes the final decision concerning future actions for improving his or her teaching.
- *Peer coaching is classroom based.* The focus is on the observation, analysis, and improvement of teaching and learning.
- *Peer coaching makes use of classroom observation data.* Depending on the model of peer coaching being used, data may serve as feedback for the observed teacher, a source of ideas for how the observer can improve his or her own teaching, or assessment of effectiveness of a new instructional strategy.
- *Peer coaching is nonjudgmental.* The coach does not express value judgments about the teacher's personal or professional qualities or instructional performance.
- *Peer coaching is based on a trust relationship among peers.* A major aspect of this trust relationship is keeping observation data and conferences confidential.

Despite these common principles, the different models of peer coaching vary significantly in both purpose and process. Next, we'll examine five different coaching models.

Models of Peer Coaching

The coaching models include technical coaching, peer coaching study teams, team coaching, cognitive coaching, and responsive coaching. As you read about these models, consider in which types of peer coaching you would be comfortable participating.

Technical Coaching. According to Garmston (1987), "Technical coaching helps teachers transfer training to classroom practice, while deepening collegiality, increasing professional dialogue, and giving teachers a shared vocabulary to talk about their craft" (p.18). The peer coaching used by Joyce and Showers in their work with schools is a technical model. In their original model, the coach observes and conferences with the teacher to assist transfer of workshop skills and strategies to the teacher's classroom. Specifically, the coach helps with technical feedback, analysis of application to the classroom situation, adaptation to students, and personal facilitation (Joyce & Showers, 1981, 1982, 1983).

Peer Coaching Study Teams. In the 1990s, Joyce and Showers made significant revisions in their peer coaching model. The revised model calls for all the teachers on a faculty to agree to be members of "peer coaching study teams." Members of the team practice agreed-upon change, support each other in the change process, and collect data on implementation and effects on students (Joyce & Showers, 1995; Showers & Joyce,

1996). In the new model, the observer no longer provides technical feedback to the teacher. "The primary activity of peer coaching study teams is planning and developing curriculum and instruction in pursuit of shared goals" (Showers & Joyce, 1996, p. 15). Joyce and Showers report that the omission of technical feedback has not reduced implementation of new strategies or resulting improvement in student growth.

Team Coaching. This model integrates peer coaching and co-teaching (Neubert & Bratton, 1987). Like the Joyce and Showers models, the purpose of team coaching is to transfer skills learned in a training program to the classroom. In this model, however, a coach who already has expertise in the teaching strategy and the teacher collaboratively plan, teach, and evaluate the lesson. Team coaching is unique among the peer coaching models discussed here in that it is the only model that calls for the teacher and coach to teach lessons side by side. Neubert and Bratton (1987) believe that it is this aspect that makes team coaching so popular among participating teachers.

Cognitive Coaching. Costa and Garmston's (1994) cognitive coaching seeks to develop teachers' cognitive skills to a level where they can "self-monitor, self-analyze, and self-evaluate" (Garmston, Linder, & Whitaker, 1993, p. 58). The cognitive coach seeks to facilitate four aspects of the teacher's instructional decision making: planning, teaching, reflection, and application (Costa & Garmston, 1994). Cognitive coaching has three stages: planning conference, lesson observation, and reflecting conference. In the *planning conference*, the coach asks the teacher to discuss the lesson's objectives, how the teacher will know that the students are meeting the objectives, the teacher's plan for teaching the objectives, and data the teacher would like the coach to collect during the lesson. During the *observation*, the coach collects the data requested by the teacher as well as data on whether the lesson's objectives are met. In the *reflecting conference*, the coach asks the teacher to assess the lesson, to recall specific aspects of the lesson on which his or her assessment is based, and to infer relationships between student achievement and teacher behaviors. The coach asks the teacher to synthesize what he or she has learned and to discuss how that learning can be applied in future lessons.

Responsive Coaching. All of the coaching models discussed thus far have a predetermined agenda. The first three models discussed assist the transfer of skills and strategies from training to practice. The agenda for cognitive coaching is to improve the teacher's cognitive skills, and the coach is expected to follow a specific protocol to achieve that purpose. In responsive peer coaching, like other models of coaching, the coach has the broad goal of facilitating the improvement of teaching and learning, and adheres to a staged coaching cycle. Beyond this broad goal and structure, however, responsive coaching has no predetermined agenda. Throughout the coaching cycle, the coach attempts to respond to the teacher's interests, goals, and concerns. This model has been referred to by other authors as *collegial coaching*. Since *all* of the coaching models discussed here are collegial in nature, *collegial coaching* seems to be too general a term to refer to this particular model. Therefore, to better differentiate this model of coaching from the others, I refer to it as *responsive coaching*.

The stages of responsive peer coaching are preconference, observation, analysis, postconference, and critique of the previous four stages. In the *preconference*, the coach asks the teacher to describe the students, the context of the lesson to be observed, and the planned lesson. Next, the coach asks the teacher to discuss aspects of the lesson about which he or she is concerned or simply curious: On what teacher behaviors, student behaviors, or teacher-student interactions would the teacher like the coach to gather data? Once the teacher has described in general terms what he or she wishes the coach to observe, the coach and teacher select or design an observation system for collecting the nonjudgmental data.

During the *observation*, the coach gathers only the data agreed upon during the preconference. Adhering to this guideline allows responsive coaching to remain teacher driven, and maintains the trust relationship between coach and teacher. Figures 3.1, 3.2, and 3.3 illustrate a few observation systems that have been used in responsive coaching. Data collection need not always involve paper-and-pencil instruments. For example, the coach might videotape the teacher's lesson or review samples of student work during the lesson.

Analysis is the next stage of responsive coaching. In analysis, the coach organizes and reviews the data in preparation for the postconference, but makes no interpretation of the data or judgments on the lesson's quality. Depending on the teacher's preference, the teacher too may review the data between the observation and the postconference.

During the *postconference*, the coach shares the observation data and explains technical aspects of the data display. Depending on the teacher's preference, the postconference may end with the sharing of data. More often, however, the observed teacher will wish to collaborate with the coach in interpreting the data and reflecting on the data's meaning. Additionally, the observed teacher may wish to discuss alternatives for improving teaching in future lessons, or even to seek the coach's assistance in designing a specific action plan for instructional improvement. Regardless of the path that the postconference takes, it is the teacher who makes the final decisions regarding interpretation of the data and future actions.

The fifth stage of responsive peer coaching is the *critique* of the coaching cycle, in which the coach seeks feedback from the teacher on the value of the previous stages as well as how the process can be improved in future coaching cycles.

Research on the various models of peer coaching indicates that technical coaching (Joyce & Showers, 1983, 1988), peer coaching study teams (Joyce & Showers, 1995; Showers & Joyce, 1996), cognitive coaching (Costa & Garmston, 1994), and responsive coaching (Gordon, 1990; Phillips & Glickman, 1991) all can result in better teacher decision making and improved instruction. Team coaching, although a promising model, has not been researched as extensively as the other four models. Ackland (1991) points out that many peer coaching programs involve a combination or choice of models. For example, sometimes teachers who participate in peer coaching between training sessions are given a choice between technical coaching for skill transfer or responsive coaching. Such "hybrid" coaching models also have proved successful at improving instruction (Munro & Elliott, 1987). A school considering a peer coaching program needs to investigate each model and choose the model that best matches its

9:30 A.M. Session

Isaac	VR	W	PB			
Felipe	PX	VR	VR	HS	VRD	S
Max	VR	VR	VR	PG	VRD	
Jacki	PB	S	PX	VR		
Gretchen	EC	W				
Sarah	VR	VRD	PB	VR		

12:15 P.M. Session

Isaac	EC	VR	PB	PX		
Felipe	PG	VRD	VR	PB	EC	PX
Max	VR	VR	PG	S		
Jacki	PG	VR	HS	CM		
Gretchen	PB	PX				
Sarah	VR	S	PB			

Key

P praise
VR verbal recognition
PB pat on the back
W wink
S sticker given
PG privilege given
VRD verbal redirect
EC eye contact
PX teacher proximity to student
HS hand signals used to redirect
CM student's clip moved to consequence
NVR nonverbal recognition

FIGURE 3.1 Observation System: Teacher Behaviors Directed toward Specific Students

Time	Name	Situation	Type of Conference	How Problem Was Dealt With
10:01	Caleb	Jumping over chairs—out of seat	1-1	C—"Caleb, sit down." Student sat quickly.
10:02	Jaclyn	Refused to go to assigned seat	1-1	C—Asked her to move to her seat. Repeated 3X. Student moved.
10:16	Chris	Refused to move to another seat	1-1	C—"Move, please." "Move right now, please." "We're all waiting for you."
10:18	Miranda	Writing on her desk	1-1	1-1 only—Walked to student & whispered. Student erased desk.
10:19	Travis	Banging pencil on desk	1-1	C—"Travis, please stop that.
10:23	Jonathan	Yelled out, "Miss, you don't ever help me!"	1-1	C—"No. No, Jonathan. I told you to do this" (pointed to board).
10:24	Betty	Making noise with empty carton	1-1	1-1 only—"Put it in the trash!" Repeated 4X. Student complied.
10:32	Jordan	Out of seat. At back of room.	1-1	C—"Jordan, go back to your seat. Now, please." Student complied.
10:45	Jesse	Out of seat. "I ain't gonna do nothing."	1-1	C—"Jesse, sit down and work." "You can do this." "Come on, Jesse."

Coding:

1-1 One on One
G Group—more than one
C Class
H Hallway

FIGURE 3.2 Observation System: Teacher Responses to Student Behaviors

FIGURE 3.3 Observation System: Open Narrative

Teacher stood at door at beginning of class.
Lesson started on time.
Began lesson with a question: "What are three numbers between one and nine that add up to equal twelve?"
Drew students' attention to board where several tic tac toe boards were drawn.
Explained nature of game and rules.
Clarified rules of game.
Demonstrated playing of game by playing with a student.
Clarified rules again.
Student question: "Isn't this a little too hard for them?" referring to primary kids with whom students will be playing game.
Teacher redirected question to students: "What can we do to make it easier?"
Students paired into partners to play game at board.
Transition from table to board was smooth, as evidenced by on-task behavior.
All students participated in the activity.
Teacher moved back and forth between student groups on an average of two to three minutes.
Teacher often skipped middle group.
Middle group seemed comfortable with the lesson, as evidenced by their ability to play the game independently.
While teacher was at right, groups on left and in middle got off task for about 30 seconds.
Transition from board back to tables with paper in groups not as smooth as first transition, as evidenced by off-task behavior during the transition.
All students were enthusiastic throughout the lesson, as evidenced by their interest and focus while playing the game.
Students were especially enthusiastic when winning, as evidenced by laughter and cheers.
Teacher questioned students about their strategies.
All students felt comfortable with lesson, as evidenced by their comments at the end of the lesson.
Closing lasted only three minutes.
Very little review was required.
All objectives were covered.

professional development needs. Another decision that must be made is concerned with the coaching relationship among participants. The two primary types of relationships, expert and reciprocal, are described next.

Expert and Reciprocal Coaching

Ackland (1991) divides all peer coaching programs into two types: coaching by experts and reciprocal coaching. *Expert coaches* have previously developed expertise in coaching and, if the coaching is for transfer of skill training, expertise in the relevant instructional skills as well. Expert coaching is "one-way" coaching; teachers coached by the experts do not coach others. Teachers involved in *reciprocal coaching* all receive training in coaching and, if relevant, in specific instructional skills. They then take turns coaching each other ("two-way" coaching). Figure 3.4 relates expert and reciprocal coaching to the five models of coaching discussed in the last section.

Technical coaching, *cognitive coaching*, and *responsive coaching* have been effective in both expert and reciprocal formats. *Team coaching* calls for one member of the team to be an expert coach. Reciprocal coaching is the appropriate format for *peer coaching study teams*, due to that model's emphasis on mutual assistance.

Suggestions for Effective Coaching Programs

Based on my facilitation of several peer coaching programs and my evaluation of several others, the following suggestions are offered:

1. Peer coaching is best used as a vehicle for helping to achieve long-term goals. Do school improvement goals include learning new instructional skills and strategies? Improving teachers' decision-making skills? Solving specific instructional problems? Increasing dialogue and collegiality among teachers? Peer coaching can be a valuable *component* of larger efforts to reach any of these goals. The most successful coaching programs I have observed are components of comprehensive improvement programs.

2. The faculty should review each model of peer coaching, then select the model they wish to use based on (a) school improvement goals, (b) other components of the professional development program, (c) their level of comfort with particular peer coaching models, and (d) available resources and expertise.

3. Once a peer coaching model is chosen, extensive planning needs to take place. A number of key questions need to be answered. Will peer coaching be expert or recipro-

FIGURE 3.4 Relationship of Expert and Reciprocal Coaching with Models of Coaching

Coaching Model	*Expert Coaching*	*Reciprocal Coaching*
Technical coaching	x	x
Peer coaching study teams		x
Team coaching	x	
Cognitive coaching	x	x
Responsive coaching	x	x

"x" designates type(s) of coaching (expert or reciprocal) appropriate for each model of coaching.

cal? Will faculty be grouped in pairs or larger teams? What will be the specific stages in a coaching cycle? How often will teachers be expected to participate in coaching? Will teachers be given released time for peer coaching? If so, how much released time, and how will it be provided? Who will coordinate the peer coaching program? What will be the coordinator's responsibilities? How will participants in the program document their activities?

4. Training in peer coaching is a must. Some common training topics include (a) an overview of peer coaching, (b) trust building, (c) conferencing skills, (d) classroom observation skills, (e) reflective problem solving, and (f) details of the specific peer coaching program chosen for the school. Initial training can be fairly basic, with additional training after participants have had an opportunity to try out peer coaching. Topics for advanced training can be suggested by program participants.

5. The peer coaching program needs to be monitored to verify the frequency and quality of peer coaching, determine if desired results are being achieved, and identify emerging participant needs and concerns. And all of this needs to be done while preserving the confidentiality that is part of the coaching process! Simple forms can be used for coaches to report frequency and duration of coaching activities. Group meetings can provide opportunities for participants to give program coordinators feedback and raise issues that need to be addressed. For example, I have never observed a peer coaching program that did not have at least a few scheduling problems. Regular group sessions give participants the opportunity to work out these and other logistical problems.

Exemplar 3.1 provides an example of a successful peer coaching program.

EXEMPLAR 3.1 *Peer Coaching at Lathrop Elementary*

Peer coaching at Lathrop Street Elementary School in Montrose (PA) School District includes aspects of technical and responsive coaching. All teachers participate in the program for their first two years in the district, after which participation is optional. Peer coaching at the school is tied to a training program at Northeastern Educational Intermediate Unit 19 (PA). The training program lasts for two years and includes the topics of peer coaching, teacher decision making, public teaching, principles of learning, systematic observation of teaching, cooperative learning, graphic organizers, and concept attainment. Teams of teachers from participating schools attend the training program. Teachers begin coaching each other in their own schools early in the first year of the program.

Coaching at Lathrop is reciprocal. Teachers choose their own partners, and each teacher is coached four times a year. During coached lessons, teachers are encouraged, but not required, to apply instructional skills and models learned during the training program. The coach collects data and provides feedback that describes student actions or responses to teaching behaviors. The coach asks the following questions during the preconference:

1. What are you teaching?
2. What are the students going to be doing during the lesson?
3. How are you going to teach the lesson?
4. What do you want me to focus on during my visitation?
5. How do you want me to collect the data?

In the postconference, the coach shares the data and the coach and teacher reflect on teacher actions and student reactions. The coach offers suggestions only if requested to do so by the teacher. The coach's role is to provide support, participate in collaborative problem solving, and learn by discussing acts of teaching and learning. Coaches are to maintain confidentiality regarding observations and conferences.

Teachers at Lathrop report that the specific focus and nonjudgmental nature of coaching makes them comfortable with assuming the coaching role. "It's an easy task because you set up one basic concept you are observing. You don't have to cast judgment.... You're really being a facilitator... there is no pressure on you." Participants are equally at ease with being coached by other teachers. "It's very positive in that there is no intimidation.... You have an observer there to communicate to you concerning an area that you have chosen on your own... it's self-reflection with the goal to improve classroom conditions."

Participants report that the program has improved their teaching in a number of ways. Peer coaching helps them to apply skills and strategies learned in the training program to their own classrooms. It also allows them to discover new techniques while observing in other teachers' classrooms. Finally, teachers perceive that coaching has increased collegiality and collaboration among participants. An administrator believes that the nonevaluative, nonthreatening nature of peer coaching helps teachers to improve their instruction:

> Most teachers know they have weaknesses but hesitate to ask for help. In the past, I think, they hoped that it wasn't noticed when they were observed. I think this [peer coaching] allows them to go to a peer, have them come in [to their classroom]... and have an objective appraisal. And it doesn't affect any kind of evaluation, it doesn't affect their performance rating. It allows them to work on improving as the year goes on. It's positive!

Collaborative Work Teams

One of the most remarkable changes that has taken place in business and industry over the last several years has been the transformation of many companies from hierarchial "command-and-control" structures to structures based on collaborative work teams (Johnson, Srinivasan, & Kemelgor, 1998; Kayser, 1994; Marshall, 1995; Orr, 2001). As so often in the past (frequently for the worse, but in this case, I believe, for the better), an idea that first became popular in the world of business has been transferred to PK–12 education. Here, we'll focus on the concept of collaborative work teams by examining three types of teams: inclusion teams, interdisciplinary teams, and vertical teams. It's important to remember that there is considerable overlap between these three types of teams. For example, an inclusion team also might be vertical or interdisciplinary.

Inclusion Teams

School-based teams consisting of regular teachers, specialists, paraprofessionals, and building administrators can assist with inclusion and meeting the needs of students at risk. Inclusion teams can focus on a variety of tasks, including:

- Adapting curriculum, instruction, and assessment to facilitate the success of special education students within regular classrooms
- Promoting respect for cultural diversity and positive relationships among students from different cultures
- Providing support services for English as a second language (ESL) students
- Promoting gender equality
- Providing interventions to assist students with severe behavioral problems
- Coordinating the school's academic, social, and health services for students at risk
- Assuring that every student at risk in the school is mentored by an adult member of the school community

All educators within a school share responsibility for assuring that each student participates fully in the educational process and meets his or her learning potential. However, there are several advantages of having a team coordinate inclusion efforts. The team becomes a visible symbol of the school's commitment to inclusion. Team members can be trained in cutting-edge inclusion practices and then share innovative practices with educators throughout the school. The team can model the collaboration and problem solving that all educators must practice if full inclusion is to become reality. Finally, team members can be available to provide individual assistance to teachers experiencing problems with inclusion.

Interdisciplinary Teams

Interdisciplinary teams are responsible for the educational program of a particular group of students. Team responsibilities include curriculum coordination, student discipline, student class assignment, class scheduling, student assessment, communication with parents, staff assignment, and program budgeting (Crow & Pounder, 1997; Manning & Saddlemire, 2000). Ehman's (1995) study identified characteristics of effective interdisciplinary teams as a strong leadership, professional growth and support, and cooperation within and among teams.

The norms of teacher individualism and separate disciplines that characterize conventional schools mean that establishing interdisciplinary teams is not a simple matter. However, when functioning effectively, such teams can provide schools with a variety of benefits. Interdisciplinary teams can increase teacher morale and collegiality (Flowers, Mertens, & Mulhall, 2000; George & Oldaker, 1985), reduce teacher isolation and foster teacher interdependence (Doda, George, & McEwin, 1987), facilitate teacher empowerment (Husband & Short, 1994), and foster integrated curriculum and instruction (Flowers, Mertens, & Mulhall, 2000; Polite, 1993; Spies, 2001).

Vertical Teams

Vertical teams can be established at the district or school level. At the district level, a team might include teachers, counselors, and principals from different school levels (elementery, middle, and high school), as well as a staff developer, a curriculum coordinator, a central office administrator, the superintendent, and a school board member. A school-based vertical team might include a teacher from each grade level, special educators, counselors, an assistant principal, and the principal. The most common purpose of vertical teams is the alignment and articulation of curriculum across school and grade levels. Curriculum-related tasks of vertical teams include assisting students in transition from one school level or grade level to another, detracking students, and, in secondary schools, increasing the number of students enrolling and succeeding in advanced courses (Ovando & Alford, 1997; Robinson, 2000). Vertical teams also are vehicles for exchanging information across organizational levels, coordinating improvement projects, and disseminating innovations.

The fact that members of vertical teams come from different organizational "subcultures" means that efforts must be made to develop a team culture. A supportive and caring environment, open and honest communication, and mutual risk taking help to create a collegial team culture. Vertical teams with collegial cultures are more likely to consider issues from varied perspectives, adopt a systems view, share expertise, and support implementation of team decisions (Cunningham & Gresso, 1993).

The three types of teams described provide only a sample of the wide variety of collaborative teams found in successful schools. Other types of teams wil be discussed in future chapters.

Co-Teaching

Brody (1994) defines *co-teaching* as "two or more teachers planning, teaching, and assessing the same students in the interest of creating a learning community and maintaining a commitment to collaboration with students and each other" (p. 32). At present, most co-teaching in PK–12 education consists of regular classroom teachers and special educators teaching students with special needs integrated within regular classrooms. Gately and Gately (1993) have identified three stages that regular classroom teachers and specialists go through when co-teaching. The *beginning stage* is marked by minimal communication and high levels of discomfort. In the *developing stage*, communication begins to open up and shared responsibility begins to emerge.

Finally, the *collaborative stage* is characterized by open communication, equal responsibility, and high levels of teacher and student comfort.

Susan Latz, a fourth-grade teacher, and Anne Dogan, a special education teacher, have provided a rich description of co-teaching functioning at the collaborative stage (Latz & Dogan, 1995). Excerpts from their self-study follow:

> Latz and Dogan worked together all day in the same room with 28 children and a teaching assistant. Although the team members were very different from each other in age, experience, background, and beliefs, they soon realized that their diversity could be unifying rather than divisive. They became more flexible in their roles as they regularly shared responsibilities for addressing the academic, social, emotional, and physical needs of all students. . . .
>
> Latz and Dogan shared the various teaching roles. Sometimes, one of them acted in a primary role, handling whole-class instruction, while the other acted as a process observer. . . . Frequently, they engaged in "parallel teaching," where both teachers and the teaching assistant, involved with a small ad hoc group of children, worked toward the same objective. In math, for example, after whole-class instruction, Latz and Dogan would break the class into small groups based on similar needs. Latz might announce, "I'll be up here by the rocking chair for anyone who needs more instruction." Dogan might say, "I'll be here at this table working with manipulatives if you want to join me." The teaching assistant might say, "I'll be wandering around. If anyone needs help just let me know." The teacher sometimes assigned children to these small groups and usually gave them the option to join or leave the group as they approached comfort or mastery. In other words, children were individually determining their needs for help and taking responsibility for making decisions about their learning. . . .
>
> At other times, each teacher and the teaching assistant worked with an individual student or group on a completely different task. The teaching assistant might have guided children on a computer program, while Latz reviewed a science trade book, and Dogan monitored children working on calligraphy. (Latz & Dogan, 1995, pp. 335, 343–345).*

Latz and Dogan reported that the inordinate amount of time spent planning and organizing for co-teaching was worth the investment; co-teaching made a positive difference in their professional and personal lives.

Calderon's (1995) study of two-way bilingual education programs illustrates how co-teaching can be integrated with other professional development frameworks. Two-person teaching teams included one monolingual and one bilingual teacher. The teaching teams participated in workshops on curriculum, teaching, and assessment for two-way bilingual education. Classes taught by the co-teachers consisted of approximately 15 Spanish-speaking and 15 English-proficient students. Teaching teams taught 50 per-

*S. Latz and A. Dogan, "Co-Teaching as an Instructional Strategy for Effective Inclusionary Practices," *Teaching and Change*, 2(4), (1995): 335, 343–345. Reprinted by permission of the National Education Association.

cent of the time in English and 50 percent of the time in Spanish. While one teacher provided direct instruction, the other facilitated group work or monitored class activities. The co-teachers coached each other and integrated coaching with ethnography: Each teacher did a classroom case study while the other was teaching. The two teachers collaboratively analyzed case-study data and outlined recommendations for follow-up study. The co-teachers rewrote curriculum, modified teaching, revised student assessment, and planned strategies for writing with parents. The co-teachers integrated their learning and experiences into workshops they designed to train other teachers to implement dual-language programs. Program outcomes identified by co-teachers included the following:

- Further development of dual-language instructional skills
- Emerging biliteracy skills for monolingual teachers
- Renewed energy and perspective on teaching
- High spirit of innovation, inquiry and research
- High level of collegiality and team teaching effectiveness. (Calderon, 1995, p. 11)

Although most co-teaching is carried out by regular classroom teachers working with special educators, Brody (1994) believes it can foster the professional development of other teachers as well. Based on Schon's (1983) concept of reflective practice, Brody recommends a three-phase model called *reflective co-teaching*. Phase One consists of two interviews intended to build trust and set goals. In the first interview, co-teachers take turns describing a memorable teaching event, interpreting its meaning and theme, and connecting the theme to the teacher's core beliefs. The second interview explores teaching styles, anticipated roles in co-teaching, teaching strengths, and professional goals.

Phase Two in Brody's model consists of teachers' *reflection-on-action* while debriefing a lesson they have co-taught. This reflection involves comparing intended instruction with its actual implementation as well as sorting out competing views of good teaching. During debriefing sessions, "co-teachers should (a) celebrate each other while giving and taking credit, (b) reciprocate expert and learner roles, and (c) develop shared understanding" (Brody, 1994, p. 35).

Phase Three consists of *reflection-in-action*; co-teachers "thinking out loud" about their teaching while in the act of teaching: "When teachers confront their uncertainties, pause to consider alternatives, share those alternatives with the students and each other, and try out the new course of action on the spot, they have engaged in reflection-in-action" (Brody, 1994, pp. 35–36).

Restructuring to permit all regular classroom teachers to co-teach on a daily basis is not a likely scenario for most schools, at least not in the near future. However, provisions can be made for regular classroom teachers to co-teach periodically, thus affording them opportunities for the collaborative planning, teaching, and reflection espoused by Brody.

Our discussion of the teacher reflection fostered by co-teaching segues us nicely to Chapter 4, which presents a variety of frameworks focused on reflective inquiry. This chapter closes with a collegial support needs assessment (Inset 3.1).

INSET 3.1 • *Collegial Support Needs Assessment*

Directions: For each item, choose the response with which you most agree. Possible responses for each item are:

A. I definitely would not choose this option.

B. This option would be acceptable, but it's not one of my favorites.

C. This would be an excellent option.

Possible Collegial Support Formats

1. Peer coaching as a follow-up to training, in which the coach observes the other teacher and provides nonjudgmental feedback in order to help the other teacher adapt new skills and strategies to his or her own classroom
2. Peer coaching as a follow-up to training, in which the coach teaches a lesson with the teacher in order to help the other teacher adapt skills and strategies to his or her own classroom
3. Peer coaching as a follow-up to training, in which the coach teaches a lesson that the other teacher observes in order to gather ideas for adapting new skills and strategies to his or her own classroom
4. Peer coaching in which the coach observes and confers with the other teacher in order to help the other teacher develop his or her decision-making skills
5. Peer coaching in which the coach observes and confers with the other teacher for the purpose of responding to the other teacher's perceived needs
6. Membership on a collaborative work team, in which teachers mutually plan, implement, and assess as well as share successes and problems, brainstorm solutions, and provide each other with moral support
7. Co-teaching, in which two or more teachers teach the same class at the same time

Summary

In this chapter we examined the roots, principles, and different models of peer coaching. Expert and reciprocal coaching were compared, and suggestions were presented for effective peer coaching programs. Three examples of collaborative work teams were given, and co-teaching was discussed both as a means of improving the instruction of regular and special educators working together and as a vehicle for improving the teaching of regular educators working with one another.

Assignments

1. Provide responsive peer coaching to a teacher. Write a report in which you reflect on your performance and the teacher's response to each stage of the coaching cycle. Attach a copy of the observation data to your paper.
2. Interview participants in a peer coaching program on (a) the specific model of peer coaching being used, (b) the types of teaching concerns addressed and observation data gathered during peer coaching, (c) any problems with the program the school has had to deal with, and (d) participant recommendations to other schools considering or planning peer coaching programs. Write a paper summarizing your interview(s) and conclusions.
3. Participate in a collaborative work team. Write a report on the team's purpose, activities, problems, and level of success, as well as the effects of the team on your own personal and professional development.
4. Observe or participate in co-teaching in a PK–12 school setting. Write a report on co-teaching activities, student responses, and the value of co-teaching as both an instructional strategy and a professional development activity.

References

Ackland, R. (1991). A review of the peer coaching literature. *Journal of Staff Development 12*(10), 22–27.

Brody, C. M. (1994). Using co-teaching to promote reflective practice. *Journal of Staff Development, 15*(3), 32–36.

Calderon, M. (1995, April). *Dual language programs and team-teachers' professional development.* Paper presented at the annual meeting of the American Educational Research Association, San Francisco.

Casalegno, L. (2000). Peer power. *Principal Leadership (Middle School Ed.), 1*(3), 42–45.

Cogan, M. (1973). *Clinical supervision.* Boston: Houghton Mifflin.

Costa, A. L., & Garmston, R. J. (1994). *Cognitive coaching: A foundation for renaissance schools.* Norwood, MA: Christopher Gordon Publishers.

Crow, G., & Pounder, D. (1997, March). *Faculty teams: Work group enhancement as a teacher involvement strategy.* Paper presented to the annual conference of the American Educational Research Association, Chicago.

Cunningham, W. G., & Gresso, D. W. (1993). *Cultural leadership: The culture of excellence in education.* Boston: Allyn and Bacon.

Doda, N., George, P., & McEwin, K. (1987). Ten current truths about effective schools. *Middle School Journal, 18*(3), 3–5.

Ehman, L. H. (1995, April). *Interdisciplinary teacher teams: A first year's experience in a restructuring middle school.* Paper presented at the annual meeting of the American Educational Research Association, San Francisco. (ERIC ED 390 845).

Elliott, V., & Schiff, S. (2001). A look within. *Journal of Staff Development, 22*(2), 39–42.

Flowers, N., Mertens, S. B., & Mulhall, P. F. (2000). What makes interdisciplinary teams effective? *Middle School Journal, 31*(4), 53–56.

Garmston, R. (1987). How administrators support peer coaching. *Educational Leadership, 44*(5), 18–26.

Garmston, R. J., Linder, C., & Whitaker, J. (1993). Reflections on cognitive coaching. *Educational Leadership, 51*, 57–61.

Gately, F. J., & Gately, S. E. (1993, April). *Positive co-teaching environments: Meeting the needs of an increasingly diverse student population.* Paper presented at the annual meeting of the Council for Exceptional Children, San Antonio.

George, P. S., & Oldaker, L. L. (1985). *Evidence for the middle school.* Columbus: National Middle School Association.

Goldhammer, R. (1969). *Clinical supervision: Special methods for the supervision of teachers.* New York: Holt, Rinehart and Winston.

Gordon, S. P. (1990, April). *Teacher-directed peer clinical supervision: Participants' reactions and suggestions.* Paper presented at the annual meeting of the American Educational Research Association, Boston.

Husband, R. E., & Short, P. M. (1994). Interdisciplinary teams lead to greater teacher empowerment. *Middle School Journal, 26*(2), 58–60.

Johnson, S., Srinivasan, S., & Kemelgor, B. (1998). Organizational structure and the role of empirical teams in U.S. business schools: An empirical assessment. *Journal of Education for Business, 73*(5), 280–283.

Joyce, B., & Showers, B. (1980). Improving inservice training: The messages of research. *Educational Leadership, 37*(5), 379–385.

Joyce, B., & Showers, B. (1981). Transfer of training: The contribution of "coaching." *Boston University Journal of Education, 163*(2), 163–172.

Joyce, B., & Showers, B. (1982). The coaching of teaching. *Educational Leadership, 40*(1), 4–8, 10.

Joyce, B., & Showers, B. (1983). *Power in staff development through research on training.* Alexandria, VA: Association for Supervision and Curriculum Development.

Joyce, B., & Showers, B. (1988). *Student achievement through staff development.* New York: Longman.

Joyce, B., & Showers, B. (1995). *Student achievement through staff development: Fundamentals of school renewal* (2nd ed.). White Plains, NY: Longman.

Kayser, T. A. (1994). *Building team power: How to unleash the collaborative genius of work teams.* Burr Ridge, IL: Irwin Professional Publishing.

Latz, S., & Dogan, A. (1995). Co-teaching as an instructional strategy for effective inclusionary practices. *Teaching and Change, 2*(4), 330–351.

Little, J. W. (1982). Norms of collegiality and experimentation: Workplace conditions of school success. *American Educational Research Journal, 19*(3), 325–340.

Manning, M. L., & Saddlemire, R. (2000). Ten guidelines for effective interdisciplinary teams. *NASSP Bulletin, 84*(620), 83–88.

Marshall, E. M. (1995). *Transforming the way we work: The power of the collaborative workplace.* New York: American Management Association.

Munro, P., & Elliott, J. (1987). Instructional growth through peer coaching. *Journal of Staff Development, 8*(1), 25–28.

Neubert, G. A., & Bratton, E. C. (1987). Team coaching staff development side. *Educational Leadership, 44*(5), 29–33.

Orr, M. T. (2001). Community colleges and their communities: Collaboration for workforce development. *New Directions for Community Colleges, 115*, 39–49.

Ovando, M. N., & Alford, B. J. (1997, February). *Creating a culture of detracking in a learner-centered school: Issues, problems, and possibilities.* Paper presented at the annual meeting of the American Association of School Administrators, Orlando. (ERIC ED 407 744).

Phillips, M. D., & Glickman, C. D. (1991). Peer coaching: Developmental approach to enhancing teachers thinking. *Journal of Staff Development, 12*(2), 20–25.

Polite, M. M. (1993). *Curricular and instructional decision making: Snapshots of team innovation at Cross Keys Middle School.* Urbana, IL: National Center for School Leadership. (ERIC ED 363 965).

Robinson, A. (2000, March). *Connecting the curriculum for excellence: English vertical teams.* Paper presented at the National Curriculum Network Conference, Williamsburg, VA. (ERIC ED 452 652).

Schon, D. A. (1983). *The reflective practitioner: How professionals think in action.* New York: Basic Books.

Showers, B. (1985). Teachers coaching teachers. *Educational Leadership, 42*(7), 43–48.

Showers, B., & Joyce, B. (1996). The evolution of peer coaching. *Educational Leadership, 53*(6), 12–16.

Slater, C. L., & Simmons, D. L. (2001). The design and implementaion of a peer coaching program. *American Secondary Education, 29*(3), 67–76.

Speck, M., & Knipe, C. (2001). *Why can't we get it right? Professional development in our schools.* Thousand Oaks, CA: Corwin Press.

Spies, P. (2001). Essential supports for sustaining interdisciplinary teams: Lessons from two departmentalized high schools. *NASSP Bulletin, 85*(624).

Resources

Barbknecht, A., & Kieffer, C. W. (2001). *Peer coaching: The learning team approach. K–College.* Arlington Hights, IL: Skylight Professional Development.

D'Arcangelo, M. (Producer), & Wurzburg, G. (Director). (1994). *Another set of eyes: Techniques for classroom observation* [Videotape set and trainer's manual]. (Available from the Association for Supervision and Curriculum Development, 1703 North Beauregard Street, Alexandria, VA 22311–1714)

Elliott, V., & Schiff, S. (2001). A look within. *Journal of Staff Development, 22*(2), 39–42.

Johnson, T. (Producer). (2002). *Improving instruction through observation and feedback* [Videotape set and trainer's guide]. (Available from Association for Supervision and Curriculum Development, 1703 North Beauregard Street, Alexandria, VA 22311–1714)

Kayser, T. A. (1994). *Building team power: How to unleash the collaborative genius of work teams.* Burr Ridge, IL: Irwin Professional Publishing.

Robbins, P. (1991). *How to plan and implement a peer coaching program.* Alexandria, VA: Association for Supervision and Curriculum Development.

Schon, D. A. (1983). *The reflective practitioner: How professionals think in action.* New York: Basic Books.

Scimonelli, G. (Producer). (1989). *Opening doors: An introduction to peer coaching* [Videotape set and facilitator's guide]. (Available from the Association for Supervision and Curriculum Development, 1703 North Beauregard Street, Alexandria, VA 22311–1714)

Slater, C. L., & Simmons, D. L. (2001). The design and implementaion of a peer coaching program. *American Secondary Education, 29*(3), 67–76.

4 Reflective Inquiry Frameworks

Study Groups

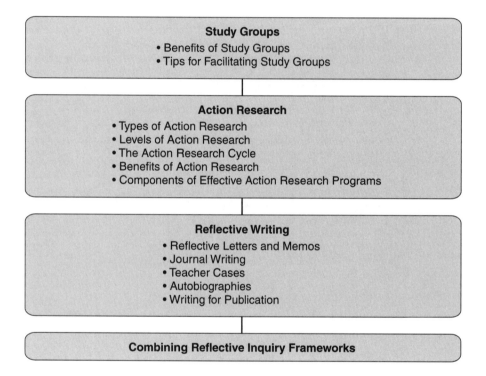

- Benefits of Study Groups
- Tips for Facilitating Study Groups

Action Research

- Types of Action Research
- Levels of Action Research
- The Action Research Cycle
- Benefits of Action Research
- Components of Effective Action Research Programs

Reflective Writing

- Reflective Letters and Memos
- Journal Writing
- Teacher Cases
- Autobiographies
- Writing for Publication

Combining Reflective Inquiry Frameworks

Reflection is careful consideration, and *inquiry* is a systematic search for knowledge and truth. Educators engaged in reflective inquiry frame meaningful questions about their practice, gather data concerning those questions, thoughtfully examine those data, and frame and test hypotheses to improve teaching and learning. This process can improve schools, yet the isolation, heavy workload, stress, and routinization present in many schools are barriers to reflective inquiry. The three frameworks discussed in this chapter can help to overcome those barriers and create environments conducive to reflective inquiry. The frameworks are study groups, action research, and reflective writing.

Study Groups

Study group is a generic term applied to a variety of types of small-group inquiry. Study groups can conduct initial exploration of theory or research and its potential application, or they can focus on planning, implementing, or assessing concrete improvement efforts. An example of the former is the guided book review, in which teachers read a book related to their professional responsibilities, take time to reflect on what they have read, and then meet to discuss their reactions in a small-group session (Goldberg & Pesko, 2000; Schmale, 1994). Guided book reviews promote self-directed learning and reflection, synthesis of theory and practice, common language, and shared meaning, all with minimal expense of time and money (Lick, 2000; Schmale, 1994). Study groups also can focus on discussion and potential application of journal articles (Belair & Freeman, 2000; Fishbaugh & Hecimovic, 1994) or educational research (Lick, 2000; Powell, Berliner, & Casanova, 1992).

Study groups also can facilitate concrete efforts at school, group, or individual improvement. Murphy (1992) recommends that the content of schoolwide study be the decision of the entire faculty, but that each small group should decide on its own specific focus. An example of this strategy is Boggs's (1996) description of study groups in a suburban elementary school. All 28 teachers in the school signed up for study related to the school's goal of "more student-directed classroom environments that meet the needs of all the learners" (p. 14). Each of the study groups chose a specific topic within that broad theme. Study group topics were the following:

- Meeting the needs of students with special learning needs
- Teaching to multiple intelligences
- Integrating math and literature into thematic units through learning centers
- Using alternative assessment/student-led conferences
- Mental health/child behavior
- Integrating instructional units with related arts
- Piloting an everyday math program (p. 14)

The groups in Boggs's (1996) study engaged in a variety of activities intended to implement change in their areas of study, including reading literature, taking courses, designing classroom activities, developing curriculum, and engaging in action research.

Study groups also can foster individual improvement. Severide (1992) describes a self-study process in which teachers discuss and rate themselves on the following criteria:

- Interaction among children and staff
- The physical environment of the classroom
- Health and safety considerations
- Parent, home, community communication
- Curriculum and instruction
- Assessment (p. 6)

Participants meet with a peer facilitator on a regular basis to discuss individual ratings, agreements, puzzlements, and disagreements. The goal is for group members to identify strengths and weaknesses and to decide on how to refine their teaching accordingly.

Keedy and Rogers (1991) describe study groups designed to facilitate teacher renewal through dialogue, informal research, and reflection. These groups "encourage professional dialogue, use teachers as a resource in promoting teacher growth, and have a specific structure encouraging teacher choice" (p. 67). Individual members establish a year-long focus for improving their teaching, and participate in 8 to 10 group meetings throughout the school year. During a group meeting, members establish "game plans," which are strategies to be tried out in two- to four-week increments. At the next group meeting, teachers update the group on the progress they have made on their game plan since the last meeting. Keedy and Rogers concluded that the groups they studied promoted individual renewal as well as cultural norms of collegiality and experimentation.

The focus of study groups can change over time. Murphy (1992) describes how study groups that originally were focused on learning new models of teaching shifted to a focus on how new math manipulatives could be integrated with various models of teaching, and later to a focus on whole language. Activities of study groups also can change over time. Rich (1992) relates how over the course of 14 years, a study group evolved from reading and discussing professional articles to curriculum development, to presenting workshops, to reviewing classroom research.

Benefits of Study Groups

Although there are many different types of study groups, some benefits are common to most effective groups. Study groups provide teachers the opportunity to choose their own focus for professional study. Since groups are small, individual members can engage in high levels of participation. Study groups can increase teacher communication, collaboration, and collegiality. They expose teachers to alternative views, increase their professional knowledge, and promote a common professional language. Study groups give teachers the opportunity to discuss with fellow professionals how new ideas can be applied in their own work settings. They can facilitate a cycle of teachers' reflections on current practice, experimentation with innovative practice, and reflection on that experimentation. They can foster the "culture of change" necessary for schoolwide improvement of curriculum, instruction, and student assessment. Finally, study groups can be used to plan, support, or assess other professional development frameworks, such as training, peer coaching, action research, reflective writing, and so on.

Many study groups have led to a variety of the benefits discussed, but others have failed to bring about any positive outcomes. The success of study groups depends to a large extent on how they are structured and supported. Next we'll take a look at suggestions for facilitating study groups.

Tips for Facilitating Study Groups

The following suggestions are offered for those considering or planning to form school-based study groups:

- *Voluntary membership.* As a general rule, participation in study groups should be voluntary. An exception to this general rule is when the predominant majority of the school community (say, 85 percent) has decided that a schoolwide improvement effort requires all teachers to belong to study groups.

- *Shared leadership.* The staff developer should serve as a facilitator to study groups, with leadership provided by group members on a rotating basis. The study group itself should be allowed to decide on its focus, although that choice might consist of identifying a specific focus within a general schoolwide focus. Group members can select their own readings or be provided a list of readings from which to choose.

- *Group rules.* Early on, the study group should establish a set of group rules. Examples of group rules are "Everyone will participate," "Everyone will use active listening skills," "We sometimes will criticize ideas, but never people," and "Individual problems, concerns, and feelings shared with the group will remain confidential."

- *Logistics.* Optimal group size is six to eight members. Meetings should be held every one to three weeks and should be at least one hour in length. They should be held in a regular place at a regular time of day. If the study group is to discuss a reading, it should be provided to members far enough in advance for all members to be able to complete the reading prior to the meeting. An agenda for the meeting should be provided. Time should be provided for structured activities (e.g., discussing a reading or the application of new ideas), unstructured activities (e.g., an in-basket session for sharing experiences, concerns, or feelings), and processing what took place in both structured and unstructured activities.

- *Diversity.* Efforts should be made to create study groups that are inclusive of teachers who are diverse in race, ethnicity, gender, and so on. The facilitator and other group members have a responsibility to ensure that all group members are treated equitably. The treatment of minorities and women in study groups should be a positive model for the treatment of all adults and students in the school community. The group facilitator should encourage a diversity of ideas by providing members with a diverse selection of readings, issues, or potential innovations from which to choose. Additionally, the facilitator should encourage members to present diverse points of view and to be open-minded about ideas presented by others.

• *Experimentation.* Risk-taking and experimentation should be supported by the group. Members should be encouraged to try out new ideas discussed in study groups, collect data on their efforts, and share both successes and failures with their groups. This means that the group needs to establish a norm that it's okay to fail, as well as a belief that individuals and groups can learn from failure.

• *Reflection.* Reflection can be fostered by the group facilitator and group members using supportive behaviors, being active listeners, and using reflective questioning. Lee and Barnett (1994) describe different types of reflective questions. *Clarifying questions* allow the teacher to clarify perceptions, beliefs, and feelings. *Purpose and consequence questions* help teachers to connect their actions to intended and unintended consequences. *Linking questions* help teachers consider relationships among variables such as their personal and professional histories, their pedagogical knowledge and skills, their professional relationships, and their beliefs, values, and goals.

• *Connections.* Members should be encouraged to make connections between theory and practice. For example, members could be asked whether a situation described in a book or journal article is similar to situations they experience in their own work setting. When discussing a new model of teaching or student assessment, members might be asked to discuss how that model could be adapted to their own content areas and students.

• *Flexibility.* The facilitator and group need to realize that sometimes special situations, interests, or concerns might necessitate deviating from the meeting agenda. Long-term flexibility also is required. Over time the group can be expected to change its focus and activities, and the staff developer should be prepared to facilitate rather than resist the study group's natural evolution.

Exemplar 4.1 provides an example of the effective use of study groups to help bring about school improvement.

EXEMPLAR 4.1 • *Study Groups*

Hamilton Park Pacesetter Magnet Elementary School is located in a predominately African American neighborhood in Richardson (TX) Independent School District. In an effort to change what previously had been a "shotgun" approach to professional development, the school initiated study groups intended to focus professional development on critical areas of curriculum and instruction. Study groups at Pacesetter Magnet School are vertical; they include representatives from each grade level (PK–12) as well as specialists. The teachers have tried out both grade-level and vertical study groups but prefer vertical groups for a number of reasons. Vertical groups allow multiple perspectives, provide teachers with an understanding of what is going on at other grade levels, and give teachers the "big picture" regarding school improvement efforts. During a recent year, there were study groups for each of the following areas:

- Leadership
- Technology
- Creativity
- Student Learning
- Student Concerns
- Customer Satisfaction
- Integrated Curriculum

There are 10 to 12 teachers in each study group, and group membership changes each year. Study groups meet once a week from 7:45 to 8:30 A.M. A teacher facilitates each group, and group norms are established during the first meeting. Early in their history, study groups read and discussed articles. More recently, they have been reading and discussing books. Study groups share their readings and reflections in an effort to tie together related areas of study. Principal Sue Francis states:

> We're doing brain research this year, we're doing integrated curriculum this year (and so on), and it all has to fit together like a puzzle. And we're constantly trying to make these connections for the teachers, just like the teachers hopefully are trying to make the connections in the classroom.

A number of schoolwide innovations at Pacesetter Magnet School initially were explored in study groups. Among these are looping (keeping a teacher with the same group of students for two years), integrated curriculum, and improvements in technology as a teaching and learning tool. Teachers reported a variety of benefits from study groups. They appreciated simply having regular uninterrupted blocks of time to reflect on readings, concerns, and ideas for improvement. Another benefit discussed by teachers was the development of a common professional language.

Additional benefits reported by teachers included improved collegiality, an increased sensitivity to the needs of minority students, better parent-teacher communication, enhanced use of technology, and curriculum and instructional improvement. The principal credits study groups with helping to improve student performance on standardized achievement tests. Study groups have gone a long way toward meeting one of the principal's goals for professional development at Pacesetter Magnet School: "I would like to get the teachers to see themselves as learners. If something doesn't work, try it again. We have to be risk-takers if we want our kids to be risk-takers."

Action Research

Action research is performed by educators for the purpose of solving a professional problem of immediate concern to them. It provides both the short-term benefits of solving immediate problems and the long-term benefit of teachers' professional development. Teachers who engage in action research on a regular basis become better theorists, more professionally active, knowledge sources for the profession, critical readers and users of published research, and collaborators with their students in the learning process (Arias, 1995; Goswami & Stillman, 1987; Speck & Knipe, 2001). In action research, teachers themselves construct knowledge about teaching and learning: "When teachers engage in their own classroom-based inquiry, they use their own expertise, experience, initiative, and leadership. This offers teachers active participation in the development of meaning and knowledge" (Miller & Pine, 1990, p. 56).

Types of Action Research

There are two broad categories of action research: collaborative and teacher driven. *Collaborative action research* involves researchers who normally are in roles different from each other. This usually means teachers collaborating with school experts or university professors who assist teachers by providing training in research skills, sharing readings or other materials on the focus area, and assisting teachers with data gathering and analysis.

Teacher-driven action research is inquiry in which teachers alone carry out all phases of the research. Teachers independently decide on the problem to be investigated, design the study, collect data, analyze data, draw conclusions, and decide on future directions. Both collaborative action research and teacher-driven action research are powerful tools for the improvement of schools, teaching, and learning. Which of these types of research is most appropriate depends on the nature of the problem being investigated as well as the expertise and preference of the teacher-researchers.

Levels of Action Research

Within a school, action research can be carried out at the individual, team, or school level. Research at any of these three levels can be collaborative or teacher driven. *Individual action research* usually involves a teacher conducting research within his or her own classroom. The research might focus on implementing a new instructional strategy, solving a classroom management problem, assisting a student with special needs, and so on. The teacher might involve his or her students in identifying an area for study, collecting and analyzing data, or action planning.

Team action research involves teachers on a grade-level, multilevel family, content area, or interdisciplinary team working together to solve a common problem. Calhoun (1993) notes that an action research team might use a wider variety of methods than an individual researcher, with different team members collecting and analyzing data on different aspects of a problem. "For example, in a study of disciplinary action, one member might survey parents, a second member might interview teachers, and a third might count referrals and organize them by cause and consequence" (p. 64). Eventually, the team compares and synthesizes data, agrees on a common action plan, and collectively implements the plan.

Schoolwide action research involves the entire faculty agreeing on a common problem and engaging in a comprehensive school improvement effort. Schoolwide action research seeks to meet agreed-upon improvement goals, increase the school's problem-solving capacity, and involve all members of the school community (including faculty, students, and parents) in collaborative inquiry (Calhoun, 1993).

It is possible for all three levels of action research to be going on in the same school at the same time. For example, teams and individuals can design their own action research that is consistent with and contributes to a broader school improvement project.

The Action Research Cycle

Action research can be carried out in a six-phase cycle:

1. *Identify the focus area.* The focus area is a general need, interest, question, puzzlement, issue, situation, or innovation chosen for study. Figure 4.1 provides a list of focus areas for research projects planned by PK–12 practioners during seminars on schoolwide action research conducted at Texas State University.

2. *Collect and analyze preliminary data.* The primary reason for collecting and analyzing data at this stage is to find out more about the focus area. Data collection methods could include questionnaires, observations, interviews, logs, journals, case studies, and review of archival data such as attendance data, referral data, student grades, standardized achievement test scores, portfolios, and so on. External data might include research literature as well as information requested from other schools, universities, or government agencies. Beyond providing information to assist in stating a specific problem and planning improvement activities, this stage can provide baseline data to be compared with postmeasures to assess the effects of problem-solving efforts.

3. *State the problem.* The next step is to formulate a specific problem statement to be solved through action research. The problem statement need not be written in formal scientific language. Let's take a look at problem statements in relation to focus areas. The first focus area listed in Figure 4.1 is "Assisting at-risk students." A problem statement related to that focus area follows:

> At ________ High School the staff continually seeks to improve the performance of at-risk students. This action research will determine if students' and teachers' understanding and application of their Learning Style Profile and Myers-Briggs Type Indicator will lead to improved performance of at-risk students.

The second focus area listed in Figure 4.1 is "Developing of an inclusion program." A corresponding problem statement follows:

FIGURE 4.1 ***Examples of Action Research Focus Areas***

- Assisting at-risk students
- Developing an inclusion program
- Improving communication between special and regular education students
- Addressing the diverse academic needs of all students on one campus setting
- Increasing motivation and achievement in reading
- Implementing an effective staff-development program
- Improving student attendance
- Developing a beginning teacher assistance program
- Improving student discipline
- Improving school climate
- Enhancing the use of technology
- Improving transition from middle school to high school
- Implementing a study skills program
- Developing a comprehensive language arts program
- Increasing student achievement in mathematics
- Using effective bilingual education practices
- Improving student achievement through team collaboration
- Implementing a student peer mentoring program
- Studying peer coaching and its efforts on instruction and students achievement
- Increasing parent involvement
- Studying efforts of clinical supervision

> In the current special education pull-out program, students at ________ Elementary School are not making adequate academic and social gains. This action research will focus on practices that can be used to promote the success of special education students in the regular classroom.

4. *Design the action plan.* Information collected in Phase 2 helps action researchers to plan activities aimed at solving the problem. In addition to improvement activities, the plan describes data that will be gathered to (a) monitor and improve the plan's implementation and (b) measure outcomes of planned activities. If the action research involves more than one researcher, the plan also describes who will be responsible for each activity. A time line should be included in order to identify the beginning and end of each activity. If the plan is complex, some type of visual diagram showing the sequence and relationship of the various activities should be prepared. Finally, resources needed to complete the action research should be listed.

5. *Implement.* Implementation includes carrying out the planned activities as well as collecting implementation and outcome data. The researchers need not wait until the problem-solving activities have been implemented to begin collecting data. Data can be collected on an ongoing basis from the beginning of implementation, although data intended to serve as postmeasures (to be compared to premeasures) cannot be gathered until the plan has been in effect long enough to produce outcomes. The methods of collecting evaluation data vary as widely as the methods of collecting preliminary data discussed earlier (questionnaires, observations, interviews, logs, journals, case studies, review of archival data, and so on).

6. *Evaluate.* At a point designated in the action plan, a comprehensive evaluation is completed, and the individual or group conducting the research makes decisions about the value of the action plan and future directions. Possible decisions include discontinuing the action research because the problem is solved; continuing the project, sometimes on a larger scale; or revising the research because the original action plan has not led to problem resolution. When the last option is chosen, Phases 4 through 6 are repeated in a new problem-solving effort.

Benefits of Action Research

A variety of benefits of action research have been reported in the literature. Regarding *benefits for students,* action research has resulted in improved student achievement, reduced referrals and suspensions, higher attendance, increased self-esteem, improved student attitudes, and student participation in schoolwide decisions (Calhoun & Allen, 1994).

Concerning *benefits for teachers,* action research has provided teachers with a structure for classroom change, helped teachers to learn from their students, and caused teachers to begin to view themselves as researchers (Cole & Knowles, 2000; Dowhower, Melvin, & Sizemore, 1990; Rock & Levin, 2002). Action research has improved teachers' abilities to identify and solve problems (Miller & Pine, 1990; Sax & Fisher, 2001; Stringer, 1999). It also has raised teachers' sense of personal satisfaction, increased their professional knowledge, helped them to become more reflective decision makers, and caused them to value research as a part of effective teaching (Bennett, 1994; Cole & Knowles, 2000; Rock & Levin, 2002).

Regarding *benefits for school culture,* action research has increased and improved shared decision making; resulted in the collection, sharing, and analysis of schoolwide data about students; led to data-based change; and fostered the study of professional literature (Calhoun & Allen, 1994). Additionally, action research has improved communication and collegiality and helped teachers develop a common body of knowledge (Carr & Harris, 2001; Miller & Pine, 1990). Diversity is an area in which action research can be an especially powerful tool. Action research teams can gather data on the treatment, concerns, and performance of different cultural groups, then design and carry out action plans aimed at the equitable treatment of these groups at the the classroom and school level. Action research can provide a variety of benefits to students, teachers, and schools. The common catalyst for achieving those benefits is the reflective inquiry running through each stage of the action research cycle.

Components of Effective Action Research Programs

The following are suggested components of long-term programs designed to support action research:

1. Prior to becoming involved in action research, teachers need training in planning, data collection, and data analysis skills. Training need not be highly technical. In fact, attempting to turn training for action research into a formal research or statistics course is a good way to kill the program before it gets started! Training in data collection should involve learning to design simple data collection instruments like short questionnaires, interview guides, and uncomplicated classroom observation systems. Training in data analysis should focus on organizing data, creating visual displays to summarize data (charts, graphs, diagrams), and comparing different types of data.

2. The school needs to set up a process for reviewing action research proposals to assure that students are never put at physical, psychological, or academic risk as a result of research, to determine if proposed research is consistent with the school's mission, and to allocate school resources to teams or individuals proposing research. The review panel should include teachers, specialists, administrators, parents, and other adult members of the school community.

3. Teachers need administrative support, including *time* to plan research, design or select data collection instruments, analyze data, implement problem-solving activities, and evaluate results. Although action research need not be overly expensive, some material support is required.

4. Eventually, *students* should become active participants in research, including helping to decide focus areas, collecting and analyzing data, defining problems, designing action plans, and evaluating problem-solving efforts.

5. Teachers willing to participate in action research should be provided public recognition. Teachers need opportunities to share research through publications, team and schoolwide meetings, and district or regional conferences.

Exemplar 4.2 provides an illustration of a successful action research program.

EXEMPLAR 4.2 • *Schoolwide Action Research*

Based on data provided by the school district and considerable discussion, the staff of Crawford Elementary School in Ames, Iowa, decided that the focus of their schoolwide action research would be the improvement of student expository writing. The problem statement that the Crawford faculty reached consensus on was "to define and study the critical attributes of expository writing in order to improve student achievement in this area." Crawford's principal summed up the teachers' rationale for the action research:

> We wanted to study expository writing ourselves: what it is, what it looks like, how we will know it when we see it.... We realized that probably the reason our kids didn't do very well was that we had very little knowledge of what the

> critical attributes of expository writing were or the best instructional practices to cause it to happen and improve.

Preliminary data collection and analysis included identifying, reading, and discussing literature on expository writing. Also, a five-point analytical scale was developed by the faculty to rate students' expository writing in three areas: *focus and organization*, *support*, and *grammar and mechanics*. The analytical scale helped teachers collect preliminary data on students' writing, served as a basis for reflective dialogue, and was used for both ongoing and comprehensive evaluation of student growth. Before using the scale for preliminary data collection, teachers practiced scoring using writing samples, then comparing their scores with scores assigned by other teachers and by trained evaluators. Collaborative practice sessions helped teachers to clarify the critical attributes of expository writing:

> Every week in our staff meetings the teachers would come and bring samples of their student work, and would try scoring them against this scheme (the analytical scale). But as we did that, we talked about it. Sometimes we would copy them and all of us would score the same ones, or sometimes we'd partner in study groups. Through that dialogue we really became much more professional in looking at our students' writing and thinking. I think that discourse in small groups was what pulled our understanding together.

The action plan called for study groups to analyze student writing samples and identify specific target areas for improvement, investigate instructional strategies, develop and implement classroom action plans, collect and analyze additional writing samples, share results, and modify actions. This process was repeated over and over again from December through May.

The first year of the program was evaluated using scores on student writing samples as well as a survey asking teachers for their perceptions of student progress in expository writing. A comparison of scores on the first and last set of writing samples from each grade level as well as the survey results indicated considerable growth in students' expository writing skills during the project's first year.

The Crawford staff used first-year evaluation data to plan for the second year of the project. Although the focus area and problem statement remained the same, during the second year the action shifted toward learning and applying instructional strategies that would improve students' expository writing. Teachers read, reflected on, and discussed research on strategies to teach expository writing: "Whenever we read an article we would process it using some kind of reflection sheet that would guide teachers' reading and get them to think. . . . What are the key points? What implications does it have for the students? For instruction?" After individual reading and reflection, the research articles were discussed in study groups or in schoolwide faculty meetings.

(continued)

EXEMPLAR 4.2 • Continued

A consultant was hired to provide training on teaching expository writing. The consultant modeled teaching strategies such as cooperative learning, inductive learning, and the group language experience. Demonstration lessons were followed by meetings with teacher-observers to debrief the lesson, analyze effects on students, share the expert instructor's thinking, and discuss how the lesson could be further developed. The consultant met with the staff as a whole as well as with each study group to clarify and answer questions about expository writing.

Teachers were organized into study groups for the purpose of planning and implementing lessons as well as evaluating progress. Student writing samples were collected on a schoolwide basis in October, January, and May. Immediate feedback on campuswide and grade-level results was provided to teachers in the form of tables and graphs. Each time this feedback was provided, study groups met to discuss and interpret the data and to plan instructional strategies based on the feedback.

In addition to the schoolwide writing samples, evaluation data for the second year included a new teacher survey and teacher journals that had been kept throughout the year. Scores for student writing samples improved considerably. Surveys administered at the end of the second year showed that, compared to the beginning of the second year, teachers enjoyed teaching writing more, were more confident in teaching writing, and were more confident in their ability to modify writing instruction based on student performance. Surveys also revealed that the professional development activities that teachers found most useful included time to plan lessons with other teachers, discussion with other teachers, reading research articles, training on instructional strategies, and time to evaluate student writing. The teacher journals showed that teacher modeling, group language experience, and inductive learning were perceived as the most effective instructional strategies for teaching expository writing.

To summerize, action research at Crawford has resulted both in teachers' professional growth and in the improvement of students' expository writing.

Reflective Writing

Writing can help teachers to reflect on their students, curriculum, instruction, and school improvement efforts (Bolton, 2001). On a personal level, writing can help teachers to consider and clarify their experiences, knowledge, emotions, and beliefs. Reflective writing need not be a solitary activity. It can be done collaboratively with other teachers. Sharing writing with each other or co-writing fosters collegial dialogue, mutual support, and collaborative problem solving. Here, we'll discuss five types of reflective writing: reflective letters and memos, journal writing, teacher cases, autobiographies, and writing for publication.

Reflective Letters and Memos

The writer of a reflective letter or memo shares his or her reflections concerning a matter that is relevant to the group or individual who receives the communication. The topic is one that the writer considers important enough to merit both the writer's and reader's thoughtful consideration. In the memo or letter, the writer discusses critical experiences, effects of these experiences, and ideas for dealing with the resulting problem or opportunity. The writer elicits some type of reader response, such as feedback to the writer, the initiation of mutual dialogue, or specific actions to address the problem or opportunity. Figure 4.2 is a reflective letter from a teacher to her class.

Journal Writing

Teachers can keep journals to reflect on daily events, critical incidents, particular students or groups, curriculum or instructional innovations, and a host of other topics. Journal writing is often one component of a larger professional development program. For example, I've facilitated a number of programs that have combined training in new instructional strategies with peer coaching. Often I will ask participants in these programs to keep journals in which they reflect on workshop activities, their experimentation with new instructional strategies, coaching and being coached, and program effects on students, teachers, and the school. Reading those portions of their journals that teachers are willing to share helps me improve my performance as a staff developer. The journals provide feedback to me on what is working in the program and what needs to be revised, and helps me provide individualized assistance when necessary.

Journal writing can be unstructured or structured. In structured journal writing, teachers are asked to respond to a set of questions related to a specific topic. For example, as part of action research at Crawford Elementary School (described in Exemplar 4.2), teachers were asked to respond to the following questions in their journals:

- Describe the strategies you used to directly teach expository writing during the last month.
- What were some things you learned about your students' progress?
- How did you modify you instruction based on what you learned?
- What strategies, suggestions, and so on, did you find most beneficial?

Journal writing can promote collaboration and collegiality. Killian (1991) describes a colleague journal network in which teacher-partners wrote and shared journals as they implemented a staff development project. Partners were asked to share reflections from journals twice weekly. Each partner wrote about what he or she was doing to implement ideas from previous workshops, as well as the problems the person encountered and the solutions he or she tried. Communication through journal writing was supplemented by letters, phone conversations, and visits to partners' classrooms. The journal network resulted in collegiality, perseverance with staff development, openness to experimentation, and opportunities for teacher leadership.

Dear Fourth Period:

It is 3:00 in the morning, and I have been awake for about an hour and a half thinking about this class. I decided to write you a letter because I do not think I will be able to sleep until I explain why I am greatly disturbed by the progress this class is making.

I am afraid that a good deal of copying answers is taking place during group work, rather than true learning. First of all, I want to make very clear the wrong reasons for working in a group. We do not work in groups so that one person can do all the work and everyone else can copy. We do not work in groups so that it is easier to talk to your neighbors. We do not work in groups so that you can easily talk to students in other groups. We do not work in groups so that a teacher can give the answers away. We do not work in groups so that you can exclude people who are assigned to your group.

There are some very good reasons for working in groups. The first reason is that there is only one of me, and over 20 of you. The teacher can talk to everyone in the classroom more often when there are five groups to talk to rather than 20 people. It also makes it easier to explain to four people at one time how to find an answer and check for understanding rather than talk to an entire class and never be sure if everyone really understood. Another reason for working in groups is that sometimes a student in your group may understand how to get an answer and actually explain it better than I do. Remember, students talk differently than teachers, and sometimes a student can explain an answer better because he or she is speaking the same language. After all, I am 30 years old, and the slang words we used 13 years ago are not necessarily used today. A third reason to work in groups is that everyone in the class has different strengths. Some people are better at reading aloud, some people learn best when they hear things, some people have good memories and can remember where they saw the answer, some people are good translators, some people are good summarizers. These are just a few characteristics that I see in this class. We need to learn to rely on other people's strengths, and to learn from other people's strengths so that our own weaknesses will be improved. A fourth reason that you need to learn how to work in groups now is that throughout your life you will be required to work with different people, and you need to learn the skills here in school. The last reason that I can think of right now — remember it is 3:31 in the morning — is that the thought processes that occur while you are finding the correct answer are the exact same thought processes that need to happen in your head on most tests and reading assignments in school.

I have been trying to think of possible reasons why I have not been able to successfully communicate this to you. I realize we have lost a lot of class time. This class has had an early release day, a talent show, and a snow day. I was sick two days, people often miss fourth period due to doctors' appointments, and I am sure there are other reasons. The point is, we have lost a lot of time together.

I know that many people in this class are ninth graders, so the state achievement test is an eternity away. So I want to take the time to tell you that your progress in this class is important to me. It may seem like we do some things that are irrelevant to your life; however, the skills you learn can be applied to other classes as well as things you do in your life. Therefore, I believe what we do in this class is important regardless of your future goals. You will always be asked to read. You will always be asked to get a job done. You will always be asked to work with others. Your future job assignments may have nothing to do with the weather, or Corizon Aquino, or Jose Antonio Navarro, but you will have to understand the job given to you and complete it correctly.

Obviously I think this class is important — otherwise I wouldn't be up thinking about this instead of getting my beauty sleep. More importantly, you are important to me. If you do not leave my class better prepared for the remainder of your high school career and your life, then our time together was not used effectively. We need to work together to learn skills that we can use throughout our lifetime.

Sincerely,
Ms. ______________________

FIGURE 4.2 Reflective Memo from a Teacher to Her Class

Teacher Cases

Cases are descriptions of practice intended to bring about learning. For example, a case might describe a teacher's efforts to help a student overcome a severe behavioral problem. Richert (1991) has concluded that having teachers themselves write cases and then discuss those cases with each other can be a powerful form of professional development. "Preparing the case and then discussing it with colleagues brought their knowledge to a new level of consciousness and understanding" (p. 126).

A process for writing and discussing teacher cases is described by Ackerman, Maslin-Ostrowski, and Christensen (1996). For a warm-up activity, teachers first are shown an example, then asked to "free-write" for seven minutes on a particular theme, such as "The obstacle to leadership for me is . . ." (p. 22). After being divided into groups of three, participants are given five minutes each to read selected portions of their writing. Time is provided for reaction and dialogue. After this warm-up, teachers are asked to write full cases. They are given 30 minutes to write about a real-life professional experience that strongly affected them. Cases are to be written like stories, with a title, lead characters, and dialogue. After the teachers are finished writing, they are assigned to groups of three. Each writer first reads and then elaborates on the case story to the other members of the triad. Then the other two group members ask clarifying questions in order to fully understand the case. Next, the teachers attempt to frame the case's central issue, identify alternative actions, and discuss alternative consequences. The triads then pair up into groups of six to reflect on the process of writing, talking, listening to, and discussing the cases. Finally, in a whole-group session, each small group reports on one major topic or finding that the members explored.

Autobiographies

Writing and sharing autobiographies can foster personal and group reflection. Raymond, Butt, and Townsend (1992) describe a process in which educators develop "collaborative autobiographies." Although the autobiographies written during this process are individual, they are developed through collaborative reflection and culminate in a common improvement project. The process has four phases of writing:

1. A description of the context of the writer's current work
2. A description of the writer's current teaching practice
3. The writer's reflections on his or her past personal and professional life
4. Based on a critical analysis of the first three phases, the writer's preferred professional future

Each member of the group shares excerpts from exploratory writing in each of the four phases. Other members of the group ask questions and share similar and different experiences. The final autobiographies are written only after exploratory writing and group dialogue on each phase. After each teacher has developed an individual professional development plan based on his or her autobiography, the group identifies its collective concerns, then designs and carries out a common project that addresses both individual and collective agendas.

Writing for Publication

Crowe (1992) presents a variety of reasons for teachers to write for professional publication: It improves their teaching, broadens their understanding, meets their obligation to improve and support the profession, and provides personal rewards. Lewis (1992) discusses personal benefits of writing for publication, including evaluating students' growth, gaining the respect of other professionals, and generating ideas that lead to new student and teacher projects.

Despite all the benefits associated with teachers writing for professional publication, few teachers do so. Lewis (1992) reviews obstacles to writing for publication, including insufficient time, writer's block, the absence of reward systems for professional writing, difficulty accepting criticism, and unwillingness to share creative ideas because of fear of losing ownership. There are a number of things that staff developers can do to overcome obstacles and to encourage writing for publication. Teachers can be encouraged to read and discuss journal articles, especially articles written by teachers. As we've seen earlier in this chapter, study groups can serve as forums for the selection, reading, and discussion of articles. Writing workshops can present teachers with information on how to select writing topics, the nuts and bolts of writing an article, how to select a target journal, the protocol for submitting articles to journals, and how to deal with rejections or requests for revisions.

Teachers having difficulty selecting a topic for writing should be encouraged to write about their own experiences and concerns. Milz (1992) provides the following advice to teachers wishing to write for publication:

> I would like to suggest that we each begin with reflecting on our own classrooms. What interesting or unusual patterns do you observe? Is there a child with special needs? What most excites you in your classroom? Is there a new technique or method you want to try? What questions do teachers ask you if they visit?

Once teachers have made a commitment to write, they can meet periodically in collaborative sessions in which they share topics they are considering, outlines of articles, and drafts of manuscripts. Some teachers may prefer to co-author articles and can spend session time sharing research, outlining articles, and co-writing.

The problem of educational journals not wishing to publish articles from PK–12 educators largely has disappeared. Many educational journals now encourage practitioners to submit articles. However, it is still difficult for novice writers to be accepted in many journals. As an alternative to submitting articles to outside journals, district or school publications can provide a means for teachers to share their experiences and ideas with each other. Finally, schools need to reward teachers for professional publication. Teachers who have had articles published can be given stipends, be recognized at school or district meetings, or include their publications in portfolios submitted for review.

Combining Reflective Inquiry Frameworks

Any of the frameworks for reflective inquiry presented in this chapter can be combined in the same program. Following are three example of programs that integrate study groups, action research, and teacher writing:

- In the Educators' Forum in the greater Boston area, teacher study groups met each week for two hours to assist each other with their classroom action research. Members helped each other select topics, design studies, analyze results, write reports, and prepare presentations on their findings to a variety of audiences. A writers' exchange established by forum members disseminated papers on teacher research (Evans, 1991).

- In the Human Education, Research, and Language Development (Herald) Project in San Francisco, site-based teams met weekly during a common planning period to work on individual and group projects to improve oral and written language skills across the curriculum. The Herald project emphasized experiential, integrated, inquiry-based learning for both students and teachers. Teachers reflected on current teaching practice and possibilities for improving teaching and learning through journal writing and discussion. Classroom-based action research enabled teachers to gain new perspectives on their students and their teaching, and led to teacher presentations and publications (Schoenbach, 1994).

- Meyer (1996) reported on a weekly study group that he facilitated that read and discussed professional literature, presented and analyzed classroom data, reflected on personal and professional problems, shared their own writing, and co-created curriculum. Eventually, group members initiated action research on student learning and their own evolving roles. "Our group was a powerful forum for thought and discussion as we read, collected data on ourselves and our classrooms, and analyzed the data (individually and within our group)" (Meyer, 1996, pp. 46–47).

Descriptions such as these show how study groups, action research, and teacher writing can be combined to create synergetic opportunities for reflective inquiry and professional development. Inset 4.1 provides a reflective inquiry needs assessment.

INSET 4.1 • *Reflective Inquiry Needs Assessment*

Directions: For each item, choose the single response with which you most agree. Possible responses for each item are:

A. I definitely would not choose this option.
B. This option would be acceptable, but it's not one of my favorites.
C. This would be an excellent option.

(continued)

INSET 4.1 • Continued

1. Membership in a study group that would read and discuss articles or books and their application to student, teacher, or school needs
2. Membership in a study group that would study and support efforts at school, group, or individual improvement
3. Individual action research, in which a teacher identifies a classroom problem, gathers and analyzes needs assessment data, designs an action plan, carries out the plan, and evaluates results
4. Team action research, in which a group of teachers identifies a common problem, gathers and analyzes needs assessment data, designs an action plan, carries out the plan, and evaluates results
5. Schoolwide action research, in which the entire school community identifies a common problem, gathers and analyzes needs assessment data, designs an action plan, carries out the plan, and evaluates the results
6. Writing reflective letters or memos to colleagues, students, parents, or community members
7. Keeping a professional journal
8. Writing, reading, and discussing cases about real-life professional experiences
9. Writing and sharing autobiographies
10. Writing for professional publication

Summary

This chapter discussed study groups, including types, benefits, and tips for facilitating study groups. Two types of action research—collaborative and teacher driven—were described. Action research was examined at the individual, team, and schoolwide levels. The six-step action research cycle was reviewed. Components of effective action research programs were proposed. Five types of reflective writing were presented: reflective letters and memos, journal writing, teacher cases, autobiographies, and writing for publication. Finally, examples were provided of programs integrating study groups, action research, and teacher writing.

Assignments

1. Interview a staff developer who has facilitated study groups on the groups' purpose(s), membership, norms, readings, activities, and benefits. Write a report summarizing what you learned from the interview.

2. Complete a small-scale individual action research project. Write a report, including your focus area, a description of preliminary data collection and analysis, your problem statement, the action plan, a discussion of your efforts to implement the action plan, a description of how you evaluated the plan's effectiveness, and evaluation results.

3. Keep a professional journal for two weeks. Submit those portions of the journal that you wish to share.

4. Write an autobiography in which you discuss (a) your current work situation and related concerns, (b) your current teaching or leadership practice and related concerns, (c) your professional history, and (d) a professional improvement plan based on your reflection on the first three topics (see Raymond, Butt, & Townsend, 1992).

5. Write an article for submission to a specific professional journal.

References

Ackerman, R., Maslin-Ostrowski, P. M., & Christensen, C. (1996). Case stories: Telling tales about school. *Educational Leadership, 53*(6), 21–23.

Arias, R. (1995). The teacher as researcher : Action research revisited. *College ESL, 5*(1), 62–76.

Belair, J. R., & Freeman, P. (2000). Active learning fostered by journal articles. *Middle School Journal, 31*(4), 3–4.

Bennett, C. K. (1994). Promoting teacher reflection through action research: What do teachers think? *Journal of Staff Development, 15*(1), 34–38.

Boggs, H. (1996, October). *Launching school change through teacher groups: An action research project.* Paper presented at the annual conferences of the Mid-western Educational Research Association, Chicago.

Bolton, G. (2001). *Reflective practice: Writing and professional deveopment.* Thousand Oaks, CA: Sage.

Calhoun, E. F. (1993). Action research: Three approaches. *Educational Leadership, 51*(2), 62–65.

Calhoun, E., & Allen, L. (1994, April). *Results of schoolwide action research in the league of professional schools.* Paper presented at the annual meeting of the American Educational Research Association, New Orleans.

Carr, J. F., & Harris, D. E. (2001). *Succeeding with standards: Linking curriculum, assessment, and action planning.* Alexandria VA: Association for Supervision and Curriculum Development.

Cole, A. L., & Knowles, J. G. (2000). *Researching teaching: Exploring teacher development through reflexive inquiry.* Boston: Allyn and Bacon.

Crowe, C. (1992). Why write for publication? In K. L. Dahl (Ed.), *Teacher as writer: Entering the professional conversation* (pp. 74–80). Urbana, IL: National Council of Teachers of English.

Dowhower, S. L., Melvin, M. P., & Sizemore, P. (1990). Improving writing instruction through teacher action research. *Journal of Staff Development, 11*(3), 22–27.

Evans, C. (1991). Support for teachers studying their own work. *Educational Leadership, 48*(6), 11–13.

Fishbaugh, M. S., & Hecimovic, T. (1994, March). Teacher study groups as a means of rural professional development. In D. Montgomery (Ed.), *Rural partnerships, Working together. Proceedings of the Annual National Conference of the American Council on Rural Special Education (ACRES)* (pp. 122–126), Austin, TX. (ERIC ED 369 600).

Goldberg, S. M., & Pesko, E. (2000). The Teacher Book Club. *Educational Leadership, 57*(8), 39–41.

Goswami, D., & Stillman, P. (1987). *Reclaiming the classroom: Teacher research as an agency for change.* Upper Montclair, NJ: Boynton Cook.

Keedy, J. L., & Rogers, K. (1991). Teacher collegial groups: A structure for promoting professional dialogue conducive to organization change. *Journal of School Leadership, 1*(1), 65–73.

Killian, V. E. (1991). Colleague journals as a staff development tool. *Journal of Staff Development 12*(2), 44–46.

Lee, G. V., & Barnett, B. G. (1994). Using reflective questioning to promote collaborative dialogue. *Journal of Staff Development, 15*(1), 16–21.

Lewis, B. A. (1992). From teacher to writer: How does it happen? *Social Education, 56*(1), 40–42.

Lick, D. W. (2000). Whole-faculty study groups: Facilitating mentoring for school-wide change. *Theory into Practice, 39*(1), 43–49.

Meyer, R. J. (1996, April). *Teachers' study group: Forum for collective thought, meaning-making, and action.* Paper presented at the annual meeting of the American Educational Research Association, New York.

Miller, D. M., & Pine, G. J. (1990). Advancing professional inquiry for educational improvement through action research. *Journal of Staff Development 11*(3), 56–61.

Milz, V. E. (1992). Reflections of a teacher writer. In K. L. Dahl (Ed.), *Teacher as a writer: Entering the professional conversation* (pp. 61–65). Urbana, IL: National Council of Teachers of English.

Murphy, C. (1992). Study groups foster schoolwide learning. *Educational Leadership, 50*(3), 71–74.

Powell, J. H., Berliner, D. C., & Casanova, U. (1992). Empowerment through collegial study groups. *Contemporary Education, 63*(4), 281-284.

Raymond, D., Butt, R., & Townsend, D. (1992). Contexts for teacher development: Insights from teachers' stories. In A. Hargreaves & M. G. Fullan (Eds.), *Understanding teacher development* (pp. 143–161). New York: Teachers College Press.

Rich, S. J. (1992). Teacher support groups: Providing a forum for professional development. *Journal of Staff Development, 13*(3), 32–35.

Richert, A. E. (1991). Using teacher cases for reflection and enhanced understanding. In A. Lieberman & L. Miller (Eds.), *Staff development for education in the 90's* (pp. 113–132). New York: Teachers College Press.

Rock, T. C., & Levin, B. B. (2002). Collaborative action research projects: Enhancing preservice teacher development in professional development schools. *Teacher Education Quarterly, 29*(1), 7–21.

Sax, C., & Fisher, D. (2001). Using qualitative action research to effect change: Implications for professional education. *Teacher Education Quarterly, 28*(2), 71–80.

Schmale, R. L. (1994). Promoting teacher reflection through guided book reviews. *Journal of Staff Development, 15*(1), 30–33.

Schoenbach, R. (1994). Classroom renewal through teacher reflection. *Journal of Staff Development, 15*(1), 24–28.

Severide, R. C. (1992). *Promoting developmentally appropriate practice through teacher self-study. Literacy improvement series for elementary educators.* Portland, OR: Northwest Regional Educational Lab.

Speck, M., & Knipe, C. (2001). *Why can't we get it right? Professional development in our schools.* Thousand Oaks, CA: Corwin Press.

Stringer, E. T. (1999). *Action research.* Thousand Oaks, CA: Sage.

Resources

Bolton, G. (2001). *Reflective practice: Writing and professional development.* Thousand Oaks, CA: Sage.

Calhoun, E. M. (1994). *How to use action research in the self-renewing school.* Alexandria, VA: Association for Supervision and Curriculum Development.

Clark, M. C. (Ed.). (2001). *Talking shop: Authentic conversation and teacher learning.* New York: Teachers College Press.

Dahl, K. L. (Ed.). (1992). *Teacher as writer: Entering the professional conversation.* Urbana, IL: National Council of the Teachers of English.

Glanz, J. (1998). *Action research: An educational leader's guide to school improvement* . Norwood, MA: Christoper Gordon.

Johnson, T. (Producer). (2002). *Improving instruction through observation and feedback* [Videotape set and trainer's guide]. (Available from Association for Supervision and Curriculum Development, 1703 North Beauregard Street, Alexandria, VA 22311–1714)

Neal, P. M. (Producer), & Watts, G. (Director). (1994). *Action research, inquiry, reflection, and decision making* [Videotape set]. (Available from the Association for Supervision and Curriculum Development, 1703 North Beauregard Street, Alexandria, VA 22311-1714)

Sagor, R. (1993). *How to conduct collaborative action research.* Alexandria, VA: Association of Supervision and Curriculum Development.

5 Teacher Leadership

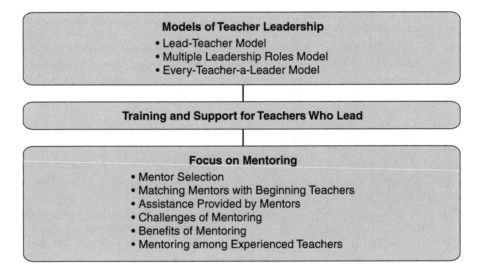

Models of Teacher Leadership

- Lead-Teacher Model
- Multiple Leadership Roles Model
- Every-Teacher-a-Leader Model

Training and Support for Teachers Who Lead

Focus on Mentoring

- Mentor Selection
- Matching Mentors with Beginning Teachers
- Assistance Provided by Mentors
- Challenges of Mentoring
- Benefits of Mentoring
- Mentoring among Experienced Teachers

Teacher leadership is not a new concept. Teachers always have been leaders within their classrooms, served as informal leaders among their collegues, and held quasi-administrative roles such as department chair. Teacher leadership per se is not a framework for professional development, but becomes a framework when it is structured in a way that intentionally promotes professional development. Teacher leadership as a professional development framework is doubly powerful: It facilitates the development of the teachers providing leadership as well as the teachers assisted through that leadership.

Models of Teacher Leadership

Although there is general agreement in the professional development literature on the potential of teacher leadership, experts disagree on the best leadership model. This section discribes three alternative models of teacher leadership: lead teacher, multiple leadership roles, and "every teacher a leader."

Lead-Teacher Model

The titles *lead teacher* and *teacher leader* are synonymous in the literature. According to Fay (1992):

> A teacher leader is a practicing teacher, chosen by fellow faculty members to lead them in ways determined by the context of individual school needs, who has formal preparation and scheduled time for a leadership role which, to preserve the teacher mission, calls for neither managerial nor supervisory duties. (p. 8)

Lead teachers sometimes are called *advising teachers*, *staff development associates*, and *helping teachers*. Smylie and Brownlee-Conyers (1992) argue that responsibilities of lead teachers should be idiosyncratic to individual schools in order to meet specific school needs. However, they also suggest broad objectives for lead teachers, including "improving professional learning opportunities for other teachers, engendering collegiality and collective responsibility among school staff members, and promoting classroom and school improvement" (p. 157).

Those considered for lead-teacher positions should have several years of teaching experience and be master teachers. Effective lead teachers have been teaching in the same school long enough to develop a thorough understanding of their schools' organization and culture. They possess strong interpersonal skills, credibility, and good working relationships with colleagues. They articulate and model philosophies of education and leadership, and display organization skills, self-confidence, and flexibility. Finally, they express a strong desire to assist other teachers.

A few years ago I was talking with a group of lead teachers about how they had been selected as leaders. One of the teachers told an interesting story. She had been suffering from repeated bouts of pneumonia. This condition had been exacerbated by the fact that she taught in a musty basement classroom. When she approached her principal with a request to change classrooms, he offered her a deal she couldn't refuse. He would allow her to move out of the basement if she agreed to fill the position of lead teacher that the district just had mandated for each campus. There are certainly better ways to choose lead teachers! One selection process that has proven effective begins with the formation of a selection commitee made up administrators, staff developers, and a majority of teachers.

The committee develops a job description and selection criteria to be disseminated to all teachers. The position should be promoted as an important and prestigious one. Service as a lead teacher should be voluntary. Teachers can nominate themselves or be nominated by colleagues. Candidates should submit application materials, including a professional portfolio. After reviewing application materials and deciding on finalists, the selection committee can conduct more in-depth selection activities such as observing the candidates teaching or engaged in leadership activities, asking them to make oral presentations, or conducting structured interviews with the applicants. The goal of the selection process should be to select the most highly qualified candidates.

Even highly qualified lead teachers can experience significant role ambiguity and role conflict when they assume their new positions. Lead teachers often are unsure of what the principal and other teachers expect of them, and how they are to balance their teaching and leadership roles. Additionally, principals may be unclear about a lead teacher's role and how it relates to the principal's role. Some principals may view lead teachers as threats to their authority. Other teachers (including some teachers that have been unsuccessful lead-teacher candidates) may be jealous of the lead teacher's position. Additionally, the lead-teacher concept contradicts long-standing norms of equality and privacy. Lead teachers are reluctant to violate these norms, and when they do, they often meet resistance from other teachers.

Lead teachers sometimes find themselves assigned to administrative tasks such as discipline, attendance, and scheduling rather than their preferred tasks of professional development, curriculum development, and instructional improvement. They may be asked to assist with monitoring and evaluating teachers rather than assisting teachers to improve teaching and learning. They often find that they lack sufficient time to fulfill both their leadership and teaching roles. This can result in work overload, less time devoted to preparing and reflecting on teaching or leadership activities, and high levels of stress.

These potential problems show the need for creating policies and procedures to facilitate the success of lead teachers. The role and responsibilities of the lead teacher must be defined clearly and disseminated to all stakeholders. School leaders need to provide support for the lead-teacher concept and individual lead teachers. Training in leadership skills is essential. Teachers should be provided incentives for becoming lead teachers and rewards for being effective leaders. Lead teachers need to be given access to individual teachers, their classrooms, and teacher groups on a regular basis. Finally, lead teachers need released time to fulfill their leadership responsibilities. An instructional day consisting of one-half time teaching and one-half time leadership seems to represent a good balance. Of course even a teacher with half-time leadership responsibilities can be overloaded, thus workload must continuously be monitored and, when necessary, adjusted.

When conditions for success are present, lead-teacher positions can provide a variety of benefits. Lead teachers experience new challenges and opportunities that lead to increased self-confidence, improved teaching, more positive attitudes, increased knowledge, and a broader view of education (Donaldson, 2001; O'Connor & Boles, 1992). Moreover, lead teachers can improve the quality of professional development at the school level by providing ongoing assistance tailored to the professional development needs of the local campus.

Multiple Leadership Roles Model

A second teacher leadership model calls for a variety of distinct leadership roles to be carried out by different specialists within the same school. This model enables more teachers to engage in leadership, allows them to focus on areas in which they have special interest and ability, and provides more opportunities for other teachers to receive professional assistance. Teachers with specialized leadership roles may be provided some released time to fulfill their leadership duties, but teaching remains their primary responsibility. The leadership roles encompassed by this model are many and varied. We've already discussed some of these roles. For example, teachers who are action researchers or peer coaches are in leadership roles. Let's take a look at some additional roles.

Preservice Teacher Educator. With the advent of professional development schools (PDS), experienced teachers in such schools have expanded opportunities as teacher educators. In many PDS, master teachers join university professors in co-teaching on-site methods courses. Clinical experiences for preservice teachers in PDS begin earlier and are more extensive than in traditional teacher preparation programs, and cooperating teachers work closely with university professors in planning, coordinating, and supervising these experiences. Master teachers at some PDS are given paid leaves from their regular teaching duties to become full-fledged members of the university teaching team. These positions usually include ongoing leadership training provided by the partner university. After serving as a full-time member of the university team for a year or two, these teachers return to their classrooms, often continuing to work with preservice teachers on a reduced basis.

Mentor of Beginning Teacher. Most beginning teacher assistance programs include the assignment of experienced teachers as mentors of new teachers. Odell (1990) proposes three primary goals of mentoring: (1) developing, (2) addressing the concerns of, and (3) retaining beginning teachers. Odell (1990) also discusses four phases of the mentoring process. Phase One is developing a trusting professional relationship with the beginner. Phase Two is determining the mentoring content. The content of mentoring should be determined by the beginner's needs over time, as identified by the beginner. Phase Three consists of the mentor applying appropriate styles and strategies while assisting the beginner. Phase Four is disengaging the mentor-beginner relationship after helping the beginner establish his or her own support network. Odell (1990) points out that mentoring has multiple benefits for both beginning teachers and mentors:

> While beginning teachers experience growth in their teaching, improved self-concepts, positive attitudes about teaching, and greater motivation to remain as teachers, they are by no means the sole beneficiaries of the mentoring process.
>
> Consider the benefits for mentor teachers. As a by-product of their mentor training, [they] become more aware of their own development as teachers and of the rationale for their own teaching practices. . . . While interacting with proteges, mentors must analyze and reflect on their own teaching. Interacting with other mentor teachers provides mentors with an appreciation for diversity in teaching styles and settings. Mentoring simply improves the teaching of the mentor. (p. 30)

A more extensive discussion of mentoring is provided later in this chapter.

Trainer. Teacher-trainers assess teachers' training needs, plan and deliver training programs, provide follow-up such as support sessions and peer coaching, and evaluate the effects of training (Cooley, 2001). Training by teachers—especially teachers from the same school—has a number of advantages over the use of outside trainers. Multiple trainers can be provided at less cost, thus increasing the types of training and the number of training sessions and allowing for small-group sessions. Teachers often prefer to be trained by other teachers. There are a number of reasons for this. Teachers can identify with teacher-trainers. They may see teacher-trainers as having a better understanding of their responsibilities, concerns, and needs than outside consultants. Since teacher-trainers are in the same role and face the same realities as other teachers, they may be viewed as having more credibility than outsiders. Participants tend to be in a more active role in sessions led by teacher-trainers, and peer trainers provide more practical ideas that can be immediately applied by other teachers (Wu, 1987). School-based teacher-trainers are more available for follow-up activities and ongoing support to assist with transfer of new skills to the classroom. Having on-site teacher-trainers enhances the development of a professional school culture (Ginocchio, 1990). Finally, the experience of being a trainer fosters the teacher-trainer's own professional growth (Cunningham, 2002; Loucks-Horsley, Harding, Arbuckle, Murray, Dubea, & Williams, 1987).

A team of teacher-trainers seems to have several advantages over an individual trainer. Team members can support each other during the training of trainers. They can practice presenting and coaching with each other. Team members can collaborate in the planning of training programs. They can each take responsibility for delivering those segments of the program with which they feel most comfortable. Each member of the team can be responsible for coaching a small group of trainees as they attempt to transfer new skills to their classrooms. Finally, team members can collaborate to assess the quality and effects of training and make appropriate changes in the training program.

School Governance Team Member. Increasingly, teachers are participating in school governance through service on democratic bodies called *school leadership councils, executive councils, site-based management teams,* or *campus improvement teams.* Those teams consist of administrators, teachers, educational specialists, and, in many cases, parents and other community members. With input from the various stakeholders they represent, governance teams make schoolwide decisions regarding staffing, professional development, curriculum, student grouping, budgets, schedules, instruction, student assessment, school-community relations, and program evaluation. School leadership councils often form committees or task forces that include a combination of council members and other educators, thus providing leadership opportunities for a large number of teachers. There are four critical requirements for teacher participation in shared governance. First, teachers should be elected for governance roles by their fellow teachers. Second, they need to be prepared for effective participation in school governance through appropriate training. Third, they always should seek input from the teachers whom they represent and other members of the school community before participating in decision making. Fourth, the governance teams on which they serve should be given real power to make schoolwide decisions.

Program Developer. Teachers can assume leadership roles in the development of:

- Professional development programs
- Curriculum
- Instructional programs
- Student assessment programs
- School improvement projects
- School-community relations programs
- Extracurricular programs
- Parent-education programs

Leadership activities in program development include needs assessment, planning, implementation, program evaluation, and revision. Program development does not always consist of creating a new program. It can involve introducing and adapting to local conditions a program that has been successful in other schools. It also can consist of revising and improving an existing program. Service as a program developer should be voluntary, preceded by appropriate training, and accompanied by administrative support. It is important that the school make a long-term commitment to the program being developed. There is nothing more damaging to teacher morale, trust, and commitment than for a group of teachers to expend time and energy on an improvement plan or curriculum guide only to find out that the administration had decided not to implement the new program.

Every-Teacher-a-Leader Model

Troen and Boles (1994) assert that teachers care more about expanding their professional roles and enhancing their careers than being assigned to a few formal leadership roles. They propose a "new paradigm for teacher leadership" in which leadership is distributed throughout the school:

> In this teacher leadership paradigm, teachers continue to feel professionally independent, the powerful norm of professional equality is maintained, and teachers develop

> expertise according to individual interests. The role of teacher leader is reconfigured to be more inclusive, rather than exclusive. (p. 282)

New paradigm teacher-leaders facilitate the development of others, challenge the status quo, and expand their influence beyond the classroom (Troen & Boles, 1994).

Gullatt (1995) points out that key functions of teacher leadership such as program, climate, and curriculum development usually take place in an informal and unstructured manner rather than through the assignment of formal roles. Duke (1994) expands on this argument: "In organizations such as schools, which consist of large numbers of professionals, the most desirable form of leadership, in fact, actually may be that which is not limited to particular roles but instead derives from expertise and experience" (p. 269). Katzenmeyer and Moller (1996) point out that when teacher leadership is based on leadership functions such as curriculum development, grant writing, or extracurricular activities rather than formal roles, leadership can be provided on an "as-needed" basis. This allows the school to match teacher talent with educational needs—something less likely with a few teachers in formal roles.

Fullan and Hargreaves (1996) define *teacher leadership* as "the capacity and commitment to contribute beyond one's own classroom" (p. 13). They argue that *all* teachers should be involved in school leadership:

> For classrooms to be effective, schools must be effective. Teachers are a big part of the school. As individuals and groups of individuals, they must therefore take responsibility for improving the whole school, or it will not improve. If they don't, their individual classrooms will not improve either, because forces outside the classroom heavily influence the quality of classroom life. (p. 11)

Consistent with Fullan and Hargreaves, Katzenmeyer and Moller (1996) call for involving a "community of leaders" in school reform efforts. They argue that including only a few teachers in leadership roles presents a negative message to other teachers; the leaders become the decision makers and the other teachers are technicians implementing these decisions.

> A better model is the involvement of all teachers as leaders in the complex and unpredictable process of school reform. . . . Teachers themselves will be engaged constantly in a process of coming to shared and deeper understandings of the change process. (p. 12)

If most or all teachers are to be involved in teacher leadership and school reform, it makes sense to move away from reliance on a few formal leadership positions or roles to a variety of leadership functions. But about what functions, specifically, are we talking? Troen and Boles (1994) provide examples of new paradigm teacher leadership:

- Teachers participate in the larger world of curriculum and pedagogy in new ways.
- They keep abreast of current research and assume a more powerful stance, affecting the development of curriculum at all levels....
- Teachers agitate for the inclusion of technology and technological advances....

- Teachers go beyond the role of teacher as "deliverer of knowledge." They create knowledge by working on research in their classrooms and across schools and communities...
- Teachers play a central role in the development and the implementation of policy....
- Teachers confront issues of how to implement change....
- Teachers write about what they do....
- Teachers hold themselves accountable for the work they do....
- Teachers learn about adult development and its ramifications, they assume that mentoring is a part of their professional lives, and they are aware of the importance of their legacy to the next generation of school teachers.
- Teachers seek to open communication with individuals and institutions outside of schools. (pp. 284–285)*

How does a school move toward the goal of "every teacher a leader"? Katsenmeyer and Moller (1996) discuss characteristics of schools in which teacher leadership is thriving. In such schools, there is a developmental focus; teachers are assisted and assist others in learning new knowledge and skills. Teachers are recognized by the school and each other for their leadership and contributions. Teacher autonomy is encouraged, but at the same time teachers are involved actively in schoolwide decision making. Communication between teachers is open and honest, and focused on problem solving. There is a positive school environment, with mutual respect and frequent teaming.

When teacher leadership is widespread, a wide variety of benefits can occur. Distributed teacher leadership fosters teacher efficacy, helps to retain effective teachers, and reduces resistance to change. Additionally, schoolwide teacher leadership enhances the teaching career, enables teachers to improve their own performance, offers opportunities to influence and assist other teachers, and leads to a collective accountability for student learning (Buckner & McDowelle, 2000; Katzenmeyer & Moller, 1996; McCay, Flora, Hamilton, & Riley, 2001).

Although the every-teacher-a-leader model clearly is based on a broader view of teacher leadership than the lead-teacher model or even the multiple leadership roles model, a school committed to encouraging leadership by all teachers may still have some formal leadership roles (preservice teacher educators, mentors, and so on), or even a lead teacher responsible for coordinating and facilitating leadership functions. However, the central focus of teacher leadership would be the involvement of all teachers in significant and personally meaningful leadership.

Regardless of the model of teacher leadership chosen, care must be taken to assure that teachers of different races, ethnicities, genders, and other cultural groups be provided equal access to leadership roles. Equality of opportunity for teacher leadership will have positive effects not only on diverse groups but on professional development and school improvement efforts, and ultimately on students. Exemplar 5.1 describes a school where the fostering of teacher leadership and equal opportunities for leadership both are high priorities.

*Donovan R. Walling, editor, *Teachers as Leaders: Perspectives on the Professional Development of Teachers.* Copyright 1994, Phi Delta Kappa Educational Foundation. Reprinted with permission.

EXEMPLAR 5.1 • *Teacher Leadership at Jose Ortega Elementary School*

Principal Debbie Sims states that Jose Ortega Elementary School has "been in the business of developing teacher leadership" for a number of years. Sims views herself as the educational leader of Ortega Elementary and sees teachers as Ortega's instructional leaders. "I can't carry the program out," she notes. "The teachers are the practitioners; they're doing it everyday." She also adds that "it is the kind of school where the culture is one of sharing, talking, and working together, and everyone has a role; it's very important that every teacher finds a place outside the classroom for leadership." Teachers agree that the principal has created a "culture of leadership" at the school:

> There is an expectation of leadership. The principal is looking around and thinking, "I've got a couple around here I think would make good leaders." I think there is a culture of leadership where people are identified to be leaders, and it's recognized that they have abilities, interests, and skills.

One formal leadership role at Ortega is the *grade-level cluster leader.* Grade-level clusters are K–1, 2–3, and 4–5. Leaders coordinate their cluster and, with the principal, constitute the school's formal leadership team. Ortega also utilizes *content-area lead teachers.* These teachers have completed, and continue to participate in, extensive professional development in particular content areas. Several of the school's lead teachers are also district lead teachers; they provide professional development opportunities to teachers throughout the district as well as to teachers at Ortega. Lead-teacher activities include assisting new teachers, coordinating curriculum development, teaching demonstration lessons, observing teachers, delivering presentations and workshops, assisting with classroom technology, working with parents, and assisting with student assessment.

Ortega was one of several schools chosen to participate in an alternative to traditional teacher education programs, the Clinical Schools Program, in which cadres of preservice teachers spend three semesters working with each other and with *master teachers* both at the school site and at their university. Principal Sims discusses the advantages of this type of program:

> There has been as much development for my teachers as for my student teachers because of the process; we had an opportunity as a school to really talk about teacher development. It provided opportunities for reflection, to look at our practices, and to look at our strategies.

Teachers at Ortega also assume *leadership of special projects.* An example is the Child Development Project, a program that uses literature as a vehicle for character education. A leadership team was appointed to sustain and support the program. The team planned and delivered extensive professional development over a four-year period.

(continued)

EXEMPLAR 5.1 • Continued

Teachers in formal leadership roles at Ortega discussed challenges they had faced as leaders. These included building trust, presenting to a group of one's peers, being a change agent, working with reluctant learners, and addressing the wide variance of needs and skill levels within a particular group of teachers. One teacher discussed the challenge of facilitating teachers' change and growth:

> You know there is going to be some resistance. . . . What are the skills I need to move a group to a place that you want them to be, and to do it in way that acknowledges and validates where they're at and what they know, and then moves them from there? I think that takes a lot of training and a lot of understanding.

Although every teacher at Ortega is assigned a specific leadership role, many types of leadership are collective in nature. All teachers at a particular grade level are considered grade-level leaders. Every teacher serves on a curriculum committee. When school portfolios were mandated by the district, all members of the school community were called on to assume some type of leadership in developing Ortega's portfolio. Another focus of collective leadership at Ortega is assisting the beginning teacher. In addition to being assigned a mentor, the new teacher is provided a schoolwide support system, including members of their grade-level cluster, content-area lead teachers, and the principal.

Beyond the formal leadership structure and roles at Ortega, there is a great deal of informal leadership. One teacher describes this "unofficial" leadership:

> There is a culture of support, and acknowledgment that there are certain people on the staff that are very knowledgeable in certain areas. And there isn't reluctance on this staff to take on, unofficially, roles of leadership. Our classroom doors are open after school, and there is an exchange, and through that sharing of ideas is a natural sort of floating to the top of people who have concentrated skills in certain areas.

Teacher leadership at Ortega is fostered not only by the principal but by other teachers:

> We are very supportive of people who take on the role. Everybody gets respect. There is an expectation here that we are all participating [in leadership] on some level. There is a grass-roots support for leadership in the school, so if you decide to take on a leadership role, you're looked at like "Wow, great!" If you know you have an environment that encourages you to take risks and put yourself out there, you're more likely to do it.

Both the principal and teachers at Ortega report numerous benefits of teacher leadership. They perceive teachers to be more committed, more skilled, and better able to articulate their craft; and the school culture to be more collaborative, collegial, and growth oriented as a result of teacher leadership. One teacher summed up what was viewed as the most important benefit of being a teacher-leader:

> The most important thing for all of us is, What happens to the students? How are they learning? How are they moving along? That's the whole purpose of what we do here, and so if my leadership role enables me to do a better job with those kids, and move them along, then that's all the benefit I need for taking on the role. It's all about the kids. That's the bottom line.

Training and Support for Teachers Who Lead

The need for teacher leadership training has been mentioned several times in this chapter. The specific knowledge and skills to be addressed in training depend on the leadership role and functions for which teachers are being prepared. Inset 5.1 provides a needs assessment for teachers considering or preparing for leadership responsibilities. Additionally, the grid in Figure 5.1 lists possible topics for leadership training as well as the examples of teacher leadership discussed in the chapter. The grid can be used to match knowledge and skill topics to particular types of teacher leadership. I predict that as you review the training topics and relate them to the various examples of teacher leadership, you'll conclude that a great many of the topics represent appropriate training content for *each* type of leadership!

Beyond training, the school and district need to provide ongoing support for teacher leadership. A number of specific factors support teacher leadership. Many of these have been mentioned in our discussions of the different types of leadership. To review and expand, the factors are:

1. *Provide incentives and rewards for teacher leadership.* Although the primary motivation for teachers providing leadership is intrinsic, extrinsic incentives and rewards let teachers know that their leadership is needed and appreciated. These can take the form of reduced course load or duties, extended contracts, special stipends, tuition for university course work, or covering the cost of registration for and travel to conferences or training programs. Additionally, lunches or dinners, award ceremonies, and special certificates or plaques can be used to recognize teacher leadership.

2. *Provide coordinated support for teacher leadership.* The district superintendent, central office staff developers, and school principal all need to provide support to teacher leaders. This includes moral as well as material support. In schools that do not have a history of teacher leadership, teachers will take the concept only as seriously as formal

(text continues on page 106)

INSET 5.1 • *Teacher Leadership Needs Assessment*

Part I: Level of Interest in Different Types of Leadership

For each item, choose the single response with which you most agree. Possible responses to each item are:

A. I definitely would not choose this option.

B. This option would be acceptable, but it's not one of my favorites.

C. This would be an excellent option.

1. Peer coach
2. Leader of a collaborative work team
3. Leader of an action research team
4. Leader of a teachers' study group
5. Lead teacher
6. Preservice teacher educator/ cooperative teacher
7. Mentor of beginning teacher
8. Trainer
9. Member of a school governance team
10. Program developer
11. Informal leadership

Part II: Knowledge and Skills You Need to Be an Effective Leader

For each item, choose the single response that most clearly indicates your need for developing or enhancing knowledge or skills in the area indicated. Possible responses for each item are:

A. No need

B. Little need

C. Moderate need

D. High need

E. Very high need

Knowledge About

12. My leadership role and responsibilities
13. Adult development
14. Adult learning
15. Self-understanding and personal philosophy
16. Problems of beginning teachers
17. The school's beginning teachers' assistance program

18. The teaching career cycle
19. The school's organization and culture
20. Community characteristics
21. District and school curriculum
22. Content-area innovations
23. Child psychology
24. Student learning theory and learning styles
25. Research on students at risk
26. Effective teaching research
27. Alternative instructional models
28. Alternative forms of student assessment
29. Effective schools research
30. Multicultural awareness and education
31. Characteristics of effective professional development
32. District and school professional development programs
33. The change process

Skills

34. Interpersonal
35. Trust building
36. Work and time management
37. Needs assessment
38. Planning
39. Resource procurement
40. Presentation
41. Modeling
42. Technology
43. Classroom observation
44. Coaching
45. Curriculum design
46. Program development
47. Advanced instructional
48. Critical thinking
49. Action research
50. Reflective writing
51. Group process
52. Problem solving
53. Conflict management
54. Program evaluation

FIGURE 5.1 ***Teacher Leadership Training Topics***

	Types of Teacher Leadership							
	Lead Teacher	*Preservice Teacher Educator*	*Mentor*	*Trainer*	*Dept. or Team Chair*	*School Governance*	*Program Developer*	*Every Teacher a Leader*
Knowledge								
Leadership role and responsibilities								
Adult development								
Adult learning								
Self-understanding and personal philosophy								
Problems of beginning teachers								
The school's beginning teachers' assistance program								
The teaching career cycle								
The school's organization and culture								
Community characteristics								
District and school curriculum								
Content-area innovations								
Child psychology								
Student learning theory and learning styles								
Research on students at risk								
Effective teaching research								
Alternative instructional models								
Alternative forms of student assessment								
Effective schools research								

Multicultural awareness and education								
Characteristics of effective professional development								
District and school professional development programs								
The change process								
Skills								
Interpersonal								
Trust building								
Work and time management								
Needs assessment								
Planning								
Resource procurement								
Presentation								
Modeling								
Technology								
Classroom observation								
Coaching								
Curriculum design								
Program development								
Advanced instructional								
Critical thinking								
Action research								
Reflective writing								
Group process								
Problem solving								
Conflict management								
Program evaluation								

leaders do. Only in schools with leaders committed to teacher empowerment will teacher leadership reach its full potential.

3. *Provide clear descriptions of roles and functions.* If a formal leadership role is to be offered, a detailed, written description of the teacher-leaders' role and functions should be created. This description should be provided to potential teacher-leaders *before* they agree to accept the role. Additionally, the description should be disseminated to all members of the school community who will be expected to collaborate with the teacher-leader. The description will go a long way toward preventing the role confusion and role conflict reported by many teacher-leaders.

4. *Structure the schedule to provide time for leadership.* Leadership responsibilities should not be add-ons to teachers' traditional workloads. Teachers need time to plan, carry out, and assess their leadership activities. Using substitute teachers, combining classes, or having an administrator or staff developer take over a teacher-leader's class are all short-term solutions to the question of time. The ultimate solution is to build time for leadership into the teacher's schedule, much as schedules now include time for instructional preparation. A strong indicator of a school system's commitment to teacher leadership is the amount of time freed up for teachers to participate in leadership activities.

5. *Create structures for continuous assistance.* In support seminars at the school or district level, teacher-leaders can share experiences, ideas, problems, and solutions; communicate concerns and needs to administrators; and receive consultation from outside experts. In Pennsylvania, for example, regional leadership centers provide leadership teams with assessments of their leadership roles and skills, leadership seminars, technical assistance with school needs assessments, workshops, school consultation, and conferences on educational leadership (Hynes & Summers, 1990). Periodicals such as Pennsylvania's *Journal of Teacher Leadership* provide teacher-leaders opportunities to share articles on their roles, experiences, and research.

We have discussed several aspects of assistance for teachers who lead, including needs assessment, training, and ongoing support. Figure 5.2 provides a training and support model for teachers who lead. This model is especially appropriate for schools adopting a multiple leadership roles model or an every-teacher-a-leader model.

Teacher leadership is one of the most exciting frameworks in professional development. It can be a direct pathway to teacher empowerment. But to flourish, it must receive genuine, ongoing support from policymakers, administrators, and staff developers.

Focus on Mentoring

Earlier in this chapter we briefly discussed mentoring as one of several possible leadership roles. Mentoring is such a vital role that it is deserves a separate and detailed discussion. In this section, we'll discuss mentor selection, matching mentors with beginning teachers, assistance provided by mentors, challenges experienced by mentors, benefits of mentoring, and mentoring among experienced teachers.

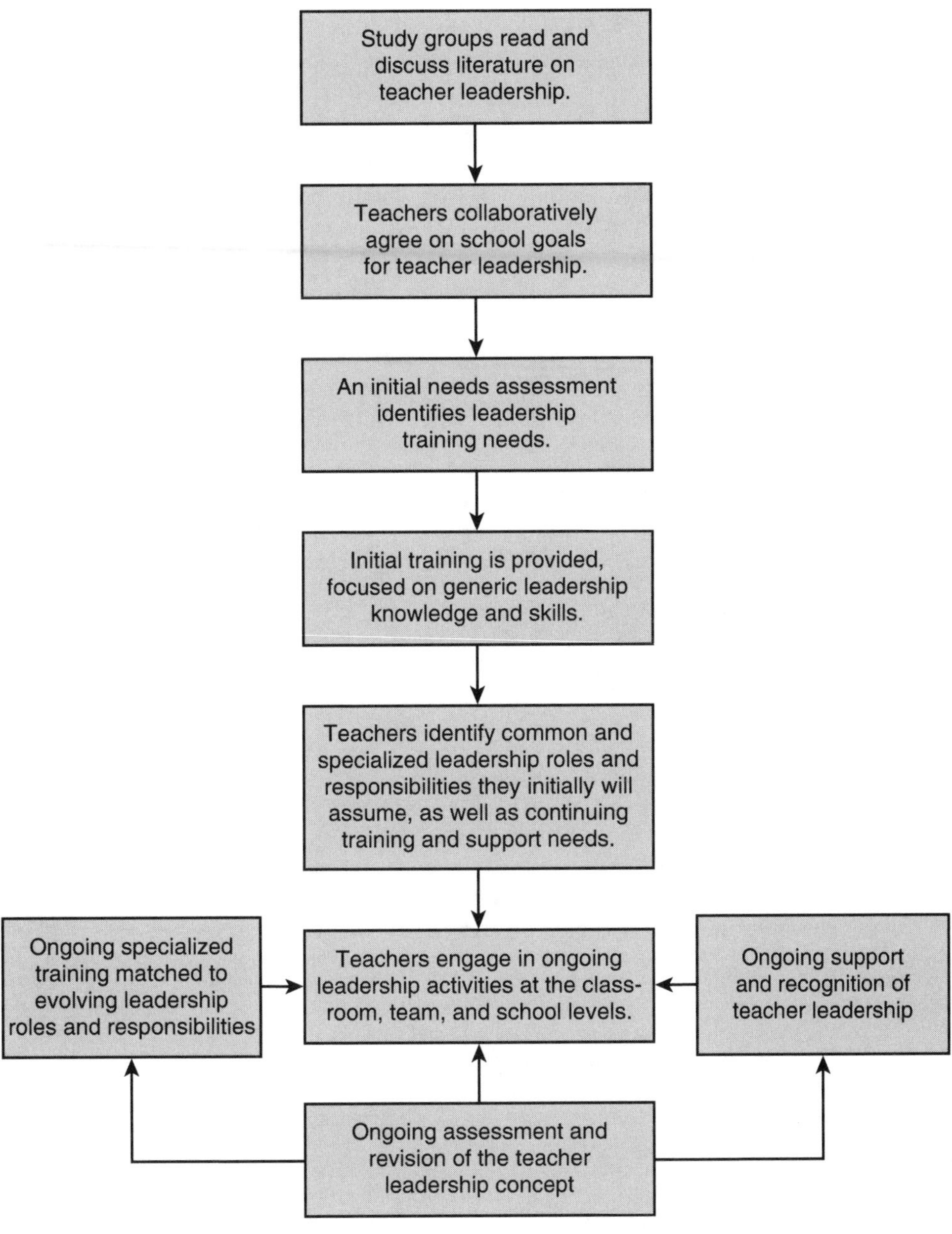

FIGURE 5.2 Training and Support Model for Teachers Who Lead

Mentor Selection

Service as a beginning teacher's mentor should be voluntary. Potential members can be nominated by principals or other teachers, or be self-nominated. An application and supporting documents (letters of support, an essay on the candidate's reasons for wishing to become a mentor, the candidate's teaching portfolio, and so on) should be submitted to a selection committee that includes administrators, staff developers, and a majority of teachers. The literature on teacher mentoring abounds with criteria for selecting mentors (Blank & Sindelar, 1992; David, 2000; Denmark & Podson, 2000; Ganser, 1992; Gordon & Maxey, 2000; Klausmeier, 1994). Figure 5.3 provides a list of personal and professional characteristics frequently suggested as selection criteria. Selection criteria and specific indicators of the presence of those criteria should be stated in writing and made available to potential mentors. Beyond reviewing application materials, the selection committee can ask mentor candidates to make oral presentations or participate in interviews to help the committee determine if they meet selection criteria.

Matching Mentors with Beginning Teachers

It is essential that the mentor and beginning teacher be matched properly— for example, they should have compatible educational philosophies and personalities. The mentor should work on the same campus as the beginning teacher and, ideally, in the same area of the building. He or she should have a teaching assignment (grade level, content area) similar to that of the beginning teacher. In small schools a content-area match might be impossible. For example, there may be only one Spanish or physics teacher in the school. One way to address this issue is for several small schools or districts to form partnerships. An experienced teacher from a partner school then can serve as the content-area mentor, meeting with the beginner on a regular basis. A second mentor on the beginner's home campus would be assigned as the beginner's regular mentor, providing daily assistance not requiring content expertise.

FIGURE 5.3 ***Characteristics of Effective Mentors***

- Teaching excellence
- District and school experience
- Knowledge of the system
- Respect of colleagues
- Influence within system
- Commitment to assist beginners
- Willingness to grow and develop
- Ability to work with adults
- Flexibility
- Problem-solving ability
- Approachability
- Interpersonal skills
- Trustworthiness
- Acceptance of other viewpoints
- Facilitative approach
- Respect for beginner
- Enthusiastiam

Assistance Provided by Mentors

The literature reports extensively on the assistance that mentors provide to beginning teachers (Bradley & Gordon, 1994; Ganser, 1992; Gordon & Maxey, 2000; Klausmeier, 1994; Stuart, 2002; Vardi & Vardi, 1995). Mentor assistance can be classified into *purposes* and *activities*. Figure 5.4 lists types of mentor assistance under these two headings.

The items listed in Figure 5.4 are all important. However, the most important aspect of mentoring is the development of a personal, trusting relationship with the beginner. This relationship is the basis for all of the meaningful assistance provided to the beginner. Meaningful mentoring can take many forms beyond formal activities. It can involve introducing the beginner to teachers and parents, dropping by the beginner's classroom to see how things are going, or taking the beginner out to discuss a problem over a cup of coffee. The effective mentor is committed both professionally and personally to the beginning teacher, and he or she is willing to expend the time and energy necessary to give the beginner the best possible opportunities for success.

FIGURE 5.4 *Types of Mentoring Assistance*

Purposes of Mentoring

- Orient beginner to community, school system, campus, curriculum
- Provide emotional support and encouragement
- Assist with classroom management
- Assist with the planning and delivery of instruction
- Assist with assessment of student learning
- Facilitate communication and collaboration between beginner and colleagues
- Mediate between beginner and "system"
- Assist with paperwork and other administrative responsibilities
- Help beginner to adapt to the school culture
- Facilitate personal and professional development
- Assist with work/time management

Specific Mentoring Activities

- Sharing information on school policies and procedures
- Collaborative problem solving
- Demonstrating teaching
- Co-teaching
- Peer coaching
- Informal discussion
- Collaborative action research
- Providing nonevaluative feedback
- Sharing resources and materials
- Modeling professional behavior
- Attending support sessions with beginner
- Directing beginner to other sources of support
- Arranging beginner observations of master teachers

Challenges of Mentoring

Often, mentors are neither well chosen nor adequately trained and supported. This can result in little meaningful contact between the mentor and the beginning teacher. The mentor might welcome the beginner, share some materials on school policies and procedures, and tell the beginner to "drop by" if he or she has any problems. Such limited involvement hardly represents the ongoing, intensive, and personal assistance provided by an authentic mentor. Beginning teachers unknowingly may contribute to the problem of inadequate mentoring. Due to a lack of understanding of the mentoring concept, fear of revealing teaching inadequacies, or simply being overwhelmed by their workload, beginners may intentionally avoid contact with the mentor. In a study of mentoring programs in a midwestern state, Bradley and Gordon (1994) found that many schools with mentoring programs placed insufficient emphasis on developing the mentor-beginner relationship and providing quality time for mentors and beginners to work together on a continuous, long-term basis. Many schools did not arrange for mutual planning time, classroom coaching of the beginner by the mentor, or opportunities for the mentor and beginner to engage in reflective problem solving.

Some of the problems experienced by mentors parallel problems of lead teachers reported earlier. Experienced teachers not chosen as mentors may resent the appointed mentor. Mentors may be unclear of their roles and responsibilities, or of the relationship of their role and the principal's role regarding the beginning teacher. Mentors may feel overworked by the combination of mentoring and teaching responsibilities. Contrary to the mentoring concept, teachers may be asked by the principal to assist in the summative evaluation of the beginning teacher. This can lead to conflict with, or resentment of, the principal.

The fact that these types of problems are often present in mentoring programs reinforces the need to select mentors carefully, using criteria and procedures like those discussed earlier, as well as the need to provide training and support to mentors. Principals, mentors, and beginners *all* need to develop a clear understanding of their roles and responsibilities relative to the mentoring process. The principal and mentor should develop a collaborative relationship in their efforts to assist the beginner, but the mentor should *not* be asked to assist in the beginner's summative evaluation. One of the mentor's goals should be to assist the beginner in developing a support network so that, once the formal mentoring relationship ends, the beginner has a variety of sources from which to draw for continued professional support.

Benefits of Mentoring

The most important support persons in beginning teacher assistance programs are mentors (Holloway, 2001). They provide beginners with social and emotional support as they help novices understand the school culture, the curiculum, and their roles as teachers. Mentors assist new teachers with classroom management by providing suggestions on how to organize the classroom, set behavioral expectations, and deal with behavioral problems. They guide beginners' instructional improvement by demonstrating effective teaching, assisting with planning lessons, procuring instructional materials, observing lessons, providing feedback, and facilitating reflection on teaching. Mentors also assist new teachers with student assessment by helping beginners set academic expectations, measure student performance, and report student progress. Finally, mentors assist beginners to become full members of the educational community by facilitating communication with parents, collaboration with faculty and staff, and the development of positive relationships with school administrators.

Mentoring beginning teachers also has many benefits for mentors (Griffin, Wohlstetter, & Bharadwaja, 2001). Mentor teachers have the opportunity to reflect on and improve their own teaching as well as to receive public recognition, enhanced professional roles, and increased collegiality (Killian, 1990; Vardi & Vardi, 1995). Teachers report that being mentors improves their confidence, broadens their perspectives, and enhances their communication skills (David, 2000; Odell, 1990). Becoming a mentor can rejuvenate the careers of experienced teachers, as they not only make new contributions to the profession but also learn about new ideas, theories, and techniques from the beginner (Ganser, 1992; Holloway, 2001).

Mentoring among Experienced Teachers

Up to this point, our discussion of mentoring has focused on providing support to beginning teachers. It is possible, of course, for experienced teachers to be mentored. Whereas mentoring of beginning teachers tends to be provided through formal programs, mentoring of experienced teachers by other teachers tends to be informal and voluntary. The best way for school administrators and staff developers to promote mentor-protege relationships among experienced teachers is to foster an environment of open communication, trust, and collegial support.

Powell and Mills (1994) discuss *reciprocal mentoring* among teachers in interdisciplinary teams. Through interviews and observations, Powell and Mills discovered five types of mentoring on the teams, all occurring simultaneously:

- *Collaborative mentoring* occurred when teachers demonstrated dispositions to willingly learn from each other. This sharing of information . . . provided an ongoing exchange of ideas for teachers to build their knowledge base.
- *Clerical mentoring* occurred when teachers helped each other learn bureaucratic procedures such as setting up grade books, taking care of attendance records, and completing regular progress reports on students.
- *Professional teacher mentoring* . . . occurred as teachers encouraged and challenged one another on a professional level. Informal conversations and personal goals often became the springboard for professional development activities.
- *Interdisciplinary content mentoring* resulted from teachers' conversations about subject areas, unit planning, instructional strategies, and student activities. Teachers felt as if they were actually learning content from other subjects as well as adapting instructional strategies which others had used; they also understood their own subject matter area more fully because of the mirror that team members provided in discussions.
- *Social informal mentoring* . . . occurred among all teachers throughout each day. Team members' sharing of ideas about students, teaching, discipline, or content often

occurred as they walked together from place to place or as they ate together during lunch breaks. (pp. 25–26, 28–29; emphasis added)*

To summarize, mentoring in schools can be offered through a formal mentoring program or informally, and can involve a relationship between a more experienced and less experienced educator or reciprocal support among teachers of equivalent levels of experience. Most efforts to develop mentors in PK–12 schools have focused on mentors for beginning teachers because of the critical need to give beginners the types of support that mentors can provide. As important as mentors are to beginning teacher assistance programs, there are other important components of such programs. We'll examine comprehensive beginning teacher support programs in Chapter 10.

Summary

This chapter reviewed three models of teacher leadership: the lead-teacher model, the multiple leadership roles model, and the every-teacher-a-leader model. In the discussion of the second of these models, several examples of formal leadership roles were discussed, including preservice teacher educator, mentor, trainer, school-governance team member, and program developer. A case study of a school focused on teacher leadership was provided. Training and support for teachers who lead was discussed. Because of the especially powerful potential of mentoring, the chapter concluded with a comprehensive discussion of that role.

Assignments

1. Write a paper reflecting on an experience you have had as a teacher-leader. The leadership can be either formal or informal. What leadership activities did you engage in? What, if any, training and support did you receive to assist you with your leadership efforts? How did other members of the school community (administrators, staff developers, other teachers, students) respond to your leadership? How successful was your leadership? To what do you ascribe your level of success? What did you learn from your leadership experience?

2. Write a paper entitled *Every Teacher a Leader?* in which you argue for or against that model of teacher leadership. Cite at least three outside references to support your position.

3. Some experts maintain that the assignment of formal mentors to beginning teachers should be unnecessary because the entire school community ought to provide a caring and supportive environment for the beginner. Write a paper in which you argue for or against this position. Cite at least three outside references in your paper.

4. Locate a school known for its emphasis on teacher leadership. Interview a small group of teacher-leaders at that school on (a) how and why they got involved in leadership, (b)

*Used with permission from National Middle School Association. The information appeared within the November 1994 issue of *Middle School Journal.*

the types of leadership they engage in, (c) training and support that is provided for teacher-leaders, and (d) the effects of teacher leadership on other teachers, the school culture, and students. Write a paper summarizing what you learned from your interview.

5. Ask 10 teachers whether they would prefer to be assisted in their professional development by a full-time staff developer or by another teacher. Ask each teacher to provide a rationale for his or her response. Write a paper reporting results and conclusions.

6. Locate a teacher known to be an effective mentor to a beginning teacher. Conduct separate interviews with the mentor and beginner on (a) the interviewee's perceptions of the characteristics of an effective mentor, (b) the types of assistance the mentor provides to the beginner, (c) the nature of the professional relationship that has developed between the mentor and beginner, and (d) the benefits of the mentoring relationship for both parties. Write a report summarizing the interviews and drawing conclusions.

References

Blank, M. A., & Sindelar, N. (1992). Mentoring as professional development: From theory to practice. *Clearing House, 66*(1), 22–26.

Bradley, L., & Gordon, S. P. (1994). Comparing the ideal to the real in state-mandated teacher induction programs. *Journal of Staff Development, 15*(3), 44–48.

Buckner, K. G., & McDowelle, J. O. (2000). Developing teacher leaders: Providing encouragement, opportunities, and support. *NASSP Bulletin, 84*(6), 35–41.

Cooley, V. E. (2001). Implementing technology using the teachers as trainers model. *Journal of Technology and Teacher Education, 9*(2), 269–284.

Cunningham, J. (2002). Building education professionals. *Leadership, 31*(4), 34–37.

David, T. (2000). Teacher mentoring: Benefits all around. *Kappa Delta Pi, 36*(3), 134–136.

Denmark, V. M., & Podsen, I. J. (2000). The mettle of a mentor. *Journal of Staff Development, 21*(4), 18–22.

Donaldson, G. A. (2001). *Cultivating leadership in schools: Connecting people, purpose, and practice.* New York: Teachers College Press.

Duke, D. L. (1994). Drift, detatchment, and the need for teacher leadership. In D. R. Walling (Ed.), *Teachers as leaders: Perspectives on the professional development of teachers* (pp. 255–273). Bloomington, IN: Phi Delta Kappa Educational Foundation.

Fay, C. (1992, April). *The case for teacher leadership: Towards definition and development.* Paper presented at the annual meeting of the American Educational Research Association, San Francisco. (ERIC ED 347–676).

Fullan, M., & Hargreaves, A. (1996). *What is worth fighting for in your school* (rev. ed.). New York: Teachers College Press.

Ganser, T. (1992, February). *The benefits of mentoring as viewed by beginning teachers and mentors in a state-mandated mentoring program.* Paper presented at the annual meeting of the Association of Teacher Educators, Orlando.

Ganser, T. (1995). Principles for mentor teacher selection. *The Clearing House, 68*, 307–309.

Ginocchio, F. L. (1990). Teacher-clinicians put credibility into staff development. *Journal of Staff Development, 11*(2), 16–18.

Gordon, S. P., & Maxey, S. (2000). *How to help beginning teachers succeed.* Alexandria, VA: Association for Supervision and Curriculum Development.

Griffin, N. C., Wohlstetter, P., & Bharadwaja, L. C. (2001). Teaching coaching: A tool for retention. *School Administrator, 58*(1), 38–40.

Gullatt, D. E. (1995, November). *Effective leadership in the middle school classroom.* Paper presented at the National Middle School Association, New Orleans. (ERIC ED 388 454).

Holloway, J. H. (2001). The benefits of mentoring. *Educational Leadership, 58*(8), 85–86.

Hynes, J. L., & Summers, P. F. (1990, November). *The southeastern teacher leadership center: A program for the development of teacher leaders.* Paper presented at the annual conference of the National Council of States of In-service Education, Orlando. (ERIC ED 326 535).

Katzenmeyer, M., & Moller, G. (1996). *Awakening the sleeping giant: Leadership development for teachers.* Thousand Oaks, CA: Corwin Press.

Killion, J. P. (1990). The benefits of an induction program for experienced teachers. *Journal of Staff Development 11*(4), 32–36.

Klausmeier, R. L. (1994). Responsibilities and strategies for successful mentors. *The Clearing House, 68,* 27–29.

Loucks-Horsley, S., Harding, C. K., Arbuckle, M. A., Murray, L. B., Dubea, C., & Williams, M. K. (1987). *Continuing to learn: A guidebook for teacher development.* Andover, MA: The Regional Laboratory for Educational Improvement of the Northeast and Islands.

McCay, L., Flora, J., Hamilton, A., & Riley, J. F. (2001). Reforming schools through teacher leadership: A program for classroom teachers as agents of change. *Educational Horizons, 79*(3), 135–142.

O'Connor, K., & Boles, K. (1992, April). *Assessing the needs of teacher leaders in Massachusetts.* Paper presented at the annual meeting of the American Educational Research Association, San Francisco. (ERIC ED 348 770).

Odell, S. J. (1990). *Mentor teacher programs: What research says to the teacher.* Washington, DC: National Education Association. (ERIC ED 323 185).

Powell, R. R., & Mills, R. (1994). Five types of mentoring build knowledge of interdisciplinary teams. *Middle School Journal, 26*(2), 24–30.

Smylie, M. A., & Brownlee-Conyers, J. (1992). Teacher leaders and their principals: Exploring the development of new working relationships. *Educational Administration Quarterly, 28*(2), 150–184.

Stuart, L. (2002). What new teachers need: A principal's perspective. *Principal, 8*(4), 18–21.

Troen, V., & Boles, K. (1994). Two teachers examine the power of teacher leadership. In D. R. Walling (Ed.), *Teachers as leaders: Perspectives on the professional development of teachers* (pp. 275–286). Bloomington, IN: Phi Delta Kappa Educational Foundation.

Vardi, D., & Vardi, Y. (1995, April). *Teacher development in urban schools: The role of transformational mentorship.* Paper presented at the Annual Meeting of the American Educational Research Assoication, San Francisco.

Wu, P. C. (1987). Teachers as staff developers: Research, opinions, and cautions. *Journal of Staff Development, 8*(1), 4–6.

Resources

Donaldson, G. A., Jr. (2001). *Cultivating leadership in schools.* New York: Teachers College Press.

Gordon, S. P., & Maxey, S. (2000). *How to help beginning teachers succeed.* Alexandria, VA: Association for Supervision and Curriculum Development.

Griffin, N. C., Wohlstetter, P., & Bharadwaja, L. C. (2001). Teaching coaching: A tool for retention. *School Administrator, 58*(1), 38–40.

Katzenmeyer, M., & Moller, G. (1996). *Awakening the sleeping giant: Leadership development for teachers.* Thousand Oaks, CA: Corwin Press.

Pellicer, L. O., & Anderson, L. W. (1995). *A handbook for teacher leaders.* Thousand Oaks, CA: Corwin Press.

Rowley, J., & Hart, P. (Producers), & Johnson, E. (Director). (1994). Mentoring the new teacher [Videotape set, facilitator's guide, and resource books]. (Available from the Association for Supervision and Curriculum Development, 1703 North Beauregard Street, Alexandria, VA 22311-1714)

Walling, D. R. (Ed.). (1994). *Teachers as leaders: Perspectives on the professional development of teachers.* Bloomington, IN: Phi Delta Kappa Educational Foundation.

6 External Support Frameworks

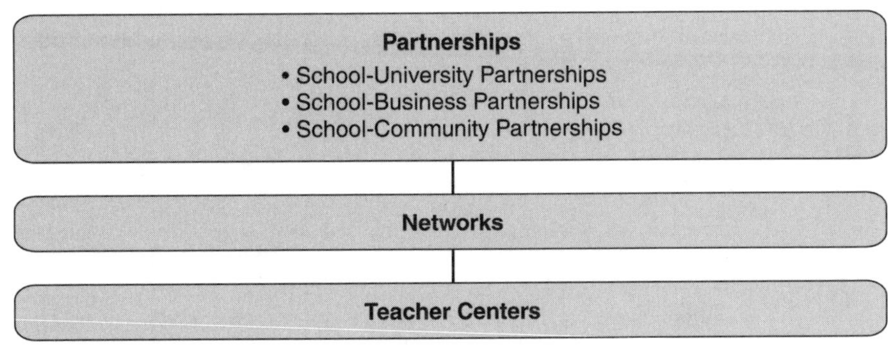

This chapter looks at professional development frameworks that extend beyond campus and often beyond district boundaries but that provide support for school-focused development. Three general categories of external support frameworks are partnerships, networks, and teacher centers. Each of these categories include a variety of specific types of support for professional development.

Partnerships

Schools can develop partnerships with universities, business and industry, and the community. Regardless of the type of partnership, it has the best chance of facilitating professional development and school improvement if it is collaborative in nature (Davies, 2000; Graves, 2001).

> In *collaborative partnerships* [collaboratives], vested interests are sublimated to the broader purposes of the partnership. The focus shifts from a power hierarchy to the strategic agenda of mutually derived goals and objectives. Because they require compromises of individual power, collaborative partnerships are difficult to create and sustain. Collaborative partnerships require an investment of time, energy, and emotion by all constituents to transcend special interests and make egalitarian decisions and equitable participation possible. (Lasley, Matczynski, & Williams, 1992, p. 257; emphasis in original)

Let's spend some time discussing different types of collaborative partnerships.

School-University Partnerships

It is not a coincidence that nearly all of the exemplars in this book involve schools that have developed professional development partnerships with nearby colleges or universities. In each school that has developed a partnership, educators consider it an essential aspect of their professional development program. Here, we'll review several different types of school-university partnerships.

Interactive Seminars. Preservice education students and university professors observe classes in PK–12 schools, then meet in seminars with teachers and school administrators. In the seminars, education students ask questions about the lessons they have observed, and teachers explain their decisions and behaviors. Professors provide teachers with feedack and ideas for improving instruction. These seminars provide education students with an awareness of the realities of teaching, teachers with the opportunities to engage in dialogue with peers and university faculty about instruction, school administrators with ideas for professional development, and professors with a better understanding of teachers' decision making (Aiken & Day, 2000; Diss, Buckley, & Pfau, 1992).

Fellowships and Residencies. Fellowships provide teachers with released time and stipends to attend graduate school in return for assisting university faculty with the development of undergraduate teacher education curriculum and teaching preservice education students. Teacher-in-residence partnerships allow master teachers to take leaves from their school districts and join university faculties as adjunct professors, usually for a period of one to two years. Teachers in residence teach undergraduate classes, supervise preservice education students' clinical experiences, and assist professors in redesigning teacher education programs. Fellowships and residencies can benefit all parties. University professors and preservice education students benefit from the practical expertise of the fellows and residents, who in turn have opportunities to reflect and articulate their own practice, work hand in hand with university professors, and examine teaching from a different perspective. When fellows and residents return to their schools, their districts benefit from their new knowledge of novice teachers and their ability to design professional development programs for in-service teachers (Auger & Odell, 1992; Cobb, 2000; Fazio, Levine, & Merry, 2000; Kagan, Dennis, Igou, Moore, & Sparks, 1993).

Exchange Programs. In teacher-intern exchange programs, a school and a university exchange experienced teachers for intern teachers. Auger and Odell (1992) describe a successful exchange program of the College of Education at the University of New Mexico and the Albuquerque Public Schools. First-year teachers, primarily recent graduates of the university, jointly are selected by the university and school district for paid internships in the district's schools. Interns also are enrolled in a tuition-free Master of Arts program at the university. The presence of the interns as fully licensed beginning teachers frees up some veteran teachers to become clinical supervisors for the college. Clinical supervisors co-teach teacher education courses with university professors and supervise preservice teacher education students. Other veteran teachers freed up by the use of interns become clinical-support teachers who work with beginning teachers in district schools. Both clinical supervisors and clinical-support teachers are chosen jointly by the university, district, and the teacher federation. Most clinical supervisors and clinical-support teachers return to the classroom following their two-year assignments, although a number of them have become principals within district schools. In this partnership, interns receive entry into the profession, a modest salary, expert assistance form the clinical-support teachers, and an opportunity to become a regular teacher within the district. Veteran teachers are provided opportunities to be teacher educators and to enhance their careers. The district has benefited from in-class and workshop support provided by the clinical-support teachers to the interns, first-year teachers, and experienced teachers new to the district. Finally, the presence of the clinical supervisors on the faculty has allowed methods courses at the university to be smaller, integrated, and team taught, with field experiences team supervised.

School-University Restructuring. Partnerships can focus on schools and universities assisting each other to restructure. In an example reported by Knight, Wiseman, and Smith (1992), faculties from a college of education and a middle school restructured their curriculum to more fully integrate the middle school concept. The effort began with selected faculty from both institutions attending a week-long seminar on school renewal and participatory decision making. Interdisciplinary teams of university professors and middle school teachers restructured courses and planned interdisciplinary units at both the university and middle school levels. Teachers and professors collaborated to integrate field-based experiences for preservice education students into interdisciplinary units. Although the project initially emphasized joint action, reflective inquiry eventually was added, with faculty and graduate students carrying out research on the effects of the restructured curriculum on teachers and students.

Professional Development Schools. Sometimes referred to as *clinical schools* or *professional practice schools*, professional development schools (PDS) are based on partnerships between universities that prepare teachers and nearby schools. Purposes of PDS include:

1. The simultaneous restructuring of schools and teacher preparation programs through school-university collaboration
2. The integration and improvement of preservice teachers' academic and clinical experiences
3. The continuing professional development of in-service educators
4. Research and development in schools to increase knowledge about and improve practice in teaching and learning
5. The creation of exemplary school sites to serve as models for professional development and school improvement

The professional development schools concept assumes collaboration between university and school personnel:

> This assumption challenges traditional status relationships in which school personnel have been expected to defer to their "better educated"colleagues at the university. In the PDS model, teachers and local administrators are no less than full partners in teacher preparation as well as school operation. The sources of authority most valued in these schools are knowledge and experience. Thus, teachers may be viewed as the most appropriate decision makers on matters affecting their classrooms. On the other hand, university personnel can bring a perspective to classroom issues that is rooted in the literature, as well as observation and reflection about practice. Teachers and faculty members in PDS will be sensitive to these differences and value them as bases for meaningful collaboration. (Nystrand, 1991, p. 10)

Proponents of PDS maintain that certain characteristics must be present if professional development schools are to achieve their purpose, including open communication and collaboration between the university and partner school (Abdal-Haqq, 1996; Clark, 1999; Nystrand, 1991; Rock & Levin, 2002), a culture of support for teacher inquiry (Lieberman & Miller, 1990; Nystrand, 1991; Sandholtz & Dadlez, 2000), and continuing renewal and improvement of all parties (Lawrence & Dubetz, 2001;

Nystrand, 1991). In PDS, methods courses often are taught on site and are integrated with clinical experiences that begin earlier, are more varied and sophisticated, last longer, and are better supervised than traditional clinical experiences. Professional development schools provide in-service teachers with a variety of opportunities. Experienced teachers can collaborate with university professors in writing grant proposals, co-authoring articles, shared teaching, workshop and conference presentations, and action research (Rosselli, Perez, Piersall, & Pantridge, 1993). Teachers collaborate with professors in mutual problem solving and the cooperative supervision of prospective educators (Abdal-Haqq, 1989; Silva & Dana, 2001). In-service teachers are also provided with opportunities to become involved in curriculum development and shared governance (Boles & Troen, 1994).

A number of concerns regarding PDS have been identified. One concern centers on the reality that considerable resources are necessary to develop and maintain PDS and the question of whether such resources can be garnered by universities and schools. Another concern relates to the cultural differences between PK–12 schools and colleges of education and whether those differences can be overcome in order to establish successful PDS. A third concern is that a variety of different types of school-university collaboratives have adopted the title PDS even though they do not adhere to the purposes or possess the characteristics of authentic PDS. Finally, there is a concern that thus far the PDS concept has been long on theory and short on research focused on the effects of PDS. Considering the ambitious agenda of PDS and the relatively short period of time that such schools have been in operation, concerns regarding their viability should not surprise us. However, these concerns do point to the need for accelerated research on PDS. Exemplar 6.1 describes a successful professional development school.

EXEMPLAR 6.1 • *Woodrow Wilson Professional Development School*

A partnership between the Manhattan-Ogden United School District and the Colleges of Education and Arts and Sciences at Kansas State University (KSU) has resulted in six K–6 professional development schools (PDS) within the district. These PDS have enabled the redesign of Kansas State's teacher preparation program, provided a variety of professional development opportunities for in-service teachers, and stimulated the improvement of curriculum, instruction, and student assessment. The exemplar described here is from one of the partnership's PDS:

In the Spring of 1989, Kansas State administered a needs assessment survey to student teachers, teachers, and parents. Based on survey results, a decision was made to focus initial restructuring efforts on the improvement of science, mathematics, and technology. A teacher from Woodrow Wilson discussed reasons for forming a school-university partnership to address these three areas:

> They [the university] knew they needed to change their courses for preservice teachers and they wanted our help in designing courses. And we knew that we

(continued)

EXEMPLAR 6.1 • Continued

> needed help in the way we were teaching math and science. And so it was kind of a merger, with no one telling anyone they were doing things the wrong way, just that we needed some help—we needed to work together.

Teachers, administrators, preservice education students, education specialists, scientists, and mathematicians all assisted in designing the PDS. The goal at Woodrow Wilson was to create a "Learning Laboratory" for observation, experimentation, and improved practice. An in-service teacher discussed initial professional development efforts:

> We needed to know our stuff first, so they started with us. They had summer institutes that were a month long where they had science professors that were involved in changing teaching preparation courses . . . they taught us chemistry, physics, they took us through courses that we had never had before.

One component of the partnership was a new elementary teacher preparation program in math, science, and technology. The program includes 31 semester hours of science and math for preservice elementary teachers, integrated with 9 semester hours of instructional methodology and 3 years of extensive school-based field experiences. In-service teachers from Woodrow Wilson served on teams that designed the new courses and field experiences. Preservice and in-service teachers became partners in field experiences at the school. A teacher elaborated on this notion:

> It's not like they [preservice teachers] come in and watch us teaching a few lessons, and then are out of there. What we've done is use them as partners in teaching. It's more of a team teaching kind of situation. We can do tons more in the classroom as far as hands-on kinds of things.

Since becoming a professional development school, Woodrow Wilson has institutionalized a variety of innovations, including a nonroutine problem-solving mathematics curriculum, an inquiry-based science curriculum, thematic teaching, multiage classrooms, and alternative assessment strategies. Two additional innovations were summer magnet schools and after-school clubs. The *summer magnet schools* provide K–6 students with hands-on activities to develop higher-order thinking and problem-solving skills, and provide professional development for teachers on activity-based instruction in science, mathematics, and technology. Assisted by KSU professors, teams of in-service and preservice teachers plan, teach, and assess the month-long magnet schools. The teams teach in the morning, then meet in the afternoon to process the morning's teaching and plan future lessons.

The *after-school clubs* are provided for K–6 students six times each semester. They last for one hour and consist of activities to increase students' problem-solving skills in math and science. The general focus of the clubs is planned by KSU methods professors and in-service teachers, but the specific planning and teaching is carried out by preservice teachers. In-service teachers are invited to observe and participate in the learning experiences, but their involvement is optional.

Clinical instructors, half-time classroom teachers and half-time university faculty, are critical leaders in PDS. They are liaisons between the school and university, teach methods courses at the university, supervise clinical experiences, lead seminars for preservice teachers, and facilitate the professional development of in-service teachers.

As a "Learning Laboratory," Woodrow Wilson Elementary makes extensive use of action research. Membership in the "Lab" includes students, teachers, administrators, parents, and university faculty. This team uses student performance data to identify discrepancies between desired and actual performance, then identifies and prioritizes specific problems to be solved. Next, action plans aimed at solving priority problems are designed and implemented.

Professional development at Woodrow Wilson is ongoing and intensive. Student assessment data, teacher surveys, and teacher interviews provide the basis for yearly site-based professional development plans. Teacher growth activities include summer institutes and courses, monthly professional development days, weekly seminars, and study groups. Professional development at Woodrow Wilson is teacher driven. As one teacher put it, "It's teachers doing the leading, teachers deciding what areas we need to improve in, and teachers deciding what kind of in-service."

Since Woodrow Wilson became a professional development school, improvements in student performance have been dramatic. Student achievement in math, science, and writing tests has steadily increased. In-service educators at Woodrow Wilson report that preservice teachers now are entering student teaching with teaching and problem-solving skills that enable them to become instructional partners with classroom teachers.

Partnerships Focused Exclusively on In-Service Educators. Each type of partnership we have discussed so far has connected the professional development of preservice and in-service teachers. There are also many school-university partnerships that focus exclusively on the development of in-service educators. For several years, other professors and I coordinated such programs through the Office of Staff Development and School Improvement at Pennsylvania State University. This office provided professional development, at cost, to schools and districts throughout the state. We focused on the collaborative planning and implementation of professional development needs assessments, long-term development programs, and program evaluations. We enlisted teams of professors, private consultants, and expert practitioners to collaborate with schools and districts wishing to enter into partnerships. Teachers involved in these programs usually had the option of earning graduate course credit for their participation.

Most of the partnerships that we developed lasted for several years. Many of the professional development programs that we facilitated included the preparation of leadership cadres—teams composed of school leaders and a majority of teachers who eventually assumed responsibility for continuing professional development programs as the university's involvement was phased out. One of the things that I learned from my involvement in these partnerships was that, although school-university partnerships are difficult to develop and maintain, they can result in significant teacher development and school improvement. Another thing I learned was that most of the expertise and energy needed for school improvement already exists among PK–12 practitioners; the university's most important role as a partner institution is the facilitation of local leaders and teachers as they articulate their own expertise and unleash their own potential for reflective action.

School-Business Partnerships

Most of the schools from which exemplars for this text were drawn are involved in partnerships with a variety of businesses. A *school-business partnership* is defined as

> a long-term, mutually beneficial relationship between a business or organization and a school. It is an exchange of personnel, expertise and resources based on a matching of the partners' interests and needs. The purpose . . . is to enrich student learning opportunities by utilizing talents unique to the business community. (Edmund Catholic Schools, in Alberta Chamber of Resources, 1994, p. 62)

There are, of course, many different types of school-business partnerships. Business partners may support professional development programs by simply providing funding or facilities for the programs. The ultimate payoff to business for such support is a better educated workforce. The best partnerships, however, involve interactive participation of business and school personnel. One type of partnership that involves interactive professional development is the *exchange program.* Exchange programs can include educators making field visits to or participating in internships at businesses in order to "learn how to integrate the world of work into the classroom and promote mutual understanding" (Reid, 1992, p. 41).

Partnerships can involve training of school personnel, business personnel, or both. For example, businesses specializing in technology may provide hardware, software, technical support, and training in the use of technology to educators. On the other hand, schools seeking to increase the number and quality of internships and other school-to-work experiences may provide adult education on effective business management and operation to local businesses (Reid, 1992). Finally, school and business personnel can engage in joint training. An example of this is the simultaneous training of teachers and tutors from local businesses to assist in the learning of students at risk. The training focuses on classroom roles and responsibilities, multiple intelligences research, and tutoring strategies (Bodinger-deUriarte, Fleming-McCormick, Schwager, Clark, & Danzberger, 1996).

In one school-restructuring effort in which I was involved as a consultant, a local corporation provided 50 percent of the funding for the effort, including its professional development component. The corporation's involvement, however, went beyond financial assistance. Corporation employees were involved in committees that conducted a comprehensive needs assessment as well as planning, implementation, and evaluation of the restructuring project. Business leaders such as those involved in this partnership have discovered that the restructuring of their own organizations has required a considerable investment in employees' professional development, hence they tend to support professional development as part of their investment in education.

Guidelines for school-business partnerships include the following:

- Involvement is voluntary
- Both partners should understand each other's management, resources, needs, and communication systems
- Business partners should recognize educators as primarily responsible for student development
- Programs and activities must be compatible with school board policies . . .
- Administrators from both organizations must take ownership, provide support, and be committed to the program
- The business partner should be viewed as an important part of the school and be included in program and curricular planning
- Programs should be planned to objectives and include an evaluation component
- Partnership contracts should last for one year and may be renewed (Edmund Catholic Schools, in Alberta Chamber of Resources, 1994, p. 66)

School-Community Partnerships

School-community partnerships can involve community institutions or individuals with special expertise providing professional development programs for educators. In Cleveland, Ohio, for example, a children's museum, education fund, environmental education institute, nature center, museum of science, and medical college joined together to provide a professional development program in science for teachers in the Cleveland School District (de Acosta, 1995). The program consisted of intensive summer workshops, monthly workshops during the first school year, and follow-up assistance from resource teams enabling teachers to explore science, assess science education in their schools, and develop a science curriculum focused on discovery learning.

School-community partnerships can focus on *bringing the community into the school.* This might mean community members coming to the school to be guest teachers, tutors, or students' mentors. Or it could mean enhancing student learning through computer links to libraries, community agencies, or local experts. Finally, bringing the community into the school might mean integrating community services with traditional school functions. Such services might include day care, after-school care, enrichment programs, health services, recreation programs, or adult education (Engeln, 2000; Kearns, 1993; Shepardson, 1994). The need to provide professional development for educators collaborating with other professionals in the delivery of community services is emphasized by Shepardson (1994):

> We need new systems of training at all levels to ensure that teachers and other front-line workers, administrators, and policy-makers are able to transform the present system. School-linked support systems will require a cadre of individuals able to build trusting

> relationships with children and families, work across professional boundaries, and respond flexibly to the needs of children and families. (p. 11)

Bodinger-deUriarte and associates describe a cross-agency professional development program for a partnership that delivered health and social services to students at risk and their families. Partners included schools and local agencies that worked with these youth. The program consisted of workshops on learning about health and social services provided by the partnership, identification and referral of students at risk, and teamwork. Participants reported that the professional development program resulted in increased knowledge of the services provided by the project as well as increased community and school collaboration (Bodinger-deUriarte et al., 1996).

School-community partnerships also can focus on *taking the school into the community*. This concept goes way beyond an occasional field trip. Units of instruction can be taught and projects carried out in museums, community agencies, universities, natural habitats, businesses, media centers, and government offices (Broda, 2002; Kearns, 1993; Lundt & Vanderpan, 2000; Purnell, 2000; Smith, 2000). Apprenticeships can be provided for older students (including college-bound students). Service learning can be part of taking the school into the community. Students can provide service to younger students, senior citizens, and the poor. They can assist in community efforts to improve neighborhoods and protect the natural environment. All of these activities can be tied to both cognitive and affective learning objectives. Taking the school into the community, of course, represents a new paradigm for teaching and learning. Educators will need to develop new skills and strategies in order to utilize effectively the community as a learning environment. Professional development will be a critical aspect of this effort. Kearns (1993) notes that "most design teams and communities see initial staff development—and ongoing teacher learning—as essential if their break-the-mold visions are to become a reality" (p. 776).

Because members of a school-community partnership have different backgrounds, occupations, and viewpoints, its important that the initial stages of the partnership focus on developing positive relationships and a sense of common purpose. The U.S. Department of Education (1996) makes the following suggestions for partners to learn about each other and the community:

- Conduct "cross-learning" exercises in which each partner tells the others who he or she is and what he or she does.
- Remember that people learn in different ways—adults as well as children. Honor different learning styles within the partnership by providing materials in many forms, verbal as well as written....
- Use small group activities to stimulate discussion between partners....
- Create opportunities for partners to learn about the community. Many partnerships rotate their meetings among different locations in the community so members can learn about their partners' organizations and clients....
- Build awareness about collaboration. Educate partners and the community about the benefits of working together....
- Make information and ideas available to all partners ... effective partnerships teach school and agency partners to avoid technical language and acronyms that may intimidate or confuse other participants....

- Build capacity for shared decision making. Partners may want to adopt a model for group decision making or devise their own approach. (pp. 32–33)

The possibilities of partnership and related professional development are almost limitless. The ultimate test of the success of a partnership, however, is not the number of partners, resources, or programs, but the improvement of teaching and learning that results from partnership efforts.

Networks

Networks of educators with common interests and needs can be formed at the local, intermediate, state, regional, national, or international level. Cooper, Slavin, and Madden (1997) describe a *network* in the fullest sense of the word:

> The concept of educational network is inclusive of, yet broader than, informal meetings of educators sharing stories about the challenges within the profession. Embedded in the concept are notions of collaboration, skill development, problem solving, collegiality, empowerment, community, motivation, information dissemination, and opportunities for retooling. (p. 5)

Networks possess common characteristics. They have a clear focus and thus serve a specific segment of the professional community. At the same time, they provide a variety of activities related to the focus area. Networks create discourse communities and provide leadership opportunities for their members (Lieberman, 1999; Lieberman & McLaughlin, 1992; Mycue, 2001). Benefits of networks include expanding members' boundaries, sharing experiences and ideas, developing a common language, continuing professional growth, supporting norms of professionalism and collegiality, increasing participants' efficacy, recognition of progress, and celebration of accomplishments (Loucks-Horsley et al., 1987). One of the most successful professional development networks with which I have been involved was the Southwest Ohio Planning Council for In-service Education (SWOPCIE). The council, funded by the Ohio Department of Education, was made up of staff development leaders from throughout the region. Council members participated in programs to enhance their own professional development, assessed regional needs, coordinated regional conferences, presented institutes for principals, made grants available for school-based professional development, and delivered workshops for teachers. Perhaps the most beneficial aspect of SWOPCIE was the dialogue and sharing that took place at our regular council meetings.

Some networks focus on content areas. For example, the National Writing Project includes teachers participating in workshops and institutes in which they analyze their teaching and write together. Other networks are centered on a particular professional development format. An example is the League of Educational Action Researchers of the Northwest, also known as Project Learn. In this network, facilitated by Washington State University, school action research teams attend workshops on action research, write action plans, receive assistance from trained volunteers with research experience, and present results of their action research to each other at a symposium held each spring (Sagor, 1991).

Some networks promote a particular approach to curriculum and teaching. The Foxfire Teacher Networks support the "Foxfire approach," based on reflective thinking, problem solving, community involvement, and the democratic process. Teachers attend an intensive course on the Foxfire approach, which includes designing a portion of curriculum based on the Foxfire principles. Foxfire networks focus on field-testing the Foxfire approach through classroom research and reflective dialogue among Foxfire coordinators and teachers. Foxfire networks include courses, workshops, small-group meetings, newsletters, and computer links (Smith & Wigginton, 1991). A number of national networks focus on whole-school reform. Accelerated Schools, the Coalition of Essential Schools, the Comer Schools, and Success for All are examples of networks promoting comprehensive models of school reform. Professional development is a critical component in each of the major school reform networks.

After discussing partnerships and networks we can see how these two frameworks are closely related. Exemplar 6.2 describes Science in Motion, a program that integrates the two frameworks.

EXEMPLAR 6.2 • *Science in Motion*

Science in Motion is a partnership between Juneata College (PA) and the rural schools within its service area, as well as a network formed among those schools. Critical components of the project include summer workshops at Juneata, science vans that make available hundreds of thousands of dollars worth of lab equipment and supplies to public school teachers, van drivers who also serve as co-teachers at the schools they visit, and ongoing support for teachers who participate in the project.

One goal of Science in Motion, supported by grants from the National Science Foundation, is to enrich high school teachers and students by exposing them to modern instrumentation and scientific techniques. Another goal is to network the teachers of the partner schools through workshops and meetings. Two weeks of introductory and advanced workshops are offered to biology and chemistry teachers. Workshops consist of lectures introducing labs that will later be brought to participants' schools by the vans, demonstrations and hands-on use of labs, debriefing of lab activities, and discussions of how labs can be integrated with the participants' curriculum. Many workshop activities are led by former workshop participants now designated as lead teachers.

The biology and chemistry van drivers are certified teachers. They schedule daily visits to partner schools. The vans visit each school at least once a month. The relationship between the van driver and local science teachers is characterized by flexibility. Sometimes the van drivers teach lessons in the teachers' classrooms. Sometimes they team teach with the regular teachers. Sometimes they drop off equipment that regular teachers use to teach lessons on their own. One van driver discussed positive aspects of team teaching:

> I really like the team teaching. Most schools you go to, the teachers are excited the same way the kids are when you're coming. They learn things from you and you learn things from them, because if you're teaching together, you bring out different things . . . you have different strengths.

Teachers who have worked with the van drivers expressed positive perceptions of their effort and flexibility:

> *Teacher 1:* One thing that really impresses me about the van drivers—I don't know if that's a good term . . . it should be co-teachers—is how hard they work and how much effort they put into it. Three different times they helped set up for a science fair. Their willingness to do anything helps make the program a success.
>
> *Teacher 2:* And their flexibility . . . coming into the classroom and being willing to do whatever you want them to do . . . the ability to work with all of the different personalities and organizational patterns . . . I think it's neat that they can do that.

The labs carried on the vans allow high school students to perform experiments in molecular biology, genetics, microbiology, and physiology. Students perform experiments using gas chromatography, spestroscopy, nuclear scalers, and microscales. Over time, teachers are able to use the labs without the on-site assistance of the van drivers. Van drivers still visit schools every day, but other vans drop off labs and equipment at schools for the use of teachers who have learned how to use requested equipment. Teachers with experience in the project can develop their own labs to teach concepts in their school's science curriculum:

> I've learned that I can develop a lab . . . that I really don't need a lab manual, but that I'm capable of saying, "This is a concept that my students need to understand with hands-on application," and I'm going from there to tailor a lab that will illustrate it. I've gotten a lot of confidence in being able to develop my own labs as I want them, and a lot of experience in trouble-shooting labs. Another thing I've learned from working with other teachers in the project is how to introduce a lab, and how to follow up the lab and tie everything together.

The last teacher's quote brings up another critical aspect of Science in Motion: networking. As one van driver noted, "At the workshops they get to talk to other teachers—and not just about their subject—about all the things that go on in the classroom." Two teachers discuss networking within the project:

> *Teacher 1:* Normally we would never cross paths, but in these workshops we get to know each other, get to share ideas, find out what works for you, for them, et cetera.

(continued)

EXEMPLAR 6.2 • Continued

> *Teacher 2:* And phone calls on science fair projects... "My student's doing this... what do you know about it?" And taking a day to go see the van working in another classroom and a different school, and how someone else is doing it. I probably wouldn't have done that if I didn't already know the teacher.

Beyond the summer workshops, van visits, and networking, Science in Motion has a number of other components. Visiting scientists conduct seminars for teachers. Teachers visit the college's field station to learn about ecology and conservation. Professors and van drivers assist teachers and students with individual science projects and school science fairs. Through all of these activities Science in Motion provides a comprehensive program, assisting teachers with instructional resources, professional development, and curriculum development.

In interviews with project staff and teachers participating in the project, a number of benefits were cited. One obvious benefit is the opportunity for science teachers to participate in professional development in their content area. As a professor explained:

> Teachers tell me it's absolutely the best professional development program they've ever had. It's the only one that relates to what they do in class. It's the only time they've ever had to work with other science teachers. One teacher said, "I never want to go back to the way it was before... so isolated... and I never talked to anyone in my area, ever."

Participating teachers I interviewed agreed with the positive reports from the Juneata College educators. The following comments were made by two different teachers:

> *Teacher 1:* It gets us, as teachers, excited. You come to the workshops here in the summers, and you get these ideas, and we get excited about it. But then they don't just leave you hanging. You have the support throughout the year. And that's the thing that's really important... follow-up.

> *Teacher 2:* For me personally, when this program started 10 years ago, I was about burned out from the isolation, from the frustration, from never having any equipment to work with... wanted out of teaching. And then when this came along... other teachers who were in the same boat in terms of lack of equipment, the isolation... and then finding the support, and having some equipment to work with that was good, totally rekindled my interest in teaching. And I probably do a better job than I've done before.

The ultimate beneficiaries of Science in Motion, of course, are the students. Teachers report that, as a result of the project, their students are more motivated to learn about science, are able to perform complex experiments, and have developed an understanding of scientific concepts and the scientific process. One teacher stated, "It's great watching them when they are in the lab—they are so excited and really get into it. They feel like scientists. And they learn they can do science."

Teacher Centers

Teacher centers are central locations where educators meet to share experiences, ideas, problems, solutions, and resources, and where they develop new curriculum, teaching strategies, instructional materials, and student assessment methods. Teacher centers are concerned with the improvement of teacher morale and the teaching profession as well as the development of teaching skills and resources; therefore, the atmosphere at such centers is collegial, nonevaluative, and supportive. Unlike networks, which tend to be focused, teacher centers usually have multiple purposes and offer a variety of activities and resources. Finally, at teacher centers teachers *lead* as well as participate in professional development activities.

During the late 1970s and early 1980s, 90 teacher centers were funded by the federal government (Public Law 94–482). In those years, the typical teacher center served a single district and was located on a school campus. Policy boards with a majority of teachers developed and assessed professional development programs that included courses, seminars, and workshops (Yarger, 1990). Once federal funding ended, many of these teacher centers went out of existence. Since the early 1980s, however, many new teacher centers have been established by school districts, universities, state agencies, and partnerships. Typical activities and resources provided by modern teacher centers are listed in Figure 6.1.

Beyond traditional "all-purpose" teacher centers, a variety of specialized centers have been established across the nation. Some of these focus on professional development in specific content areas. Others specialize in teacher leadership. One unique teacher center is the North Carolina Center for the Advancement of Teaching (NCCAT) in Cullowhee, North Carolina. The center, located at Western Carolina University, was created to reward and support outstanding teachers. Kirk (1991) describes the NCCAT experience:

> Participants are treated to an all-expense trip to the mountains. From the moment they arrive, NCCAT employees pet and pamper their guests, as if they were Hollywood celebrities (Graves, 1988). They are served breakfast in bed. Newspaper and fresh fruit are brought to their private quarters daily. They have free access to tennis courts, swimming pools, library facilities, and walking trails. Such treatment can go a long way toward bolstering self-esteem and engender a sense of importance. (p. 6)

FIGURE 6.1 Typical Teacher Center Activities and Resources

Activities	*Resources*
Workshops	Computers and Internet links
Courses	Audiovisuals to preview and borrow
Seminars	Distance education facilities
Symposiums	Professional books, journals, teacher writings
Conferences	Facilities for individual study
Distance education programs	Group meeting facilities
Curriculum development	Sample curricula
Development of instructional materials	Commercially made instructional materials
Grant writing	Teacher-made instructional materials
Action research	Equipment and supplies to develop units, lessons, instructional materials
Individualized study	Labs to preview and borrow
Self-assessment	Photocopy machines
Consultation	Information on community resources
Networking	Exhibitions/displays
Study groups	Work areas
Support for beginning teachers	National, state, and district mandates
Training of trainers	Information on associations, networks, outside professional development
Leadership training	Recreational facilities
Demonstrations	Dining facilities
Expert presentations	
Teacher writing	

> Because of their experiential or hands-on approach, seminars at NCCAT are sometimes referred to as "living seminars." They involve a varied range of activities. Examples include such things as repelling off mountain sides, gem mining, participating in anthropology digs, star gazing, scientific field studies, visits to a local Indian reservation, day trips to historical sites, story telling, folk dancing, and poetry writing. These highly participative activities are augmented by readings, media presentations, demonstrations, and addresses by visiting experts. The idea is to immerse participants in a more natural environment and rekindle the child-like curiosity and creativity that was once theirs. To help participants escape the myopia which sometimes prevents them from looking at everyday events in a holistic manner. (p. 5)

It is fitting to end our discussion of external support frameworks with a description of such a creative program.

Summary

This chapter discussed examples of school-university partnerships, including interactive seminars, fellowships, residencies, exchange programs, school-university restructuring, professional development schools, and partnerships focused solely on in-service educators. We examined school-business partnerships and reviewed guidelines for such partnerships. We saw how school-community partnerships can bring the community into the school as well as take the school into the community. Common characteristics and examples of networks were described. Finally, we explored attributes and purposes of teacher centers.

Assignments

1. Read three articles on professional development schools. Write a report summarizing each article and discussing commons themes across the three articles.
2. Read three articles on school-university partnerships that include a significant emphasis on the professional development of in-service teachers. Write a report summarizing each article and discussing common themes across the three articles.
3. Write a paper entitled "A Brief History of Teacher Centers." Include at least five references from sources other than this text.
4. Interview a teacher who is or has been a fellow, exchange teacher, or university resident as part of a school-university partnership. Ask questions about (a) the overall partnership; (b) the interviewee's experiences as a fellow, exchange teacher, or resident; and (c) the interviewee's perceptions of the effects of the special role on his or her professional development.
5. Visit a professional development school (PDS). Your visit should include discussions with (a) a university professor working with the PDS, (b) the principal, and (c) an in-service teacher engaged in university field experiences at the PDS. Write a paper discussing the design of the PDS, professional development opportunities made available by the PDS, and the impact of the PDS on the professional development of preservice and in-service teachers.
6. Visit a teacher center. Discuss the center's purpose, typical activities, and available resources with the center's director and at least two teachers who participate in center activities. Also conduct an inspection of the center's facilities and resources. Write a report describing the center and your perceptions of the center's impact on participating teachers' professional development.

References

Abdal-Haqq, I. (1989). The nature of professional development schools. *ERIC Digest*, 4–89. (ERIC ED 316 548).

Abdal-Haqq, I. (1996). An information provider's perspective on the professional development school movement. *Contemporary Education*, *67*, 237–240.

Aiken, I., & Day, B. D. (2000). Teachers for a new century: Two premiere programs. *Kappa Delta Pi*, *36*(3), 124–127.

Alberta Chamber of Resources. (1994). *Partnerships in education: Skill development. Mobilizing community resources phase II.* Edmonton, Alberta: Author.

Auger, F. K., & Odell, S. J. (1992). Three school-university partnerships for teacher development. *Journal of Teacher Education*, *43*, 262–268.

Bodinger-deUriarte, C., Fleming-McCormick, T., Schwager, M., Clark, M., & Danzberger, J. (1996). *A guide to promising practices in educational partnerships.* Washington, DC: Institute for Educational Leadership. (ERIC ED 392 980).

Boles, K. L., & Troen, V. (1994, April). *Teacher leadership in a professional development school.* Paper presented at the annual meeting of the American Educational Research Association, New Orleans.

Broda, H. W. (2002). Learning in and for the outdoors. *Middle School Journal, 33*(3), 34–38.

Clark, R. W. (1999). School-university partnerships and professional development schools. *Peabody Journal of Education, 74*(3–4), 164–177.

Cobb, J. (2000). The impact of professional development schools on preservice teachers preparation, inservice teachers' professionalism, and children's achievement: Perceptions of inservice teachers. *Action in Teacher Education, 22*(3), 64–76.

Cooper, R., Slavin, R. E., & Madden, N. A. (1997). *Success for all: Exploring the technical, normative, political, and socio-cultural dimensions of scaling up.* Report No. 16. (ERIC ED 412 324).

Davies, D. (2000). Powerful partnerships among schools, parents and communities. *The Education Digest, 66*(2), 41–44.

de Acosta, M. (1995). *Enhancing science education in the primary grades through a community-based collaborative: Lessons from the CLASS (children learning about science and self) Program.* Occasional Paper No. 16. (ERIC ED 396 959).

Diss, R. E., Buckley, P. K., & Pfau, N. D. (1992). Interactive reflective teaching: A school-college collaborative model for professional development. *Journal of Staff Development, 13*(2), 28–31.

Engeln, J. (2000). The complete turnabout. *The High School Magazine,* 7(6), 28–31.

Fazio, R. P., Levine, C., & Merry, D. (2000). Cultivating a garden of educators. *Journal of Staff Development, 21*(2), 16–19.

Graves, B. (1998, February 28). Teachers get petted at N.C. center for rejuventing frazzled educators. *The News and Observer,* pp. 29–30A.

Graves, D. H. (2001). Build energy with colleagues. *Language Arts, 79*(1), 12–19.

Kagan, D. M., Dennis, M. B., Igou, M., Moore, P., & Sparks, K. (1993). The experience of being a teacher in residence. *American Educational Research Journal, 30,* 426–443.

Kearns, D. T. (1993). Toward a new generation of American Schools. *Phi Delta Kappan, 74,* 773–776.

Kirk, J. J. (1991). *Cullowhee: A place of renewal and professional growth.* (ERIC ED 340 544).

Knight, S. L., Wiseman, D., & Smith, C. W. (1992). The reflectivity-activity dilemma in school-university partnerships. *Journal of Teacher Education, 43,* 269–277.

Lasley, T. J., Matczynski, T. J., & Williams, J. A. (1992). Collaborative and noncollaborative partnership structures in teacher education. *Journal of Teacher Education, 43,* 257–261.

Lawrence, A. T., & Dubetz, N. (2001). An urban collaboration: Improving student learning through a professional development network. *Action in Teacher Education, 22*(4), 1–14.

Lieberman, A. (1999). Networks. *Journal of Staff Development, 20*(3), 43–44.

Lieberman, A., & McLaughlin, M. W. (1992). Networks for educational change: Powerful and problematic. *Phi Delta Kappan, 73,* 673–677.

Lieberman, A., & Miller, L. (1990). Teacher development in professional practice schools. *Teachers College Record, 92*(1), 105–122.

Loucks-Horsley, S., Harding, C. K., Arbuckle, M. A., Murray, L. B., Dubea, C., & Williams, M. K. (1987). *Continuing to learn: A guidebook for teacher development.* Andover, MA: The Regional Laboratory for Educational Improvement of the Northeast and Islands.

Lundt, J. C., & Vanderpan, T. (2000). It computes when young adolescents teach senior citizens. *Middle School Journal, 31*(4), 18–22.

Mycue, S. (2001). The professional circle. *Kappa Delta Pi, 38*(1), 28–31.

Nystrand, R. O. (1991). *Professional development schools: Toward a new relationship for schools and universities.* Trends and Issues Paper No. 4. (ERIC ED 330 690).

Purnell, J. (2000). Get students started on social change. *The Education Digest, 65*(7), 33– 36.

Reid, M. E. (1992). *Partnership for progress: Development and implementation of a framework for increasing partnerships between business and school districts.* Ed.D. Practicum Report, Nova University. (ERIC ED 363 002).

Rock, T. C., & Levin, B. B. (2002). Collaborative action research projects: Enhancing preservice teacher development in professional development schools. *Teacher Education Quarterly, 29*(1), 7–21.

Rosselli, H., Perez, S., Piersall, K., & Pantridge, O. (1993). Evolution of a professional development school: The story of a partnership. *Teacher Education and Special Education, 16*(2), 124–136.

Sagor, R. (1991). What project LEARN reveals about collaborative action research. *Educational Leadership, 48*(6), 6–10.

Sandholtz, J. H., & Dadlez, S. H. (2000). Professional development school trade-offs in teacher preparation and renewal. *Teacher Education Quarterly, 27*(1), 7–27.

Shepardson, B. (1994). Beyond books. *Spectrum: The Journal of State Government, 67*(4), 6–14.

Silva, D. Y., & Dana N. F. (2001). Collaborative supervision in the professional development school. *Journal of Curriculum and Supervision, 16*(4), 305–321.

Smith, H. J. (2000). A world of ideas: Creating an interdisciplinary museum of history. *Middle School Journal, 31*(4), 5–12.

Smith, H., & Wigginton, E. (1991). Foxfire teacher networks. In A. Lieberman & L. Miller (Eds.), *Staff development for education in the 90's* (pp. 193–220). New York: Teachers College Press.

U.S. Department of Education. (1996). *Putting the pieces together: Comprehensive school-linked strategies for children and families.* Washington, DC: Author.

Yarger, S. J. (1990). The legacy of the teacher center. In B. Joyce (Ed.), *Changing school culture through staff development* (pp. 104–116). Alexandria, VA: Association for Supervision and Curriculum Development.

Resources

Dana, N. F., Silva, D. Y., Gimbert, B., Nolan, J., Jr., Zembal-Saul, C., Tzur, R., et al. (2001). Developing new understanding of PDS work: Better problems, better questions. *Action in Teacher Education, 22*(4), 15–27.

Jacobson, D. L. (2001). A new agenda for educational partnerships: Stakeholder learning collaboratives. *Change, 33*(5), 44–53.

Levine, M. (1997). Can professional development schools help us achieve what matters most? *Action in Teacher Education, 19*(2), 63–73.

Lieberman, A., & McLaughlin, M. W. (1992). Networks for educational change: Powerful and problematic. *Phi Delta Kappan, 73*, 673–677.

Silva, D. Y ., & Dana, N. F. (2001). Collaborative supervision in the professional development school. *Journal of Curriculum and Supervision, 16*(4), 305–321.

Von Frank, V. (Ed.). (2000). Partners: Teaming up to improve adult learning [entire issue]. *Journal of Staff Development, 21*(2).

Review of Professional Development Model, Part II

Part II presented frameworks for professional development: training, collegial support, reflective inquiry, teacher leadership, and external support. These frameworks, along with the three themes discussed in Part I, are listed in Figure II.1 below. Part III will focus on capacity-building functions of professional development, including professional development for school leaders, cultural development, team development, and individual teacher development.

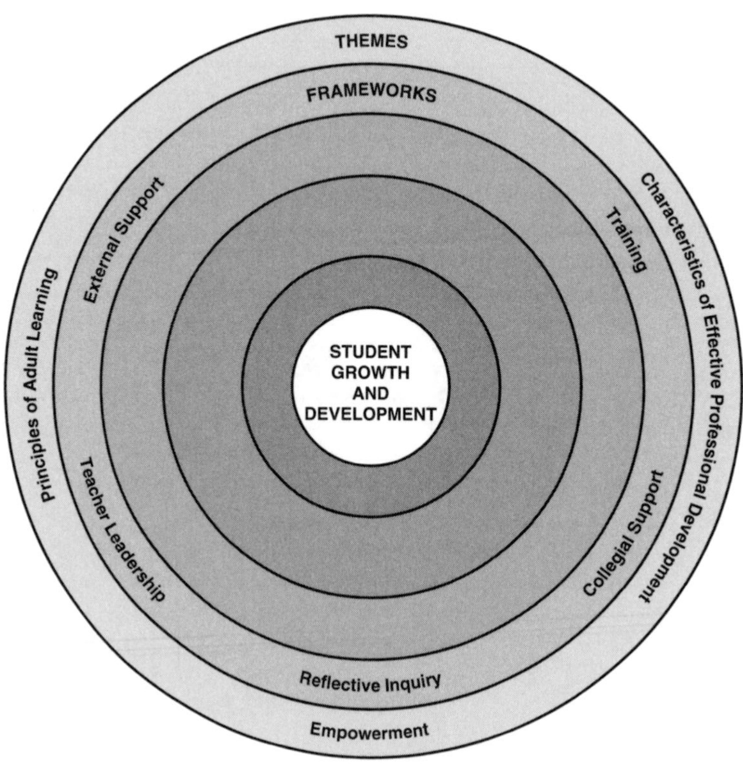

FIGURE II.1 Comprehensive Model: Professional Development for School Improvement

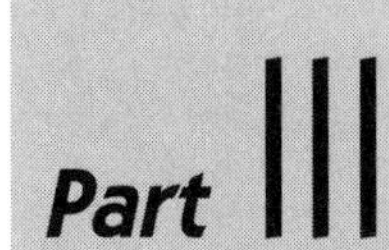

Capacity-Building Functions of Professional Development

7 School Leader Development

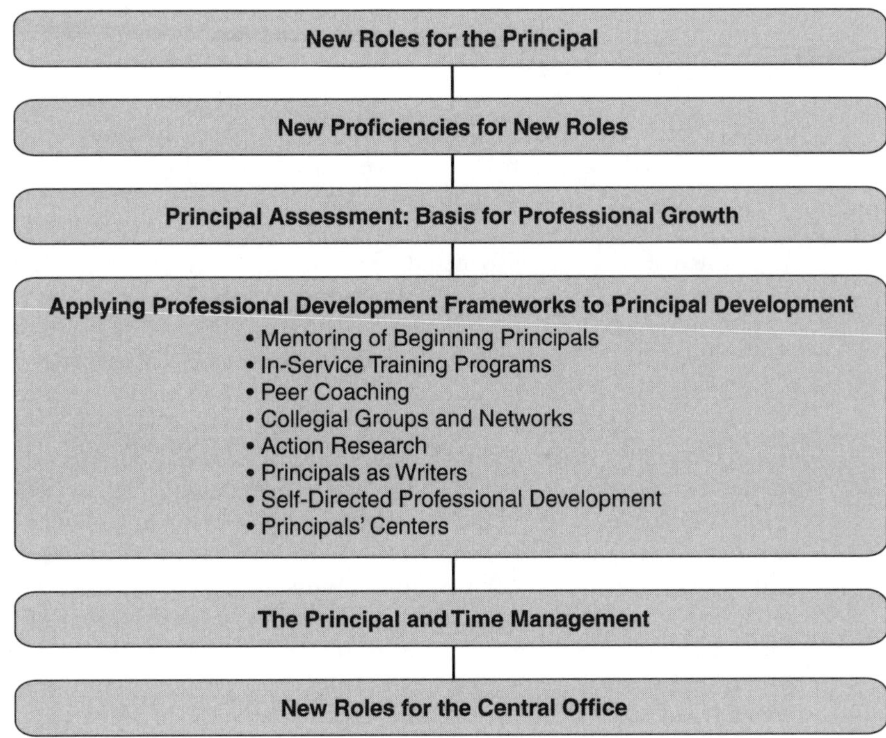

New Roles for the Principal
New Proficiencies for New Roles
Principal Assessment: Basis for Professional Growth
Applying Professional Development Frameworks to Principal Development
• Mentoring of Beginning Principals
• In-Service Training Programs
• Peer Coaching
• Collegial Groups and Networks
• Action Research
• Principals as Writers
• Self-Directed Professional Development
• Principals' Centers
The Principal and Time Management
New Roles for the Central Office

We have established that teachers, parents, and students all can be school leaders. This chapter, however, will focus on school principals (including assistant and associate principals) and central office personnel charged with facilitating professional development and school improvement. If formally designated school leaders are going to facilitate the professional development of teachers and the empowerment of all members of the school community, then they must become *empowered leaders*. To be successful in the twenty-first century, school leaders will need to assume new roles, develop new skills, and establish new relationships with other members of the learning community. Professional development will be an essential tool in the development of new leaders for the new millennium.

New Roles for the Principal

Chapter 1 proposed that principals need to become empowered leaders, teachers, and learners. This three-part role includes *transformational leadership*, in which the principal helps teachers create a collaborative culture, fosters teacher development, and facilitates group problem solving (Blase & Blase, 2001; Leithwood, 1992; Siegrist, 1999). The principal's new role also includes being the *principal teacher* by modeling important behaviors such as creativity, risk taking, and collegiality. Finally, the "new" principal must be the *principal learner* in the school (Brewer, 2001; Ellis, 1995; Rallis & Goldring, 2000). Barth maintains that by becoming *"sustained, visible learners"* principals can unlock energy and learning throughout the school community (Sparks, 1993a).

Unfortunately, a number of barriers hinder the professional development of principals. One of these barriers is the conventional preparation program for educational administrators, with its focus on what Behar-Horenstein (1995) refers to as the "technology of managerial practice." To make matters worse, professional development for in-service principals traditionally has been inadequate or nonexistent: "Knowledge and skills for effective leadership are either fragmented and piecemeal or are lacking altogether in in-service training programs" (Johnson, Snyder, & Johnson, 1991–92, p. 41). Barth discusses several reasons why many principals have failed to become serious learners. First, there is the belief that professional development for principals siphons school resources away from students. A second reason is principals' reluctance to admit that they have learning needs. Another has been the poor quality of previous in-service programs. A final reason is that principals do not feel that they have time to assume any new responsibilities (Pierce, 2001; Sparks, 1993a).

Principals' attitudes toward their own professional development, however, have begun to change in recent years. The site-based management movement has made principals aware of their need to develop collaborative skills. Increasing calls for school accountability have brought home to principals the need to effect school change through transformational leadership. The new emphasis in the literature on effective schools as "communities of learning" or "learning organizations" has helped principals realize the value of being their school's principal learner. For these same reasons, central office administrators have begun to provide encouragement and resources for principals' development. If the professional development of in-service principals is an idea whose time has come, then what should be the nature of that professional development?

The next several pages will discuss proficiencies for the "new" principal and formats for developing those proficiencies.

New Proficiencies for New Roles

The new roles of the principal require a new set of proficiencies. Each of these proficiencies requires knowledge, skills, and dispositions. For example, *knowledge* of the research on effective group process is insufficient if the principal does not also possess group process *skills*. Furthermore, being able to demonstrate group process *skills* during a principals' workshop is of no value if the principal does not have a *disposition* toward using those skills to facilitate collaborative teams back at his or her campus. The new proficiencies are:

- *Personal proficiencies*, including intrapersonal communication, interpersonal communication, understanding of the principal's role, reflective inquiry, modeling ethical behavior, self-confidence, collaborative leadership, risk taking, technology, and time management
- *Organizational development proficiencies*, including site-based management, shared governance, school assessment, cultural development, collaborative vision setting, organizational planning, and change facilitation
- *Group process proficiencies*, including facilitation of communication, role development, decision making, conflict management, problem solving, and creativity within groups
- *Professional development proficiencies*, including facilitation of professional development needs assessment, readiness, program planning, program implementation, and program evaluation
- *Curriculum development proficiencies*, including facilitation of curriculum needs assessment, identifying intended learning outcomes, designing multicultural curriculum, designing interdisciplinary curriculum, curriculum mapping, curriculum implementation, and curriculum evaluation
- *Instructional development proficiencies*, including collaboration with teachers on developing a schoolwide instructional program, developing generic as well as content-specific teaching skills, and meeting the developmental, cultural, and individual learning needs of students; more specific proficiencies include conferencing, classroom observating, and collaborating in schoolwide, team, and individual action plans for instructional improvement
- *Student assessment proficiencies*, including facilitating assessment at the individual, group, classroom, and school level; more specific proficiencies include facilitating development of performance standards; designing and analyzing traditional tests; assessing student presentations, projects, interviews, and other forms of alternative assessment; developing rubrics; and developing individual, group, and school portfolios

- *Parent and community outreach proficiencies*, including collaborating with various stakeholders in school improvement efforts, "bringing the community into the school," "taking the school into the community," celebrating diversity, and collaborating fully with parents in the education of their children

You no doubt have noticed that traditional management proficiencies are not present in the preceding list. That is because most graduate programs in educational administration already teach management proficiencies fairly effectively. But for principals to fulfill their new roles successfully, the proficiencies just listed must be developed as well. Many principal preparation programs across the nation are beginning to place more emphasis on the new proficiencies (Lauder, 2000). As we wait for the reform of principal preparation programs to become a widespread reality, however, professional development must play a critical role in transforming the practice of in-service principals.

Principal Assessment: Basis for Professional Growth

The first step in principal growth and development is assessment. This assessment should be based primarily on self-appraisal rather than judgments by external assessors. An example of principal assessment based on reflection and self-appraisal is the Educational Leadership Appraisal (ELA) process, offered by the Dade County (FL) public schools as part of a larger program called the Executive Training Program (Ellis & Macrina, 1994). In Phase I of the appraisal process, participants engage in structured activities that allow them to identify things that make them unique educational leaders. Participants also learn how to articulate what they have observed about themselves and how "being in the present" is necessary for awareness, which is the beginning of leadership. Phase II of the process includes an in-basket activity in which participants organize a variety of memos, reports, phone messages, and so on; establish priorities; and plan actions. After the in-basket, participants analyze and reflect on their decisions. In Phase III, participants identify their own behavior styles, then learn how different styles shape the individual's frames of reference regarding leadership. Phase IV includes learning a process for identifying problems and developing problem-solving strategies. This process is practiced in a school improvement simulation. Finally, in Phase V, participants learn to foster uniqueness and diversity within groups, practice group process skills, and observe their own behavior within groups. The ELA process treats self-appraisal as an essential aspect of professional growth that must continue throughout the principal's career.

Seller (1993) proposes an assessment model focused specifically on the principal as staff developer. In this model, principals reflect on their present activities as staff development leaders and are then presented with new images of principals. Principals reflect on these new roles in relation to their current activities, then they identify areas of strength and weakness relative to the new roles. The principals then participate in staff development (workshops, presentations, readings, etc.) in areas they have targeted for improvement. The next phase of the model calls for principals to collect data on professional development needs at their schools. This assessment eventually expands to include principals observing at each other's schools to obtain a more valid description of the present state of professional development. Next, principals are assisted in developing three-year plans for their own professional development and for facilitating the professional development of their school's staff.

There are a variety of assessment programs like the two just described. Most of these programs include the use of inventories designed to assist principals to assess their personal styles. One of several such inventories is the Life Styles Inventory, or LSI (Human Synergistics, 1989, 1990). The LSI measures 12 patterns of thinking, some of which are effective, others of which are ineffective. Figure 7.1 groups each of these styles into one of three broad categories:

> The *Constructive Styles* (11, 12, 1, and 2 o'clock positions) characterize self-enhancing thinking and behavior that contribute to one's level of satisfaction, ability to develop healthy relationships and work effectively with people, and proficiency in accomplishig tasks.
>
> The *Passive/Defensive Styles* (3, 4, 5, and 6 o'clock positions) represent self-protecting thinking and behavior that promote the fulfillment of security needs through interaction with people.
>
> The *Aggressive/Defensive Styles* (7, 8, 9, and 10 o'clock positions) reflect self-promoting thinking and behavior used to maintain status/position and fulfill security needs through task-related activities. (Human Synergistics, 1989, p. 7; emphasis in original)

The LSI 1 is an inventory completed by the participant. It yields a score for each of the 12 styles. The scores are plotted on a circular profile that converts them to percentile points and shows whether the participant's score for each style is in the high, medium, or low percentile range. Viewing the circular profile allows the participant to compare scores on the 12 styles and to reflect on how the various styles combine to influence the participant's behavior. The LSI 2 is an inventory completed by others who know the participant well, in order to provide feedback to the participant on his or her use of the 12 styles. The self-description profile (LSI 1) can then be compared to the description-by-others profile (LSI 2) to see whether scores are in agreement or disagreement. A comparison of the two profiles can identify "confirmed strengths," "unrecognized strengths," "stumbling blocks," and "blind spots." The presence of the latter three indicate developmental needs or, put positively, opportunities for self-improvement. The LSI results, then, can serve as data for a principal's self-assessment as well as the basis for planning personal and professional development.

There are, of course, numerous other inventories that can be used to assist principals to assess their professional development needs. I offer the LSI as an example of an inventory that both preservice and in-service principals with whom I have worked have found particularly helpful. Another assessment, found in Inset 7.1, consists of multiple-choice items based on the new proficiencies proposed earlier in this chapter.

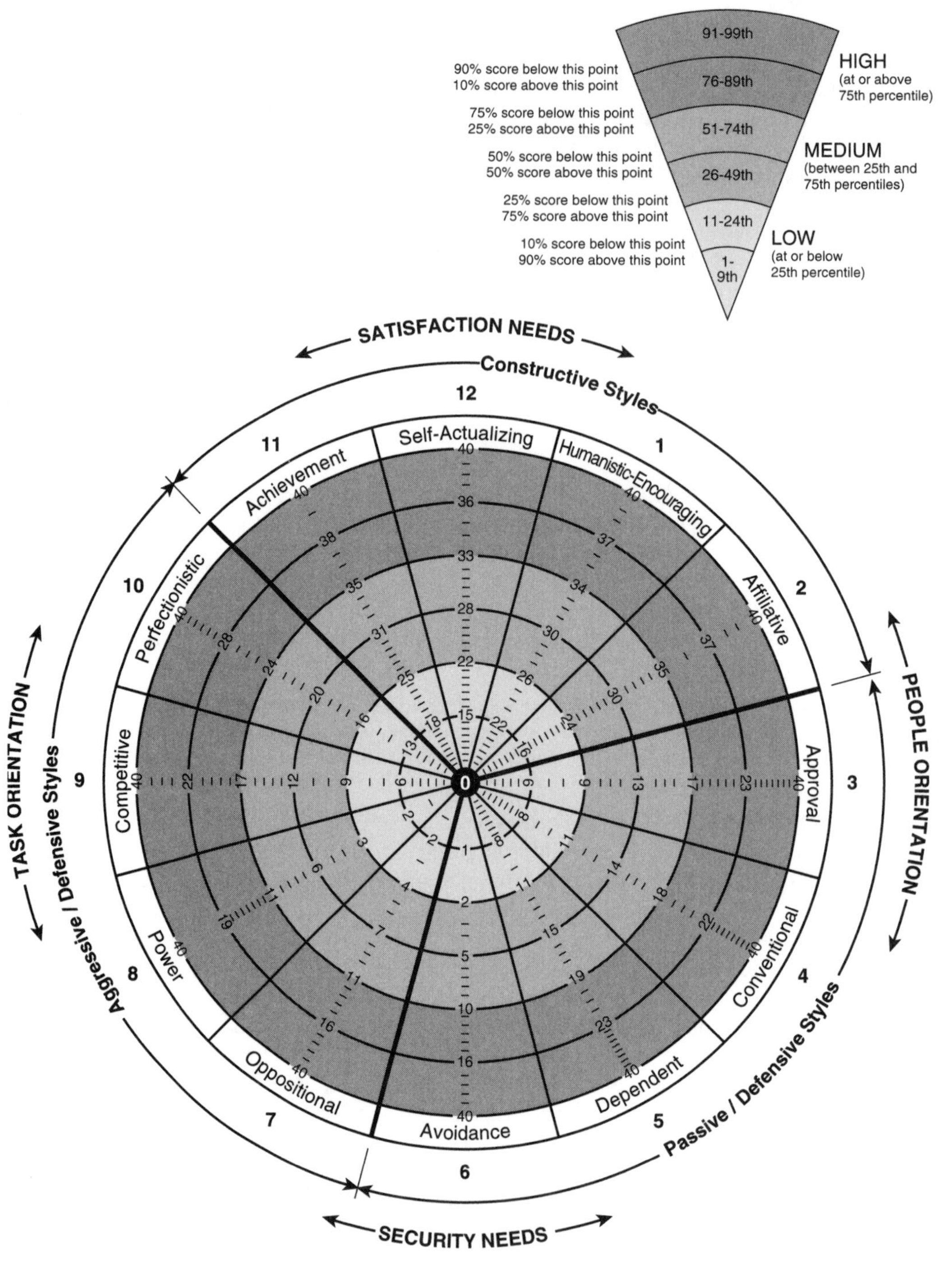

FIGURE 7.1 Life Styles Categories

Source: Life Styles Inventory (LSI) Profile Supplement, © 1989, Human Synergistics, Inc. Reproduced with permission of authors and publisher.

INSET 7.1 • *Principals' New Proficiencies Needs Assessment*

Directions: Respond to each item by selecting the response that most nearly reflects your level of need for professional development relative to the stated proficiency. Possible responses are:

A. No need
B. Some need
C. Moderate need
D. High need
E. Very high need

Personal Proficiencies

1. Intrapersonal communication (understanding self)
2. Interpersonal communication
3. Understanding the principal's role
4. Reflective inquiry
5. Modeling ethical behavior
6. Self-confidence
7. Multicultural awareness
8. Collaborative leadership
9. Risk taking
10. Technology
11. Time management

Organization Development Proficiencies

12. Site-based management
13. Shared governance
14. School assessment
15. Facilitation of a collegial culture
16. Collaborative vision setting
17. Organizational planning
18. Change facilitation

(continued)

INSET 7.1 • Continued

Group Process Proficiencies

19. Facilitation of communication within groups
20. Role development within groups
21. Group decision making
22. Conflict management
23. Group problem solving
24. Creativity within groups

Professional Development Proficiencies

25. Professional development needs assessment
26. Readiness for professional development
27. Planning professional development programs
28. Professional development program implementation
29. Professional development program evaluation

Curriculum Development Proficiencies

30. Curriculum needs assessment
31. Identifying intended learning outcomes
32. Multicultural curriculum design
33. Interdisciplinary curriculum design
34. Curriculum mapping
35. Curriculum implementation
36. Curriculum evaluation

Instructional Development Proficiencies

37. Development of a schoolwide instructional program
38. Development of generic teaching skills
39. Development of content-specific teaching skills
40. Meeting the developmental, cultural, and individual learning needs of children
41. Conferencing with teachers for instructional improvement
42. Classroom observation
43. Collaboration in schoolwide, team, and individual action plans for instructional improvement

Student Assessment Proficiencies

44. Assessment of individual students
45. Assessment of student teams
46. Assessment at the classroom level
47. Schoolwide assessment of student learning
48. Development of performance standards
49. Design and analysis of traditional tests
50. Design of alternative assessments (student presentations, projects, interviews, etc.)
51. Development and use of assessment rubrics
52. Development of individual, group, and school portfolios

Parent and Community Outreach Proficiencies

53. Collaboration with various stakeholders in school improvement efforts
54. Bringing the community into the school
55. Taking the school into the community
56. Celebrating diversity
57. Collaboration with parents in the education of their children

Applying Professional Development Frameworks to Principal Development

Part II of this text discussed a variety of professional development frameworks to promote teacher development. Here, we'll discuss how several frameworks can be adapted for principal development.

Mentoring of Beginning Principals

Role ambiguity, conflicting expectations from different stakeholders, inadequate skills, excessive workload, and professional isolation can combine to overwhelm the beginning principal. In response to the problems faced by new principals, some states have mandated internships or induction programs for entry-year principals. Such programs might include orientations, skill training, support groups, and individualized professional development plans. A key component in most of these programs is the assignment of a mentor to work with the beginning principal throughout the entry year.

Principal mentors, like teacher mentors, must be chosen carefully. Characteristics of effective mentors reported by principals include being knowledgeable, experienced, supportive, reliable, flexible, accessible, and trustworthy (Casavant & Cherkowski, 2001; Grover, 1994; Hopkins-Thompson, 2000). Even when possessing these characteristics, mentors need to complete preparation programs before beginning to assist new principals. Daresh and Playko (1991) recommend that mentor training include five domains:

> 1. *Orientation to mentoring*, including characteristics and responsibilities of effective mentors, matching mentors with proteges, and benefits of mentoring programs for mentors and proteges
> 2. *Instructional leadership skills*, including new conceptions of leadership, personal educational platforms, and forms of inquiry
> 3. *Human relations skills*, including proteges as adult learners, adult learning styles, and personality and social styles
> 4. *Mentor process skills*, including problem-finding and problem-solving, interviewing techniques, and observation techniques
> 5. *Contextual realities and district needs*, including an analysis of issues and concerns unique to the mentor's individual school district. (pp. 25–27)

Daresh and Playko (1992) discuss a number of general benefits of mentoring. Having a mentor can increase a protege's confidence, help the protege integrate theory with practice, and increase the protege's communication skills. Proteges learn from mentors practical techniques and strategies that they can use to address the daily challenges of leadership. Finally, having a mentor greatly reduces the protege's professional isolation.

School systems have been slower to develop mentoring programs for beginning principals than for beginning teachers, despite the obvious need for assisting new administrators. In recent years, districts finally have begun to address this need, with positive results. Another area districts have been slow to explore is the mentoring of midcareer principals. Currently, such mentoring tends to be informal, and largely ignored in the professional literature.

In-Service Training Programs

Guiding principles for leadership training were drawn from the research literature by Moller and Bohning (1992). Staff development for principals should be based on what they perceive to be their training needs. An implication is that principals be involved in planning their own training programs. Training programs need to be ongoing and long term. Programs involving major change should last two or more years, with continuous support provided for principals throughout the program. Training should include opportunities for collegial learning. The school district may provide recognition and awards to principals involved in training and related school change. Finally, the effectiveness of training programs should be evaluated over time, with the evaluation including assessment of the program's effects on student learning.

Training programs can foster major changes in a principal's behavior. For example, in a district training program on instructional leadership described by Jones (1990), principals were trained in a variety of instructional improvement models as well as clinical supervision. As a result of this program, the amount of the instructional day that principals spent working with teachers on curriculum and instruction increased from under 10 percent to 60 percent. Principals also shifted from a one-to-one ratio of formative evaluations (evaluations for the purpose of assisting teachers to improve their instruction) to summative evaluations (evaluations to rate the performance of the teacher) to a ratio of five formative evaluations to one summative evaluation.

Peer Coaching

Typically associated with teachers, peer coaching can be adapted for use by principals wishing to assist each other to improve their leadership. In a principal peer coaching program described by Roberts (1991), principals selected one or two areas of instructional leadership in which they wished to improve, were paired with partners, and agreed to coach for four clinical cycles and be coached for four cycles. In a preobservation conference, the coached principal identified an instructional leadership task he or she wished to have observed. Types of observation data included existing records, frequency charts, diagrams, open-ended notes, videotapes, and audiotapes. After the coach analyzed the observation data, it was reported and discussed during a postobservation conference, during which the coach asked the observed principal to reflect on the meaning of the data, possible improvement goals, and behaviors validated by the data. The final step in the process was a collaborative critique of the previous steps. Principals in this peer coaching program reported that they had grown as instructional leaders as a result of their participation in the program. Interestingly, coaching matches made across different districts, ages, experience levels, genders, and positions (principal and assistant principal) all were successful.

The components of successful principal peer coaching programs are similar to those of teacher peer coaching, discussed in Chapter 3. The purpose of the program as well as the commitment required by participants should be made clear from the outset. Participants should be trained in the principles and process of peer coaching, observation techniques, and conferencing skills. Principals assigned to the same coaching pairs or teams need to have compatible personalities, and pairing principals with strongly conflicting educational or leadership beliefs probably should be avoided. A flexible coaching schedule needs to be worked out in advance, and principals need to reserve time for travel, observations, data analysis, and conferencing. Participants should be brought together periodically to discuss successes, problems, concerns, and needed modifications in the program.

Collegial Groups and Networks

Principals, like teachers, have a strong sense of isolation, and yearn for time to reflect on and improve their practice (McCay, 2001; Wilmore, 2001). Yet, unlike teachers—who across the nation are joining their peers in collegial groups to study, dialogue, and problem solve—principals remain isolated, with few opportunities for collaboration or reflective inquiry with their fellow principals. Fineman (1996) attempts to explain this phenomenon:

> That might be because many administrators are hesitant to participate in group support systems. In fact, one study of administrators found their culture to be "clan-like" and

> isolated; anther found that principals say they fear that participating in support groups to better understand instructional issues would be perceived as an admission of incompetence or lack of adequate training. (p. 34)

Fineman goes on to say that when principals *do* become part of collegial groups, they become less isolated, more reflective, collaborative problem solvers, and role models for life-long learning. She recommends making participation in a group voluntary, focusing on topics of mutual interest of which participants already have some knowledge. Initially, a facilitator can schedule and plan meetings, but once the group is up and running, a group member can assume responsibility for planning agendas. Fineman also recommends that the group's format vary over time. Possible formats include review of previous training, discussion of readings or videotapes, skill practice and peer feedback, case-study analysis, problem solving, or discussion of a demonstration or class session.

Successful principal networks possess the same features as successful teacher networks. They are focused, provide a variety of activities, establish discourse communities, and provide leadership opportunities (Lieberman & McLaughlin, 1992). Krovetz (1995) demonstrates how these four features are present in a principals' support network for high school restructuring in San Jose (CA). The network is focused on professional development to help the principal work effectively with the school community "to improve the quality of life for students and adults" (p. 71). In monthly sessions, the network addresses a variety of topics, including student assessment, curriculum, scheduling, student grouping, change, interpersonal skills, and interdisciplinary teaming. The network attempts to be a discourse community by creating a safe, confidential environment for dialogue and fostering principal reflection. Finally, the network provides leadership opportunities by allowing principals to share ideas with and learn from colleagues. Participating principals reported that the network helped them to develop a better understanding of the change process, more comfort with shared decision making, expanded teacher leadership in their schools, and a more critical approach to decision making.

The advent of the Internet means that principals easily can become part of electronic networks within which new ideas can be shared and discussed, problems can be framed and solved, and data can be collected and disseminated. Universities, government agencies, and educational associations can initiate electronic networks and serve as "brokers" of information and professional assistance. Ongoing communication on the Internet can complement other forms of networking, such as traditional conferences, newsletters, and journals.

Action Research

Principals, of course, should be involved as facilitators of teacher action research and as collaborators with teachers in schoolwide action research. But principals also can use action research as a vehicle for their own professional development. A case study of teacher action research at Crawford Elementary School in Ames (IA) Community School District was presented in Chapter 4. Principals in Ames are involved in their own action research as part of the district's administrator professional development program. Principal action research at Ames has been supported through district training and support sessions. At the professional development sessions, principals read and share literature, view and discuss videotapes, and engage in extensive dialogue about the action research process. Principals develop belief statements concerning the role of action research in their buildings. They meet with district support teams to identify student achievement goals and develop action research plans based on those goals. The principals integrate ideas for improving shared decision making, time management, and instructional leadership with their action research plan. Principals' action research in Ames is integrated with existing schoolwide action research and school improvement efforts. I have a personal bias in favor of principals' action research that is integrated with teachers' action research. However, action research also can be focused exclusively on the development of the individual administrator. For example, the principal could use action research to improve his or her time management, interpersonal communication, or instructional supervision skills.

Principals as Writers

Like teachers' writing, principals' writing can take many forms (reflective letters and memos, journals, cases, autobiography, or professional publication). The various forms of writing all can foster reflective inquiry, and, if done in collaboration with other principals or teachers, reflective dialogue and collegiality. Like teachers' writing, principals' writing can be structured or unstructured, formal or informal, collaborative or individual. Regardless of the format, writing can stimulate reflective thinking—an essential process for the "new" principal.

Self-Directed Professional Development

Self-directed professional development involves the administrator engaging in self-assessment, setting personal/professional improvement goals, planning learning activities designed to meet the stated goals, implementing the plan, assessing progress, and then entering into a new cycle of action planning. The principal involved in self-directed learning may carry out any phase of the professional development cycle by himself or herself, or the principal may (preferably) request assistance for any phase of the cycle from a mentor, coach, or collegial support group. What makes the professional development cycle *self-directed* is that, in each phase of the cycle, the principal makes all of the key decisions required to proceed through that phase.

Principals can incorporate into self-directed development any of the frameworks discussed in this section. They can request mentoring, attend training, partner with a peer coach, join a collegial group, become part of a network, engage in action research, do reflective writing, or attend a principals' center. They also can engage in less formal activities, such as reading, visiting other schools, completing nonevaluative observations of classrooms in their own school, and so on. The district's role in self-directed principal development is to provide encouragement, resources, a menu of learning opportunities, a collegial support system, and recognition for those who engage in self-directed learning.

Principals' Centers

Principals' centers typically are sponsored by universities, state agencies, associations, or business and industry. Centers usually serve principals from a number of districts. Levine (1989) compares effective teachers' and principals' centers. They both involve members in program development, consider members' individual characteristics, and base program content on member-perceived needs. Teachers' and principals' centers both provide modeling of new skills, build on members' strengths, provide feedback, and offer ongoing support. Many principals prefer meeting in a neutral site away from their work setting, and having an eclectic array of program offerings. The Harvard University Principals' Center has for many year been a model for other centers. The majority of the centers' advisory board are principals. Members are involved in all aspects of program development. The center offers dozens of professional development activities, with participation in any of these activities voluntary. Principals are providers as well as receivers of professional assistance.

The preceding discussion illustrates that there are a variety of professional development models available to facilitate principal development. The real challenge is to convince school districts and principals that professional development for campus administrators is worth the resources and personal commitment that it requires. One school district that has made a committment to principals' professional development is the San Francisco Unified School District. Exemplar 7.1 describes San Francisco's program, called The Leadership Connection.

EXEMPLAR 7.1 • *The Leadership Connection*

The Leadership Connection is a districtwide leadership development program for in-service administrators, jointly developed by the Stupski Family Foundation and the San Francisco Unified School District. The program better equips principals to analyze their school's reality and apply their leadership skills and practices to the development of strategies that positively impact student achievement in the area of literacy. The program partly is based on Kouzes and Posner's (1987, pp. 8–14) five fundamental practices of exemplary leadership:

Challenging the process. Accepting challenges and meeting those challenges through experimentation, innovation, and change

Inspiring a shared vision. Enlisting people in their vision through belief in, enthusiasm for, and articulation of an image of the future

Enabling others to act. Enlisting the support and assistance of others through teamwork, trust, and empowerment

Modeling the way. Establishing guiding principles and operational plans, and modeling through hard work, persistence, and attention to detail

Encouraging the heart. Recognizing individuals, holding group celebrations, linking rewards with performance, and self-encouragement

The program includes an annual summer institute for all district administrators that also serves as the initiation for administrators wishing to participate in the program the following school year. Principals connect their own professional growth goals and strategies to their school's goals, objectives, and strategies. During the school year, administrators meet monthly in day-long sessions that build sequentially to assist them to meet professional development and school goals.

The leadership program also includes a coaching component. District personnel complete a training program on the art of effective coaching. They attend monthly coaches' meetings to reinforce coaching skills and techniques, and strengthen subject matter expertise. The coaches facilitate monthly network meetings and provide one-to-one site-based coaching to network members. The specific nature and times of the coaching are determined by the coach and the network member.

A preliminary review found that participants increased their knowledge and confidence, and applied program skills in the strategic development of strategies to impact the academic achievement of students.

The Principal and Time Management

A common complaint from principals is that, although they would *like* to spend more time on things such as professional development, curriculum development, and instructional leadership, their time is so consumed with things such as paperwork, phone calls, and student discipline referrals that they simply don't have time to deal with leadership tasks that most directly impact teaching and learning. It is ironic that many principals don't have time to provide leadership for the improvement of curriculum, instruction, and student assessment, since most of us would agree that these are the core activities of schools! One way to address the problem of lack of time for core school functions is improvement of the principal's time management.

Covey (1989) offers the time management matrix in Figure 7.2 as a tool for self-management. The matrix is divided into quadrants, with activities assigned to particular quadrants based on the factors of urgency and importance. *Urgent* matters demand immediate attention. They are usually highly visible and popular activities. *Important* matters, when addressed, help principals reach their high-priority goals. Quadrant I activities are both urgent and important. They are significant and require immediate attention. Many principals spend much of their day in crisis management, reacting to Quadrant I situations.

Quadrant III activities are urgent but not important. The problem is that many principals mislabel Quadrant III activities as Quadrant I activities, because they are popular or expected by others. Thus, many principals spend an inordinate and unnec-

	URGENT	NOT URGENT
IMPORTANT	I *Activities:* Crises Pressing problems Deadline-driven projects Dealing with parental complaints Discipline referrals Central office requests Some calls	II *Activities:* Self-renewal Improving communication Long-range planning Professional development Meet with curriculum teams Classroom observations Improve school-parent collaboration
UNIMPORTANT	III *Activities:* Interruptions, some calls Some mail, some reports Some meetings Proximate, pressing matters Popular activities Some paperwork	IV *Activities:* Trivia, busy work Some mail Some phone calls Time wasters Some Internet surfing Some pleasant activities

FIGURE 7.2 The Time Management Matrix

Source: Excerpted from *The 7 Habits of Highly Effective People*, © 1989 by Stephen Covey, www.franklincovey.com. Used with permission. All rights reserved.

essary amount of time dealing with Quadrant III matters. Quadrant IV activities are neither urgent nor important. A principal may engage in these activities because they are pleasant diversions or because the principal is procrastinating regarding important activities.

Quadrant II activities are important but not urgent. Principals who spend most of their time in Quadrant II are visionary, self-disciplined, and proactive. Their focus on Quadrant II activities reduces the number of Quadrant I situations with which they must deal. For example, facilitating long-term professional development for improving instruction and classroom management (Quadrant II activity) will tend to reduce referrals to the principal's office (Quadrant I). Likewise, ongoing efforts to improve school-parent communication (Quadrant II) will reduce the frequency of parents calling or visiting the office to complain about school policies or actions (Quadrant I).

A principal can use the time management matrix as a basis for her or his professional development. After collecting data on daily activities over a period of two to three weeks, the principal clarifies professional values and identifies priorities, reflects on the relationship of typical and potential activities to those priorities, then creates lists of typical activities for Quadrants I, III, and IV, and desired activities for Quadrant II.

Next, the principal designs a long-range plan to avoid activities in Quadrants III and IV, focus on activities in Quadrant II, and reduce activities in Quadrant I. This process of prioritization and planning is best done in a collegial setting, facilitated by dialogue with and feedback from fellow administrators.

New Roles for the Central Office

School-focused professional development requires the support of central office administrators, supervisors, and staff developers. To provide effective support in a new era of professional development, central office personnel must assume new roles. Let's start with the superintendent, who should assume the role of the district's primary support person for professional development. This, of course, includes providing resources and discussing on a regular basis the importance of professional development. It also requires modeling. Barth maintains that the superintendent should be the "head learner" in the school system (Sparks, 1993b). The effective superintendent models support for professional development by attending planning sessions, participating and sometimes leading professional development for teachers and administrators, and visiting schools and classrooms to assess the progress of professional development efforts. The superintendent who is an effective staff developer develops extensive knowledge about organizational culture, research on learning, and the change process. Additionally, the successful superintendent is highly skilled in communication, human relations, and long-range planning. Effective superintendents are able to assume roles of champion, coach, and cheerleader for professional development (Sparks, 1993b).

Let's turn our attention now to central office staff developers. The single biggest change in the role of the central office staff developer is the shift from *director* to *facilitator* of professional development (Grove, 2002; Killion & Simmons, 1992). The facilitative staff developer first attempts to gain an in-depth understanding of the school's culture. Next, the facilitator assists the school community as it builds its own vision and selects its focus for school improvement and professional development. The facilitator collaborates with the school community in designing a development program, and supports the program with services, resources, and opportunities for reflection and feedback (Nowak, 1994; Slavin, 2001). Another aspect of facilitation is helping to eliminate barriers to change, such as an inflexible budgeting process or insufficient time for professional development (Corcoran, Fuhrman, & Belcher, 2001; Middleton, Smith, & Williams, 1994). To help eliminate barriers, the staff developer may need to become a broker between the school and the central office. Another part of the central office staff developer's new role is that of liaison between the district's schools. The staff developer can facilitate networks of teachers and principals, help schools to share effective practices, and help elementary, middle, and high schools articulate programs. Some "centralization" of professional development still is desirable. School-focused programs should be consistent with the district's broad philosophy, vision, and mission, and the central office staff developer can help schools meet that requirement.

Summary

This chapter proposed that principals in today's schools need to assume new roles and develop new proficiencies. It described principals' self-assessment as the basis for professional growth. A variety of frameworks for principal development were reviewed. Time management for principals was addressed. Finally, the changing roles of superintendents and central office staff developers were discussed.

Assignments

1. Write a paper on mentoring of beginning principals, including at least three references not listed in this chapter.
2. Administer the Principal's New Proficiencies Needs Assessment (Inset 7.1) to three different principals and/or assistant principals. Based on the data collected by the needs assessment, write a report on each administrator's perceived needs.
3. Interview a principal or assistant principal regarding professional development activities that he or she has participated in over the last two years and the perceived benefits of these activities. Write a paper summarizing your interview and discussing whether the principal's professional development has been consistent with the ideas presented in this chapter.
4. Based on reflection on your personal activities, create your own time management matrix (see Figure 7.2), classifying each of your typical work activities into one of the four quadrants.
5. Interview a central office staff developer on his or her role in teachers' professional development, including any ways in which his or her role has changed in recent years, and any ways in which he or she anticipates his or her role will change in the future. Write a report on the interview, including a discussion of whether the staff developer's perceptions are consistent with the ideas presented in this chapter.

References

Behar-Horenstein, L. L. S. (1995). Promoting effective school leadership: A change-oriented model for the preparation of principals. *Peabody Journal of Education, 70*(3), 18–40.

Blase, J., & Blase, J. (2001). The teacher's principal. *Journal of Staff Development, 22*(1), 22–25.

Brewer, H. (2001). 10 steps to success. *Journal of Staff Development, 22*(1), 30–31.

Casavant, M. D., & Cherkowski, S. (2001). Leadership: Bringing mentoring and creativity to the principalship. *NASSP Bulletin, 85*(624), 71–81.

Corcoran, T., Fuhrman, S. H., & Belcher, C. L. (2001). The district role in instructional improvement. *Phi Delta Kappan, 83*(1), 78–84.

Covey, S. R. (1989). *The 7 habits of highly effective people.* New York: Simon and Schuster.

Daresh, J. C., & Playko, M. A. (1991). Preparing mentors for school leaders. *Journal of Staff Development, 12*(4), 24–27.

Daresh, J. C., & Playko, M. A. (1992). Entry year programs for principals: Mentoring and other forms of professional development. *Catalyst for Change, 21*(2), 24–29.

Ellis, A., & Macrina, A. M. (1994). Reflection and self-appraisal in preparing new principals. *Journal of Staff Development, 15*(1), 10–14.

Ellis, S. S. (1995). "The principal must be the principal learner in the school" : An interview with Edna Varner. *Journal of Staff Development, 16*(4), 52–55.

Fineman, M. P. (1996). Learning together. *The Executive Educator, 18*(5), 34–35.

Grove, K. F. (2002). The invisible role of the central office. *Educational Leadership, 59*(8), 45–47.

Grover, K. L. (1994, April). *A study of first year principals and their mentors in the New York City public schools.* Paper presented at the Annual Meeting of the American Educational Research Association, New Orleans.

Hopkins-Thompson, P. A. (2000). Colleagues helping colleagues: Mentoring and coaching. *NASSP Bulletin, 84*(617), 29–36.

Human Synergistics. (1989). *Life Styles Inventory (LSI) 1: Self-development guide.* Plymouth, MI: Author.

Human Synergistics. (1990). *Life Styles Inventory (LSI) 2: Description by others staff development guide.* Plymouth, MI: Author.

Johnson, W. L., Snyder, K. J., & Johnson, A. M. (1991–92). Development of an instrument for the continuing educational needs of principals. *Teacher Education and Practice,* 7(2), 39–49.

Jones, R. R. (1990). An instructional leadership training program for principals. *Journals of Staff Development, 11*(4), 60–62.

Killion, J. P., & Simmons, L. A. (1992). The Zen of facilitation. *Journal of Staff Development, 13*(3), 2–5.

Kouzes, J. M., & Posner, B. Z. (1987). *The leadership challenge: How to keep getting extraordinary things done in organizations.* San Francisco: Jossey-Bass.

Krovetz, M. L. (1995). Principal support network: Collegial support for school restructuring. *NASSP Bulletin, 73*(574), 69–74.

Lauder, A. (2000). The new look in principal preparation programs. *NASSP Bulletin, 84*(617), 23–28.

Leithwood, K. A. (1992). The move toward transformational leadership. *Educational Leadership, 49*(5), 8–12.

Levine, S. L. (1989). *Promoting adult growth in schools: The promise of professional development.* Boston: Allyn and Bacon.

Lieberman, A., & McLaughlin, M. W. (1992). Networks for educational change: Powerful and problematic. *Phi Delta Kappan,* 673–677.

McCay, E. (2001). The learning needs of principals. *Educational Leadership, 58*(8), 75–77.

Middleton, J. A., Smith, A. M., & Williams, P. (1994). *Journal of Staff Development, 15*(3), 6–9.

Moller, G., & Bohning, G. (1992). School improvement leadership training. *Journal of Staff Development, 13*(1), 36–39.

Nowak, S. J. (1994). New roles and challenges for staff development. *Journal of Staff Development, 15*(3), 10–13.

Pierce, M. (2001). Support systems for instructional leaders. *Leadership, 30*(5), 16–18.

Rallis, S. F., & Goldring, E. B. (2000). *Principals of dynamic schools: Taking charge of change.* Thousand Oaks, CA: Corwin Press.

Roberts, J. (1991). Improving principals' instructional leadership through peer coaching. *Journal of Staff Development, 12*(4), 30–33.

Seller, W. (1993). New images for the principal's role in professional development. *Journal of Staff Development, 14*(1), 22–26.

Siegrist, G. (1999). Educational leadership must move beyond management training to visionary and moral transformation leadership. *Education, 120*(2), 297–303.

Slavin, R. E. (2001). Expecting excellence: Comprehensive school reform brings with it a revolution in professional development. *American School Board Journal, 188*(2), 22–25.

Sparks, D. (1993a). The professional development of principals: A conversation with Roland S. Barth. *Journal of Staff Development, 14*(1), 18–21.

Sparks, D. (1993b). Three superintendents speak out on planning and their role as staff developers: A conversation with Mary Nebgen, David Sousa, and Ray Williams. *Journal of Staff Development, 14*(2), 22–25.

Wilmore, E. L. (2001). Reflecting on reflection. *Principal, 81*(2), 44–45.

Resources

Blase, J., & Anderson, G. (1995). *The micropolitics of educational leadership: From control to empowerment.* New York: Teachers College Press.

Blase, J., & Blase, J. (1998). *Handbook of instructional leadership: How really good principals promote teaching and learning.* Thousand Oaks, CA: Corwin Press.

Casavant, M. D., & Cherkowski, S. (2001). Leadership: Bringing mentoring and creativity to the principalship. *NASSP Bulletin, 85*(624), 71–81.

Cherniss, C. (1998). Social and emotional learning for leaders. *Educational Leadership, 55*(7), 26–28.

DuFour, R. P. (2001). In the right context. *Journal of Staff Development, 22*(1), 14–54.

Fullan, M. (1998). Leadership for the 21st century: Breaking the bonds of dependency. *Educational Leadership, 57*(7), 6–10.

Hopkins-Thompson, P. A. (2000). Colleagues helping colleagues: Mentoring and coaching. *NASSP Bulletin, 84*(617), 29–36.

Lauder, A. (2000). The new look in principal preparation programs. *NASSP Bulletin, 84*(617), 23–28.

McCay, E. (2001). The learning needs of prinicpals. *Educational Leadership, 58*(8), 75–77.

Mohr, N. (1998). Creating effective study groups for principals. *Educational Leadership, 55*(7), 41–44.

Wanzare, Z., & DaCosta, J. L. (2001). Rethinking instructional leadership roles of the school principal: Challenges and prospects. *Journal of Educational Thought, 35*(3), 269–295.

8 Improvement of School Culture

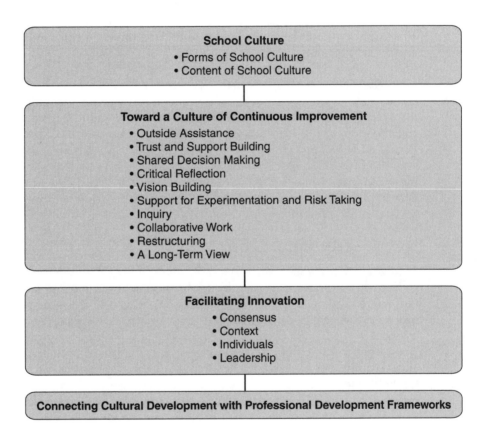

School Culture
- Forms of School Culture
- Content of School Culture

Toward a Culture of Continuous Improvement
- Outside Assistance
- Trust and Support Building
- Shared Decision Making
- Critical Reflection
- Vision Building
- Support for Experimentation and Risk Taking
- Inquiry
- Collaborative Work
- Restructuring
- A Long-Term View

Facilitating Innovation
- Consensus
- Context
- Individuals
- Leadership

Connecting Cultural Development with Professional Development Frameworks

Historically, professional development has maintained a curious dichotomy of process and goals. The traditional *process* has involved group learning, sometimes including all teachers in the school—sometimes all teachers in the district—in the same professional development activities. The *goals* of traditional programs, however, usually have been the improvement of the individual teacher's classroom instruction. Even when professional development has attempted to facilitate schoolwide change, it has tended to be specific instructional change rather than systemic organization development or school improvement. Only in recent years have many in the field come to accept slowly, sometimes grudgingly, the role of professional development in the improvement of school culture. This change in perspective has come none too soon in view of the negative effects that the conventional school culture has had on teaching and learning. These effects can be summarized in three disturbing statements:

1. *The traditional school provides a poor culture for student learning.* Goodlad's (1984) classic study of schools across the nation found that students typically are listening to the teacher, doing seatwork, or taking quizzes or tests. Usually they work alone, without collaboration with other students or initiation of interaction with teachers. Owen, Loucks-Horsley, and Horsley (1991) site a number of conditions that make schools poor places for learning, including isolation without privacy, poor assessment, rewarding of conformity, discouragement of independence and creativity, scheduling not conducive to engaged learning, and little connection between school and the real world. Sarason (1990) sums up schools as learning environments in blunt terms: "Schools generally are and have been uninteresting places for students and others. They are intellectually boring places" (p. 111).

2. *The traditional school provides a poor culture for teacher growth and development.* My colleagues and I have discussed this problem in depth in a different text (Glickman, Gordon, & Ross-Gordon, 2001), but a summary of why this statement is true is in order. Teachers typically spend most of their workday in isolation from their colleagues, and thus without the collaboration and collegiality needed for professional growth. Their workload and routinized schedules do not allow for reflection of teaching or creative planning, but do result in incessant psychological dilemmas and stress. Beginning teachers tend to enter this hostile environment with little support from their experienced colleagues. They typically begin teaching with inadequate resources, difficult work assignments, and unclear expectations, and are left alone by their colleagues to "sink or swim." Inadequate induction leads many promising teachers to leave the profession, and causes many teachers who remain in teaching to develop "survival" teaching strategies. Teachers move through upstaged careers, without new challenges, responsibilities, or rewards commensurate with their years of experience, expertise, or accomplishments. The conventional school organization makes no effort to accommodate teachers' development as adults. Teachers typically engage in little dialogue about curriculum and instruction and have little involvement in schoolwide curriculum and instructional decisions. Teachers in conventional schools seldom possess the common purpose, performance standards, analysis and problem solving expertise, and technical language found in the shared technical cultures that characterize true professions. Rather, they tend to rely on their personal experiences, preferences, and traditions.

3. *The same school culture that is so hostile to student and professional growth is extremely resistant to change. Indeed, the vast majority of efforts at significant schoolwide change have failed.* Weissglass (1991) identifies four obstacles to change, including the culture of schools, personal resistance to change, lack of awareness of the need for change, and working conditions of teaching. Many would argue that Weissglass's last three obstacles are really part of or a result of school culture. Fullan (1996) argues that "existing school cultures and structures are antithetical to the kinds of activities envisioned by system reform" (p. 422). Heckman (1993) states that "the unwritten norms and regularities of classroom and school life (the culture of school) transcend the written rules, regulations, and alternative ideas of the most ambitious and innovative administrators, policy makers, and curriculum developers" (p. 265). Indeed, some writers on organizational culture argue that the primary purpose of culture is to resist change! The conventional school culture is such an obstacle to change that we who are interested in school improvement must attempt to better understand organizational culture before we begin to think about organizational development. The next section attempts to help develop that understanding.

School Culture

School culture is the heart and soul of the school organization (Gratch, 2001; Marriott, 2001). Any school improvement effort must take the school's culture into account. School culture and professional development are interactive. The culture to some extent determines what types of professional development are feasible, and certainly can impact the success level of development programs. Conversely, professional development has been a significant factor in almost all successful school improvement efforts. Thus, it behooves those committed to professional development and school improvement to closely examine school culture. In this section we'll take a look at two aspects of culture: form and content.

Forms of School Culture

Hargreaves (1992) defines the *form of cultures* as "the characteristic patterns of relationship and forms of association between members of those cultures" (p. 219). He has identified three forms of culture: the culture of individualism, balkanized cultures, and collaborative cultures. In his discussions of collaborative cultures, Hargreaves distinguishes between fully functioning collaborative cultures, "comfortable collaboration," and "contrived collegiality" (Hargreaves, 1992; Fullan & Hargreaves, 1996). Let's take a closer look at each of Hargreaves's forms of culture.

Cultures of Individualism. This is the dominant form of school culture. In the conventional school, teachers almost never observe each other teaching and receive little feedback or support from other professionals. Although teachers may share a few "tricks of the trade" and resources, they seldom collaborate in serious analysis of and reflection on their teaching. The only feedback they typically receive is from their students. Such limited, unreliable feedback leads to teachers' uncertainty about their instructional practice. Root causes of individualism include the physical isolation caused by "egg crate" classrooms, teachers equating professional interaction with teacher evaluation and its negative connotations, and increasing expectations of teachers that leave little time for collegiality and make collaboration risky.

Balkanized Cultures. Hargreaves (1992) describes *balkanized cultures* as "made up of separate and sometimes competing groups, jockeying for position and supremacy like loosely connected, independent city states" (p. 223). These separate groups usually consist of teachers who work and socialize together. Balkinization can lead to poor communication, inconsistent expectations of students, poor long-term monitoring of student growth, and conflicts over school resources. Balkanization is most apparent in high schools, due in part to their division into specialized subjects and departments. Hargreaves concludes that a root cause of balkanization is the fact that some groups are valued more than others.

Fully Functioning Collaborative Cultures. Collaborative cultures are characterized by mutual acceptance, trust, openness, sharing, support, and recognition. They are not developed just for specific projects, but rather are found in day-to-day human relationships and interactions. Collaborative cultures possess agreement on core values, but tolerate and even encourage disagreements within the parameters of the agreed-upon values. Leadership is critical to creating and sustaining collaborative cultures, including leadership by example and dispersion of leadership throughout the school. Hargreaves points out that collaborative cultures are difficult to create and sustain and rarely are found in schools. One reason he cites for this is that collaborative cultures are inconsistent with the traditional context of teachers' work. In particular, (1) teachers have almost no scheduled time for collaboration and (2) highly detailed curriculum mandates leave little room for teacher collaboration. Despite the difficulty of developing collaborative cultures, they are clearly the type of cultures most congruent with ongoing school improvement (Hargreaves, 1992).

Comfortable Collaboration. This type of collaboration, also referred to as *bounded collaboration*, is described by Hargreaves (1992) as "restricted in its depth, its scope, its frequency or persistence, or a combination of these factors" (p. 228). Collaboration in this type of culture is limited to providing routine advice, trading practical "tricks of the trade," and sharing resources. Comfortable collaboration does not extend across classroom boundaries for such collegial activities as co-teaching, peer observation, or collaborative action research. There is no critical inquiry, reflection, or dialogue among teachers. Collaboration is focused on immediate issues and short-term initiatives, and is limited to individual units of instruction or particular subjects rather than wider and deeper issues concerning the quality and long-term improvement of curriculum and instruction. In short, although teachers in comfortable cultures enjoy a high level of congeniality, they fail to ask the tough questions and do the hard work needed for fully functioning collaboration. Hargreaves asserts that most schools purporting to possess collaborative cultures in fact possess bounded collaboration (Hargreaves, 1992).

Contrived Collegiality. When administrators attempt to create collaboration through mandatory programs and bureaucratic procedures, contrived collegiality results. Hargreaves (1992) argues that, "at its worst, contrived collegiality can be little more that a quick, slick administrative surrogate for more genuinely collaborative cultures" (p. 230). He maintains that contrived collegiality may affront the dignity of teachers, lead to unwanted meetings and teacher administrative overload, and stifle teachers' informal collaboration. As one reads Hargreaves's thoughts on contrived collegiality, at times it seems that he considers any type of structured program or formal assistance from educational leaders as an impediment to true teacher collaboration. Yet, in studies found throughout the professional development literature, teachers report that structured programs such as peer coaching, mentoring, and action research—if well conceived, voluntary, and adequately supported—lead to authentic teacher collaboration. Teachers certainly don't appreciate being forced to attend meetings or participate in programs they find irrelevant, or that are used by administrators to manipulate and control faculty. Yet, when teachers are committed to programs or projects that they believe will promote their professional development, improve collaboration, and lead to improved student learning, they are grateful for assistance provided by facilitative leaders. Although Hargreaves might disagree, it seems to me that the important distinction between contrived and authentic collegiality is not whether collaboration is formal or informal, or whether school leaders are involved or uninvolved. Both formal and informal collaboration can be successful. In fact, they can complement each other. Moreover, authentic collaboration can occur between school leaders and teachers as well as among teachers. The important distinction, I believe, is between controlling leadership, which leads to contrived collegiality, and facilitative leadership, which fosters true collegiality.

Our discussion of the forms of school culture has helped us understand the differences between fully functioning collaborative cultures and other types of cultures. Clearly, fully functioning collaboration should be every school's aim (Foley, 2001). But *why* are some cultures fully collaborative and others not? And *how* does a school with a culture of individualism, a balkanized culture, or a culture of comfortable or contrived collaboration move to a fully functioning collaborative culture? The following discussion on the content of school culture hopefully will answer the first question, and begin to answer the second.

Content of School Culture

For a fuller understanding of school culture, we need to go beyond the forms of culture to its content. Edgar Schein has been a pioneer in the study of organizational culture, and much of this discussion is based on his work. One of Schein's (1990) significant contributions has been his descriptions of the different levels of content within a culture. Figure 8.1 is an adaption of Schein's levels of culture.

To explain the levels of culture illustrated in Figure 8.1, let's imagine we are going to visit a school to explore the content of its culture. Let's further assume that we're going to begin our exploration by simply observing what's going on in the school, in its classrooms, hallways, offices, meeting rooms, teachers' lounge, cafeteria, and so on. With our eyes and ears we will be able to investigate *observable artifacts*—the surface level of the culture. On the first day of our observation, we will note obvious artifacts, including the physical layout and appearance of the school, how classrooms are organized, how students are grouped, and our general impression of the school's climate. Over the following few days, we might examine archival documents, such as the school's mission statement, strategic plan, written rules and procedures, the master schedule, curriculum guides, student achievement data, and so on.

Although it will be relatively simple to determine *formal* roles, rules, and relationships, determining *informal* roles, norms, and relationships—which often have more powerful effects on the culture than formal ones—will take weeks of observing behavioral patterns. What informal leadership roles do various teachers assume? What interpersonal roles do administrators and teachers display during group interaction? What informal working relationships exist between various individuals and various groups, and how do things get done in the school? At this stage of exploration, we need to remain tentative about our interpretation of the meanings of observed artifacts. We should not be surprised to observe behaviors and other artifacts within the culture that seem contradictory, but we also need to keep in mind that as we dig deeper into the school's culture we may find that seemingly contradictory behaviors are in fact consistent with the culture's basic underlying assumptions.

As a result of our observation of artifacts, we will have acquired some understanding of the school's culture. Even at this early stage, we should have a fairly good idea of the school culture's form (individualism, balkanization, collaboration). However, if we wish to find out more about the culture, we need to exam its second level—*espoused values*. To do this, we would have to return to the school to ask members of the school community questions about their perceptions and beliefs. Data collected during our initial observations can be used to frame questions on the meaning of the observed artifacts, as well as any seeming inconsistencies between artifacts. Additionally, we would ask

Surface Level: *Observable Artifacts*

- -

Deeper Level: **Espoused Values**

Deepest Level: **Basic Underlying Assumptions**

FIGURE 8.1 The Content of School Culture

Source: E. H. Schein, "Organizational Culture," *American Psychologist, 45*(2), 109–119. Copyright © 1990 by the American Psychological Association. Adapted with permission.

members of the school community to share their philosophical values, such as what the mission of the school should be, what the curriculum should consist of, what constitutes effective teaching, the value placed on different subjects, groups, and programs within the school, and so on. Although written surveys can provide us with some information on espoused values, in-depth interviews with key informants are preferable. We can expect to find apparent contradictions between espoused values and observed artifacts, or even between values espoused by different members of the culture. To discover the underlying meaning of espoused values, to explain apparent contradictions, and to examine the deepest level of the school culture, we must continue our investigation still further.

As we work with the school community to uncover its *basic underlying assumptions*, we often will find that apparent contradictions among and between observed behavior and espoused values are not really contradictions at all. For example, teachers who report that they value learning about educational technology but who never attend district professional development programs on technology may share the assumption that district-based programs will be irrelevant to their school and classroom needs, and that the best way for them to learn needed skills is to receive informal assistance from peers at their own school. Identifying underlying assumptions helps us understand the meaning of observed behaviors and espoused values. Consider, for example, the forms of culture describe by Hargreaves. If teachers assume that their classrooms are their private domain, that losing their privacy might call into question their established teaching practice or even threaten their professional reputation, then we can understand why a culture of individualism has developed. If teachers assume that different levels of respect are assigned to different grade levels, teams, disciplines, experience levels, or other subgroups within the culture, and that the group they identify with needs to "hunker down" to protect itself or compete for scarce resources, we can understand why a balkanized culture has emerged.

Again, assumptions are taken for granted—so much so that they no longer are examined consciously by members of the culture. We begin to see now why changing school culture, or introducing specific innovations not consistent with the culture, is so difficult. Leaders often attempt to convince teachers to change their behaviors without realizing that those behaviors ultimately are based on assumptions that contradict the proposed change. These assumptions have been controlling and protecting the culture for a considerable period of time. Significant changes in or within the culture will not take place until the underlying assumptions are changed! Prerequisites for changing assumptions include understanding what they are, as well as helping members of the school community examine the assumptions in light of what they want their school to be, and what they want their students to learn. Although some have argued that the very purpose of culture is to resist change, a more accepted view is that the purpose of the culture is the survival of the organization and, more specifically, the solving of problems that threaten its well being. When educators in a school become convinced that their assumptions no longer are meeting that purpose—that other assumptions will better serve them and their students—then they will finally be ready to discard their old assumptions and adopt new ones. Staff developers and other educational leaders cannot mandate such a change; they can only facilitate it. The next section will provide some ideas for the long-term improvement of school culture.

Toward a Culture of Continuous Improvement

My own observations and study of school culture have led me to one overarching conclusion: *The primary focus regarding change in schools should not focus on any particular innovation, but rather on changing the traditional school culture to one that promotes continuous improvement.* Once we have achieved a culture of continuous improvement, specific changes in the best interest of the school and its students will be far less difficult to implement. Based on our previous discussion of school culture, the following three things need to take place to develop and maintain a culture of continuous improvement:

1. Members of the school community need to engage collaboratively in ongoing, critical analysis of their behaviors, espoused values, and underlying assumptions, especially in regard to the school's curriculum, instruction, and student assessment.
2. Members of the school community need continously to envision the ideal learning environment for students, explore the gaps between the ideal and the present environment, and consider alternatives for bridging those gaps.
3. Members of the school community need collaboratively to plan, implement, assess, modify, and integrate change aimed at continuous improvement at both the school and classroom levels.

This list is consistent with both Schein's content of school culture and Hargreave's collaborative culture. However, to repeat a question asked earlier in this chapter, *How* does a school move from a less than fully functioning collaborative culture to one that includes the three factors listed above? Simply developing an understanding of school culture, its forms and its content, is a good start, but it is not enough. There are specific practices that principals, staff developers, and teachers interested in movement toward a collaborative culture can foster (not mandate). The remainder of this section discusses those practices.

Outside Assistance

School cultures cannot be changed from the outside, but outside assistance can support change (Fullan, 2001). The first line of support for the individual school is the school district. It is essential that the superintendent actively supports reculturing efforts. Indeed, if the superintendent is unwilling to support practices such as collaborative decision making at the district level, they are not likely to succeed at the school level (Ferguson, 2001; Holloway, 2001; Prestine, 1991). In the districts where the exemplary programs presented in this text were carried out, the primary unit of change was the school, but the primary source of support for school change was the district. Furthermore, the shared decision making, reflective inquiry, vision building, and collaboration that was taking place in the school was invariably taking place at the district level as well. Modeling, provision of resources, and encouragement from the central office all help individual schools to succeed in building cultures of continuous improvement.

All of the external support frameworks discussed in Chapter 6 are relevant here. Schools can seek *partnerships* in reculturing efforts with universities, business, and the community. Also, a variety of national, state, and regional *networks* are concerned with school improvement through reculturing. All of the major national school improvement networks offer a model for changing school culture, professional development for change facilitators, and ongoing support and sharing among network members. Most of the schools involved in the exemplars for this text had joined one of the national networks early on in their reculturing efforts. However, in each case, the school adapted the network's school improvement model to local needs and context.

Another source of assistance for reculturing is an organization development (OD) consultant. Although OD consultants can be from within the organization, they traditionally have been from outside the system. The consultant typically has an advanced degree in group dynamics or organizational psychology. The consultant's purpose is to help the organization to improve itself by changing its roles, norms, and procedures and by improving its communication, decision making, and problem-solving processes. The OD consultant helps members of the school community to assess and transform their own organization (Schmuck & Runkel, 1994).

Less structured external support for reculturing can be provided by "critical friends," experienced volunteers from outside the school community who are available on request to assist with reculturing. Critical friends may be administrators, staff developers, teachers, professors, or retired educators. It is important that critical friends be highly trusted by members of the school community. The role of the critical friend is to gather data and provide feedback on the school's culture, give advice on how to improve the culture, and critique reculturing efforts. Critical friends develop informal but close, long-term relationships with the school community.

Trust and Support Building

To build a culture of continuous improvement, mutual trust and support must be present throughout the school community. The road toward an ethos of trust begins with open, honest communication. This includes establishing and maintaining communication channels among principals, teachers, staff, students, and parents. It also includes the development of effective communication skills. Operational roles for fostering mutual trust can be agreed upon. Chance, Cummins, and Wood (1996) list a set of roles developed by Altus Middle School in southwestern Oklahoma:

- People are important and should be listened to and recognized.
- Feelings are important so any criticism should always be focused on issues and ideas, not on individuals.
- Feelings, behaviors, and concerns should be openly, freely acknowledged and discussed.
- Honesty is a valued commodity among the "family" members at Altus Middle School.
- We all learn from doing things together, deciding on issues as a group, and analyzing ideas that create an effective school work culture. (pp. 45–46)

Obviously, the principal plays a key role in building trust within the school community. Ferris (1994) reports on an action research project to build trust among teachers and administrators in Harwich, Massachusetts. Teachers developed and completed a questionnaire for rating administrators on their trust-building behaviors. Based on questionnaire results, administrators collaboratively planned and implemented year-long trust-building plans. Re-administration of the questionnaire showed that trust between teachers and administrators was enhanced. Although we need to avoid generalizing from this small-scale study, it does indicate the possibility of principals increasing their trust-building capacity through collaboratively designed improvement plans.

Shared Decision Making

There are four primary reasons for shared decision making in schools. First, better decisions will result if the principal involves other members of the school community in the decision-making process. The principal and other members of the school community together have more knowledge and expertise than the principal alone. Second, shared decision making will increase collaboration among members of the school community, thus moving the school closer to a collaborative culture. Third, if allowed to participate in decisions about change, members of the school community are far more likely to develop a sense of ownership in the decision and thus support implementation of the change. Fourth, if we really wish to empower students to be contributing members of a democratic society, they need to be members of a school community that empowers all of its members.

Sharing decision making is sharing power. One way to encourage principals to share power is to help them cease viewing power as a "zero sum game." Administrators need to accept the principle that, rather than losing some of their own power when they involve others in decision making, they are in fact increasing their power as change agents by increasing the capacity of the school to change. Thus, in terms of school improvement (which should be the principal's real focus), *power with* is simply more effective than *power over*.

We must be careful to differentiate between structures intended to promote shared decision making and authentic shared decision making. For example, site-based management is a structure for shared governance, but it may or may not be accompanied by authentic shared decision making. To find out if shared decision making is really taking place, we need to spend time in a school talking to teachers, watching decision making in action, and observing who makes what types of decisions. At present, it seems that this critical aspect of reculturing is observed more in the breach than in the main.

Critical Reflection

In a study of eight secondary schools attempting to reculture their organizations to support teacher and student learning, Hannay, Ross, and Brydges (1997) found that *initiating schools*—schools that made more fundamental changes more quickly—engaged in questioning past school structures and classroom learning experiences. Schools that are serious about reculturing "commit to creating and sustaining a culture of continued self examination" (Conley, 1993, p. 24). They openly exchange ideas and debate issues (Peterson & Brietzke, 1994).

Heckman (1993) describes four conditions that support reflection:

1. *Group dialogue*, in which teachers, principals, and others discuss school and classroom practices and the underlying reasons for those practices
2. *Public mindfulness*, in which participants make public the meanings underlying their practices and efforts to change those practices
3. *Outsiders* who facilitate dialogue by raising questions, offering alternative ideas, encouraging participants to ask questions, and probing for clarification
4. *Enactment*, in which participants try out new practices, discuss results, and consider alternative explanations—especially for unexpected outcomes

One way to structure dialogue is to agree in advance on what types of analysis will take place. Heckman (1993) has proposed a series of questions to be considered in dialogue concerning school practice.

> Analysis is not merely confined to questions of effectiveness, i.e., Does a practice "work"? Does the practice produce a predetermined outcome criterion? Instead, questions are raised about the reasons for a criterion of effectiveness and the practices that are being evaluated: Why this criterion? What conceptions of effectiveness undergird this criterion? Why these conceptions? What alternative ideas of effectiveness could guide the creation of other practices, and what other criteria could be invoked? (pp. 266–267)

Whether dialogue is structured or open ended, when used as a vehicle for reculturing, its primary purpose is always the same: to critically examine the behaviors, espoused values, and assumptions of the culture, and to consider alternative assumptions, values, and behaviors.

Vision Building

There is agreement across the literature that vision building is an essential characteristic in school cultures of continuous improvement (Bulach, 2001; Campo, 1993; Chance, Cummins, & Wood, 1996; Conley, 1993; Fullan, 1992; Hannay, Ross, & Brydges, 1997; Marriott, 2001; Snyder & Snyder, 1996). Chance, Cummins, and Wood (1996) assert that "a shared vision provides a focus for school personnel and results from an intensive process of self-evaluation, consensus building, and identification of strengths, weaknesses, and needs by stakeholders for the school" (p. 45). Here, we are definitely *not* talking about the principal selling (or worse yet, mandating) his or her vision to others. Rather, the principal should foster collaborative vision building by the school community (Fullan, 1992). Nor should vision building merely consist of a committee of teachers writing a vision statement to be reviewed and approved by others. True vision building consists of repeated cycles of study, practice, and dialogue that will enable teachers to develop ownership in a gradually emerging vision (DuFour, 2000; Lewis, Watson, & Schaps, 1997). Fullan (1992) puts it well:

> The message is not the traditional "Plan, then do," but "Do, then plan . . . and do and plan some more." Even the development of a shared vision that is central to reform is better thought of as a journey in which people's sense of purpose is identified, considered, and continuously shaped and reshaped. (p. 749)

There is no need to fear that the continuous shaping and reshaping of vision will delay reculturing. The journey itself fosters a culture of continuous improvement (Hannay, Ross, & Brydges, 1997).

Support for Experimentation and Risk Taking

Critically examining one's own practice is risky business (Sparks, 2001a). Attempting to change one's practice is riskier still. Working with others to assess and change the school culture multiplies risk exponentially. To engage in experimentation and risk taking requires extensive support from administrators and staff developers. Supporting experimentation and risk taking by teachers, of course, creates risks for leaders. The ideal of a predictable, stable school culture where no one challenges the status quo must be thrown out forever as principals and staff developers become models of experimentation and risk taking.

Inquiry

Inquiry is the natural companion of experimentation and risk taking. At the heart of inquiry is a commitment to data-based decision making. Data can come from a variety of sources, including classroom and school processes, learning outcomes, best educational practice going on inside and outside the school, and societal trends (Conley, 1993). In schools committed to continuous improvement, data gathering and analysis are ongoing. Moreover, the school community is willing to pursue inquiry into all areas of its culture and to initiate necessary change in any of those areas.

Collaborative Work

Earlier in this chapter we read about collaborative school cultures and Hargreave's cautions that some cultures, although collaborative on the surface, are not fully functioning collaborative cultures. Little (1990) has proposed a continuum of collegiality ranging from independence (lowest level of collegiality) to interdependence (highest level). At the low end of Little's continuum is *story telling and scanning of ideas*, in which teachers tell brief stories of classroom events in order to receive information or reassurance. At the next level on the continuum is *aid and assistance*. At this level, teachers provide each other with help and advice only when asked to do so. This type of assistance tends to be sporadic and piecemeal. *Sharing*, the next level on Little's continuum, consists of the routine exchange of materials, methods, ideas, and opinions. The highest stage of collegiality on Little's continuum is *joint work*. This represents true collaboration or "shared responsibility for the work of teaching" (Little, 1990, p. 519). It includes (1) continuous and precise discussion of teaching; (2) peer observation and critique; (3) collaborative design, development, and evaluation of instructional materials; and (d) teachers teaching each other about effective teaching (Little, 1982). Collaborative work is at the center of the culture of continuous improvement.

Restructuring

Here we are talking about restructuring with a small *r* as opposed to the general concept of school reform. Structures within the school culture include rules and procedures, formal roles and relationships, curriculum organization, student organization, schedules, and so on. We must remember that structures are part of the surface level of school culture. Unless changes in beliefs and assumptions occur, structural changes by themselves will not lead to a culture of continuous improvement. Changes in assumptions and beliefs naturally will lead to structural changes, which will in turn enhance and support continued reculturing.

One type of restructuring involves assigning teachers new roles such as mentor or team leader. These roles of course must be authentic rather than mere titles, and teachers must be provided training, support, and rewards. Another type of restructuring involves teacher grouping and teaming. School governance councils, vertical teams, and interdisciplinary teams are examples. Such teams can increase communication, collegiality, and collaboration. Merely assigning teachers to groups and mandating meetings will not lead to reculturing. Providing opportunities for such groups to form and facilitating group process and team development are essential to cultures of continuous improvement.

Restructuring time is another critical aspect of reculturing. It might include restructuring teachers' work schedules so they have more time for collaborative work, moving to a block schedule to facilitate interdisciplinary curriculum, or changing the primary focus of faculty meetings from information sharing to dialogue about teaching and learning. Although the provision of time alone will not assure reculturing, it is difficult to imagine a culture of continuous improvement without this most valuable resource.

A Long-Term View

The school wishing to move toward a culture of continuous improvement must overcome the desire for a quick fix so prominent in American schools and, for that matter, American culture. (I'm reminded of the story about the superintendent who ordered the district's principals to institute new cultures in their schools by the end of the semester!) The fact of the matter is that, when it comes to reculturing, there is no magic bullet. Many of the exemplars in this text involve schools that transformed from traditional cultures to cultures of continuous school improvement. Such transformations usually took at least five years.

The long-term nature of reculturing means that schools need to escape the fadism that results in teachers being asked to implement innovations that are forgotten within the year because of an even "hotter" innovation that takes center stage. Innovations should be chosen based on the school's vision, integrated with other improvement efforts, and given time to succeed. Another aspect of a long-term view is the need to frame and solve problems in a way that enhances the school culture. When a problem arises, professionals need to analyze it in terms of its potential effects on the culture. Finally, the length of time that it takes to transform a school culture underlies the need for staff stability. Fortunately, once the culture begins to improve, staff retention is likely to improve as well. Exemplar 8.1 tells the story of continuous improvement at Leander (TX) Middle School.

EXEMPLAR 8.1 • *Continuous Improvement at Leander Middle School*

Perhaps the most salient characteristic of Leander (TX) Middle School's culture is the trust, respect, and support found among educators at the school. One teacher articulated this as follows:

> There is a high level of respect because they [administrators] trust us to do our job. They are not breathing down our necks all the time. They respect you as adults and as professionals, and that creates this incredible level of trust, where you feel like you can make a difference in your school, and you can come forward and express your ideas in the process.

Teachers at the middle school report that they feel comfortable discussing problems that they encounter, and that individual problems quickly become mutual problems to be solved by administrators and teachers working together. Mutual trust, respect, and support have led to a strong sense of community at the school, and efforts are made to socialize newcomers into the community:

> One of the things that sets this particular school apart from other schools is that there is a family or a community feeling. Whenever we have new people coming into the system we embrace them and make them aware of what we stand for and what our culture is. There is a certain energy or morale that you feel from our school.

Shared governance has become such an integral part of the school culture that it is taken for granted by teachers. One teacher made the following comment: "We pretty much insist on being part of the decision-making process. I think that's expected. That's what we've become accustomed to, and we're very empowered in that respect." Administrators are equally adamant that teachers be involved in school governance. Much of the decision making at Leander Middle School is made by academic teams serving groups of approximately 150 students. The teams include core content teachers and specialists and are facilitated by an assistant principal. The teams make decisions about the learning environment, curriculum, instruction, student assessment, assistance for students at risk, student discipline, and communication with parents. Decisions are based on data gathered by the teams, including student achievement data and input from students and parents. A teacher discussed the value of delegating decision making to academic teams: "Because your team only has responsibility—even in a huge and growing school—for 150 students, you know every one of them. You know what their needs are, and you can best assess what you need to do for them." The same teacher goes on to discuss the relationship between the principal and the academic teams:

> The principal never says, "I want everybody to do student-run conferences" or "I want everybody to do student portfolios." The principal says, "Here's the data on this. If your teams feel that it's value-added, something you want to do, then go for it. I'll support you either way."

In addition to the academic teams, schoolwide improvement teams develop proposals for faculty review. There are standing improvement teams for academic excellence, student discipline, and special needs. Shared decision making at Leander Middle School extends to students. Students are involved in identifying their academic goals, designing learning activities, assessing their academic growth, developing their portfolios, and planning student-parent conferences. A teacher discussed the effects of shared governance:

> As long as you're being enabled and empowered by the people that you report to, whether it's the kids reporting to the teachers or the teachers reporting to the administration, that totally changes the whole culture of the school, from the top down *and* from the bottom up.

Another aspect of the school's culture is vision building. Administrators, teachers, students, and community members have developed a vision of learning that would take place on an ideal campus. On their perfect campus, students would be *responsible citizens, effective communicators, academically prepared individuals*, and *productive learners.* But visioning building has gone beyond imagining the ideal school. For each of these desired characteristics, specific student learning outcomes, professional development programs, instructional strategies, and student assessment methods have been developed. In short, there's a continuing effort to create a system with all of its components aligned with the school vision.

At Leander, educators are willing to take a hard, honest look at practices that are not working. Assignment of blame as well as quick administrative fixes are avoided:

> There are so many things that happen that we don't want and don't like, but one thing that we don't do is hide them. We search for the harder answers; we don't go the blame route, and we don't rely on power. If you don't blame people and you don't power out, then you're forced to find a better solution.

(continued)

EXEMPLAR 8.1 • Continued

Improvement efforts at the middle school are data based. Learning matrices are developed for both academic and affective learning goals. Academic teams have developed a variety of rubrics for authentic assessment of student work. Students develop their own portfolios. Benchmark tests are administered three times a year. Another example of data-based improvement is the school's efforts to improve student discipline. Based on analysis of discipline reports, comparison of student behaviors across grade levels, and student and teacher surveys, the school has identified particular problem areas, environmental inhibitors to self-discipline, and suggestions for improvement. Teachers at the middle school continuously gather feedback from each other, students, and parents. Feedback is provided through informal discussions, brainstorming sessions, and surveys. A teacher summed up her experiences with data-based improvement as follows: "The whole thing I've learned from working here at Leander is not to be afraid of the data. You simply cannot function without it."

The intensive collaboration at Leander Middle School is no accident. Through such structures as vision building, school-wide data analysis, and goal setting, as well as academic and improvement teams, common planning periods, and peer coaching, the school is *designed for collaboration!*

Facilitating Innovation

Although movement toward a culture of continuous improvement is more important than any specific change, particular innovations still need to be fostered. This section will take a look at facilitating innovations through attention to consensus, context, individuals, and leadership.

Consensus

Innovation has the best chance for success if all stakeholders are involved from the beginning of and throughout the change process. Stakeholders need to agree on (1) the need for change, (2) the specific nature of the desired change, and (3) how to achieve the change. Through a process of collaborative inquiry and reflection, destination and journey need to be visualized with increasing clarity. In addition to a shared vision, various stakeholders must understand and agree to responsibilities, risks, sacrifices, and rewards associated with the innovation. Authentic consensus is the basis for the shared ownership and shared commitment necessary to implement any meaningful innovation, and thus well worth the required time and effort.

Context

Innovation must be planned and implemented with attention to the context of the school (Ellsworth, 2001). One way of attending to context is being realistic about the scope and pace of the innovation in light of the school's structure, faculty, and resources. The trick is to attempt innovation that is meaningful but not beyond the capacity of the organization to achieve. All meaningful innovations take time, but the same type of innovation might take two years to implement in one school, and three years in another. Another contextual variable is teacher workload. Teachers must be provided time to implement the change. This can be done through restructuring teachers' schedules so they have built-in time to work with the innovation, providing released time, or eliminating other teacher responsibilities that have outlived their usefulness. If the innovation is one that has been successful in other schools, it must be adapted to fit the school's culture, vision, and goals. Of course, sometimes the school must make adaptions to *itself* in order to prepare for the innovation. Existing priorities, programs, or structures that are inconsistent with the innovation may need to be modified or eliminated to accommodate the desired change. To quote a number of experts on school innovation, change is a process, not an event. Meaningful change cannot be mandated, declared, or dropped into an existing school culture. It must be developed and integrated into the culture over an extended period of time.

Individuals

School cultures are composed first and foremost of individuals, and thus individuals need to be the focus of schoolwide innovations. A long line of research shows that for individuals, change is both a personal and developmental experience. Individuals move through several stages of concern when dealing with innovations. A teacher must first become aware of an innovation's purpose and of what it consists. Next, the teacher must develop an understanding of his or her role regarding the change. Once implementation is underway, the teacher must learn how to manage the tasks he or she is expected to complete to make the innovation successful. Next, the teacher must attend to the impact of the change on his or her students. Eventually, the teacher will need to work with other educators to assist with schoolwide implementation. And finally, at the end of the developmental continuum, the teacher works with others to find new applications for the innovation, to modify the innovation itself, or even to replace the innovation with a more powerful one (Hall & Hord, 1987; Hord, Rutherford, Huling-Austin, & Hall, 1987; Loucks-Horsley & Stiegelbauer, 1991; Sipe, 2001).

The developmental nature of the individual's concerns about innovations has several implications. First, a single innovation of any significance requires extensive "readiness" activities prior to implementation. Second, implementation and institutionalization of an innovation is a long-term proposition requiring ongoing assistance. Third, the assistance needs to be differentiated. Even if every teacher in a school starts at the "awareness" level of concern, individual teachers will move through the stages of concern at different rates, requiring different types of assistance for different teachers during any given period of time. Therefore, we cannot assist individuals with innovations according to a predetermined schedule.

Leadership

Administrative and teacher leadership are required if meaningful innovations are to succeed. The most successful innovations are supported by *coordinated administrative leadership* by central office personnel and the school principal (Gordon, Nolan, & Forlenza, 1995; Sparks, 2001b). Administrators must show through word and deed that they take the innovation seriously (Dull, Pagon, & Smith, 1999; Sparks, 2001b). This includes obtaining resources as well as encouraging and recognizing those involved in the change effort. It also involves monitoring the change effort and assisting with problem solving when necessary (Heller & Firestone, 1994). For example, conflicts should be viewed as not only inevitable but necessary for meaningful change. Leaders need to admit this to themselves, and help teachers deal with conflict in an open and constructive manner (Evans, 1996; Green & Etheridge, 2001).

Teacher leadership also is essential for innovation. Teachers should be encouraged to initiate change. Regardless of who initiates innovation, it is unlikely to succeed without strong teacher advocates early on. Additionally, leaders should provide as many opportunities as possible for both formal and informal teacher leadership throughout the change process. In the schools selected as exemplars for this text, innovations sometimes were initiated by administrators, sometimes by teachers. But always it was teachers who were primarily responsible (with administrator support and encouragement) for implementing and institutionalizing meaningful change.

Inset 8.1 provides a school culture needs assessment that addresses needs relative to cultural improvement as well as school innovations.

INSET 8.1 • *School Culture Needs Assessment*

Part I : Cultural Improvement

Directions: Respond to each item by selecting the response that you believe most nearly corresponds with the school's level of need for the type of assistance described. Possible responses for items 1 through 10 are:

A. No need
B. Little need
C. Moderate need
D. High need
E. Very high need

1. Need for support from the central office for efforts to improve your school's culture

2. Need for support from outside the district (partnerships, networks, consultants, etc.) to improve your school's culture
3. Need for trust and support building at your school
4. Need to increase the level of shared decision making at your school
5. Need for professionals at your school to engage in thoughtful self-examination of the school culture
6. Need to build a shared vision of long-term goals at your school
7. Need for support for experimentation and risk taking at your school
8. Need for data-based decision making at your school
9. Need for collaborative work among teachers to improve your school
10. Need for your school to move from a short-term to a long-term view of school improvement

Part II: School Innovations
Directions: Respond to each item by selecting the response that you believe most nearly corresponds with the school's current practice. Possible responses for items 11 through 16 are:

A. Never
B. Sometimes
C. Often
D. Always

11. Consensus is reached on the need for innovations.
12. Consensus is reached on how to achieve innovations.
13. Innovations are adapted to fit the school's culture.
14. The concerns and needs of individuals are taken into account when planning and implementing innovations.
15. Innovations are supported by district and school leaders working together.
16. Teachers assume leadership roles regarding innovations.

Connecting Cultural Development with Professional Development Frameworks

Each of the professional development frameworks discussed in Part II can be used to facilitate cultural development. For example, study groups might deal with how to foster practices that build trust. Action research or collaborative work teams might be used to solve an immediate problem (such as how to improve students' study skills) while also fostering long-term cultural improvment goals such as shared decision making. Peer coaching or team teaching can have the immediate objective of adopting an instructional innovation while also fostering the experimentation, risk taking, and collaborative work essential for cultures of continuous improvement. Figure 8.2 relates professional development frameworks with practices associated with cultural improvement as well as specific innovations. As you review Figure 8.2, consider which frameworks could be used to facilitate each factor listed under the headings Cultural Improvement and Specific Innovations.

Summary

School culture was described as the heart and soul of the school organization. Arguments were presented that the conventional school culture has negative effects on students, teachers, and change efforts. Different forms of school culture were described, including individualistic, balkanized, fully functioning collaborative, comfortable collaborative, and contrived collegiality. Three levels of cultural content were discussed, including observable artifacts, espoused values, and basic underlying assumptions. A culture of continuous improvement was described, and 10 practices for promoting such a culture were presented. Finally, the chapter discussed facilitating innovations through attention to consensus, context, individuals, and leadership.

Assignments

1. Write a paper in which you agree or disagree with my contention that the traditional school provides a poor culture for student learning, teacher professional growth, and change.
2. Read an article or chapter on school culture written by someone other than me. Write a paper comparing and contrasting what this text has to say about school culture with your other reading.
3. Write a paper in which you describe your direct observations of a school with one of the following types of cultures: (a) culture of individualism, (b) balkanized culture, (c) comfortable collaboration, or (d) contrived collegiality. Also include in your paper suggestions for how the culture you describe eventually could be transformed into a fully functioning collaborative culture.
4. Administer the School Culture Needs Assessment (Inset 8.1) to a group of teachers from a selected school. After analyzing the results of the written needs assessment, conduct either small-group or individual interviews with a subset of those who completed the survey in order to gather more information on the school's cultural needs. Based on both written needs assessment and interview results, write a paper describing needs assessment results, suggested cultural improvement goals for the school, and a suggested plan for researching those goals. Include your interview questions as an appendix to the paper.
5. Write a paper briefly describing a school you are familiar with as well as an innovation the school attempted to adopt. Review in your paper the extent to which the school

FIGURE 8.2 *Matrix for Relating Professional Development Frameworks to Cultural Development*

	Train	*Peer Coach*	*Work Team*	*Team Teach*	*Study Group*	*Action Research*	*Teacher Writing*	*Teacher Leadership*	*Partnership*	*Network*	*Teacher Center*
Cultural Improvement											
Outside Assistance											
Trust and Support Building											
Shared Decision Making											
Critical Reflection											
Vision Building											
Experimentation and Risk Taking											
Inquiry											
Collaborative Work											
Restructuring											
Long-Term View											
Specific Innovations											
Consensus											
Context											
Individual											
Leadership											

attended to (a) consensus, (b) context, (c) individuals, and (d) leadership during the adoption process. Finally, describe in your paper the school's level of success in adopting the innovation, as well your perceptions of the major reasons for that outcome.

References

Bulach, C. R. (2001). Reshaping school culture to impower its partners. *The Education Digest, 67*(1), 8–11.

Campo, C. (1993). Collaborative school cultures: How principals make a difference. *School Organization, 13*(2), 119–127.

Chance, E. W. (1992). *Visionary leadership in schools: Successful strategies for developing and implementing an educational vision.* Springfield, IL: Charles C. Thomas.

Chance, E. W., Cummins, C., & Wood, F. (1996). A middle school's approach to developing an effective school work culture. *NASSP Bulletin, 80*(576), 43–49.

Conley, D. T. (1993). Managing change in restructuring schools. *OSSC Bulletin, 36*(7). (ERIC ED 356 537)

DuFour, R. (2000). Data put a face on shared vision. *Journal of Staff Development,21*(1), 71–72.

Dull, F. A., Pagon, R., & Smith, D. L. (1999, March). *Turn around strategies for an urban, culturally diverse high school.* Paper presented at the national conference of the Association for Supervision and Curriculum Development, San Francisco.

Ellsworth, J. (2001). A survey of educational change models. *Teacher Librarian, 29*(2), 22–24.

Evans, R. (1996). *The human side of school change.* San Francisco: Jossey-Bass.

Ferguson, F. A. (2001). Welcome to the circus: The superintendent as ringmaster. *School Administrator, 58*(2), 62.

Ferris, C. H. (1994, April). *A program for building trust between teachers and administrators to enhance the supervision/evaluation process.* Paper presented at the annual meeting of the American Educational Research Association, New Orleans. (ERIC ED 370 930)

Foley, R. M. (2001). Professional development needs of secondary school principals of collaborative-based service delivery models. *The High School Journal, 85*(1), 10–23.

Fullan, M. G. (1992). Visions that blind. *Educational Leadership, 49*(5), 19–22.

Fullan, M. G. (1996). Turning systemic thinking on its head. *Phi Delta Kappan,* 77, 420–423.

Fullan, M. G. (2001). *The new meaning of educational change* (3rd ed.). New York: Teachers College Press.

Fullan, M., & Hargreaves A. (1996). *What's worth fighting for in your school?* New York: Teachers College Press.

Fullan, M., & Miles, M. (1992). Getting reform right: What works and what doesn't. *Phi Delta Kappan, 73,* 745–752.

Glickman, C. D., Gordon, S. P., & Ross-Gordon, J. M. (2001). *Supervision and instructional leadership: A developmental approach.* Boston: Allyn and Bacon.

Goodlad, J. I. (1984). *A place called school.* New York: McGraw-Hill.

Gordon, S. P., Nolan, J. F., & Forlenza, V. A. (1995). Peer coaching: A cross-site comparison. *Journal of Personnel Evaluation in Education, 9*(1), 69–91.

Gratch, A. (2001). The culture of teaching and beginning teacher development. *Teacher Education Quarterly, 28*(4), 121–136.

Green, R. L., & Etheridge, C. P. (2001). Collaboration to establish standards about accountability: Lessons learned about systemic change. *Education, 121*(4), 821–829.

Hall, G. E., & Hord, S. M. (1987). *Change in schools: Facilitating the process.* Albany: State University of New York Press.

Hannay, L. M., Ross, J. A., & Brydges, B. (1997, March). *The complexity of secondary school curriculum change: The reculturing / restructuring shuffle.* Paper presented at the annual meeting of the American Educational Research Association, Chicago.

Hargreaves, A. (1992). Cultures of teaching: A focus for change. In A. Hargreaves & M. G. Fullan (Eds.), *Understanding teacher development* (pp. 216–240). New York: Teachers College Press.

Heckman, P. E. (1993). School restructuring in practice: Reckoning with the culture of school. *International Journal of Education Reform*, *2*(3), 263–272.

Heller, M. F., & Firestone, W. A. (1994). *Heroes, teams, and teachers: A study of leadership for change*. (ERIC ED 371 445).

Holloway, J. H. (2001). Setting standards for the school superintendent. *Educational Leadership, 58*(5), 85.

Hord, S. M., Rutherford, W. L., Huling-Austin, L., & Hall, G. E. (1987). *Taking charge of change*. Alexandria, VA: Association for Supervision and Curriculum Development.

Lewis, C. C., Watson, M. S., & Schaps, E. (1997, March). *Conditions for school change: Perspectives from the child development project*. Paper presented at the annual meeting of the American Educational Research Association, Chicago.

Little, J. W. (1982). Norms of collegiality and experimentation: Workplace conditions of school success. *American Educational Research Journal, 19*(3), 325–340.

Little, J. W. (1990). The persistence of privacy: Autonomy and initiative in teachers' professional relations. *Teachers College Record, 91*, 509–536.

Loucks-Horsley, S., & Stiegelbauer, S. (1991). Using knowledge of change to guide staff development. In A. Lieberman & L. Miller (Eds.), *Staff development for education in the 90's* (2nd ed.). New York: Teachers College Press.

Marriott, D. (2001). Managing school culture. *Principal, 81*(1), 75–77.

Owen, J. M., Loucks-Horsley, S., & Horsley, D. L. (1991). Three roles of staff development in restructuring schools. *Journal of Staff Development, 12*(3), 10–14.

Peterson, K. D., & Brietzke, R. (1994). *Building collaborative cultures: Seeking ways to reshape urban schools*. Oak Brook, IL: North Central Regional Educational Laboratory.

Prestine, N. A. (1991). Shared decision making in restructuring essential schools: The role of the principal. *Planning and changing, 22*(3–4), 160–177.

Ruder, R. (2001). The mark of leadership: Thinking outside the box. *Middle Ground, 5*(1), 29–30.

Sarason, S. B. (1990). *The predictable failure of educational reform*. San Francisco: Jossey-Bass.

Schein, E. H. (1990). Organizational culture. *American Psychologist, 45*(2), 109–119.

Schmuck, R. A., & Runkel, P. (1994). *The handbook of organization development in schools*. Prospect Heights, IL: Waveland Press.

Sipe, R. B. (2001). The not-so-secret formula for successful change. *Principal, 80*(30), 35–37.

Snyder, K. M., & Snyder, K. (1996). Developing integrated work cultures: Findings from a study on school change. *NASSP Bulletin, 80*(576), 67–77.

Sparks, D. (2001a). Change: It's a matter of life or slow death. *Journal of Staff Development 22*(4), 49–53.

Sparks, D. (2001b). Why change is so challenging for schools. *Journal of Staff Development, 22*(3), 42–47.

Weissglass, J. (1991). Teachers have feelings: What can we do about it? *Journal of Staff Development, 12*(1), 28–33.

Resources

Bulach, C. R. (2001). Reshaping school culture to empower its partners. *The Education Digest* 67(1), 8–11.

Evans, R. (1996). *The human side of school change*. San Francisco: Jossey-Bass.

Foley, R. M. (2001). Professional development needs of secondary school principals of collaborative-based service delivery models. *The High School Journal, 85*(1), 10–23.

Fullan, M. G. (2001). *Leading in a culture of change*. San Francisco, CA: Jossey-Bass.

Fullan, M. G. (1996). Turning systemic thinking on its head. *Phi Delta Kappan*, 77, 420–423.

Fullan, M. G., & Hargreaves, A. (1996). *What's worth fighting for in your school?* New York: Teachers College Press.

9 Team Development

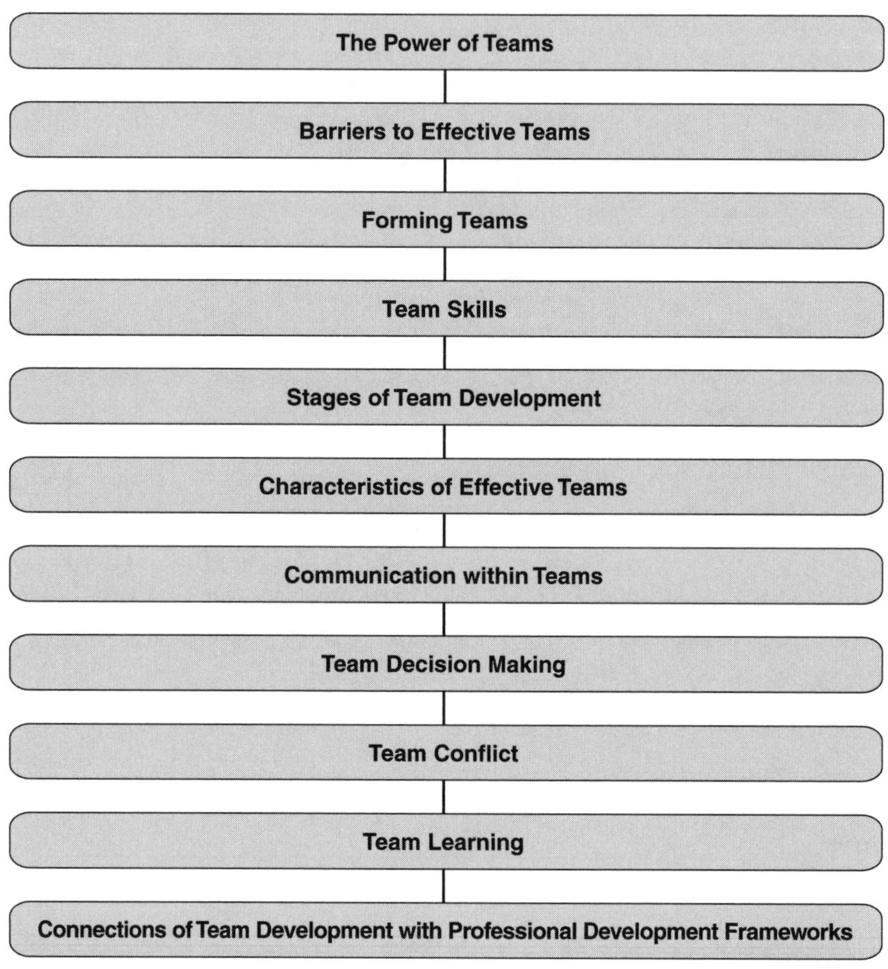

The Power of Teams
Barriers to Effective Teams
Forming Teams
Team Skills
Stages of Team Development
Characteristics of Effective Teams
Communication within Teams
Team Decision Making
Team Conflict
Team Learning
Connections of Team Development with Professional Development Frameworks

The previous chapter emphasized that a schoolwide culture of continuous improvement is necessary for significant school improvement to take place. Within this type of culture, much of the day-to-day work of school improvement is carried out by collaborative teams. The different types of teams that can form as part of professional development and school improvement are myriad. Teams can be vertical or horizontal. They can be temporary or permanent. Their purpose can be school governance, the improvement of school culture, teacher development, curriculum development, instructional improvement, student support, parent-teacher collaboration, and so on. In this chapter we will examine the power of teams, forming teams, team skills, stages of team development, barriers to team success, effective teams, communication within teams, team conflict, decision making, team learning, and connections of team development with professional development frameworks.

The Power of Teams

Before discussing the benefits of collaborative teams, we need to take a moment to define further what is meant by *teams* and *teamwork*, particularly within the context of PK–12 schools. Rees (1997) has compared traditional work with teamwork. Figure 9.1 summarizes her comparison. Note Rees's emphasis on shared goals, collaboration, interdependence, and mutual accountability. For Rees, and for improving schools, a team is not merely a collection of individuals. A real team develops an identity of its own. The whole (team) becomes greater than the sum of its parts (members). There is a shift from the traditional emphasis on individualism and competition to cooperation and team success.

Although traditional departments still have value, the most exciting work in school improvement taking place today is being done by nontraditional teams. Much of the recent literature on school teams has focused on interdisciplinary, cross grade-level, and cross-functional (made up of members with different work roles) teams. Regardless of their membership and organization, teams on the cutting edge of school improvement are collaborative in three ways. First, they have a collaborative relationship with the school administration. Second, team members work collaboratively with each other. Third, they work collaboratively with other teams within the school and district.

Effective teams provide a variety of benefits to team members, the school, and students. Team membership gives individuals a sense of identity and belonging (Trimble & Miller, 1996). For teachers, teams provide emotional and moral support, dignity, intellectual assistance, and encouragement (Harris, 2000; Kruse & Louis, 1997). Teaming increases involvement in decision making, reduces isolation, facilitates the sharing of concerns and problem solving, and improves self-esteem (Burnette, 2002; Deason, 1992). In short, team membership fosters teacher empowerment. Nontraditional teams are more likely to facilitate empowerment than departmentally organized teachers in the areas of decision making, professional growth, status, self-efficacy, autonomy, and impact (Husband & Short, 1994).

Teams also can be vehicles for school improvement. Kruse and Louis (1997) maintain that teaming can lead to a "professional community," equivalent to the culture

FIGURE 9.1 Traditional Work and Teamwork Compared

Traditional Work	*Teamwork*
Individual accountability	Mutual accountability
Individual goals	Shared team goals
Focus on individual performance	Focus on team performance
Independence	Interdependence
Infrequent, unfocused interaction with peers	Frequent, focused interaction with peers
Individual jobs defined	Output of team defined
Competition valued and encouraged	Collaboration and cooperation valued and encouraged
Functional roles given to groups and individuals	Teams take on several functions
Individual, professional skills needed	Team skills also needed
Headset: Please your supervisor	Headset: Respect your teammates
"This is my job."	"This is our job."
"This is not my job."	"How can I make the whole team successful?"

Source: F. Rees, *Teamwork from Start to Finish: 10 Steps to Results*, p. 57. Copyright © 1997 by Pfeiffer/Jossey-Bass, Inc., San Francisco. This material is used by permission of Jossey-Bass, Inc., a subsidiary of John Wiley & Sons, Inc.

of continuous improvement described in Chapter 8. Critical elements of a professional community that teaming can foster include reflective dialogue, collegiality, a collective focus on student learning, collaboration, and shared norms and values. Additionally, teaming fosters more knowledge about the school curriculum, better coordination of the curriculum, and curriculum integration (Deason, 1992; McGehee, 2001; Vasudeva & Ryan, 1997).

Finally, and most importantly, teacher teaming has positive effects on students. Teams can lead to stronger relationships between teachers and students (Kew, 2000; Vasudeva & Ryan, 1997) and better student discipline (Deason, 1992). With administrative support, teaming can improve classroom practice and student learning (Burnette, 2002; Trimble & Peterson, 1999). Collaborative teams thus can be powerful vehicles for improving schools, teaching, and learning (Vann, 2000). But often, teams fail to reach their potential. Next, we will look at roadblocks to effective teams.

Barriers to Effective Teams

Most of us have served on teams that were a waste of time. Why are some teams ineffective? One reason is that team members don't understand or don't support the team's mission. This often occurs when a team is formed by an administrator without sufficient dialogue with the school community and potential team members. Team failure can also result when individuals don't understand their roles and responsibilities as team members. A lack of collaborative planning is responsible for this problem. Incompatibility between the school culture and team purpose is another cause of ineffective teams. Some teams fail because an administrator pays lip service to team decision making while attempting to manipulate the team into doing what the administrator wanted all along.

Sometimes members lack the team skills necessary for effective team functioning. (Later in this chapter we will discuss skills needed for effective teamwork.) An inability to manage conflict is a cause of many dysfunctional teams. Depending on a team's make-up, a lack of conflict management skills may lead to negative conflict, or to team members avoiding productive conflict, an equally dysfunctional behavior. Teams may not be provided sufficient time for collaboration, or they may not have the material resources they need to fulfill their mission. Staff turnover may create problems of continuity. All of these potential problems do not diminish the potential for teams as powerful vehicles for professional development and school improvement. But they do point to the need for careful attention to forming, developing, and supporting teams. The rest of this chapter will focus on how to perform these critical tasks.

Forming Teams

The first decision to make when considering forming a team is its mission. The formation of a new team should be the result of extensive dialogue within the school community, and should be based on a need that can best be met through a team approach. Once the mission of the team has been established, it's time to consider the team's composition. Decisions need to be made concerning what groups within the school will be represented (different content areas, grade levels, job roles, ethnic groups, and so on). The approximate size of the team needs to be decided on, and a process for selecting team members determined. Depending on the team's mission and desired size, membership can be open, elected, or appointed. Regardless of the selection method, members should not be required to serve on a team against their will.

Teams may assign formal roles to their members. Some examples of formal roles are team leader, recorder, timekeeper, and liaison(s) to groups or individuals outside the team. The role of team leader obviously is a critical one (Burnette, 2002). Rottier (1996) recommends strong leadership from a single person for teams in the initial stages of development. Once the team reaches a more advanced stage of development, leadership can be rotated among team members.

It is important for a team to establish its own ground rules; some typical ground rules follow:

- Members will attend all team meetings unless causes beyond their control prevent them from doing so.
- All proposals made by team members will be considered worthy of consideration.

- Conflict will be considered an essential part of the team's decision-making process, but will not include personal criticism.
- Requests for confidentiality will be honored.

Finally, a team needs to set goals that are consistent not only with its mission but also with the mission and goals of the school. Goals should be reachable and measurable. A note of caution considering mission and goals: As the team evolves, its goals and even its mission are subject to change. Performance measures may change along with mission and goals. Rees (1997) recommends creating a team charter that includes many of the components of team formation discussed here. Her team charter would include a list of team members, the team's mission statement, a statement of how the team's mission supports organizational goals, team goals, and ground rules.

Team Skills

Team skills are the *sine qua non* of team success. Given this reality, should all teams be provided training in team skills? The answer to this question depends on the current skill levels of a particular team. Given the history of isolation and norms of privacy in most schools, however, skill training most likely will be needed. One approach to schools considering teaming is to provide generic training in team skills before forming teams with specific responsibilities. Once a team is formed, a team facilitator or critical friends can observe the team in action, assess team skills, and recommend any additional skill training needed for the team to complete its mission. Skills displayed by effective teams—and possible topics for team skill training—include the following:

- Leadership
- Interpersonal communication
- Group process
- Goal setting and planning
- Collaboration
- Conflict management
- Decision making
- Problem solving
- Team self-assessment
- Presentation
- Critical thinking
- Change process

Note the presence of leadership skills on this list. All members of a truly collegial team are involved in both individual and collective leadership; thus they need to develop leadership skills. Most successful teams do not spend an inordinate amount of time in skill training. Rather, continued skill development is based on a combination of experience, feedback from facilitators or critical friends, reflection, and experimentation with new strategies and techniques.

Stages of Team Development

Experts on team development are in agreement that teams pass through different stages of development as they attempt to complete their mission. There are five stages of team development (Tuckman & Jenson, 1977; Spiegel & Torres, 1994; Rees, 1997).

1. *Forming.* This is an orientation stage when members are trying to determine if they wish to be a part of the team, how they will relate to other team members, and what their role and responsibilities will be. The forming stage can be a period of confusion and anxiety. To get through this stage, team members need information about the team's mission.
2. *Storming.* This stage is characterized by conflict, as team members assert their individuality and debate over the team's goals, norms, and decision-making process. At this stage, open communication remains vital. Additionally, conflict management skills are essential. To get through this stage, the team needs to deal with issues that surface, as well as agree on a decision-making process.
3. *Norming.* This stage is characterized by the development of trust and collaboration among team members. The team agrees on rules, roles, relationships, responsibilities, processes, and tasks to be accomplished.
4. *Performing.* At this stage the team is fully functioning. Team members identify with the team and are committed to its mission. The team continuously engages in reflective dialogue, consensus building, and self-assessment.
5. *Transforming.* The team determines that its mission is complete, celebrates its accomplishments and its members' growth, and either adjourns or renews itself by establishing a new mission. If the team reconstitutes and commits to a new mission, it will revert to the first stage of team development and begin a new cycle.

Some teams never make it to the later stages of team group development. They may break apart as a result of conflict or apathy, or continue sputtering along as ineffective groups with no hope of achieving their mission. What makes some teams successful while others fail? The next section will address this question.

Characteristics of Effective Teams

Despite the various types of teams that can be formed within schools, successful teams of all types have several common characteristics. Effective teams possess a shared identity, a clear focus, diversity, role clarity, a high level of collaboration, administrative support, effective decision-making strategies, and a process of continuous self-assessment.

One characteristic of effective teams is a *shared identity.* This trait includes shared responsibilities, experiences, concerns, challenges, successes, and failures. The single-most important aspect of a shared identity is a set of common values.

A characteristic related to the concept of team identity is a *clear focus.* The first step in developing a clear focus is an understanding and acceptance of the team mission. The team becomes more focused as it reaches consensus on goals and objectives consistent with its mission. True consensus on the team's goals and objectives does not emerge from a single meeting, but is developed as a result of team reflection and dialogue over a period of time.

Another characteristic of effective teams is *diversity.* This means diversity of people, including individuals of different work roles, races, ethnicities, genders, content areas, grade levels, and years of experience. It also means that group members represent different points of view.

Members of effective teams possess *role clarity.* They know what the team expects of them to help the team achieve its mission. Members understand and accept the structure of the team, its ground rules, and its processes.

Effective teams are characterized by *high levels of collaboration.* Members share information, brainstorm ideas, work toward consensus, and support each other in the completion of team tasks. Collaboration is based on mutual trust, so trust building may be necessary before collaboration can take root. Since collaborative teams are unlikely to thrive outside of a collaborative school culture, schoolwide cultural development also may be a prerequisite.

Administrative support is another characteristic of effective teams. Teams need to be provided adequate resources to complete their mission. First and foremost among needed resources is adequate time. Leaders should be responsive to concerns and requests of teams, letting teams know that their missions are high priorities. Finally, school leaders need to recognize both team accomplishments and contributions by individual team members.

Effective teams develop *effective decision-making strategies.* On major issues, they reach decisions by consensus. They recognize the inevitability of conflict, and use conflict management skills to make conflict constructive. Effective teams pay attention both to the task they are working to complete and to interpersonal relationships within the team.

A final characteristic of effective teams is that they *continuously assess themselves* with an eye toward team improvement. This self-assessment includes gathering and analyzing data on team performance, taking time at the end of team meetings to process activities and discussions, and accepting critiques from outside observers. In short, effective teams do not rest on their laurels; they are continually examining ways that they can become more effective!

Communication within Teams

The quality of communication within a team goes a long way toward determining the level of team success (Beebe & Masterson, 1997). Formulating, sending, receiving, and interpreting messages are all important components of effective communication.

One aspect of effective communication described in almost all publications and training programs is *active listening*, which includes maintaining eye contact with the message sender, leaning toward the sender, asking clarifying questions, and paraphrasing the sender's messages through statements such as, "What I hear you saying is . . . ," "It sounds like . . . ," "In other words . . . ," and so on. Some have criticized the techniques of active listening as artificial and condescending. I can remember attempting to use active listening with a friend who had just been left by his significant other. I said something like "So you feel terrible that she left you without warning?" My friend's response: "Don't use that psychological crap with me!" One problem with active listening is that some techniques like paraphrasing can be used inappropriately (e.g., "So you wish to know what time it is?"). One way to make better use of active listening is to focus on the messages you are trying to send rather than merely on the mechanics of your message. Spiegel and Torres (1994) review the basic messages people should be trying to send with active listening:

- I understand what you are saying.
- I want to hear what you are telling me.
- I am paying attention and I am concerned.
- I respect you as a person.
- I understand your thoughts.
- I am not trying to either change or evaluate your message. (p. 49)

By focusing on the intent of active listening and using its verbal and nonverbal messages as means to an end, active listening will become more authentic and effective.

As important as active listening is, teams would not reach any decisions or complete any tasks if they used only active listening. The literature on teams presents a whole set of behaviors needed for effective team functioning. Kayser (1990), for example, classifies essential team behaviors into three categories: task behaviors, group maintenance behaviors, and gatekeeping. Kayser's *group task behaviors* include the following:

> *Proposing.* A behavior that initiates a new idea, proposition, or suggestion . . .
>
> *Building.* A behavior that takes a group member's proposal, suggestion or idea and then extends, develops, or expands it . . .
>
> *Information seeking.* A behavior that solicits values, beliefs, or sentiments from others . . .
>
> *Information giving.* A behavior that offers facts, data, experiences, or clarification . . .
>
> *Opinion giving.* A behavior that offers values, beliefs, or sentiments . . .
>
> *Disagreeing.* A behavior that provides direct opposition to, or raises doubts and objectives about, an issue (NOT the person who presents it) . . .
>
> *Summarizing.* A behavior that reiterates the content of previously shared dialogue in condensed form . . .
>
> *Testing comprehension.* A behavior that poses a question in order to establish whether a previous communication has been correctly understood . . .

> *Consensus testing.* A behavior that periodically tests whether the group has reached consensus or whether more discussion of the issue is required . . . (pp. 87–89)

Group maintenance behaviors described by Kayser include the following:

> *Encouraging.* A behavior that supports, agrees with, or recognizes the contributions of others . . .
>
> *Harmonizing.* A behavior that attempts to reconcile disagreements . . .
>
> *Performance checking.* A behavior that suspends task operations in order to examine where the group stands in relation to achieving its desired outcomes . . . or to evaluate the session and its conclusion . . .
>
> *Standard setting.* A behavior that expresses standards for the group and applies these standards to improve the quality of the group process . . .
>
> *Tension relieving.* A behavior that eases tensions and increases the enjoyment of group members by joking, suggesting breaks, or proposing fun approaches to group work . . . (pp. 90–91)

Finally, Kayser (1990) describes two *gatekeeping processes* that can occur only in combination with a task or maintenance behavior:

> *Gate opening.* This process utilizes a task or maintenance behavior as a means for directly including another individual in the discussion . . .
>
> *Gate closing.* This process uses a task or maintenance behavior as a means for directly excluding another individual from the discussion . . . (p. 92)*

The effective team includes a balance of group task and group maintenance behaviors. A team focused on task behaviors alone without attention to group maintenance will soon experience interpersonal problems, a lack of personal satisfaction, and reduced motivation to participate in group activities. On the other hand, a team that attends only to group maintenance behaviors at the expense of task behaviors will experience a positive work climate and great interpersonal relations but will never make any critical decisions or complete any significant tasks.

An issue regarding task, personal, and gatekeeping functions is whether they should be roles, assigned to particular individuals, or behaviors used by a variety of group members as the need arises. McCrimmon (1995) points to problems with assigning exclusive roles to particular team members. Assigning roles leads to restrictive obligations, rigidity, territoriality, abdication from making contributions that are not part of one's role, and annoying predictability. McCrimmon considers the suggestion that individuals can periodically shift roles "simply a defensive move to salvage a bad idea" (p. 36). Since role assignments inhibit flexibility and creativity, McCrimmon recommends that team members should simply be trained to use each behavior whenever appropriate. McCrimmon argues that "if employees (at all levels) are to be fully empow-

*T. A. Kayser, *Mining Group Gold* (El Segundo, CA: Serf Publishing, 1990). Copyright © 1990 The McGraw-Hill Companies, Inc. Used with permission of McGraw-Hill.

ered they need fluid, evolving skills sets and criteria for effective team work, not roles" (p. 41).

In addition to the necessary task, group maintenance, and gatekeeping behaviors, there are *negative process behaviors* displayed by team members that can adversely affect team functioning. Spiegel and Torres (1994) describe five negative process behaviors:

> *Withdrawing.* Acting passive or indifferent, daydreaming, doodling, whispering while others talk, and wandering from the subject of discussion.
>
> *Blocking.* Wandering from the subject of discussion, citing personal experiences unrelated to the problem, arguing too much on the point, and rejecting expressed ideas without consideration.
>
> *Joking.* Excessive playing around, telling jokes, mimicking other members, and other playful behavior that interferes with the team's work.
>
> *Dominating.* Excessive talking, interrupting others, trying to gain status by criticizing or blaming others, showing open hostility toward other team members, and deflating the status of others.
>
> *Self-Seeking.* Putting one's personal needs before the team's needs, trying to induce other team members to be sympathetic to one's misfortunes, developing one's situation, and disparaging one's own ideas to gain support. (pp. 77–78)

Even one team member displaying a negative behavior on a regular basis can disrupt a team. There are a number of techniques for addressing negative behaviors. One technique is to establish eye contact with the dysfunctional individual. Another is for everyone else to become silent until the behavior ceases. A third possible response to negative behavior is to describe the behavior in objective terms and then to initiate a discussion with the entire team (including the dysfunctional team member) to determine the extent to which the behavior is harming the team process. A final alternative for dealing with negative behavior (not possible in all situations) is removal of the offending member from the team. When removal is a viable option, it should be done only after all other options have failed.

Part of improving communication within teams is to assess the level of task behaviors, group maintenance behaviors, gatekeeping behaviors, and negative behaviors within the team. Figure 9.2 provides a data collection instrument for recording individual behaviors, tallying overall team behaviors, and comparing frequency of behaviors across categories. The data can be collected and tallied by an observer, then discussed by the entire team. Team and individual improvement goals can be based on analysis of the observation data.

Team Decision Making

There are a variety of ways to make a team decision. The team facilitator could make the decision. Given the fact that one-person rule is antithetical to the types of teams discussed in this book, as a general rule this is not advised. However, there are exceptions. For example, if the team facilitator has an emergency situation (e.g., whether to

FIGURE 9.2 ***Observation of Team Communication***

Member →	*A*	*B*	*C*	*D*	*E*	*F*	*G*	*H*	*I*	*J*	*Team Total*
Task Behaviors											
Proposing											
Building											
Information seeking											
Information giving											
Opinion giving											
Disagreeing											
Summarizing											
Testing comprehension											
Consensus testing											
Overall Team Total, Task Behaviors:											
Maintenance Behaviors											
Encouraging											
Harmonizing											
Performance checking											
Standard setting											
Tension relieving											
Overall Team Total, Maintenance Behaviors:											
Gatekeeping Behaviors											
Gate opening											
Gate closing											
Overall Team Total, Gatekeeping Behaviors:											
Negative Behaviors											
Withdrawing											
Blocking											
Joking											
Dominating											
Self-seeking											
Overall Team Total, Negative Behaviors:											

Directions: Step 1 involves making a tally mark under each individual team member's name for each specific behavior demonstrated. For Step 2, add tally marks for each behavior for each individual, and enter numerals for each individual cell on a new form. Step 3 consists of entering a team total for each specific behavior, and entering overall team totals for task, maintenance, gatekeeping, and negative behaviors.

postpone a meeting because of a tornado warning), then he or she simply has to make a decision immediately. Also, when members of the team don't care about a minor issue (e.g., in which room a meeting will be scheduled), then it's fine for the facilitator to simply make the decision.

A minority subgroup of team members can make a team decision. Again, this is generally not advisable, with some exceptions. For example, a school's professional development planning team might delegate a small group of math teachers from the team to plan a math workshop.

A decision could be made by majority vote or by averaging. Majority vote is self-explanatory. Averaging might consist of members voting for their top three alternatives, assigning their top alternative three points, their second choice two points, and their third choice one point. The team would then average all ratings. Both majority vote and averaging sound like highly desirable ways to make decisions. With both methods, each member of the team has an equal vote. Also, both methods reflect the "democratic way." Yet, both majority vote and averaging have drawbacks. With either of these methods, there is a probability that the "team" decision will not be supported by all members. This may, in turn, result in problems with implementing the decision.

Unanimity and consensus are two additional ways for a team to make decisions. *Unanimity* means that all members are in full agreement with a decision. *Consensus* means that, although different team members express varying levels of support for a decision, all three of the following criteria are present:

1. Each member must feel he or she has been heard and understood by the rest of the team.
2. Each member must be able to live with the decision or solution.
3. Each member must be willing to commit to his or her role in carrying out the decision or implementing the solution. (Harrington-Mackin, 1994, p. 10)

Unanimity is difficult to achieve when teams make decisions on complicated matters. Consensus is easier to achieve than unanimity and once consensus has been reached, we can be reasonably confident that all team members will support the decision's implementation. Consensus decision making provides a "climate of empowerment" and legitimizes team decisions (Green & Etheridge, 2001; Spiegel & Torres, 1994). If consensus is to work, it's important that all team members fully understand what consensus means. Figure 9.3 presents Rees's (1997) summary of what a consensus is and is not.

Team Conflict

Some level of conflict is necessary if a team is to achieve meaningful goals. The challenge is to manage the conflict so that it involves the surfacing and examination of diverse views and synergistic solutions rather than personal animosity and team dysfunction. One key to managing conflict is to understand what type of conflict is taking place. Harvey and Drolet (1994) have identified five different types of conflicts. *Value conflicts* result from differences in personal beliefs. *Tangible conflicts* are disagreements

FIGURE 9.3 ***What a Consensus Is and Is Not***

Consensus Is	*Consensus Is Not*
A point of maximum agreement so action can follow	Voting
A win-win solution	A win-lose situation
A decision everyone can support	Compromising (a settlement of differences by mutually giving in)
Creative collaboration	Dictating the conclusion
A team effort to achieve an agreed-upon team goal	Everyone agreeing on every point
	Forced unanimity
	Suppression of minority views and dissent

Source: F. Rees, *Teamwork from Start to Finish: 10 Steps to Results*, pp. 155–156 (format adapted).

over measurable resources (time, money, facilities). *Interpersonal conflicts* result from team members' personal feelings toward one another. *Boundary conflicts* result from a disagreement over an individual or group's role and responsibilities. Finally, *perceptual conflicts* result from misunderstanding and are based on miscommunication.

Strategies for managing conflict are described here. Although specific ways of resolving conflict (e.g., clarifying perceptions, expanding or sharing resources, redefining roles and responsibilities) will depend on the type of conflict, the following strategies represent a generic model for conflict management.

Use Communication Skills. When conflict begins to surface, active listening by all team members becomes critical. Teams should not attempt to avoid emerging conflict by ignoring it or pressuring the team to make a premature decision. Training in communication and conflict management skills is one way to prepare for conflict. Another idea is to establish as part of the team's charter a set of ground rules for dealing with conflict.

Define the Conflict. It is essential that the team facilitator and team members who are not in conflict over the issue at hand help to clarify the conflict. A good starting point is to have each individual involved in the conflict state to the entire team his or her perception of what the conflict is all about. If the team is dealing with a perceptual conflict, this strategy can resolve the conflict by clearing up what is essentially a failure to communicate. Even if the stating of perceptions reveals a more serious type of conflict, there will in all likelihood be some areas of agreement. By emphasizing and building on those agreements, the team already has made progress toward resolving the conflict. It is especially important to recognize broad goals on which conflicting parties agree. The discussion then can focus on means of reaching the agreed-upon goals.

Seek Information. Once areas of agreement and disagreement have been clarified, it is important to develop as much additional information about the conflict as possible. What are the undisputed *facts* concerning the conflict? What information can other members of the team provide? Everyone on the team should become involved in a discussion of the relevant issues. The stance of all parties, including those in direct conflict, should be that the entire team is addressing a problem to be solved through inquiry and dialogue, not a battle to be won or lost.

Examine Alternatives. If the conflict is to be resolved in a win-win manner, then the team needs to meet the needs of the team members who are in conflict as well as the overall team. First, the various needs (individual and team) relative to the conflict are recognized. Next, barriers to meeting those needs are identified. Finally, multiple alternatives for removing barriers and meeting needs are considered.

Agree on a Solution. Alternative solutions unacceptable to individual team members should be ruled out. This does not mean that an alternative that a member does not favor should be dismissed, but rather that solutions a member could not support under any circumstances should be removed. Remaining alternatives should be analyzed until the best alternative can be agreed upon. Sometimes, especially, when dealing with value conflicts, it will be impossible to agree on a solution. In such cases, after intense efforts to reach a mutually agreeable solution, the team may have to "agree to disagree," in the interest of long-term relationships and the team's larger mission.

Team Learning

All effective teams need to make decisions. Action research teams need to decide what areas to research, what data to collect, what improvement activities to implement, and how to evaluate their action plans. Interdisciplinary teams need to decide what curriculum to integrate, how to teach interdisciplinary content, and how to assess student growth. Even study teams need to make decisions. They need to decide on meeting formats and ground rules, what area of study they wish to focus on, and how to apply what they are reading and discussing to their classrooms and school. In educational settings, however, teams need to go beyond making decisions and completing tasks. In schools, teams should also be vehicles for personal, professional, and cultural development. They should be models of learning for the larger learning community.

In his best-selling book *The Fifth Discipline*, Senge (1990) discusses the concept of "team learning." He argues that team learning has three critical dimensions:

- First, there is the need to think insightfully about complex issues. Here teams must learn how to tap the potential for many minds to be more intelligent than one mind . . .

- Second, there is the need for innovative, coordinated action. The championship sports teams and great jazz ensembles provide metaphors for acting in spontaneous yet coordinated ways . . .
- Third, there is the role of team members on other teams. For example, most of the actions of senior teams are actually carried out through other teams. Thus a learning team continually fosters other learning teams through inculcating the practices and skills of team learning more broadly. (pp. 236–337)

To further explain his concept of the learning team, Senge (1990) reviews physicist David Bohm's views on discussion and dialogue. Participants in a *discussion* present and defend their different points of view on a subject of common interest. The individual's goal is for his or her view to prevail. The purpose of a *dialogue*, in contrast, is to go beyond any individual participant's understanding of the subject. Those involved in a dialogue engage in "participatory thought," become observers of their own thinking, and develop common meaning. For dialogue to take place, participants must suspend their assumptions and regard each other as colleagues. Senge notes that discussion and dialogue are counterparts, and that both must be present for team learning to take place. He considers reflection and inquiry skills an essential foundation for successful discussion and dialogue.

Examples of teams in action at Everett Middle School in San Francisco are provided in Exemplar 9.1.

EXEMPLAR 9.1 • *Teaming at Everett Middle School*

At Everett Middle School in San Francisco, teams are viewed as vehicles for shared governance, professional development, and school improvement. At the heart of Everett's team structure is the *Governance Council*, with a membership of five faculty, four administrators, and five community members (including one student). The primary role of this group is to provide a forum for schoolwide decision making, and the delegation of actions to groups responsible for moving toward the school's mission and goals.

Everett has a plethora of other teams involved in collaborative improvement efforts. *Issues groups* meet twice a month to discuss schoolwide issues that can be submitted by any member of the school community. Each issues group includes a cross-section of educators, including representatives from different content areas and grade levels, student support services, and administration.

Action groups are teams formed to address specific school improvement efforts, including areas such as the school environment, school safety, literacy, curriculum, the master schedule, diversity, grant writing, and community outreach. Action groups propose schoolwide plans for faculty approval.

Everett's teachers have a common planning period each day for *grade-level teams*. One thing these teams use common periods for is the planning of interdisciplinary units that integrate math, science, the arts, and social studies. Grade-level teams also discuss individual student problems, assistance plans, and progress.

Everett also has discipline-based *departments* that take a team approach to improvement. Departments are responsible for curriculum articulation across grade levels as well as schoolwide portfolios in each of the content areas. Unlike traditional schools where departments constitute the primary team structure, at Everett, departments are just one part of a complex network of teams that collaborate for professional development and school improvement.

Early in the process of team development, teachers at Everett participated in training to develop team skills. However, in recent years, team skills have been enhanced through the actual experience of serving on collaborative teams. A critical aspect of team collaboration at Everett is a commitment to decisions by consensus. Ground rules established by the teams aid consensus building. The teachers at Everett agree that collaboration and consensus building are difficult, but they believe that the resulting empowerment is worth the time and effort. A teacher at Everett stated, "The power you feel with decisions not coming down from the top is the biggest advantage and probably the biggest reason we've been able to stick with it, despite it being a very difficult process."

Teaming among faculty at Everett Middle School has spread to parents, community members, and students. Parents and community members have representatives on schoolwide teams, and parent teams provide a variety of services to the school such as after-school programs for students, cultural awareness activities, and parenting classes. Students have a representative on the Governance Council, have their own student council, and serve on a variety of schoolwide teams. The teaming and consensus decision making so apparent at the school level are becoming increasingly evident in individual classrooms.

Connections of Team Development with Professional Development Frameworks

Any of the professional development frameworks discussed in Part II can be used as vehicles for team development. Training can provide teams with fundamental skills in communication, group process, conflict resolution, and decision making (Manouchehri, 2001). Yet, for most successful teams that I have observed in schools, training represents only the initial phase of team development. Teams become highly developed by working together over time within collegial support frameworks (peer coaching, collaborative work teams, team teaching), reflective inquiry frameworks (study groups, action research, teacher writing), teacher leadership, and external support frameworks (partnerships, teacher centers, and networks). As teams use these various frameworks, they further develop team skills by engaging in reflective dialogue, conflict management, decision making, and problem solving.

Team development is vital to the core function of professional development: the improvement of teaching and learning. Schoolwide change in curriculum, instruction, and student assessment is dependent on highly sophisticated teamwork (Crow &

Pounder, 2000). Schools that do not develop effective teams simply will not have the capacity to make significant, lasting improvements in teaching and learning.

Both newly formed teams and long functioning teams need to assess their needs as a basis for team growth and development. Inset 9.1 provides a team development needs assessment.

INSET 9.1 • *Team Development Needs Assessment*

Directions: For each item, choose one of the following responses:

A. No need
B. Little need
C. Moderate need
D. Great need
E. Very great need

To what extent does the team need to:

1. Clarify its mission?
2. Clarify the roles and responsibilities of team members?
3. Receive administrative support?
4. Be provided time for team activities?
5. Secure needed resources?
6. Establish ground rules for meetings?
7. Establish specific goals consistent with its mission?
8. Improve leadership skills?
9. Improve communication?
10. Improve collaboration?
11. Improve conflict management?
12. Improve decision making?
13. Improve problem solving?
14. Increase critical thinking?
15. Learn about the change process?
16. Increase trust among team members?
17. Increase reflective dialogue?
18. Develop self-assessment skills?
19. Develop a sense of team identity?

20. Become more focused?
21. Benefit from more diverse members and diverse views?
22. Increase behaviors that help the team complete its tasks?
23. Increase behaviors that improve the team's interpersonal relationships?
24. Decrease the team's dysfunctional behaviors?

Summary

Teamwork was defined, and the benefits of effective teams for team members, the school, and students were reviewed. Barriers to effective teams were discussed. These include a lack of purpose, team members not understanding their roles and functions, incompatibility between team purpose and school culture, an absence of administrative support, inadequate team skills, and insufficient resources, including time. Decisions relative to team formation were considered, including team mission, membership, formal roles, ground rules, and goals. A variety of skills necessary for effective teams were reviewed. Five stages of team development—forming, storming, norming, performing, and transforming—were presented. Characteristics of effective teams were discussed. These include clear focus, diversity, role clarity, collaboration, administrative support, effective decision-making strategies, and continuous self-assessment. Effective communication within groups was addressed, including the need for active listening, task behaviors, group maintenance behaviors, and gatekeeping. Dysfunctional behaviors were explained, and strategies for reducing them were proposed. Team decision making was discussed, with a focus on consensus building. Different types of group conflict were outlined, and strategies for resolving conflict were presented. The concept of team learning was described. Finally, team development was related to professional development frameworks.

Assignments

1. Interview a school-based team—one that has been functioning for at least several months—on the benefits and challenges of school teams. Write a paper summarizing your interview and drawing conclusions.
2. Write a paper on the life span of a school team on which you have served. Did the team go through the five stages of team development (forming, storming, norming, performing, transforming) discussed in this chapter? If so, describe details of how the team progressed through each stage. If the team did not go through the typical stages, describe the different stages that the team *did* go through, create your own name for each stage, and describe in detail how the team progressed through each stage.
3. Write a paper describing one effective and one ineffective team on which you have served. In your paper discuss why one team was effective and the other team was not. Relate your discussion to relevant material from this chapter.

4. Use the observation system in Figure 9.2 to collect data on behaviors displayed during a team meeting. Write a paper in which you discuss the behaviors you recorded and their effects on the team. Include in the paper your perception of the team's level of effectiveness, and the relationship between the team's effectiveness and the behaviors you recorded.

5. Read at least three articles or chapters on any one of the following topics: (a) team skills, (b) conflict management, (c) team decision making, or (d) reaching consensus. Write a paper comparing and contrasting what the authors had to say about the chosen topic.

References

Beebe, S. A., & Masterson, J. T. (1997). *Communication in small groups: Principles and practices* (5th ed.). New York: Longman.

Burnette, B. (2002). How we formed our community. *Journal of Staff Development, 23*(1), 54–55.

Crow, G. M., & Pounder, D. G. (2000). Interdisiciplinary teacher teams: Context, design, and process. *Education Administration Quarterly, 36*(2), 216–254.

Deason, J. C. (1992). *The development of effective teaming practices to meet the needs of seventh graders.* Practicum report, Nova University. (ERIC ED 354 605).

Green, R. L., & Etheridge, C. P. (2001). Collaboration to establish standards about accountability: Lessons learned about systemic change. *Education, 121*(4), 821–829.

Harrington-Mackin, D. (1994). *The team building tool kit.* New York: AMACOM.

Harris, S. L. (2000). Behave yourself. *Principal Leadership, 1*(3), 36–39.

Harvey, T. R., & Drolet, B. (1994). *Building teams, building people: Expanding the fifth resource.* Lancaster, PA: Technomic Publishing.

Husband, R. E., & Short, P. M. (1994). Interdisciplinary teams lead to greater teacher empowerment. *Middle School Journal, 26*(2), 58–61.

Kayser, T. A. (1990). *Mining group gold.* El Segundo, CA: Serf Publishing.

Kew, D. W. (2000). Middle level teaming: Strength in collaboration. *Schools in the Middle, 9*(9), 39–40.

Kruse, S., & Louis, K. S. (1997). *Teacher teaming—Opportunities and dilemmas.* (ERIC ED 383 082).

Manouchehri, A. (2001). Collegial interaction and reflective practice. *Action in Teacher Education, 22*(4), 86–97.

McCrimmon, M. (1995). Teams without roles: Empowering teams for greater creativity. *Journal of Management Development, 14*(6), 35–41.

McGehee, J. J. (2001). Developing interdisciplinary units: A strategy based on problem solving. *School Science and Mathematics, 101*(7), 380–389.

Rees, F. (1997). *Teamwork from start to finish.* San Francisco: Pfeiffer.

Rottier, J. (1996). The principal and teaming: Unleashing the power of collaboration. *Schools in the Middle, 5*(4), 31–36.

Senge, P. M. (1990). *The fifth discipline: The art and practice of the learning organization.* New York: Currency Doubleday.

Spiegel, J., & Torres, C. (1994). *Manager's official guide to team working.* San Diego: Pfeiffer.

Trimble, S., & Miller, J. W. (1996). Creating, invigorating, and sustaining effective teams. *NASSP Bulletin, 80*(584), 35–40.

Trimble, S. B., & Peterson, G. W. (1999, April). *Beyond the process of teaming: Administrative support, classroom practices, and student learning.* Paper presented at the annual meeting of the American Educational Research Association, Montreal.

Tuckman, B. W., & Jenson, M. A. (1977). Stages of small group development revisited. *Group and Organization Studies, 2*(4), 419–427.

Vann, A. S. (2000). Shared decision-making committees: Power without power. *The Education Digest, 65*(6), 67–69.

Vasudeva, A., & Ryan, S. (1997, March). *Why some teams work: The role of social capital in teacher efficacy.* Paper presented at the annual meeting of the American Educational Research Association, Chicago.

Resources

Beebe, S. A., & Masterson, J. T. (1997). *Communication in small groups: Principles and practices* (5th ed.). New York: Longman.

Crow, G. M., & Pounder, D. G. (2000). Interdisciplinary teacher teams: Context, design, and process. *Education Administration Quarterly, 36*(2), 216–254.

Rees, F. (1997). *Teamwork from start to finish.* San Fransisco: Pfeiffer.

Senge, P. M. (1990). *The fifth discipline: The art and practice of the learning organization.* New York: Currency Doubleday.

Trimble, S., & Miller, V. W. (1996). Creating, invigorating, and sustaining effective teams. *NASSP Bulletin, 80*(584), 35–40.

Vann, A. S. (2000). Shared decision-making committees: Power without power. *The Education Digest, 65*(6), 67–69.

10 Individual Teacher Development

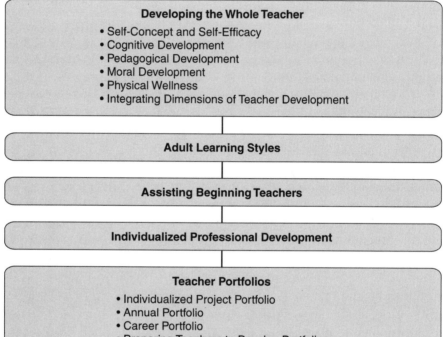

Developing the Whole Teacher
- Self-Concept and Self-Efficacy
- Cognitive Development
- Pedagogical Development
- Moral Development
- Physical Wellness
- Integrating Dimensions of Teacher Development

Adult Learning Styles

Assisting Beginning Teachers

Individualized Professional Development

Teacher Portfolios
- Individualized Project Portfolio
- Annual Portfolio
- Career Portfolio
- Preparing Teachers to Develop Portfolios

The literature on school improvement calls for collegial dialogue, shared vision, reculturing, and collaboration. Yet, experts on the change process remind us that an organization is made up of individuals and that change within an organization ultimately takes place at the individual level. Who is right: the proponents of collective development or those of individual development? The answer is both! In schools operating at full capacity, development is taking place simultaneously at the school, team, and individual levels. The optimal professional development program maintains a balance of the three (with individual development, of course, often taking place within a collaborative framework).

For most of its history, professional development (although delivered in a one-size-fits-all, group setting) was centered on the individual teacher's classroom practice. In recent years, the field finally has recognized the need for team and organization development and shifted its emphasis in that direction. It will be a shame, however, if the pendulum swings too far in this new direction and educators begin to ignore the need for individual development. This chapter recommends a holistic approach to teacher development, provides an overview of adult learning styles, and describes beginning teacher assistance programs. Additionally, the chapter examines individualized development projects and discusses teacher portfolios as a vehicle for teacher growth.

Developing the Whole Teacher

Traditional professional development programs often have focused on assisting teachers to comply with state or district directives, training in the latest teaching fad, or attempting to remediate administrator-perceived weaknesses in classroom instruction. Few would argue that one purpose of professional development should be to ensure the effective teaching of essential knowledge and skills. However, if we see the purpose of schools to be the development of the whole student and we recognize the complexity of the teaching-learning process, then professional development needs to go beyond the skills needed to transmit "the basics." If we believe that one purpose of teaching is to improve the self-concept of students, then it is important that teachers themselves maintain a healthy self-concept. If we wish our schools to help students develop higher-level thinking skills, then the cognitive development of teachers becomes critical. Teachers cannot assist their students in developing moral reasoning skills unless they themselves are functioning at higher levels of moral development. A teacher who is not in reasonably good physical health will find it difficult to deal with the demands of the teaching day, let alone serve as a model of healthy living for students. In this section, we'll take a look at each of these areas of teacher development, then discuss how they can be integrated within the school's professional development program.

Self-Concept and Self-Efficacy

Kelly Sykes is a highly motivated, enthusiastic teacher. She has a positive view of herself and her students. Not only does she *want* to make a differ-

> ence with her students, she is confident that she *will* make a difference! To that end, Sykes works hard at developing a warm, supportive classroom environment, and is particularly concerned with developing positive relationships with her low-achieving students. But she is no pushover. She maintains high standards for student performance, and continuously monitors student academic progress. Sykes uses a variety of creative teaching methods, and emphasizes collaborative learning. She does not respond to less than successful lessons by blaming students, becoming angry, or becoming stressed out. Rather, she views them as problems to be solved. Sykes considers parents to be her partners, and works closely with them to improve student learning.
>
> The attitude and actions of Kelly Sykes have positive effects on her students. They realize that she views them favorably and thus view themselves and each other favorably. Sykes's image of herself and her students helps to improve their academic achievement. Her positive self-image assists her in extending her influence beyond her own classroom. She sees herself as having shared responsibility for schoolwide decision making, and works with other teachers and administrators to create a more positive school environment.
>
> Sykes possesses both high self-concept and high self-efficacy, two related but different constructs. *Self-concept* is a person's general perception of himself or herself; *self-efficacy* is a person's belief that he or she can behave in a manner that will produce desired results. Each of the professional characteristics demonstrated by Kelly Sykes is positively related to positive self-concept and high self-efficacy.*

The historical context of teaching, as well as current political and social conditions, work against teachers developing a positive self-concept and self-efficacy. Historically, teachers have worked in isolation, possessed little power to change their work environments, and have been part of a profession with few economic rewards and little social recognition (Connolly, 2000). These are precisely the conditions that impede the development of a positive self-image! In recent years, teachers have been blamed by policymakers and the public alike for what has been perceived as an inadequate educational system. In response to this perception, state legislatures have mandated curriculum, high-stakes achievement tests, and teacher evaluation systems that have restricted teacher choice, added to teachers' workloads, and increased teacher stress. The perception by policymakers and the public that teachers need to be remediated and the corresponding efforts to control teachers' practice has had a devastating effect on many teachers' self-concept and efficacy.

Given the fact that the current environment puts many teachers "at risk" in the areas of self-concept and self-efficacy, how can professional development improve

*See Ashton, Webb, & Doda, 1983; Aspy, 1969; Chase, Germundsen, Brownstein, & Distad, 2001; Chwalisz, Altmaier, & Russell, 1992; Cole & Knowles, 2000; Curtis & Altmann, 1977; Edwards & Newton, 1995; Garmston, 2001; Gratch, 2001; Kitsantas & Baylor, 2001; Pintrich, 1990; Relich, 1996; Thomson & Handley, 1990; Wilson & Coolican, 1996.

teacher self-image? We know that participation in study groups can make teachers feel more in control of classroom situations, in charge of their own professional development, and more confident in their ability to meet professional challenges (Beatty, 1999). Training in problem solving can improve teacher efficacy (Moss, 1997). Including peer sharing and peer feedback in training programs can meet teacher esteem needs (Bennett, 1991). Team teaching of multiaged groups (Ashton, Webb, & Doda, 1983; Heins, Tichenor, Coggins, & Hutchinson, 2000), peer coaching (Edwards & Newton, 1995; Tolan, 2001), and participation in school decision making (Ash & Persall, 2000; Grafton, 1993; Green & Etheridge, 2001) also have been associated with higher teacher self-efficacy. As important as self-concept and self-efficacy are, they are not enough to guarantee a successful teacher. Cognitive growth is another critical aspect of individual teacher development.

Cognitive Development

Teacher cognitive development involves the growth of teachers' information processing and decision-making skills. There are several different theories of cognitive development. A number of well-established theories explain adult cognitive development as growth from lower to higher developmental stages (Keagan, 1994; King & Kitchener, 1994; Sprinthall, Reiman, & Thies-Sprinthall, 1996). As individuals move from lower to higher stages of cognitive development, they perceive problems more broadly, have a wider repertoire of problem-solving strategies, and respond to problems more effectively. We know that it is possible to stimulate teacher growth from lower to higher stages of cognitive development. One way to do this is to provide teachers with new, challenging roles and to facilitate guided reflection on the experiences that come with the new roles. Let's use peer coaching as an example. In an effective peer coaching program, the teacher-coach will learn a variety of new skills, including alternative approaches to conferencing, varied classroom observation techniques, and a variety of new teaching methods. Participants will engage in multiple peer coaching cycles, allowing observation of different classroom situations, exposure to different teaching strategies, and dialogue with colleagues. In the best programs, coaches will be involved in reflective debriefing sessions between coaching cycles. When all of these elements are present, the peer coaching program can result in significant cognitive growth for the participants (Phillips & Glickman, 1991).

A related theory of adult cognitive development has focused on reflective thinking. Dewey (1933) defined *reflective thinking* as intellectualizing a problem or perplexity being experienced into a problem for which the individual is compelled to seek a solution. According to Schön (1983), reflection goes beyond problem solving. It includes "problem setting":

> In real world practice, problems do not present themselves to the practitioner as givens. They must be constructed from the materials of problematic situations which are puzzling, troubling, and uncertain. Problem setting is a process in which, interactively, we *name* the things to which we will attend and *frame* the context in which we will attend to them. (p. 40)

Reflective teachers examine their classroom practice to determine the gap between the ideal and the real, plan how to bridge the gap, take action, and assess their efforts. Ash (1993) considers reflective teaching to be a continuous cycle of reflecting, planning, acting, observing, reflecting, and so on. Figure 10.1 depicts the reflective teaching cycle. There is really no beginning or end to the cycle. Each stage of the cycle is based on the previous stage and serves as the basis for the following stage.

A variety of strategies can be used to improve teacher reflection. Langer and Colton (1994) suggest strategies for promoting reflective thinking for individuals, pairs, and small groups. At the individual level, they recommend the writing of personal histories, video or audio self-assessments, and journal writings. Suggestions for pairs of teachers include cognitive coaching, action research, and interactive journaling. Suggested small-group activities include case discussions, case writing, action research, and role playing. Moss (1997) describes a study in which a group was provided training on a problem-solving model, then was asked to use a self-reflection rubric to analyze their performance on each component of the problem-solving process. Moss found that participants who employed the rubric to engage in systematic reflection displayed significantly higher levels of problem identification, goal setting, and accuracy of intervention than either the control group or the group that had received training on the problem-solving model alone. This study is consistent with the idea that reflection goes beyond technical problem solving; it includes not only the ability to frame and reframe problems but also to systematically self-assess one's actions during each stage of the problem-solving process.

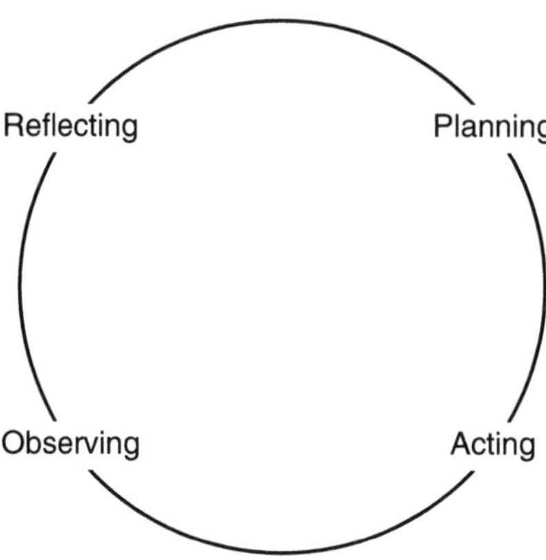

FIGURE 10.1 The Reflective Teaching Cycle

Source: Tom Ash, *Reflective Teaching: What Am I Doing? Why Am I Doing It This Way? Instructional Strategies Series No. 11.* © Copyright, 1993, The Saskatchewan Instructional Development and Research Unit and the Saskatchewan Professional Development Unit, Regina, Saskatchewan, Canada. Reprinted by permission.

Pedagogical Development

Effective pedagogical development assists teachers in the development and integration of expert knowledge, performance, and dispositions through systematic, ongoing development. Here, we will review characteristics of expert teachers, as well as pedagogical models that integrate the knowledge base on expert teaching. Also, we will connect pedagogical development to professional development frameworks.

The research literature reports numerous characteristics of expert teachers (Barnes, 1981; Cruickshank, 1990; Graber, 1995; Haberman, 1995; Moreira, 1996; Shanoski & Hranitz, 1992; Shulman, 1987; Steffy & Wolfe, 2001; Walls, Nardi, & von Minden, 2002). Figure 10.2 provides some frequently reported characteristics. Despite the importance of the characteristics listed in Figure 10.2, pedagogical development should not be dominated by checklists of discreet knowledge areas, performances, and dispositions. Rather, we need coherent models of pedagogical growth that integrate the various characteristics listed in Figure 10.2. We will discuss three such models here, including two traditional models and one more recent model.

FIGURE 10.2 Characteristics of Expert Teacher

Knowledge	*Performances*	*Dispositions*
Content knowledge	Organize and manage classroom	Believes all students can learn
Knowledge of the curriculum	Communicate effectively	Takes responsibility for student learning
Pedagogical knowledge (general principles and strategies)	Create positive classroom climate	Professional attitude toward students (teacher is diagnostician and problem solver)
Pedagogical content knowledge (blending of content and pedagogy)	Diagnose student needs	High expectations of students
Knowledge of the learner	Motivate students	Persistent
Knowledge of educational contexts (classroom, school, community, social, cultural)	Provide for individual differences	Likes and respects students
Knowledge of one's own educational beliefs	Use a variety of teaching strategies	Listens to students' concerns and opinions
	Use academic time efficiently	Flexible and open-minded
	Respond effectively to unanticipated events	Takes risks for students
	Assess student learning	Enthusiastic about teaching
		Good sense of humor

David Berliner's (1988) model of pedagogical skill development is one of the traditional schemas. Berliner's model has five stages: novice, advanced beginner, competent, proficient, and expert. As teachers develop through Berliner's five stages, they move from minimal to fluid and seamless application of skills, from rule-oriented to contextualized decisions, and from trial and error to experience-based problem solving, and ultimately to rational, intuitive problem solving. A teacher moving from lower to higher stages also increasingly accepts responsibility for the effects of his or her teaching.

Another traditional model of pedagogical development was developed by Frances Fuller and colleagues (Fuller, 1969; Fuller & Bown, 1975) and extended by other researchers (Adams & Martray, 1981; Atkins & Vasu, 2000; Lasley, 1992). Fuller's model is focused on stages of teacher concern. At the *self-adequacy stage*, teachers are concerned about their professional survival. They are concerned about managing their workload, controlling their class, and how their supervisor will evaluate them. At the *teaching tasks stage*, teachers are concerned about organizing and managing their classroom for effective teaching, developing teaching materials, and effectively using different teaching methods. Finally, teachers at the *teaching impact stage* are student centered. They are concerned about diagnosing student needs, motivating students, and addressing individual differences. They teach the whole student, fostering the student's intellectual, emotional, and physical development.

Berliner's and Fuller's developmental models have much in common. In both models, teacher growth involves moving from narrow to wider perspectives on teaching, from unconnected to holistic practice, and from minimal to primary teacher responsibility for student learning. Both models require a differentiated approach to professional growth.

A more recent pedagogical model is proposed by Barone, Berliner, Blanchard, Casanova, and McGowan (1996). Their "visionary pedagogy" includes the following elements:

- *Noble and purposeful.* Teachers should articulate a moral vision centered on students' present and future well being.
- *Integrative and holistic.* Teaching should soften the boundaries between disciplines and connect content areas.
- *Constructivist.* Learning is constructed by the student rather than delivered by the teacher. The focus is on depth, not breadth, of content as students engage in reflection, decision making, and problem solving.
- *Active and engaging.* Teaching promotes social interactions, classroom movement, and manipulation of resources. Experiential learning is important for all students, regardless of their culture. Teaching is related to student needs and interests.

Visionary pedagogy incorporates much of the modern research on teaching and learning, as well as addressing the moral dimension of teaching.

Figure 10.3 illustrates the three models of pedagogical development just described. Which of the three models is the best one to guide teachers' professional

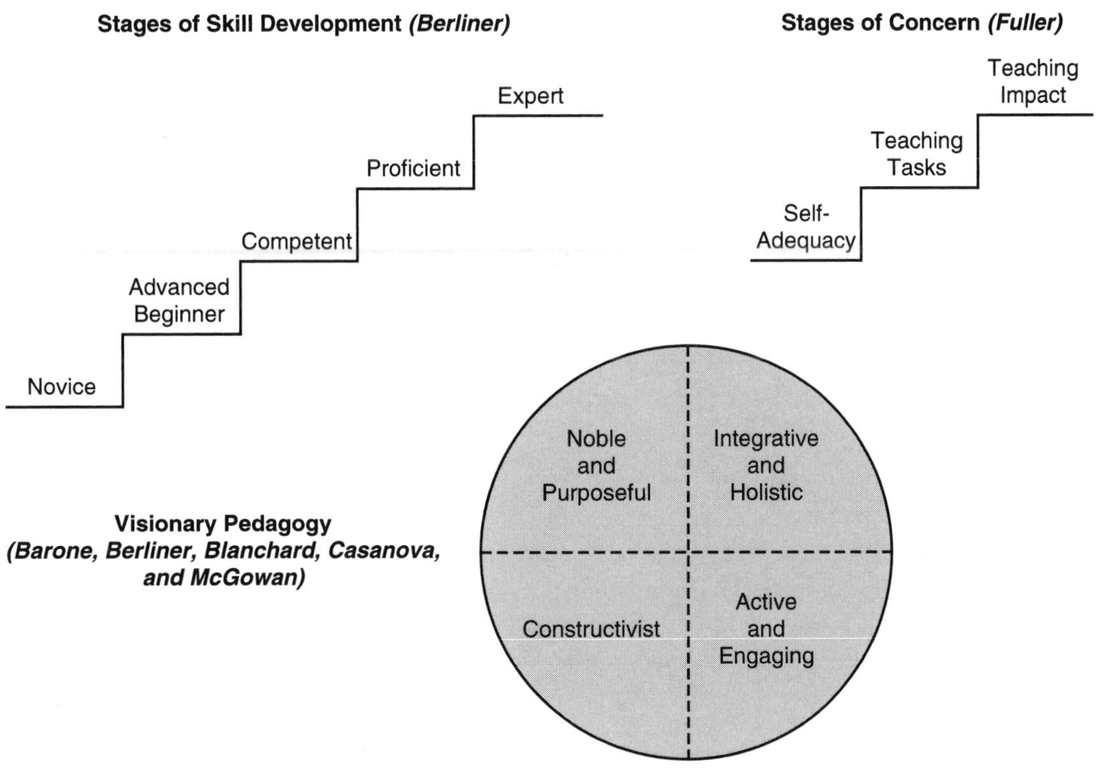

FIGURE 10.3 Models of Pedagogical Development

growth? Although visionary pedagogy is a more recent model, both Berliner's skill development model and Fuller's stages of concern have a solid research base and remain highly relevant to teacher development. The characteristics of expert teachers listed in Figure 10.2 can be integrated within any of the three models. The choice of pedagogical model should be based on the school's improvement goals, other aspects of the school's professional development program, and the comfort level of the faculty with potential models. The school may wish to create its own model for pedagogical growth, borrowing from existing models, and integrating its model with relevant professional development frameworks.

Visionary pedagogy calls for teachers to articulate a moral vision. The idea of moral vision leads us to a consideration of teacher moral development, a concept so important that it deserves in-depth discussion.

Moral Development

A study group at Ross High School is considering the topic "Teaching as a Moral Activity" for its next focus area. Participants are discussing what meanings they attach to the proposed topic.

Tom: To me, teaching as a moral activity includes adhering to professional codes of ethics like those promoted by the educational associations, but they provide minimal expectations. Teaching as a moral activity somehow has to go beyond codes of conduct.

Keisha: I agree, Tom. A graduate class I'm taking just finished the topic of moral development. According to Kohlberg, as persons develop from lower to higher stages, they change in the way they deal with moral dilemmas. They progress from a focus on self, to maintaining group or societal norms, to responding to dilemmas based on universal ethical principles and equal human rights.

Zach: I'm interested in learning more about adult moral development, but disappointed with any discussion that doesn't consider the reality that sometimes the highest of ethical principles conflict with each other. My view is that teachers' moral growth means they get better and better at dealing with moral dilemmas that require a balancing of conflicting values.

Liz: So far everyone's been equating teaching as a moral activity to teachers' moral development. My view is that our discussions ought to focus on teachers' fostering the moral development of students.

Keisha: Liz, I'm not sure that you can separate teachers' and students' moral development. It seems to me that the best way to teach morality and ethics is to model them in one's day-to-day teaching.

Robyn: I agree with Keisha. A teacher makes all types of decisions that affect daily classroom life. Most of the decisions seem to have a moral dimension. Zach is right when he says that teachers need to learn how to deal with moral dilemmas, but to me it goes beyond that, to intentionally creating a classroom climate that will foster students' moral growth.

Andrew: Why stop at the classroom level? Much of what goes on in the classroom seems to me to be controlled by the school, and by district and state directives. Don't teachers have a moral obligation to stand up to the powers that be if these powers hinder our capacity to create the type of classroom climate that Robyn is talking about?

Liz: We have little or no influence over districtwide decisions, let alone state mandates. Why waste out time talking about issues over which we have no control?

Scott: I think it's important that we examine the effects of state and district mandates on our teaching behaviors, and we can all work for more democratic school and classroom communities. To me, democracy is the best path to moral decisions, and the best way to learn how to deal with barriers to moral development.

The study group's discussion illustrates differing conceptions of "teaching as a moral activity." Which of the educators in the study group has the accurate perception? At different levels, all of the participants are correct. Certainly, Tom is correct when he states that professional ethics are part of moral teaching, as well as when he says that simply following professional codes of conduct is insufficient. Liz, too, is correct when she argues that the moral development of students is a primary purpose of teaching. However, the teacher who implements a character education program precisely as described in the curriculum guide but lacks compassion and fairness with students is not likely to inspire students toward higher levels of moral development.

Stage theories of moral development like the one described by Keisha also are relevant to teaching as a moral activity. Research on the relationship of teachers' moral reasoning with their thought and behavior shows that teachers functioning at higher stages of moral reasoning develop a more democratic view of classrooms and think about their teaching in more complex and reflective ways (Collinson, 2001; Lampe, 1994). Robyn's comment about the moral implications of teachers' daily decisions reflects Boostrom's (1998) concept of teaching as a moral activity:

> Every teacher defines the social quality of conduct, a way of looking at the world, and a social perspective. He or she decides how time will be spent, interprets the rules of classroom life, and establishes the language of the classroom.... Every act of a teacher—from how he or she greets (or does not greet) students in the morning to how he or she grades papers before going to sleep at night—helps to shape what will be done, how it will be done, and what the doing means. (pp. 63, 64)

Toward the end of the scenario, both Andrew and Scott express a critical perspective on teaching as a moral activity. They believe that the moral development of teachers includes facing and dealing with moral problems caused by institutional factors, as well as the social and political contexts of schooling. A critical approach calls for teachers to recognize that their teaching has been morally compromised by institutional or contextual factors. As teachers identify moral problems, express feelings, and seek solutions, they become "moral exemplars" for their students (Collinson, 2001; DeVries, 2000; Huebner, 1996).

The study group members expressed different conceptions of teaching as a moral activity. Yet, all of them agree that there is a moral aspect to good teaching. Qualitative research on outstanding teachers documents this moral dimension For example, Ponticell and Zepeda (1995) examined 90 teachers who had received rewards for teaching. Their study revealed that the teachers possessed characteristics traditionally associated with expert teachers, but also revealed a moral dimension:

> These teachers saw touching lives in the deepest personal and spiritual sense as a "given" in teaching.... Beyond knowledge, active learning, and risk taking, these teachers intended for their students to become caring human beings. Thus, classroom interactions were reviewed as primary teaching opportunities, as important as academic content.... Knowledge would mean little if its application was not tempered by compassion for others, concern for world problems, caring in personal interactions, and commitment to the building of a better, more humane world. (pp. 10, 14, 15)

Given the differing conceptions of teaching as a moral activity it is not surprising that there are a variety of different strategies for fostering moral development. One strategy is *dilemma discussion*. Dilemmas can be hypothetical or real life. Hypothetical dilemmas typically involve a conflict between two or more goods (e.g., compassion and truthfulness). Real-life dilemmas can be borrowed from other settings or based on the personal experience of participants. In the discussion, participants choose what they consider the morally appropriate response to the dilemma and their reasons for that response. The facilitator uses Socratic dialogue to help participants examine their reasoning. The dialogue, including exposure to alternative viewpoints, can create moral disequilibrium among group members, which in turn can lead to changes in moral thinking. There is a tendency for moral reasoning to advance to the higher levels of moral thinking present in the group. Oser's (1991) *discourse approach* is a variation of dilemma discussion in which participants consider possibilities for a synthesis of conflicting moral responses to a dilemma. "Complete discourse" addresses conflicting needs, rules, and principles as it works toward an equilibrium among care, justice, and truthfulness.

Kohlberg's *Just Community* is a schoolwide, ongoing strategy for facilitating moral development. In a "Just Community," all students and teachers meet every two to three weeks for a democratic community meeting regarding issues of school policy, justice, responsibility, and behavior (Kohlberg and others, 1975). Oser (1991) found that students involved in a Just Community experienced impressive moral growth, but that it was the teachers who developed most dramatically. The teachers interacted more, helped each other more, made more efforts to assist troubled students, and developed respect for students' reasoning. These teachers, initially functioning at no more than average levels of moral development, progressed to the complete discourse stage (the highest stage) of moral problem solving. Rulon (1992) explored Just Community as a specific method for professional development, and found that teachers involved in the professional development program experienced a significant increase in moral judgment test scores, whereas a control group showed no change.

Smyth (1989a,1989b) describes a professional development program that takes a critical perspective on teachers' moral development. Participants write about, then engage in group discussions on critical teaching incidents that alienated and confused them. Then participants develop "local theories" of the meaning behind the critical incidents they have described. Next, teachers focus on the causes of the local theories expressed in their practice. In the final phase of Smyth's model, teachers focus on what they might do differently in the future, including actions to overcome the external forces that have influenced past practice.

A critical approach to moral development that I have used begins with teachers collaboratively envisioning and describing their "ideal teacher." Then, based on their own experiences and observations, the teachers describe the *conventional teacher.* I ask individuals to draw a line segment on a sheet of paper and to write the words *conventional teacher* on one end and *ideal teacher* at the other end. The line segment represents a continuum between the conventional and the ideal. Each teacher is asked to privately place an *x* where they believe they belong on their individual continuum. The teachers will almost always place themselves somewhere between the two endpoints of the continuum. Participants next focus on the gap between where they have placed themselves and their conception of the ideal teacher. The teachers are asked to reflect on their classroom practices (omissions and commissions) that illustrate the gap between the real and the ideal.

After identifying and discussing classroom practices that they consider less than ideal, teachers are asked to reflect beyond their classroom behavior to the *causes* of undesirable practice. During this phase it becomes increasingly apparent to teachers that organizational, cultural, political, and social forces have had considerable impact on their classroom teaching, and have contributed to the gap between ideal and actual teaching practice. The next phase of the exercise consists of the teachers designing action plans for improving their classroom practice, including plans for ameliorating negative influences of organizational, cultural, political, and social forces. Such plans by necessity involve a commitment to collaboration with other professionals within the teacher's school. The final phase of this activity is implementation of the action plan, with ongoing self-assessment, revision, and group support.

Physical Wellness

Many who would readily agree with the other dimensions of teacher development discussed in this section might scratch their heads at the inclusion of teachers' physical wellness in a professional development program. After all, teachers are academics, not athletes! But one only needs to consider the tremendous stress that teachers experience on a daily basis to realize that they belong to a physically and emotionally at-risk profession! Corporate leaders long have realized that wellness programs provide a significant return in terms of employee morale, attendance, and performance. It's high time that school leaders come to the same realization.

One program dedicated to the wellness of its professional staff is Bastrop (TX) Intermediate School. The focus of the program is stress reduction. A needs assessment revealed that 67 percent of the teachers said they would participate in an after-school exercise program to reduce stress. The wellness program that the school developed included a variety of fitness activities, including a teacher walking program, a weight-loss program, an alternative exercise class, and regular stress reduction sessions. Other initiatives included the creation of a new faculty lounge with comfortable furniture and soft background music, a healthy-eating cookbook with recipes contributed by teachers, and a special cafeteria lunch menu for faculty. The Bastrop program views physical and emotional well being as interrelated and sees both of them as necessary for optimal professional performance. Other schools around the country include offerings such as massage therapy, meditation, and yoga. Many wellness programs are made available not just to faculty but to all adult members of the school community.

Integrating Dimensions of Teacher Development

All of the dimensions of teacher development discussed in this section should be viewed as interrelated, and integrated into a holistic program. Not every dimension needs to be addressed in every professional development activity, but most activities can address several dimensions, and all dimensions should be attended to throughout the school year. Figure 10.4 provides a simple grid for thinking about how the different dimensions of teacher development can be integrated across multiple professional development activities.

Adult Learning Styles

A critical aspect of individual teacher development is adapting professional development to teachers' individual learning styles. Teachers, like students, have individual learning preferences. The era of one-size-fits-all professional development is quickly drawing to a close. There are myriad instruments designed to measure adult learning styles. In this section, we'll review four instruments widely used in professional development programs across the nation—the Myers-Briggs Type Indicator, the Kolb Learning Style Inventory, the Gregorc Style Delineator, and the Productivity Environmental Preference Survey. After brief descriptions of each instrument, ways of using learning style measures to promote individual development will be discussed.

1. *The Myers-Briggs Type Indicator (MBTI)* (Briggs & Myers, 1987; also see Johnson, Mauzey, Johnson, Murphy, & Zimmerman, 2001) is based on Jungian theory and measures individuals on four continuums:
   - *Extraversion (E)* (attention focused on outer world) to *Introversion (I)* (attention focused on one's inner world)
   - *Sensing (S)* (perceives present, concrete world through senses) to *Intuition (N)* (perceives future, relationships, and generalities through intuition)
   - *Thinking (T)* (bases decisions on objective analysis and logic) to *Feeling (F)* (bases decisions on personal values and concern for others)

FIGURE 10.4 Integrating Dimensions of Teacher Development

Professional Development Activity	*Self Concept/ Self-Efficacy Objective*	*Cognitive Development Objective*	*Pedagogical Development Objective*	*Moral Development Objective*	*Physical Wellness Objective*

Note: An individual activity may meet multiple objectives.

- *Judging (J)* (planned, organized, stable lifestyle) to *Perceiving (P)* (spontaneous, flexible, open lifestyle)

  Scores on the MBTI indicate which end of each continuum the individual is closest to, so that he or she has four preferences. The person's four preferences combined place him or her into one of 16 types. Each type has some characteristics in common with other types, but the *combination* of characteristics for any of the 16 types is unique.

2. *Kolb's Learning Style Inventory (LSI)* (Kolb, 1985; also see Healey & Jenkins, 2000) measures the adult's learning modes on two continuums:
   - *Concrete Experience (CE)* (emphasis on feeling, uniqueness, intuition, relations with others, real situations, artistic approach, openness) to *Abstract Conceptualization (AC)* (emphasis on logic, ideas, generalities, scientific approach, planning, analysis, precision).
   - *Reflective Observation (RO)* (emphasis on description, understanding, meaning, implications, alternative perspectives, impartiality, thought) to *Active Experimentation (AE)* (emphasis on change, application, practicality, implementation, impact, results)

   Based on scores for each of the four learning modes, the individual is classified into one of four learning styles:

   - *Diverger* (higher scores on concrete experience and reflective observation). The Diverger is imaginative, people oriented, sensitive, open-minded, and capable of generating multiple alternatives.
   - *Assimilator* (higher scores on reflective observation and abstract conceptualization). The Assimilator organizes information, develops theories, designs models, and creates plans.
   - *Converger* (higher scores on abstract conceptualization and active experimentation). The Converger sets goals, defines problems, seeks solutions, and makes decisions.
   - *Accommodator* (higher scores on concrete experience and active experimentation). The Accommodator is a committed leader, explorer, and risk taker who becomes personally involved and influences others.

3. *Gregorc's Style Delineator* (Gregorc, 1982; also see Ross, Drysdale, & Schulz, 2001) classifies adults into one of four styles:
   - *Concrete Sequential (CS).* Adults with a CS learning style relate to the world around them through their five senses. They complete tasks methodically, and learn best through hands-on activities with concrete objects.
   - *Abstract Sequential (AS).* These adults use abstract symbols to represent concrete reality. They learn best through analysis and synthesis of available knowledge. They are highly logical and highly verbal.
   - *Abstract Random (AR).* Adults with an AR learning style focus on feelings and emotions. They live in the present moment, and rely on their intuition to make decisions. They place great value on personal relationships and they are imaginative and artistic.

- *Concrete Random (CR).* These adults focus on the interrelationship of past, present, and future. They are independent, rely on their instincts, and are process oriented, creative, and holistic.

4. *The Productivity Environmental Preference Survey (PEPS)* (Dunn, Dunn, & Price, 1989; also see Dunn & Dunn, 1999) measures adults' learning styles across four types of stimuli, including several elements within each type:
   - *Environmental stimuli*, including noise level, light (dim vs. bright), temperature, and design (informal vs. formal seating).
   - *Emotional stimuli*, including motivation (self-motivated vs. required breaks), persistence, responsibility (conformity vs. nonconformity), and structure (internal vs. external).
   - *Sociological stimuli*, including alone vs. peer, authority figures (absent vs. present; requiring feedback vs. not requiring feedback), and variety (patterns and routines vs. variety).
   - *Physiological stimuli*, including perceptual preference (auditory, visual, tactile, kinesthetic), intake (eating/drinking), time (morning, afternoon, or evening), and mobility (passive vs. mobile).

How can the results of learning style measures be used to improve professional development programs? Simply assessing and understanding one's style promotes self-understanding. Sharing results and reflecting on what happens when teachers with different styles work together can help colleagues to better understand each other as well as the dynamics taking place within work groups.

Teams can be organized so that all styles are represented on a given team. This balanced approach means that a variety of viewpoints will be expressed and a wide range of alternatives considered. Alternatively, if a heterogeneous group is working on a project that can be divided into distinct phases or tasks that require different strengths, the group can be split into homogeneous subgroups. Each subgroup can then perform its part of the project utilizing the strengths associated with their particular learning style. Thus, whether taking a "balanced" approach or a "different strengths" approach, forming teams based on learning styles can allow teachers to display their strengths, expose teachers to other learning styles, and help achieve team goals.

Learning styles can be used to organize learning activities. One way to do this is to match differentiated professional development sessions with different learning styles. A variation of the style-activity match is incremental movement from matched to "optimally mismatched" activities. The idea here is to begin with learning sessions that match the teacher's learning style, and eventually shift to sessions that will cause the teacher to stretch to new learning styles without creating an extreme mismatch between natural style and learning activity.

There are strategies other than differentiated sessions for adapting professional development to teachers' learning styles. A variety of activities can be provided during the same session, addressing each teacher's learning style some of the time. An advantage of this approach is that the extra resources required for a differentiated program need not be expended. A disadvantage is that only some of a session's learning activities will match any individual's learning style.

A strategy that goes beyond merely offering a variety of activities representing different learning styles is to sequence such activities into a developmental process or learning cycle. This approach is based on the theory that different learning styles reflect different aspects of a holistic learning experience. To be fully effective learners, adults need to develop the strengths associated with each learning mode. Thus, each phase of a learning cycle requires the use of a different learning style. The best example of this type of learning process is Kolb's adult learning cycle. In this cycle, the learner goes through each of Kolb's learning modes in the following order: concrete experience, reflective observation, abstract conceptualization, and active experimentation. Figure 10.5 illustrates Kolb's adult learning cycle.

For an example of Kolb's learning cycle used in a professional development program, consider the case of teachers wishing to make more effective use of cooperative learning in their classrooms. At the concrete experience stage, teachers could share their experiences of having tried out cooperative learning in past lessons and their feelings about those experiences. The reflective observation stage could involve teachers critically examining theory and research on cooperative learning, attempting to better understand the cooperative model and its implications for teaching and learning. Abstract conceptualization might consist of teachers designing cooperative units of

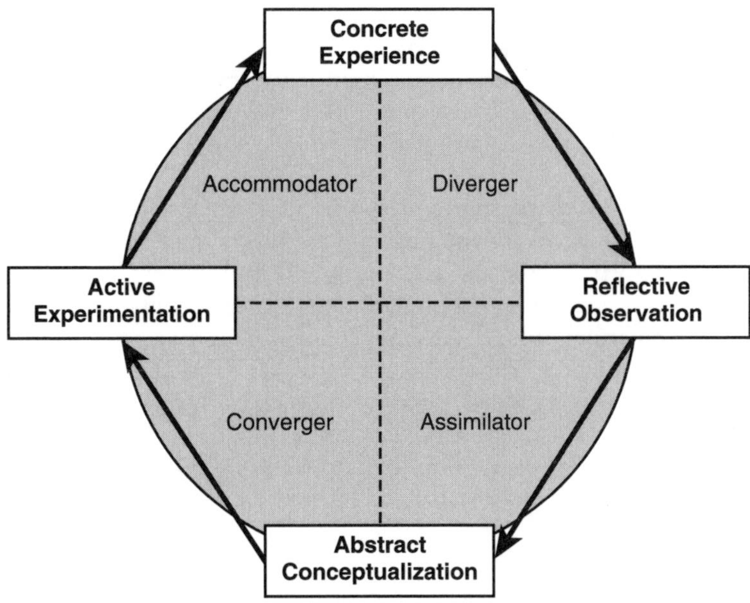

FIGURE 10.5 Kolb's Learning Cycle

Source: Adapted from David A. Kolb, Irwin M. Rubin, and James M. McIntyre, *Organizational Psychology: An Experiential Approach to Organizational Behavior* (Upper Saddle River, NJ: Prentice Hall, 1984). The Learning Style Inventory is copyrighted by David A. Kolb, 1976. Used by permission of David A. Kolb.

instruction or lesson plans, then evaluating each other's designs. Finally, the active experimentation stage of Kolb's learning cycle could involve teachers actually trying out cooperative learning strategies in their classrooms, sharing teaching materials with each other, and providing reciprocal peer coaching.

The types and uses of learning style models are many and varied. Ultimately, the educators at each school must decide which learning style inventories to use and how learning style information will help to shape the school's professional development program. The advantages of using one or more of the learning style models include better understanding of ourselves, our colleagues, and adult learning, and more effective professional development programs.

Assisting Beginning Teachers

Individualized professional development is important for all teachers, but it is especially critical for beginning teachers. Traditionally, teachers' first years in the profession have been "trial by fire." With little information about what was expected of them, few resources, and no special assistance, beginners have been expected to fulfill the same teaching responsibilities as the 20-year veteran. In fact, because they are assigned students, courses, and classrooms that veteran teachers do not want, many beginners have more difficult work assignments than their experienced colleagues! It is no wonder that many beginners experience frustration, fatigue, low self-esteem, and even depression and physical illness, and that around 15 percent of them leave the profession by the end of their first year, with up to 50 percent leaving within six years (Gordon & Maxey, 2000). Fortunately, the long history of the profession's sink-or-swim attitude appears to be drawing to an end. Beginning teacher assistance programs gradually are becoming the norm in schools across the nation. Much work remains, however, in order to make assistance programs universal and to improve the quality of many existing programs.

A beginning teacher assistance program ought to be a formal component of the school's professional development program. A program development team should develop a written plan for the assistance program. Roles and responsibilities of those involved in the program (administrators, staff developers, mentors, beginning teachers, and so on) need to be delineated. As noted in Chapter 5, a process for selecting, preparing, and assigning mentors should be put in place. A process for ongoing program assessment and revision is needed. Finally, necessary resources should be identified.

What are the typical needs of novice teachers that a beginning teacher assistance program can meet? A review by Gordon and Maxey (2000) identified the following needs as common to most new teachers:

- Managing the classroom
- Acquiring information about the school system
- Obtaining instructional resources and materials
- Planning, organizing, and managing instruction as well as other professional responsibilities
- Assessing students and evaluating student progress

- Motivating students
- Using effective teaching methods
- Dealing with individual students' needs, interests, abilities, and problems
- Communicating with colleagues, including administrators, supervisors, and other teachers
- Communicating with parents
- Adjusting to the teaching environment and role
- Receiving emotional support (p. 6)

A needs assessment can identify the individual beginner's needs relative to self-concept, cognitive, pedagogical, moral, and physical development. The needs assessment can also identify the beginner's learning preferences. The assessment might include formal surveys and interviews, but can also include informal discussions among the beginner, the mentor, and other members of the support team. The individualized assistance plan resulting from the needs assessment should be viewed as tentative and flexible. It will almost certainly need to be revised as the school year continues.

A novice's support needs are best addressed through a team approach to beginning teacher assistance. In most successful programs, the beginner's mentor is the center of the support team (you might wish to review the discussion of mentoring in Chapter 5); however, all the teachers who work with and around the beginner should be considered members of the team. Informal mentoring can be provided anytime by teachers who teach at the same grade level, on the same team, or in the same content area. Important members of the support team include the principal and assistant principal, professors from universities that prepare teachers, educational specialists, staff developers, parents, and community members. Once a support team is in place, it makes sense for the mentor to coordinate team activities.

Although each new teacher should have an individualized professional development plan, some forms of assistance should be provided to all beginners. One of these is an orientation to the school district and school. Another is assistance with a detailed plan for the first week of school. Additionally, all new teachers need to be provided adequate classroom resources. Starting one's teaching career is difficult enough without having to deal with broken desks, computers that don't work, and missing materials. Perhaps most importantly, all beginners deserve the moral support of their colleagues. Little things like helping the beginner complete a form, listening to the novice discuss a classroom problem, or letting the newcomer know you're glad to have him or her on the faculty can make all of the difference in the world.

In addition, a variety of professional development frameworks and activities can be tailored to the beginners' individual needs. Training can be provided in areas such as classroom management, planning for instruction, motivating students, and communicating with parents. The support team can organize various types of group meetings for beginners, including support groups, seminars, and study groups. The novice can engage in reflection on teaching through analyzing videos of his or her teaching, journal writing, or debriefing critical incidents with the mentor. Developing an entry-year portfolio allows the beginner to reflect on experiences and assess personal and professional growth throughout the year.

To summarize, some support activities that the beginner participates in will be provided for all of the school's novice teachers, others will be individualized. The goal is a comprehensive program that will help both the beginning teacher and the beginner's students to have a successful school year. Inset 10.1 provides a beginning teacher needs assessment that can be one source for determining the beginner's needs.

INSET 10.1 • *Beginning Teacher Needs Assessment*

Directions: Indicate your level of need for assistance in each of the numbered items below by selecting one of the following responses:

A. No need
B. Little need
C. Moderate need
D. High need
E. Very high need

1. Managing the classroom
2. Acquiring information on district and school rules and procedures
3. Obtaining instructional resources and materials
4. Planning, organizing, and managing professional responsibilities
5. Assessing student learning
6. Motivating students
7. Using effective teaching methods
8. Meeting individual student needs
9. Communicating with administrators and peers
10. Communicating with parents
11. Adjusting to the teaching role
12. Receiving emotional support

Individualized Professional Development

The attention finally being given to the individual needs of beginning teachers hopefully signals a movement toward providing individualized support to all teachers. At first blush, individual professional development might seem inconsistent with the modern emphasis on common vision, collegiality, and collaboration. Nothing could be further from the truth. Most of the exemplary programs described in this text include individualized professional development plans that are tied to schoolwide visions and goals. Individualized professional development can take several different forms. These forms can be viewed on continuum from intensive individual assistance to independent development:

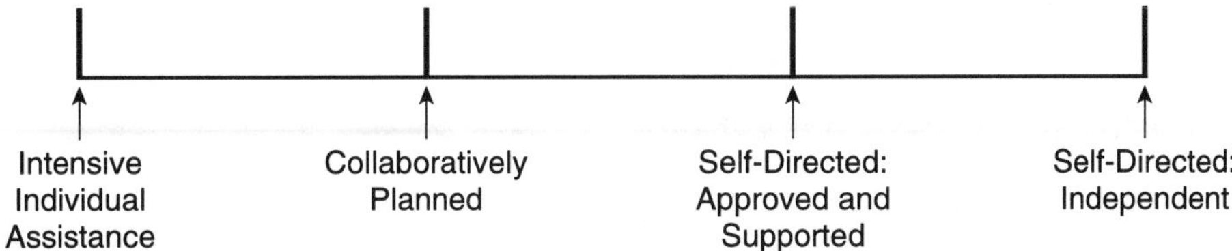

Intensive individualized assistance is reserved for the teacher who is having serious professional difficulty. It is remedial assistance, and should be provided only until the teacher has reached a level of basic competence. Collaboratively planned individual development is appropriate for the teacher who is moving toward autonomy but still needs some assistance from a staff developer or colleague in planning and implementing his or her professional development. Self-directed professional development can be planned by the teacher and then reviewed, approved, and supported by the school, or it can be carried out independently. Independent professional development might consist of the teacher participating in a graduate program, conference, or network unassociated with the school, or in private reading, research, or reflective writing. Inset 10.2 provides a preliminary needs assessment for individualized professional development.

INSET 10.2 • *Preliminary Needs Assessment for Individualized Professional Development*

Directions: Respond to each of the numbered items below by selecting one of the following responses:

A. No need
B. Little need
C. Moderate need
D. High need
E. Very high need

What is your level of need to explore each of the following topics:

Understanding Self

1. My self-concept and self-efficacy
2. My cognitive development

(continued)

INSET 10.2 • Continued

3. My pedagogical development toward expert teaching
4. The moral dimension of teaching
5. My physical-emotional wellness
6. My learning styles
7. Developing my own educational philosophy

Designing an Individualized Professional Development Project

8. Selecting a focus for individual professional development
9. Connecting my focus area to team and school goals
10. Collecting data on my focus area
11. Assessing my learning style
12. Planning my individualized professional development project
13. Evaluating my individualized professional development project
14. Sharing benefits of my individualized professional development project

Professional Portfolio Development

15. Purposes and benefits of professional portfolios
16. How to organize a portfolio
17. What to include in a portfolio

The remainder of this section will describe a process for planning individualized professional development that I have been using with teachers for several years. The process can be adapted to collaborative or self-directed development. In the first phase of the process, the teacher selects a focus area for individual development. The focus area initially is fairly broad. It is made more precise later on in the process. The focus area should also relate to collaboratively agreed upon school and team goals.

The second phase is the self-assessment and consists of two types of assessment. One type gathers data to better understand and narrow the focus area. I encourage teachers to collect a variety of self-assessment data on their focus area. Data gathering might consist of videotaping classroom lessons, keeping a reflective journal for several weeks, asking students to complete feedback questionnaires, and so on. Figure 10.6 is an example of a student feedback questionnaire designed by a teacher wishing to gather information on the affective dimension of her teaching. The second part of the self-assessment concerns the teacher's learning style. I encourage teachers to complete several learning style inventories like those described earlier in this chapter, and to identify broad themes running through those results. The teacher then writes a summary of his or her learning style and implications for individual professional development.

Dear Students:

Please circle the response that you feel is most nearly true for each item.

1. The teacher makes me feel good about being in her class.

   never *seldom* *sometimes* *often* *always*

2. The teacher allows students to disagree with her.

   never *seldom* *sometimes* *often* *always*

3. The teacher acts as if she likes being with my class.

   never *seldom* *sometimes* *often* *always*

4. The teacher treats students fairly.

   never *seldom* *sometimes* *often* *always*

5. The teacher goes out of her way to help students who have special problems or questions.

   never *seldom* *sometimes* *often* *always*

6. The teacher listens to students who feel that they have something important to say even if it might not have to do with the subject being taught.

   never *seldom* *sometimes* *often* *always*

7. I would be willing to go to the teacher and discuss a personal problem.

   never *seldom* *sometimes* *often* *always*

8. When the teacher asks a question, she is willing to accept different opinions, rather than accepting only one "right" answer.

   never *seldom* *sometimes* *often* *always*

9. The teacher praises students who are trying to learn.

   never *seldom* *sometimes* *often* *always*

10. The teacher treats students like "real people" rather than little children.

    never *seldom* *sometimes* *often* *always*

FIGURE 10.6 Teacher-Designed Student Feedback Questionnaire

Based on the self-assessment, the teacher is now ready to write specific objectives aimed at self-improvement. I tell teachers not to worry about writing formal behavioral objectives, that the important thing about this third phase of the process is conceptualizing and articulating in their own words improvements they wish to make in their professional lives. Next, the teacher creates an action plan for meeting the improvement objectives. The purpose is to plan growth activities that the teacher will be comfortable with and excited about. The fact that this is an individualized plan does not mean that the growth activities must be carried out individually. The teacher might elect to attend a training program, participate in peer coaching, join a study group, and so on. What makes the program individualized is the fact that it is tailored to the individual's own growth objectives, learning style, and preferred activities.The teacher also describes in the plan how the individualized project will assist in the attainment of school and team goals. The plan should be long term, but one that can be completed within one to two years.

The next phase is for the teacher to design an evaluation of the individualized project. One part of the evaluation should be formative and ongoing. The teacher also plans a final evaluation, to be carried out at the end of the project. As with the self-assessment, the self-evaluation should include a variety of data. Some of the same types of data collected for the self-assessment can be gathered during the evaluation phase. Some formative data collected over a year or two can become a cumulative record used in the final project evaluation. The self-evaluation might take the form of a portfolio that tracks needs assessment, planning, implementation, and results (individual portfolios will be discussed in detail in the next section).

The last phase of the project is the listing of major resources needed for the project, and the creation of a budget. An individualized professional development plan should be so exciting that the teacher is bound and determined to implement it, even if school funding is not available. Given the reality of both school budgets and teachers' salaries, the plan needs to be as economical as possible.

I have recommended that a teacher's plan be for a period of one to two years. The end of that time period, however, does not necessarily mean the end of the project. The teacher's next individualized plan might well be an extension of the previous one, with revised objectives and growth activities based on the teacher's self-evaluation. Often, however, the teacher will wish to venture into an entirely new project. Everything depends on the teacher's needs, concerns, and interests, which may well have changed since the initiation of the previous cycle. Inset 10.3 provides a format for planning an individual professional development project.

INSET 10.3 • *Format for Individualized Professional Development Project*

1. What is your focus area?

2. Why did you choose this focus area?

3. How will professional growth within the focus area support the school vision?
4. How will professional growth within the focus area be beneficial to one or more school teams to which you belong?
5. What data have you gathered on the focus area? What has the data told you about the focus area?
6. What data have you gathered on your learning styles?
7. What are your professional development objectives?
8. Describe your plan for meeting your objectives. Include activities and a time line for completing activities.
9. How will you evaluate your project to determine if your objectives have been met?
10. How will you share the results/benefits of your project with other educators?

Teacher Portfolios

There are two broad purposes of teacher portfolios: teacher evaluation and professional development. Specific purposes within the former category include evaluation to determine if a teacher is eligible for certification, licensure, employment by a school district, continued employment, tenure, a career ladder step, or a merit pay increase. In contrast, professional development portfolios are concerned with reflection on practice, self-assessment of professional needs, and self-monitoring of professional growth. Professional development portfolios can focus on individualized professional development projects, annual professional development, or professional development throughout the teacher's career. I'll describe in detail these three types of professional development portfolios, then conclude with a discussion of the need to prepare teachers for portfolio development

Individualized Project Portfolio

The project portfolio goes hand in hand with the individualized professional development project discussed in the previous section. The portfolio is a vehicle for recording the project's context and history, reflecting on the project, and self-assessment of professional growth during the project. Sections within the portfolio can parallel the stages of the individual project. Possible section titles and types of artifacts within each section are provided here:

- *Focus area*, including a reflective essay describing the community, school, and teaching context; and the focus area, why the focus area was chosen, and how the focus area relates to school and team goals
- *Self-assessment*, including copies of instruments used to collect data on the focus area; summaries and interpretation of focus data; results of learning-style inventories; and interpretation of learning-style data
- *Plan*, including objectives, activities to meet objectives, activities for ongoing and final project evaluation, a time line for implementation, a plan for sharing results and benefits with others, resources needed, and a project budget
- *Implementation*, including logs tracking growth activities, project artifacts, reflections on the implementation process, samples of feedback from mentor or coach, and so on
- *Self-evaluation*, including student achievement data, samples of student work, summaries of survey and interview data, classroom observation data, and so on
- *Learning and future directions*, including a reflective essay on what the teacher has learned from the project, and how the teacher would like to extend his or her professional growth either through project continuation or initiation of a new project

Project portfolios might cover a period of a semester, an entire school year, or even two years. The length of portfolio development depends in the length of the project.

Annual Portfolio

A project portfolio and an annual portfolio could be one in the same, if a teacher's individual development program consists of completing an individual project over the course of a school year. Another version of the annual portfolio is less focused, including entries in several broad areas of professional development, such as educational philosophy, curriculum development, instructional development, student assessment, teacher and parent collaboration, and professional service. The teacher developing a comprehensive annual portfolio would use it as a vehicle for planning, reflecting on, and self-assessing individual growth in each broad area (Tolan, 2001). After a section on the teacher's educational philosophy, each remaining section of the portfolio could address one of the other areas listed above, with each section including an individual improvement objective, an essay connecting the objective to school and team goals, a plan for the year, as well as artifacts and reflections on growth activities. Examples of artifacts relevant to each of the six areas listed in this paragraph are provided in Figure 10.7.

Career Portfolio

In one form of the career portfolio, each section of the portfolio represents a different phase of the teacher's career, as defined by the teacher. The career portfolio is thus autobiographical and developmental. The teacher selects artifacts and reflections that represent each career stage. As the teacher gains experience, the career portfolio becomes a richer and deeper resource for reflecting on one's experience and growth.

FIGURE 10.7 ***Examples of Sections and Artifacts for Annual Portfolio***

Educational Philosophy
- Readings influencing philosophy
- Artifacts from professional development (PD)
- Written philosophy
- Lesson plans or videos that demonstrate philosophy
- Student work that reflects philosophy
- Reflective writing on philosophy-reality gaps

Student Assessment
- Readings influencing assessment
- Artifacts from PD activities on student assessment
- Examples of student learning-style assessments
- Teacher-made displays of student achievement data
- Samples of tasks/directions for performance-based assessments
- Samples from student projects, performances, presentations, portfolios
- Samples of student peer assessment
- Samples of student self-assessment
- Reflective writing on student assessment

Curriculum Development
- Curriculum readings
- Artifacts from PD activities on curriculum development
- Curriculum maps designed
- Interdisciplinary curriculum designed
- Reflective writing on curriculum
- Curriculum guides designed
- Sample curriculum units designed
- Artifacts from curriculum evaluation
- Reflective writing on curriculum

Teacher-Parent Collaboration
- Readings influencing teacher-parent collaboration
- Artifacts from PD activities on teacher-parent collaboration
- Sample written communications
- Logs of phone communication
- Artifacts of teacher-parent, student-parent, and three-way conferences
- Artifacts of parent involvement
- Samples of family information gathered
- Log of home visits
- Examples of parent input/feedback
- Artifacts of parent information sessions
- Reflective writing on teacher-parent collaboration

Instructional Development
- Readings on instruction
- Artifacts from PD activities on instructional development
- Artifacts from instructional innovations
- Artifacts from technology enhanced instruction
- Sample lesson plans
- Videos and photos of lessons
- Logs from demonstration lessons, coaching, co-teaching, team teaching, action research
- Examples of differentiated instruction
- Reflective writing on instruction

Professional Service
- Readings on professional service

Artifacts from:
- National service
- State service
- Community service
- School district service
- Service to school
- Service to department/team
- Mentoring
- Professional writing
- Reflective writing on professional service

An alternative form of the career portfolio is divided into sections representing broad areas such as the annual portfolio described earlier (e.g., educational philosophy, curriculum development, instructional development, student assessment, teacher-parent collaboration, and professional service). As the teacher's career continues, each area of the portfolio is periodically updated or revised. For example, the teacher might write a new educational philosophy every two to three years, and reflect on changes in educational beliefs through the years. The career portfolio might show how the teacher's units of instruction, or instructional strategies, or student assessment methods have evolved over the years, and could track changing relationships with parents, increasing leadership responsibility, and so on.

In either type of career portfolio it is vital that the teacher be the one to determine what areas of his or her career to focus on, and what artifacts to include in the portfolio. Adequate preparation in how to develop a portfolio will assist the teacher in constructing a meaningful portfolio that will facilitate the teacher's ongoing professional growth.

Preparing Teachers to Develop Portfolios

Preparation for portfolio development is essential. Teachers need to become familiar with the different types of portfolios and their respective purposes, and how to organize portfolios. Sample portfolios and discussions with teachers who have developed portfolios are invaluable. A big part of the preparation process should be teachers making their own decisions about portfolio content and taking their own first steps in constructing portfolios. This is best done in collaboration with other teachers. Exemplar 10.1 describes professional portfolio development at Leander (TX) Middle School.

EXEMPLAR 10.1 *Portfolios at Leander Middle School*

Teacher portfolios at Leander Middle School are tied to annual individual improvement projects, which in turn are tied to the school's improvement plan. Teachers are prepared to work with portfolios at team meetings. Topics addressed during preparation include the following:

1. How to self-assess professional needs using a set of learner-centered proficiencies developed by the school community
2. How to select a topic for professional development
3. How to relate individual learning objectives to school and district objectives
4. How to use a resource matrix developed by the school community to select professional development activities, relevant learning resources, and peer coaches
5. Sharing ideas for data collection and self-evaluation of learning
6. Establishing a supportive environment to share ideas and experiences

Portfolios at the middle school are large, three-ring binders organized into sections corresponding to the PDSA cycle (Plan, Do, Study, Act). The *Plan* section includes artifacts of self-assessment and planning. The *Do* section documents participation in learning activities, changes in professional practice, and collegial support. The *Study* section includes data assessing progress of the teacher's annual project. A variety of teacher-developed data displays on teacher and student growth are found in this section. The final part of the portfolio is the *Act* section. The focus of this section is the portfolio conference with a school administrator. Included in this section are written teacher reflections on what took place during the improvement project, what the teacher learned, and how the teacher intends to continue his or her professional development. The teachers whom I interviewed were not worried about sharing their portfolios with an administrator. In fact, they were quite excited about the portfolio review conference:

> I couldn't wait to get in there to show my principal what I was doing. It gave me an audience, and a portfolio is more valuable if you have an audience and you can get feedback. I can tell the principal things that have not worked for me . . . and if I had felt that I was being graded, I would not do that. It's back to the trust thing. I put every artifact that I valued in my portfolio. It was the most incredible thing to have this time with an administrator who had been in a classroom and who has done a portfolio this year.

Teachers were highly positive about the overall portfolio development process:

> My portfolio was not just something that I got together in April. For me, it's a driver. It's something that's helping me guide my own development. You need a focus, a direction to go, and the portfolio gives me that. With a portfolio, you're constantly working on and learning about your teaching.

At Leander Middle School, portfolios assist educators to plan, implement, and assess their own professional development. The portfolio is a showcase for reflective practice and continuous improvement.

Summary

This chapter argued for the need to develop the whole teacher, including the dimensions of self-concept and self-efficacy, cognitive development, pedagogical development, moral development, and physical wellness. Different learning-style measures were examined, and we discussed how an understanding of learning styles can improve professional development. Providing individual professional development to novice teachers is critical, hence we discussed beginning teacher assistance programs. The individualized professional project was explored, and a process for facilitating long-range projects was outlined. Finally, we examined the professional development portfolio as a vehicle for assisting individual development.

Assignments

1. Write a paper on one of the topics listed below. The paper should include information not provided in this chapter. Use and cite at least three references other than this text.
   a. Adult development
   b. Reflective teaching
   c. Expert teaching
   d. Adult learning styles
   e. Assisting beginning teachers
   f. Individualized teacher professional development
   g. Teacher portfolios
2. Based on Berliner's stages of skill development, observe a novice, a competent, and an expert teacher teaching a lesson. Write a report comparing the performance of each teacher. Include in your paper specific examples of each teacher's classroom behaviors.
3. Complete at least three different adult learning-style inventories. Write a paper in which you discuss the results of each inventory, identify themes about your learning style that run through the various results, and compare inventory results with your past experiences as a learner. Finally, discuss how the information derived from the inventories might facilitate your future learning.
4. Engage in a learning project that takes you through the four stages of Kolb's learning cycle: concrete experience, reflective observation, abstract conceptualization, and active experimentation (see Figure 10.5). Write a report describing your experiences and reactions, as well as your perceptions concerning the validity of Kolb's model.
5. Interview a beginning teacher on the teacher's experiences as a beginner, his or her perceived support needs, and the types of support the teacher has received. Write a report summarizing the interview and relating the information you gather to this chapter's discussions of beginning teachers' needs and support programs.
6. Create a career portfolio.
7. Design your own individual professional development project. Use the questions in Inset 10.3 as a guide for designing the project.

References

Adams, R. D., & Martray, C. (1981, April). *Teacher development: A study of factors related to teacher concerns for pre, beginning, and experienced teachers*. Paper presented at the annual meeting of the American Educational Research Association, Los Angeles.

Ash, R. C., & Persall, J. M. (2000). The principal as chief learning officer: Developing teacher leaders. *NASSP Bulletin, 84*(616), 15–22.

Ash, T. (1993). *Reflective teaching. What am I doing? Why am I doing it this way? Instructional strategies series No. 11*. Regina, SK: The Saskatchewan Instructional Development and Research Unit and the Saskatchewan Professional Development Unit. (ERIC ED 360 309).

Ashton, P. T., Webb, R. B., & Doda, N. (1983). *A study of teachers' sense of efficacy. Final report, executive summary*. Gainesville: University of Florida. (ERIC ED 231 833).

Aspy, D. N. (1969). *The effect of teachers' inferred self concept upon student achievement.* (ERIC ED 031 300).

Atkins, N. E., & Vasu, E. S. (2000). Measuring knowledge of technology usage and stages of concern about computing: A study of middle school teachers. *Journal of Technology and Teacher Education, 8*(4), 279–302.

Barnes, S. (1981). *Synthesis of selected research on teacher findings.* Austin, TX: Research and Development Center for Teacher Education.

Barone, T., Berliner, D. C., Blanchard, J., Casanova, V., & McGowan, T. (1996). A future for teacher education: Developing a strong sense of professionalism. In J. Sikula (Ed.), *Handbook of research on teacher education* (2nd ed., pp. 1108–1149). New York: Macmillan.

Beatty, B. R. (1999, April). *Teachers leading their own professional growth: Self-directed reflection and collaboration and changes in perception of self and work in secondary school teachers.* Paper presented at the annual meeting of the American Educational Research Association, Montreal.

Bennett, C. K. (1991). Staff development in light of Maslow's theory. *Journal of Staff Development, 12*(4), 10–14.

Berliner, D. C. (1988, February). *The development of expertise in pedagogy.* Paper presented at the annual meeting of the American Association of Colleges for Teacher Education, New Orleans.

Boostrom, R. E. (1998). What makes teaching a moral activity? *Educational Forum, 63*(1), 58–64.

Briggs, K. C., & Myers, I. B. (1987). *Myers-Briggs Type Indictor—Form G.* Palo Alto, CA: Consulting Psychologists.

Chase, B., Germundsen, R., Brownstein, J. C., & Distad, L. S. (2001). Making the connection between increased student learning and reflective practice. *Educational Horizons, 79*(3), 143–147.

Chwalisz, K. D., Altmaier, E. M., & Russell, D. W. (1992). Causal attributions, self-efficacy cognitions, and coping with stress. *Journal of Social and Clinical Psychology, 11*, 377–400.

Cole, A. L., & Knowles, J. G. (2000). *Researching teaching: Exploring teacher development through reflexive inquiry.* Boston: Allyn and Bacon.

Collinson, V. (2001). Intellectual, social and moral development: Why technology cannot replace teachers. *The High School Journal, 85*(1), 35–44.

Connolly, R. A. (2000). Why do good teachers leave the profession? What can be done to retain them? *Momentum, 31*(3), 55–57.

Cruickshank, D. R. (1990). *Research that informs teachers and teacher educators.* Bloomington, IN: Phi Delta Kappa Educational Foundation.

Curtis, J., & Altmann, H. (1977). The relationship between teachers' self-concept and the self-concept of students. *Child Study Journal*, 7(1), 17–27, 77.

DeVries, R. (2000). The teacher's role in establishing a constructivist sociomoral atmosphere. *Scholastic Early Childhood, 14*(7), 12–14.

Dewey, J. (1933). *How we think: A restatement of the relation of reflective thinking to the educative process.* Boston: D. C. Heath.

Dunn, R., & Dunn, K. (1999). *The complete guide to the learning styles inservice system.* Boston: Allyn and Bacon.

Dunn, R., Dunn, K., & Price, G. E. (1989). *Productivity Environmental Preference Survey.* Lawrence, KS: Price Systems.

Edwards, J. L., & Newton, R. R. (1995, April). *The effects of cognitive coaching on teacher efficacy and empowerment.* Paper presented at the annual meeting of the American Educational Research Association, San Francisco.

Fuller, F. (1969). Concerns of teachers: A developmental conceptualization. *American Educational Research Journal, 6*, 207–226.

Fuller, F. F., & Bown, O. H. (1975). Becoming a teacher. In K. Ryan (Ed.), *Teacher education: The seventy-fourth yearbook of the National Society for the Study of Education* (pp. 25–52). Chicago: University of Chicago Press.

Garmston, R. J. (2001). Newly hatched: Beginning teachers become professionals through coaching, consulting. *Journal of Staff Development, 22*(4), 54–55.

Gordon, S. P., & Maxey, S. (2000). *How to help beginning teachers succeed.* Alexandria, VA: Association for Supervision and Curriculum Development.

Graber, K. C. (1995). The influence of teacher education programs on the beliefs of student teachers: General pedagogical knowledge, pedagogical context knowledge, and teacher education coursework. *Journal of Teaching in Physical Education, 14,* 157–178.

Grafton, P. E. (1993). The relationship of selected school organizational variables and beginning teachers' sense of efficacy (teacher efficacy). Doctoral dissertation, Bowling Green State University. *Dissertation Abstracts International*, *54/07A*, AAD93–34553.

Gratch, A. (2001). The culture of teaching and beginning teacher development. *Teacher Education Quarterly, 28*(4), 121–136.

Green, R. L., & Etheridge, C. P. (2001). Collaborating to establish standards and accountability: Lessons learned about systemic change. *Education, 121*(4), 821–829.

Gregorc, A. (1982). *Gregoric Style Delineator.* Columbia, CT: Gregorc Associates, Inc.

Haberman, M. (1995). Selecting "star" teachers for children and youth in urban poverty. *Phi Delta Kappan, 76*(10), 777–781.

Healey, M., & Jenkins, A. (2000). Kolb's experiential learning theory and its application in geography in higher education. *Journal of Geography, 99*(5), 185–195.

Heins, E. D., Tichenor, M. S., Coggins, C. J., & Hutchinson, C. J. (2000). Multiage classrooms: Putting theory into practice. *Contemporary Education, 71*(3), 30–35.

Huebner, D. E. (1996). Teaching as a moral activity. *Journal of Curriculum and Supervision, 11,* 267–275.

Johnson, W. L., Mauzey, E., Johnson, A. M., Murphy, S. D., & Zimmerman, K. J. (2001). A higher order analysis of the factor structure of the Myers-Briggs Type Indicator. *Measurement and Evaluation in Counseling and Development, 35,* 96–108.

Kegan, R. (1994). *In over our heads: The mental demands of modern life.* Cambridge, MA: Howard University Press.

King, P., & Kitchener, K. (1994). *Developing reflective judgement: Understanding and promoting intellectual growth and critical thinking in adolescents and adults.* San Francisco: Jossey-Bass.

Kitsantas, A., & Baylor, A. (2001). The impact of the instructional planning self-reflective tool on preservice teacher performance, disposition, and self-efficacy beliefs regarding systematic instructional planning. *Educational Technology Research and Development, 49*(4), 97–106.

Kohlberg, L., and others (1975). *The just community school: The theory and the Cambridge cluster school experiment.* (ERIC ED 223 511).

Kolb, D. A. (1985). *Learning Style Inventory* (rev.ed.) Boston: McBer.

Kolb, D. A., Rubin, I. M., & McIntyre, J. M. (1984). *Organizational psychology: An experiental approach to organizational behavior.* Englewood Cliffs, NJ: Prentice Hall.

Lampe, J. R. (1994, April). *Teacher education, students' moral development and ethical reasoning processes.* Paper presented at the annual meeting of the American Educational Research Association, New Orleans.

Langer, G. M., & Colton, A. B. (1994). Reflective decision making: The cornerstone of school reform. *Journal of Staff Development, 15*(1), 2–7.

Lasley, T. J. (1992). Promoting teacher reflection. *Journal of Staff Development, 13*(1), 24–29.

Moreira, J. M. (1996). Approaches to teacher professional development: A critical appraisal. *European Journal of Teacher Education, 19*(1), 47–63.

Moss, C. M. (1997, March). *Systematic self-reflection: Professional development for the reflective practitioner.* Paper presented at the annual meeting of the American Educational Research Association, Chicago.

Oser, F. K. (1991). Professional morality: A discourse approach (the case of the teaching profession). In W. M. Kurtines & J. L. Gewirtz (Eds.), *Handbook of moral behavior and development. Volume 2: Research* (pp. 191–228). Hillsdale, NJ: Lawrence Erlbaum.

Phillips, M. D., & Glickman, C. D. (1991). Peer coaching: Developmental approach to enhance teacher thinking. *Journal of Staff Development, 12*(2), 20–25.

Pintrich, P. R. (1990). Implications of psychological research on student learning and college teaching for teacher education. In W. Robert Houston (Ed.), *Handbook of research on teacher education* (pp. 826–857). New York: Macmillan.

Ponticell, J. A., & Zepeda, S. J. (1995, October). *What matters to great teachers: What's not the focus of teacher education and evaluation.* Paper presented at the annual convention of the University Council for Educational Administration, Salt Lake City.

Relich, J. (1996). Gender, self-concept and teachers of mathematics: Effects of attitudes to teaching and learning. *Educational Studies in Mathematics, 30*(2), 179–195.

Ross, J. L., Drysdale, M. T., & Schulz, R. A. (2001). Cognitive learning style and academic performance in two postsecondary computer application courses. *Journal of Research on Computing in Education, 33*(4), 400–412.

Rulon, D. (1992). The just community: A method for staff development. *Journal of Moral Development, 21*(3), 217–224.

Schön, D. A. (1983). *The reflective practitioner: How professionals think in action.* New York: Basic Books.

Shanoski, L. A., & Hranitz, J. R. (1992, February). *Learning from America's best teachers: Building a foundation for accountability through excellence.* Paper presented at the annual meeting of the Association of Teacher Educators, Orlando.

Shulman, L. S. (1987). Knowledge and teaching: Foundations of the new reform. *Harvard Educational Review, 57*(1), 1–22.

Smyth, J. (1989a). A critical pedagogy of classroom practice. *Journal of Curriculum Studies, 21*(6), 483–502.

Smyth, J. (1989b). A research agenda: An alternative vision and an "educative" agenda for supervision as a field of study. *Journal of Curriculum and Supervision, 4*(2), 162–177.

Sprinthall, N. A., Reiman, A. J., & Thies-Sprinthall, L. (1996). Teacher professional development. In J. Sikula (Ed.), *Handbook of research on teacher education* (2nd ed., pp. 666–703). New York: Macmillan.

Steffy, B. E., & Wolfe, M. P. (2001). A life-cycle model for career teachers. *Kappa Delta Pi Record, 38*(1), 16–19.

Thomson, J. R., & Handley, H. M. (1990, November). *Relationship between teacher self-concept and teacher efficacy.* Paper presented at the annual meeting of the Mid-south Educational Research Association, New Orleans.

Tolan, M. (2001). The new kids on the block. *Middle Ground, 5*(1), 10–13.

Walls, R. T., Nardi, A. H., & von Minden, A. M. (2002). The characteristics of effective and ineffective teachers. *Teacher Education Quarterly, 29*(1), 39–48.

Wilson, S. M., & Coolican, M. J. (1996). How high and low self-empowered teachers work with colleagues and school principals. *Journal of Educational Thought, 30*(2), 99–117.

Resources

Boostrom, R. E. (1998). What makes teaching a moral activity? *Educational Forum, 63*(1), 58–64.

Cranton, P. (1996). Strategies for self-directed development. In *Professional development as transformative learning: New perspectives for teachers as adults.* San Francisco: Jossey-Bass.

Dell'Olio, J. M. (1998). Hearing myself: Reflections-in-action in experienced teachers peer-assistance behaviors. *Journal of Curriculum and Supervision, 13*(2), 184–204.

Dunn, R., & Dunn, K. (1999). *The complete guide to the learning style inservice system.* Boston: Allyn and Bacon.

Gordon, S. P., & Maxey, S. (2000). *How to help beginning teachers succeed.* Alexandria, VA: Association for Supervision and Curriculum Development.

Gratch, A. (2001). The culture of teaching and beginning teacher development. *Teacher Education Quarterly, 28*(4), 121–136.

Huebner, D. E. (1996). Teaching as a moral activity. *Journal of Curriculum and Supervision, 11*, 267–275.

McLaughlin, M., Vogt, M. E., Anderson, J. A., DuMez, J., Peter, M. G., & Hunter, A. (1998). *Professional portfolio models: Applications in education.* Norwood, MA: Christopher-Gordon.

Steffy, B. E., & Wolfe, M. P. (2001). A life-cycle model for career teachers. *Kappa Delta Pi Record, 38*(1), 16–19.

Walls, R. T., Nardi, A. H., von Minden, A. M., & Hoffman, N. (2002). The characteristics of effective and ineffective teachers. *Teacher Education Quarterly, 29*(1), 39–48.

Review of Professional Development Model, Part III

Part III discussed four capacity-building functions of professional development: school leader development, improvement of school culture, team development, and individual teacher development. These functions now are included in the evolving professional development model illustrated in Figure III.1 below. In Part IV, Chapter 11 addresses the core function of professional development: the improvement of teaching and learning. Chapter 12, the concluding chapter, presents a comprehensive model for program development.

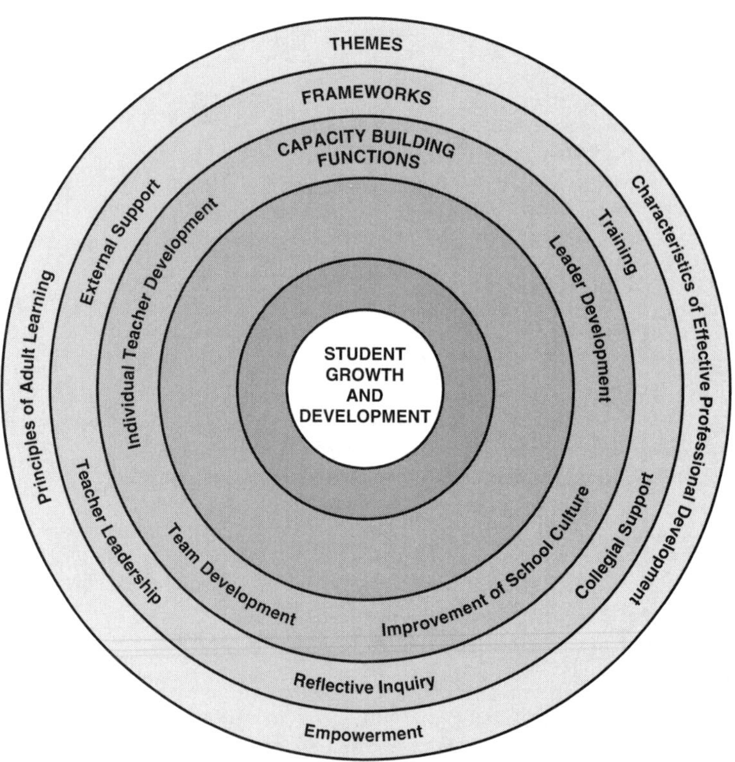

FIGURE III.1 Comprehensive Model: Professional Development for School Improvement

Part IV

Conclusion

11 Core Function of Professional Development

Improvement of Teaching and Learning

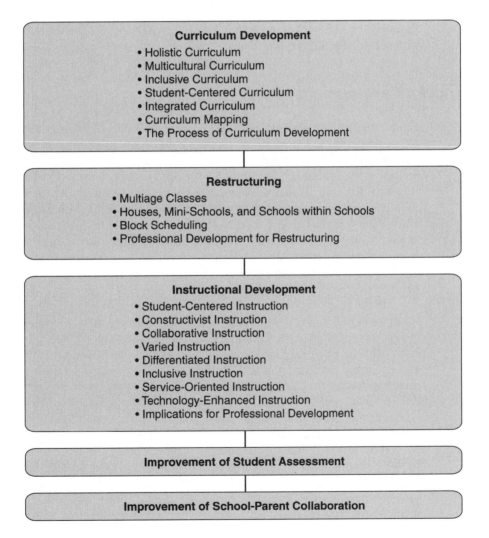

Curriculum Development
- Holistic Curriculum
- Multicultural Curriculum
- Inclusive Curriculum
- Student-Centered Curriculum
- Integrated Curriculum
- Curriculum Mapping
- The Process of Curriculum Development

Restructuring
- Multiage Classes
- Houses, Mini-Schools, and Schools within Schools
- Block Scheduling
- Professional Development for Restructuring

Instructional Development
- Student-Centered Instruction
- Constructivist Instruction
- Collaborative Instruction
- Varied Instruction
- Differentiated Instruction
- Inclusive Instruction
- Service-Oriented Instruction
- Technology-Enhanced Instruction
- Implications for Professional Development

Improvement of Student Assessment

Improvement of School-Parent Collaboration

The improvement of teaching and learning has several dimensions, including curriculum development, restructuring, instructional development, improvement of student assessment, and collaboration with parents. The five dimensions are present in each of the professional development and school improvement programs presented as exemplars in this text. Moreover, in each of the exemplary programs, continuous effort was made to align the dimensions to create coherent improvement programs. Although for the purpose of discussion we will treat these dimensions as separate topics, in successful schools they are treated as different aspects of a unified, synergistic improvement process. The five dimensions represent the core of both professional development and school improvement. It is in the improvement of teaching and learning that the reciprocal nature of professional development and school improvement becomes most apparent. Professional development can foster significant changes in any of the five dimensions, and, in turn, meaningful work across the five dimensions will result in significant professional development.

Curriculm Development

Some years ago I was preparing to teach a graduate course on curriculum design. As part of my preparation, I visited a curriculum consultant at a state agency. The purpose of my visit was to review the state's latest curriculum standards and to see what curriculum resources the agency might have available for use in the course. Early in my conversation with the consultant I was astonished when she declared that there was no reason for me to be teaching a curriculum design course to future educational leaders! The consultant reminded me that state-mandated curricula for each content area were in place. She stated that the task of educational leaders and teachers was to implement the state-mandated curriculum, not design new curriculum. She declared that at the school level, creativity and decision making should be focused not on *what* to teach but on *how* to teach the required curriculum.

In the years since my conversation with the consultant, a growing number of state legislatures have mandated statewide curricula, enforced through high-stakes standardized achievement tests. Students who fail the state tests may not be permitted to graduate. Schools usually are rated based on student test scores, rewarded for high ratings, and penalized for low ratings. Both the consultant I visited several years ago and the state legislatures that have mandated statewide curricula are wrong in their assumption that teachers and other local stakeholders should not design curriculum. Different communities, groups of students, and even individual students have different needs that a one-size-fits-all curriculum simply cannot address.

The nature of most state-mandated curriculum is, in fact, a good argument for increased rather than decreased teacher involvement in curriculum development. The required curriculum usually consists of laundry lists of "basic" facts and skills at the lower end of Bloom's Taxonomy, with no design for connecting those narrowly defined proficiencies into broader, more meaningful learning outcomes. State-mandated proficiencies are usually limited to declarative knowledge (information within a particular discipline) and procedural knowledge (discipline-based skills), with scant attention paid to life-long learning skills that "cut across all disciplines and are applicable to life outside the classroom" (Marzano, Pickering, & McTighe, 1993, p. 15; see also Yeh, 2001; Dounay, 2000). Not only do most state-mandated curricula fail to address higher-level cognitive development but they also pay little attention to the social, moral, physical, or artistic development of students.

If state-mandated curricula are inadequate for meeting the educational needs of students, what are districts and schools to do? They could simply throw in the towel and focus on covering the seemingly endless lists of state proficiencies. They could announce that they will ignore the state standards and develop their own superior curriculum (probably not the wisest political move). Or (the preferable alternative) they could to design a curriculum that meets the state standards but that also:

- Provides for the development of the whole child, including interpersonal, cognitive, moral, social, artistic, and physical development
- Is relevant to and promotes the success of diverse cultures within the school community
- Integrates state proficiencies with each other and with higher-level capacities to create meaningful learning experiences
- Is sufficiently flexible to be adapted to the special needs of individual students
- Prepares students to be life-long learners

Curriculum development is the cornerstone of school improvement, and meaningful curriculum development must involve teachers. It is teachers who are best able to assess students' educational needs, assess the curriculum's strengths and weaknesses, and plan needed change. Teachers who have been involved in curriculum design develop a sense of ownership and thus are far more likely to understand and effectively apply new curriculum. Curriculum development is a natural vehicle for teacher reflection. It can lead to better understanding of one's content area as well as how that content relates to other parts of the curriculum. Involvement in curriculum improvement helps teachers articulate their own educational beliefs and pedagogical practice, and consider possible changes in what and how they teach. Curriculum design is a collaborative venture, and collaboration provides a number of additional benefits. Teachers cooperating in curriculum development can share knowledge, create new knowledge, engage in mutual problem solving, and help each other integrate content (Martin, 1995; Palma, 2001).

What, precisely, should teachers do to improve their school's curriculum? Teachers can work to design a curriculum that is holistic, multicultural, inclusive, student centered, and integrated.

Holistic Curriculum

A quality curriculum addresses the development of the whole person. Caine and Caine (1997) argue that the purpose of education needs to be changed from acquiring knowledge and skills to the "development of more complex and integrated people" (p. 97).

Marzano, Pickering, and McTighe (1993) propose life-long learning standards of complex thinking, information processing, effective communication, cooperation and collaboration, and effective habits of mind (metacognition). These experts are not telling us that students no longer need to learn any knowledge and skills from traditional disciplines, but that such knowledge and skills must be folded into a larger view of the curriculum—a view that calls for the development of the whole student in a way that fosters life-long learning and a society of learners.

In an age of state-mandated curriculum, high-stakes achievement tests, and increasing demands on teachers, it is not surprising that many teachers initially may not be overly excited about developing a holistic curriculum that goes well beyond the scope of state standards. The *Ideal Graduate* is a professional development activity that fosters realization of the need of a more holistic curriculum. In this exercise, teachers are asked to envision their school systems' current kindergartners as high school graduates, over 16 years into the future. What characteristics would the "ideal graduate" possess? After some individual reflection, the teachers are asked to write down the desired characteristics. Teachers then share and discuss the characteristics. In an extension of this activity, teachers take parents and other members of the community through the same exercise. After each teacher has gathered several lists of characteristics, the teachers reconvene to share their lists. Invariably, the composite list goes beyond "basic" content knowledge and skills to include thinking skills, social skills, moral virtues, intrapersonal skills, and all of the characteristics cited in the literature on holistic curriculum.

If the school curriculum is going to address the development of the whole person, teachers must engage in professional and curriculum development in areas such as the following.

Intrapersonal Development. Armstrong (1994) defines *intrapersonal intelligence* as "self-knowledge and the ability to act adaptively on the basis of that knowledge" (p. 3). Intrapersonal growth includes developing self-esteem, learning to understand and manage one's emotions, and developing self-motivation. In a curriculum that fosters intrapersonal growth, students are encouraged to relate course content to their own lives and discuss that relationship. Time and space are provided for self-reflection and self-expression.

Higher-Level Cognitive Development. A curriculum that develops higher-level thinking skills provides opportunities for inquiry, perspective taking, interpreting and synthesizing, and discovering and explaining relationships. A curriculum fostering cognitive development presents opportunities for dealing with uncertainty and contradiction, creating stories about the past and predictions about the future, and constructing novel solutions to complex problems.

Social Development. The need to develop social skills, to work cooperatively with others, and to build community begins in childhood and continues throughout one's life. Communication skills are the heart of social development, and they need to be taught and modeled across the curriculum. Team building, consensus building, and conflict management skills all are essential. A curriculum stressing social skills will include regular opportunities for interpersonal interaction and cooperative learning. Social learning can be extended beyond the classroom through student participation in school and community projects. With the technology now available in most schools, social interaction and community building may even extend to the national and international levels.

Moral Development. Personal honesty, integrity, responsibility, and commitment to equality, freedom, and justice are not measured on high-stakes achievement tests, yet we all desire that young people develop such characteristics. Teachers can develop democratic processes in their classrooms that allow students to examine and resolve moral issues that arise from day-to-day interaction among students and between the teacher and students. A curriculum that adequately addresses moral development will gradually lead students to consider moral issues present within the local community, and eventually to examine moral issues within the larger society.

Physical Development. A holistic curriculum not only includes health and physical education classes but it also connects these to a range of services, including health services, nutrition programs, school-community wellness programs, and school-family support services (Marx & Northrop, 2000). A variety of activities should be provided, including creative movement, sports, recreation, and fitness (Lambert, 2000). Professional and curriculum development should involve teachers in collaboration with school health professionals, community agencies (recreation, social, and health), and parents.

Artistic Development. Schools traditionally have shortchanged education in the visual and performing arts. Since learning in the arts is not tested on state exams, in many districts art budgets have been cut and programs reduced or eliminated. Perhaps the best hope for a revival of art education is a movement toward integrating art with other subjects. When this is done effectively, "art is not an add-on that interrupts the existing curriculum, or an unnecessary frill. Rather, art becomes a potent stimulus for a thoughtful exploration and communication of complex ideas" (Aschbacher, 1996, p. 40).

Multicultural Curriculum

From time to time I have heard individuals declare that they "don't believe in multiculturalism." This is equivalent to saying that they don't believe in reality! Multiple cultures (different races, classes, genders, religions, sexual orientations, and exceptionalities) are already in our schools and our society, for everyone to see. The purpose of a multicultural curriculum is to align curriculum with multicultural reality! One goal of multicultural education is for all students to respect each culture represented in the school community and the larger society. A related goal is to improve communication and interpersonal relationships among members of different cultures. A third goal is to improve achievement of students from victimized cultures by eliminating cultural bias from the curriculum, to provide students with equal opportunity to learn, and to empower students to achieve.

The lofty goals of multicultural education will not be achieved by "Cultural Awareness Days." Discreet units, readings, projects, or even entire courses appended to the existing curriculum also are inadequate. True multicultural education is integrated across the curriculum and throughout the school year. Multicultural education should be part of the formal and informal curriculum at each grade level, for each content area, in each classroom. Eventually, the curriculum must provide opportunities for students to become involved in examining and solving multicultural problems within their school and community. At this social action stage, multicultural education and moral education merge.

Teachers involved in developing a multicultural curriculum first need to become more knowledgeable about different cultures, how curricula across the various content areas can meet the goals of multicultural education, and how the school climate and curriculum are interrelated. Professional and curriculum development for multicultural education can involve a wide range of activities. Teachers can infuse multicultural education throughout the curriculum's scope and sequence. Interdisciplinary units of instruction can be planned. Curriculum materials can be examined to ensure that different cultures are represented and bias eliminated. The curriculum can be connected to existing cultural issues and problems within the school and community.

Inclusive Curriculum

An inclusive curriculum goes beyond allowing students to be part of the "regular school environment" and provides all students with equal opportunities for learning. A school wishing to develop an inclusive curriculum must do away with tracking, segregated classes, and extensive pullout programs. Often, attitudinal changes must precede the development of an inclusive, adaptive curriculum. Professional development activities can help educators place greater value on diversity and the need for special needs students to be fully integrated with the school community. Later, skill development programs can provide teachers with the tools to design and test curriculum that will "personalize education for every student" (Villa & Thousand, 1995, p. 54).

An inclusive curriculum benefits non-English speaking, learning disabled, and physically handicapped students, of course, but its effects go beyond special needs students:

> Inclusion is not just for students with disabilities, but rather for all students, educators, parents, and community members. Experience tells us that as communities and schools embrace the true meaning of inclusion, they will be better equipped to learn about and acquire strategies to change a segregated special education system to an inclusive service delivery system, with meaningful, child-contoured learning. In the process, a society and world intolerant and fearful of difference may change to one that embraces and celebrates its natural diversity. (Falvey, Givner, & Kimm, 1995, p. 10)

Student-Centered Curriculum

Student-centered curriculum means that teachers who are developing curriculum are more concerned with students than with content to be covered, objectives to be written, or curriculum materials to be chosen. Student-centered curriculum is relevant to students' lives and connects students to their local community. One way to design student-centered curriculum is to involve students in curriculum development. Keedy and Drmacich (1994) describe a process for teacher-student collaboration in curriculum development. Teachers and students design "essential questions" to be answered, identify available resources, determine a unit of study for each question, sequence learning activities within each unit, and evaluate the units at the end of the course. All students can participate in curriculum design at some level. At the very least, teachers need to seek student input and adapt the curriculum to students' life experiences and evolving interests.

Integrated Curriculum

How can teachers add all of the content we have discussed to the declarative and procedural knowledge mandated by state legislatures and tested by high-stakes achievement tests? How can teachers add goals for students' higher-level cognitive, social, moral, physical, and artistic development, and then find time to teach all of the resulting content? How can multicultural education and content focused on special student needs be added to an already crowded curriculum? The answer is that it is absolutely impossible to *add on* all of this desired content to the existing curriculum! Only by folding basic competencies into larger, more meaningful learning experiences can educators hope to develop a teachable, learnable curriculum. Research on the human brain reveals that people cannot separate learning into discrete competencies (Caine & Caine, 1997). In the real world, individuals are faced with complex problems that can be solved only through a combination of academic knowledge, complex thinking skills, social skills, and moral principles. It makes sense, then, to integrate the various dimensions of learning within the school curriculum.

To meet state mandates while creating meaningful learning opportunities, several competencies can be integrated within a single theme, problem, or project. For example, Rothman (1996) reports on a staff-development program that assists teachers in integrating national, state, and district standards within essential questions that students investigate as they prepare an integrated product or performance to be presented to teachers and community members.

Although integration can take place within content areas, a high level of integration requires an *interdisciplinary* curriculum, which can be accomplished on a number of levels:

1. *Within a course.* A teacher can teach a course focused on a particular content area with some integration of other content areas. For instance, a social studies teacher might make use of art projects, dance, and music during the study of world cultures.

2. *Coordinated curriculum.* Teachers in different content areas teach related units the same time of year. For example, during the same month a science teacher teaches about space travel, the English language arts class reads and writes stories about space travel, and the math class learns about measurement by solving problems focused on space travel.
3. *Skills across the curriculum.* Examples are writing across the curriculum, thinking skills across the curriculum, technology across the curriculum, and so on.
4. *Interdisciplinary units or courses.* The different content areas remain but teachers collaboratively plan an entire unit or course around a theme or series of themes.
5. *Broad fields.* Related courses are combined. For instance, Eggebrecht and associates (1996) describe a three-semester, double-period course that integrates biology, chemistry, earth and space sciences, and physics into a general science program.
6. *Transdisciplinary curriculum.* In a transdisciplinary curriculum, separate disciplines disappear entirely. The entire curriculum is built around themes, problems, or projects.

The first three levels in the preceding list (within a course, coordinated curriculum, skills across the curriculum) can be viewed as preliminary steps leading to the fourth level and beyond. Once teachers are ready to move to the fourth level, there exists a fairly well-defined process for developing interdisciplinary units (Campbell & Harris, 2001; Erickson, 1998; Jacobs, 1989; Thompson, 2000). The first step is to select a theme. The obvious place to look for a theme is the required curriculum content. Campbell and Harris (2001), however, recommend additional considerations, including current events, the uniqueness of the community, and the experiences and interests of teachers, parents, and students.

The second step in the process is to select concepts to be taught in the unit and to create a *concept web* showing the relationships of these concepts. Jacobs's (1989) concept web for the theme "Flight" is shown in Figure 11.1. Note that this concept web relates the unit theme, content areas to be included in the interdisciplinary unit, and concepts to be addressed in the unit.

Step three involves the preparation of *essential questions*. Questions for the unit on flight illustrated in Figure 11.1 include:

1. What flies?
2. How and why do things fly in nature?
3. What has been the impact of flight on human beings?
4. What is the future of flight? (Jacobs, 1989, p. 59)

Essential questions provide a scope and sequence for the interdisciplinary unit. The questions provide scope by placing parameters on the unit's content. They provide sequence by moving from simple to more complex topics. The fourth phase of the process is to design learning activities for the unit. The last step consists of designing methods for assessing student learning. Assessments should be varied, allowing students to demonstrate what they have learned in a variety of ways and producing a rich documentation of student growth (Campbell & Harris, 2001; Clark & Clark, 2000).

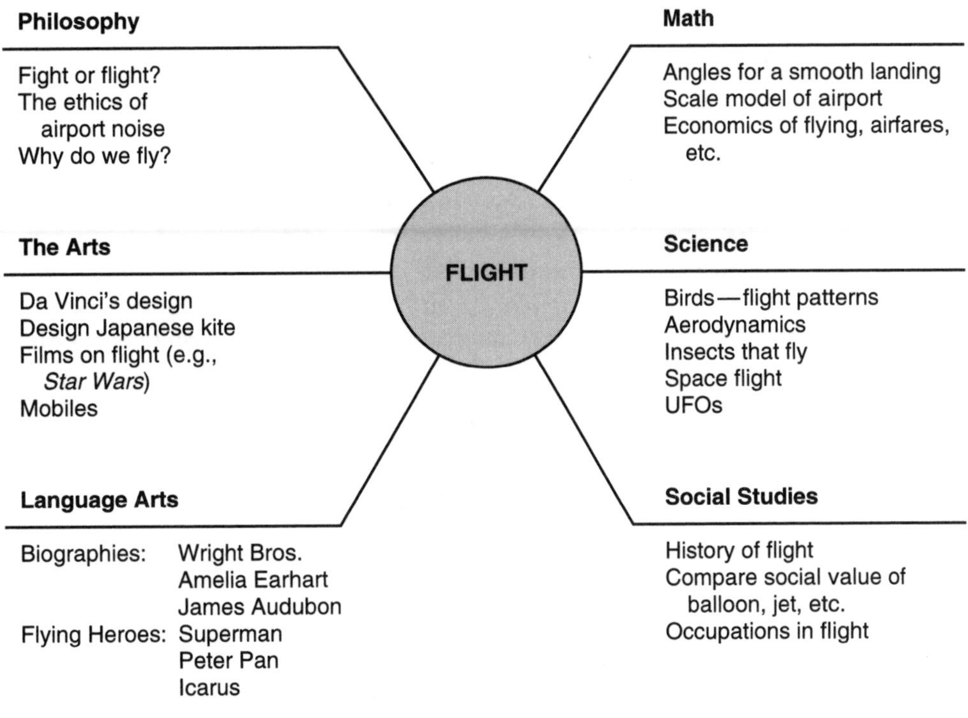

FIGURE 11.1 Concept for Interdisciplinary Unit on Flight

Source: Adapted from Heidi Hayes Jacobs (Ed.), *Interdisciplinary Curriculum: Design and Implementation* (Alexandria, VA: Association for Supervision and Curriculum Development, 1989), p. 57.

Teachers' work toward integrated curriculum is most likely to be successful if it takes an incremental path. Teachers who previously have not participated in developing integrated curriculum could start by getting assistance from colleagues in integrating some simple content from other disciplines into the courses they teach. Next, teachers could begin to coordinate courses, first for one or two units during the school year, and eventually for the entire year. Interdisciplinary teams can begin more comprehensive integration with a few thematic, interdisciplinary units of instruction, and eventually move to integrated curriculum throughout the school year. It is difficult to predict the extent to which traditional disciplines one day will be fused into broad fields or transdisciplinary curriculum, but the current movement toward interdisciplinary curriculum has opened exciting possibilities.

Curriculum Mapping

Curriculum mapping, as conceived by Fenwick English (1980, 1983), consists of experts interviewing and surveying teachers to determine what topics they teach and how much time they spend on each topic. The taught curriculum is then mapped out and compared to the district's written curriculum, state curriculum mandates, or standardized achievement tests. The map is used as a basis for aligning the taught curriculum with the required curriculum. Heidi Hayes Jacobs (1997) has developed a different version of curriculum mapping in which teachers themselves prepare calendar-based maps of the curriculum they teach. The maps are overviews of curriculum content, not detailed reports. Maps are used to identify gaps and repetitions, identify potential areas for integration, match the taught curriculum with curriculum standards, and revise the curriculum (Jacobs, 1997).

In many schools I have visited in recent years, teachers have gone beyond both the English and the Jacobs models of curriculum mapping and have used calendar-based maps to plan an entirely new curriculum. Teachers establish intended student learning outcomes, then map out a scope and sequence of content, including unit topics and time lines for each school year or course. This form of curriculum mapping is especially helpful for planning interdisciplinary curriculum.

The Process of Curriculum Development

The single-most important thing to remember about moving toward a holistic, multicultural, inclusive, student-centered, and integrated curriculum is that it cannot be created overnight (or even over the summer!). Effective curriculum development is a long-term, incremental process. A precursor is developing knowledge and skills for curriculum design. Since curriculum improvement is a collaborative endeavor, developing team skills is essential. An understanding of the change process is necessary.

Some general principles apply to the curriculum development process. One of these is *participation*. Every teacher in the relevant content areas should be involved in the curriculum development process! Students, parents, and other community members need to be involved at some level. This could mean having representatives on curriculum development teams, providing input to the planning process, or giving feedback on draft curriculum products. Another general principle of curriculum development is *communication*. An infrastructure must be set up to provide communication among the curriculum designers, the school administration, the rest of the school, the community, and the central office. A third general principle is *support* (a recurring theme throughout this text). As in other areas of professional development and school improvement, the most important type of support is the provision of *time* to participate in the curriculum development process. Moral, technical, and material support also are important.

Restructuring

Restructuring with a small *r* (as opposed to restructuring the entire educational system) means reorganizing students, teachers, facilities, and time for improved teaching and learning. Although "small *r*" restructuring is more focused than the broader term, it is itself a complex undertaking that cannot be achieved without extensive professional development. In this section we'll discuss three types of restructuring that have been proposed by reformers for years, have had periods of popularity and unpopularity, and now are experiencing a resurgence as part of the current reform movement. These three types of restructuring are multiage classes, schools within schools, and block scheduling.

Multiage Classes

Multiage classes include students from two or more traditional grade levels. The students in such a class are not considered to be in any particular grade. Multiage classes typically stay with the same teacher or teachers for the duration of their stay in the assigned unit. Classes faithful to the multiage concept are not made up exclusively of high needs or gifted students, but rather reflect the diversity of the school's population (Forsten, Grant, & Richardson, 1999). Daniel and Terry (1995) provide a rationale for multiage classes:

> Children develop at different rates, at different times, and in different ways. . . . Our traditional system of education has been very inflexible. Each student has had a set amount of time to "get it" or to fail. The multiage classroom gives students time to develop, to grow, to get it, not unlike the one-room school of the past. (p. 8)

If we wished to visit a multiage classroom to see what was going on, we would have to schedule several visits to get a good understanding of the multiage concept. This is because the organization of a multiage classroom keeps changing. On any given day, students might be receiving whole-group or small-group instruction, working in cooperative groups, engaged in peer tutoring, or involved in individual projects. How students are grouped at any time might depend on the problem to be solved, specific learning needs, student interests, or learning styles (Heins, Tichenor, & Coggins, 2000). Learning usually would be interdisciplinary. Different classes in a learning unit would often be combined, allowing team teaching and team learning. Students would work at their own pace and be assessed on their individual progress.

Multiage classes have resulted in fewer retentions, fewer special education referrals, and improved attendance for students and teachers. Additionally, multiage grouping has reduced disciplinary problems, made for more efficient use of instructional time, and enabled parents to become more involved in their children's education (Fortsen, Grant, & Richardson, 1999; Holloway, 2001). Stone (1998) argues that the cross-age learning that takes place in multiage classes enables cognitive, social and emotional growth.

Houses, Mini-Schools, and Schools within Schools

The expanding size of individual schools across the nation, combined with research indicating that small schools better promote students' academic and affective growth (Raywid, 1995; Wasley, 2002), has generated a movement to create subschools within larger schools. There are different types of subschools, depending on how distinct and autonomous the subschool is.

- *Houses* are groups of teachers and students who remain together for one to several years. The teachers within the house teach the students all of their core courses, with students often leaving the house for "specials," such as physical education and music. Houses can be horizontal (e.g., a middle school might have four houses, each with grades 4 through 6) or vertical (e.g., a ninth-grade house within a high school). Traditional schoolwide academic departments usually remain in schools with houses.
- *Mini-schools* group teachers and students for several years and have developed their own curriculum and instructional program distinct from other mini-schools within the larger school.
- *Schools within schools* have separate administrators, faculties, and budgets, and report to the principal of the larger school regarding schoolwide resources, operations, and safety. Thus, schools within schools are the most autonomous of the three types of subschools.

A variety of positive benefits of subschools have been reported, including better student attendance, improved student behavior, increased satisfaction with school, higher student self-esteem, more student participation, fewer dropouts, and higher academic achievement (Ark, 2002; Dewees, 1999; Raywid, 1995). Positive effects seem to increase with the level of subschool autonomy; schools within schools, the most independent type of subschool, seem to have the most positive effects.

Block Scheduling

Nichols (2000) asks us to "imagine adults going to work each day having to work for seven or more supervisors, in many workplaces, in seven or more areas of expertise" (p. 3). Few adults could be productive workers under such conditions, and yet this is exactly what many junior and high school students must deal with every school day. The traditional seven-period schedule can lead to impersonal teacher-student relationships, create discipline problems, and limit the use of innovative teaching strategies (Nichols, 2000).

An increasingly popular alternative to the traditional seven-period schedule is the block schedule, especially the 4 × 4 block: four courses a semester taught in four 90-minute periods each day. Perhaps the single-most important thing that the block schedule does is provide more *time* for a daily class (Stokes & Wilson, 2000). The increased time can bring with it a number of direct benefits, including more interaction between teachers and students, a greater variety of instructional strategies, more student participation, more opportunities for higher-level thinking, and more in-depth study of important topics. These direct benefits can, in turn, lead to a number of indirect benefits, including better relationships between teachers and students, more positive students, a less stressful environment, more energized teaching, improved student behavior, and higher student achievement (Freeman, Maruyama, Frederickson, & Walkowiak, 1997; Veal & Flinders, 2001).

Even proponents of block scheduling admit that it is no panacea. Rather, block scheduling presents an opportunity for school improvement that can be realized only if a number of supporting factors are in place. These factors include:

- Extensive planning and preparation
- Resources
- Professional development
- Visionary leadership and administrative support
- A positive school culture (McCoy & Taylor, 2000)

Professional development for a successful shift to block scheduling must help teachers to develop "knowledge and skill in authentic, multidimensional instructional strategies, such as cooperative learning, graphic organizers, multiple intelligences and higher order thinking, and in curricular frameworks that use subject matter in meaningful projects and performances" (Nichols, 2000, p. 9).

Exemplar 11.1 describes the transition to block scheduling at Conrad-Weiser Junior-Senior High School in Robesonia, Pennsylvania.

EXEMPLAR 11.1 • *Block Scheduling at Conrad-Weiser Junior-Senior High*

Conrad-Weiser's commitment to professional development was in large part responsible for the decision to move toward block scheduling. Professional development had helped teachers develop a variety of new teaching skills and instructional models, yet teachers realized that the traditional schedule hampered their application of innovative classroom practices. Teachers found that they had too many students and too few minutes per class to properly implement strategies such as interdisciplinary curriculum, cooperative learning, higher-level thinking, and performance-based learning. The school community decided that a block schedule would be more consistent with the innovative practices they were learning.

Training for block scheduling included developing skills for teaching within longer class periods, planning varied learning activities, transitioning from one activity to the next, working with special needs students during longer class periods, and so on. Teams of teachers spent many hours designing lessons appropriate for a block schedule. Teachers were trained in peer coaching as a means of gathering data and providing feedback on innovative teaching strategies for extended lessons. For an entire year, the school's professional development program focused on preparation for the block schedule.

Despite all the hard work in implementing the block schedule, teachers at Conrad-Weiser clearly believe it has been worth the effort. One benefit reported by educators is that the range of students that individual teachers teach each day has been reduced from the 180 to 220 range to 90 to 110. This allows for more teacher interaction with individual students. Block scheduling gives teachers at Conrad-

(continued)

EXEMPLAR 11.1 • Continued

Weiser more planning time and allows them to use better teaching strategies: "All of those great ideas that I had stuck away in my file, now I have time to use," one teacher noted. The new schedule has required traditional teachers to become more creative. As one teacher put it, "You learn that you can't stand in front of a group of kids for 82 minutes and give notes." Students receive more individual assistance from teachers, as well as more peer assistance. Teachers also report that expectations for student achievement have increased.

Block scheduling at Conrad-Weiser also has led to interdisciplinary curriculum. Learning is now performance based, and often takes the form of community service and student projects. One teacher noted, "Instead of doing the project to show they have learned, students do the project *in order to learn.*"

Teachers at Conrad-Weiser offered several tips to make block scheduling successful. A team approach is necessary. This means that administrators must be willing to share power with teachers, and teachers must be willing to share power with students. Extensive planning is necessary, and teachers need to be part of the planning process from the very beginning. Teachers should be encouraged to take risks: "You're willing to be a risk-taker if you're not going to get nailed if you come up short." Finally, ongoing administrative support is necessary, including support for extensive professional development.

Professional Development for Restructuring

Professional development is a critical aspect of all types of restructuring. Most restructuring efforts (including multiage grouping, subschools, and block scheduling) can follow one of a variety of models, and professional development includes research and dialogue about which model is best for the school, and how particular models can be adapted to meet local needs. Restructuring initially can take the form of action research that tests out the desired change and indicates needed revisions. Restructuring directly linked to the improvement of teaching and learning nearly always involves the development of new instructional and student assessment strategies. Training programs help teachers develop new skills, collegial support assists teachers as they transfer new skills to the classroom, and reflective inquiry enables teachers to assess progress and revise restructuring efforts. Teacher leadership as well as external support from those experienced in restructuring both are essential. The types of restructuring discussed in this section cannot be completed overnight. From one to two years of planning are necessary before initial implementation, and it may take several additional years for new structures such as multiage classrooms, subschools, or block schedules to be functioning smoothly.

Instructional Development

Keeping in mind that curriculum and instruction are interdependent concepts, a general distinction between the two is that *curriculum* is "what" gets taught and *instruction* is "how" it gets taught. Instructional development, then, is an extension of curriculum development. This section will describe the characteristics of quality instruction as well as implications for professional development programs. When we combine expert teachers like those described in Chapter 10 with high-level curriculum as described in this chapter, the result is quality instruction. Quality instruction is student centered, constructivist, collaborative, varied, differentiated, service oriented, inclusive, and technology enhanced. Professional development that leads to quality instruction mirrors what goes on in successful classrooms. As we consider the characteristics of quality instruction, keep in mind that they are not totally discrete concepts. Rather, they are overlapping, interactive aspects of a complex instructional process.

Student-Centered Instruction

Student-centered instruction actualizes the student-centered curriculum discussed earlier. Paris and Combs (2000) describe five elements of learner-centered instruction. The first element is a focus on the learner's interest and experiences. Another element is that the teacher guides and facilitates learning—the teacher monitors from "backstage," ready to provide assistance when necessary. Promoting active engagement is the third element. Actively engaged students are "excited, active participants in their own learning" (Paris & Combs, 2000, p. 12). The fourth element is the teacher as reflective learner. The final element is the promotion of learner ownership and responsibility by involving students in making decisions about how they will learn.

What does a student-centered classroom look like? Kohn (1996) describes the student-centered classroom in sharp contrast to a traditional classroom. In the learner-centered classroom, the walls are covered with examples of student work, collaboration, and decisions. Students are sitting around tables or in comfortable work areas. They speak directly to each other and often initiate questions for the teacher or other students. Often, different learning activities are occurring simultaneously. Classroom meetings are held on a regular basis to decide learning activities, solve problems, and resolve conflict. Thus, student-centered classrooms are democratic learning communities (Evans, 1996; Kira, 1997; Landau & Gathercoal, 2000; Schneider, 1996).

Constructivist Instruction

Constructivism holds that persons create new knowledge through the interaction of existing knowledge, beliefs, or values with new ideas or experiences. Learning takes place as a result of the learner resolving cognitive conflict caused by encountering an idea or experience that contradicts the learners' previous conception of reality. Many constructivists also maintain that the individual cannot create new knowledge alone, but learns only through interaction with his or her social context.

In the constructivist classroom, the teacher and students together choose complex problems relevant to the students. Through open discussion, the teacher seeks to understand the students' prior understanding of the problem under consideration. As students engage in a problem-solving process, assumptions are challenged, cognitive conflict emerges, solutions are tested, and the conflict eventually is resolved. After the problem has been solved, students reflect together on both the solution and the problem-solving process. The teacher's assessment of student learning includes analysis of both students' solutions and the process by which they develop solutions. Put differently, the teachers seek to understand how students have constructed meaning from the learning experience.

Collaborative Instruction

Collaborative instruction means that knowledge, authority, teaching, and learning are shared by teachers and students, and among students. In collaborative instruction, students are involved in diagnosing their learning needs, setting learning goals, planning instructional units and lessons, peer teaching, co-learning, and assessing instruction. Students must be prepared to participate successfully in collaborative instruction. An essential part of that preparation is trust building. Learning social skills and group processing skills also is necessary. Some direct teaching of collaborative skills is required, but the teacher prepares students for collaborative instruction primarily through structuring collaborative lessons, modeling, and facilitating. Collaborative lessons can be structured through such techniques as physically setting up the rooms for optimal interaction, forming appropriate groups, assigning group roles, establishing positive interdependence, and providing time and techniques for students to process their learning.

Varied Instruction

Quality instruction includes the use of a variety of instructional strategies. Although some use of traditional strategies such as direct instruction is appropriate, teachers should make greater use of strategies more consistent with student-centered, constructivist, collaborative instruction. Some examples are cooperative learning, problem-based learning, role playing, and project-based learning. (For extensive reviews of the variety of instructional strategies available to teachers, see Fogarty, 1997; Gunter, Thomas, & Schwab, 1998; Harris, 2000; Joyce, Weil, & Calhoun, 1999.) Possessing an extensive repertoire of instructional strategies is essential but not sufficient for the successful use of varied strategies. Different strategies must be combined expertly within the same unit of instruction or even the same lesson. The idea of "mixing and matching" instructional strategies leads us to a discussion of differentiated instruction.

Differentiated Instruction

Differentiated instruction means using different instructional environments, strategies, and activities in the lesson. One purpose of differentiated instruction is to address different learning styles within the same group of students. The Learning Style Inventory

(Dunn, Dunn, & Price, 1996) is an instrument designed to measure the preferred learning styles of students in grades 3 through 12 across four types of stimuli: environmental, sociological, emotional, and physical. (The Productivity Environmental Preference Survey discussed in Chapter 10 is the "adult version" of the LSI.) Classroom use of LSI results usually involves creating different classroom conditions. For example, quiet areas for some students and music headsets for others, brightly and dimly lit areas of the classroom, a formal learning environment (desks or tables and chairs) for some and informal environment (carpets, bean bags, easy chairs) for others, and so on (Braio, Beasley, Dunn, Quinn, & Buchanan, 1997).

Bernice McCarthy's (1997) 4 MAT is an instructional model based on Kolb's learning style model (presented in Chapter 10) and brain hemisphericity. The 4 MAT model includes four learning styles or types. Type 1 learners perceive information concretely and process it reflectively. They prefer to learn by "talking about experiences, listening and watching quietly, then responding to others and discussing ideas" (p. 46). Type 2 learners perceive information abstractly and process it reflectively. They learn best "through lectures and objective explanations, by working independently and systematically, and by reading and exchanging ideas" (p. 47). Type 3 learners perceive abstractly and process actively. Their learning preferences are "active problem solving step-by-step procedures; touching, manipulating, and construction" (p. 48). Type 4 learners perceive concretely and process actively. They learn best through "self-discovery, talking, convincing others, looking for creative solutions to problems, and engaging in free flights of ideas" (p. 48). The 4 MAT model calls for learners to complete a learning cycle in which they utilize each of the four learning styles in sequence (experiencing, conceptualizing, applying, and creating). Additionally, McCarthy recommends both left- and right-brain learning activities in each stage of the cycle.

Both LSI- and 4 MAT-based instruction have been used for years in U.S. classrooms and remain popular among PK–12 educators. Currently, however, Howard Gardner's (1999) multiple intelligences (MI) is the differentiated instruction model that is receiving the most attention. Gardener's eight intelligences are verbal-linguistic, logical-mathematical, visual-spatial, musical-rhythmic, bodily-kinesthetic, interpersonal, intrapersonal, and naturalistic. Gardner holds that each person possesses all eight intelligences, but that each individual is more highly developed in some intelligences than others. Since solving real-life problems usually requires using several intelligences in combination, education should help students to develop adequate competency in each intelligence. Figure 11.2 includes differentiated strategies and activities used by teachers to support multiple intelligences in an action research project described by Goodnough (2000).

Inclusive Instruction

The discussion of inclusive curriculum earlier in this chapter called for doing away with tracking, segregated classrooms, and extensive pullout programs, and instead providing all students with equal opportunities for learning. Let's assume that a school has committed to including as many students as possible in its regular educational program. How does this commitment play out in daily classroom instruction? First, it's important

FIGURE 11.2 ***Strategies and Activities to Support Multiple Intelligences***

Verbal-Linguistic	*Logical-Mathematical*	*Visual-Spatial*	*Musical-Rhythmic*
Lecturing Reading and writing activities (reports, summaries, poems, skits) Debating (science-society-technology issues) Presenting projects (students) Discussing (small group and whole group) Brainstorming Learning new vocabulary Questioning (teacher-led)	Critiquing news articles Sequencing events Comparing and contrasting Testing hypotheses Observing Collecting data Analyzing data Graphing data Categorizing Performing calculations Using inductive and deductive reasoning	Creating mind maps (individual and small groups) Viewing videos Creating collages and posters Demonstrating (teacher) Creating Venn diagrams Using overhead transparencies (teacher) Engaging in guided visualization Making models Using computer software	Writing songs, raps, or jingles Listening to background music Changing the words to a song (teacher includes facts about a scientific concept)
Bodily-Kinesthetic	***Interpersonal***	***Intrapersonal***	***Naturalist***
Experimenting Inventing Playing games Using activity centers Performing a skit Role playing (behavior of molecules in solids, liquids, and gases) Manipulating equipment	Using think-pair-share Working on projects in pairs and small groups Planning as teams for a debate Discussing with a partner Giving feedback Assuming different roles in completing a collaborative task Doing group presentations	Engaging in guided visualization Recording personal reflections based on MI theory Organizing portfolios Selecting assessment projects (students) Taking positions based on STS issues Reading silently Writing about learning Describing feelings about a topics or situation	Observing (planets, stars, and space) Classifying and categorizing Using graphic organizers Going to an environmental center

Source: From Karen Goodnough, *Using Multiple Intelligences to Create a More Meaningful Science Curriculum: An Action Research Approach* (pp. 14–15). Paper presented at the annual meeting of the American Educational Research Association, New Orleans, April 2000. Used by permission of the author.

that teachers have high expectations of all students, including students at risk. Second, it's critical that teachers treat all students in an equitable manner. Inclusive instruction often takes the form of co-teaching by regular and special educators. Effective co-teaching involves high levels of communication, relationship building, and sharing of experiences by the teaching partners (Monroe-Baillargeon, 1999; Whitbread, 1999). In fully inclusive classrooms, the traditional norm of the regular classroom teacher providing general instruction and the special educator assisting only special education students has been replaced by *the norm of giving and receiving assistance*—any member of the classroom community is expected to provide and receive assistance from any other member (Arguelles, Hughes, & Schumm, 2000; Federico, Herrold, & Venn, 2000; Pugach & Wesson, 1995; Whitbread, 1999).

At times it is necessary to adapt instruction to meet special learning needs. The challenge is to adapt instruction without lowering the quality of learning. Deschenes, Ebeling, and Sprague (1994) recommend alternative adaptations, including reducing the size of the task, increasing the time allotted, increasing support, changing instructional delivery, decreasing difficulty, adapting the level of student participation, and modifying learning goals. Palmer, Stough, Holbein, and Gesek (1997) found that effective teachers working with students with special needs used a combination of content knowledge and knowledge of the student to diagnose the student's learning difficulty, then made an instructional adaptation intended to assist the student. The teachers closely monitored the effect of the adaptation and, when necessary, rediagnosed the learning difficulty and applied a new adaptation.

Service-Oriented Instruction

Service learning is a way for students to extend their growth and development by applying what they have learned in school to the real world (Alvarado, 1997). In service learning, not only the local community but the entire world becomes a "classroom under construction" (Des Marais, Yang, & Farzanehkia, 2000, p. 680). Toole (2000) distinguishes service learning from a traditional community service project:

> While the prototypical school "community service" project is a competition between classes about who can collect the most canned foods during the holidays, service-learning would deepen and transform the meaning and outcome of the same project. Students might conduct a critical analysis of the local causes of hunger and homelessness, apply nutritional and cultural knowledge to the foods that they select, and educate the community through multiple media about the results of their investigation. (pp. 7–8)

The National Service-Learning Cooperative (1998) has identified "essential elements" of effective service learning. These elements include the application of academic learning, student growth, tasks that meet school or community needs, value for diversity, interaction and collaboration with the community, and critical student reflection before, during, and after the service project.

Technology-Enhanced Instruction

In quality instruction, technology is not a substitute for teachers, but rather "a means of enhancing and transforming their instructional practices" (Mayer-Smith, Pedretti, & Woodrow, 1997, p. 5). In effective instruction, "student use of learning techniques is woven integrally into the patterns of teaching" (Pisapia, 1994, p. 3). Technology can be integrated with and enhance a variety of instructional foci, including higher-level thinking, multiple intelligences, thematic instruction, cooperative learning, and project-based learning (Burton & Prest, 1997; Seline, 2001).

Quality instruction has moved well beyond using computers for skill drill or as a reward for students finishing their work or being well behaved. Technology can immerse students in virtual reality experiences, enabling them to better learn complex scientific concepts like motion, molecular structures, electricity, and space (Dede, Salzman, Loftin, & Sprague, 1997). Students can take electronic field trips around the world, communicating with experts in various fields, visiting the world's great museums and libraries, and gathering real-time data from archeological sites, ecosystems, and human relief efforts around the globe.

Closer to home, teachers can set up webpages for their classes, placing class materials and assignments online, and providing chat rooms and forums for discussions of course topics and projects. Electronic mentors can use the Web to communicate with student mentees, and parents can use the Web to keep abreast of class activities and their children's progress. Finally, students can develop their own webpages to share biographic information, display their favorite academic or artistic work, and communicate with other students in their local communities and around the world.

Technology tends to evolve over time. Initially, technology may be limited to keyboarding and skill drill. In time, students begin to compose on computers and some individual activities beyond drill are assigned. Gradually, teachers will begin to experiment with interdisciplinary projects, team teaching, and student grouping. At its highest stage of evolution, technology will be fully integrated with the curriculum, there will be a balance of direct teaching and project-based teaching, and technology will be integrated with alternative methods of student assessment (Sandholtz, Ringstaff, & Dwyer, 1997; Smith, 2001).

Implications for Professional Development

All of the professional development frameworks described in Part II, often used in combination, can assist instructional development. *How* the frameworks are used to promote improved instruction is critical to whether improvement efforts succeed. The characteristics of quality instruction we've reviewed have important implications for how professional development for instructional improvement should be delivered. An overarching theme is that professional development should mirror the quality instruction that it seeks to foster. This means that professional development should be teacher centered, constructivist, collaborative, varied, differentiated, inclusive, service oriented, and technology enhanced.

Improvement of Student Assessment

Critics argue that most statewide, high-stakes tests lead to restricted curriculum, poorer instruction, and narrowed student learning (Kohn, 2001; Popham, 2001; Thompson, 2001). In studies that my colleagues and I have conducted, teachers tend to agree with these critics (Gordon & Reese, 1997; Reese & Gordon, 1999). As long as high-stakes testing is in place, teachers have an obligation to prepare students for the test. If the critics of high-stakes testing are correct (and I believe they are), educators also have an obligation to educate parents, the general public, and policymakers about the negative effects of high-stakes testing with an eye toward either improving or eliminating such tests. At the same time, and in the meantime, educators need to do everything they can to make sure that high-stakes testing does not deter them from providing students with a quality education. Regardless of one's position on the value of high-stakes testing, we can all agree that additional, contextual types of student assessment are necessary, and that educators need to work at continuously improving local assessment.

The enhancement of traditional teacher-made tests is one way to improve student assessment at the classroom level. Professional development programs can help teachers learn how to write higher-order test items, construct clear test items that accurately measure student learning, and modify tests for at-risk learners. Teachers also can learn how to better analyze test results to diagnose students' learning needs and to improve instruction.

Traditional teacher-made tests have their place in student assessment, but will always have their limitations because of their measurement of isolated learning and their focus on recognition and recall (Dorfman, 1997; Josephsen, 2000). Authentic assessment is an alternative to traditional testing. "In authentic assessment, a student demonstrates an ability to apply a desired behavior in a real life context and is evaluated on the basis of that performance" (Wooster, 1993, p. 48). Although some experts make distinctions between authentic assessment, performance assessment, and alternative assessment—across the literature these terms are used interchangeably. Authentic performance tasks usually require students to display higher-level cognition and integrate different types of knowledge and skills as they solve real-world problems. Assessment of student performance is based on established criteria that the student is aware of in advance. Students usually are involved in the design of performance tasks, the establishment of performance criteria, and the assessment of their own performance.

One general argument in favor of using authentic assessment is that it provides a more valid assessment of the holistic learning argued for in this chapter. Since authentic assessment requires the integration and application of skills necessary to solve complex problems, successful performance provides better evidence of the ability of students to be successful in real-life situations. Authentic assessment usually gives students opportunities to explain their performance, thus it provides teachers with a deeper understanding of students' learning processes. Another broad rationale for using authentic assessment is the interaction and reciprocity of good teaching and authentic assessment. Since authentic assessment involves students in decisions about their own assessment and is integrated with active learning, students become more motivated to learn. Because authentic assessment provides students with clear criteria in advance of the learning performance task, they are more likely to understand learning expectations. Authentic assessment allows the teacher to assess student learning while the student is engaged in learning, and to provide immediate feedback and assistance. Finally, since authentic assessment includes student self-assessment through reflection on the learning process, it promotes metacognition.

At the heart of authentic assessment is the performance task. First and foremost, performance tasks should be aligned directly with curriculum objectives. Interdisciplinary curriculum requires interdisciplinary assessment tasks. Performance tasks should include several different types of learning, with basic knowledge and skills enveloped within higher-level knowledge and skills. The task should allow students to demonstrate growth and development. It should culminate with a product or performance. Over time, a variety of different performance tasks should be required

There are various techniques for analyzing performance tasks. Outcomes can be measured by analyzing student projects, presentations, artistic creations, performances, exhibitions, interviews, conferences, or student-made videos. Rubrics are instruments that assist the assessment of performance tasks. Rubrics can be used to assess the learning process, student products, and student progress over time. All rubrics include "(1) a list of criteria, or 'what counts' in a project or assignment, and (2) gradations of quality, with descriptions of strong, middling, and problematic student work" (Andrade, 2000). Rubrics can be designed and utilized by teachers, peers assessing a student's work, or a student assessing his or her own work. Often, teachers and students collaboratively design rubrics. Figure 11.3 provides an example of a rubric for student self-assessment of performance on a persuasive essay. Rubrics serve as aids for instruction as well as assessment. A well-designed rubric serves as an advanced organizer for learning, helping the students to understand what is expected of them (Andrade, 2000; Pate, Homestead, & McGinnis, 1993). During the learning process, the rubric provides ongoing guidance for students as they work toward meeting the rubric's various criteria (Standford & Siders, 2001).

In authentic assessment, student products usually are gathered and displayed in portfolios, which are "purposeful collections of children's work that illustrate their efforts, progress, and achievements" (Dorfman, 1997, p. 13). Some schools have different types of student portfolios, such as working portfolios (works in progress), showcase portfolios (the student's best work), and assessment portfolios (proofs of learning) (Danielson & Abrutyn, 1997). In other schools, these different types of work are integrated within a single portfolio. A portfolio might contain student work at various stages of development, final products, feedback from teachers and peers, student reflections on his or her work, and plans for the future. Students are involved in the organization of the portfolios, the selection of content, and the overall portfolio assessment. Portfolios have a variety of uses. They provide a vehicle for the discussion of learning among students, teachers, and parents. Portfolios assist students in reflecting on their learning and in demonstrating their learning to others. They help students set long-term learning goals and they document student growth over time (Burke, 1998; Stix, 2000).

FIGURE 11.3 ***Instructional Rubric for a Persuasive Essay***

Gradations of Quality ←→

Criteria	*4*	*3*	*2*	*1*
The claim	I make a claim and explain why it is controversial.	I make a claim but don't explain why it is controversial.	My claim is buried, confused, and/or unclear.	I don't say what my argument or claim is.
Reasons in support of the claim	I give clear and accurate reasons in support of my claim.	I give reasons in support of my claim, but I overlook important reasons.	I give 1 or 2 weak reasons that don't support my claim and/or irrelevant or confusing sentences.	I don't give reasons in support of my claim.
Reasons against the claim	I discuss the reasons against my claim and explain why it is valid anyway.	I discuss the reasons against my claim but neglect some or don't explain why the claim still stands.	I say that there are reasons against the claim, but I don't discuss them.	I don't acknowledge or discuss the reasons against the claim.
Organization	My writing has a compelling opening, an informative middle, and a satisfying conclusion.	My writing has a beginning, a middle, and an end.	My organization is rough but workable. I may sometimes get off topic.	My writing is aimless and disorganized.
Voice and tone	It sounds like I care about my argument. I tell how I think and feel about it.	My tone is OK, but my paper could have been written by anyone. I need to tell how I think and feel.	My writing is bland or pretentious. There is either no hint of a real person in it, or it sounds like I'm faking it.	My writing is too formal or informal. It sounds like I don't like the topic of the essay.
Word choice	The words that I use are striking but natural, varied, and vivid.	I make some fine and some routine word choices.	The words that I use are often dull or uninspired or sound like I'm trying too hard to impress.	I use the same words over and over. Some words may be confusing.
Sentence fluency	My sentences are clear, complete, and varying lengths.	I have well-constructed sentences. My essay marches along but doesn't dance.	My sentences are often awkward, run-ons, or fragments.	Many run-on sentences and sentence fragments make my essay hard to read.
Conventions	I use correct grammar, punctuation, and spelling.	I have a few errors to fix, but generally use correct conventions.	I have enough errors in my essay to distract a reader.	Numerous errors make my paper hard to read.

Source: H. G. Andrade, "Using Rubrics to Promote Thinking and Learning." *Educational Leadership*, 57(5) (2000): 17. Reprinted with permission of the Association for Supervision and Curriculum Development.

Professional development on authentic assessment is essential for teachers inexperienced in its use. Teachers can work together to improve validity and reliability of authentic assessments by creating and trying out performance tasks and rubrics, rating the same student work separately, then comparing and discussing their ratings. Through dialogue, revision, and practice, they can become better and better at creating performance tasks that measure intended learning and at inter-rater reliability in scoring student performance. Experimenting, sharing, practicing, and reflecting all are critical elements in professional development for improving authentic assessment.

The professional fruits of using and improving authentic assessment are many. The use of authentic assessment helps teachers better understand how students think and learn. Successful implementation of authentic assessment brings with it improved teacher collegiality and collaboration, and increases teacher inquiry and reflection. The broad use of assessment strategies typical of authentic assessment naturally leads to a broader range of instructional strategies, and improves the quality and clarity of learning activities. With well-designed authentic assessment, quality teaching, learning, and assessment merge.

Improvement of School-Parent Collaboration

Joyce Epstein, in her classic typology, has described six types of school-family involvement that can have a positive impact on student learning. These include parenting, communicating, volunteering, learning at home, decision making (sharing in school governance), and collaborating with the community (Epstein, Coates, Salinas, Sanders, & Simon, 1997). Advocates of parent empowerment note that certain types of involvement are more empowering than others. For example, Epstein's fifth type of involvement, decision making, is often described as more empowering than the other categories in her typology. Henry (1996) contrasts "emerging" types of involvement, such as parent advisory councils and parent membership on school committees, with more traditional types of involvement. Olmstead (1991) found that the most successful types of parent involvement were those that empowered parents, including parents as advocates, parents as decision makers, and parents as teachers.

Parent involvement in their children's education has been shown to improve student academic achievement, attitudes toward school, discipline, attendance, and self-efficacy. Additionally, parent involvement leads to positive changes to curriculum and better information exchange between home and school (Lopez & Scribner, 1999; Nichols-Soloman, 2001). Despite the positive effects of parent involvement, a number of barriers to involvement exist. School barriers include the bureaucratic nature of schools, educators' lack of knowledge about how to involve parents, educators' fear that parent involvement will threaten their role of expert, and the perception that fostering parent involvement would take too much time and effort (Baker, 2000; Lopez & Scribner, 1999). Home barriers include a lack of time due to parent work schedules or single parenting responsibilities, parents' perception that it is not part of their role to become involved, past negative experiences with schools, feelings of inadequacy, and a lack of transportation (Black, 1993; Dwyer & Hecht, 1992; Hargreaves, 2001; Lopez & Scribner, 1999).

There are a number of ways to break down the barriers to school-parent collaboration. Educators need to acknowledge that both school and home are necessary for successful student learning, and commit to collaborative relationships with parents. This means nothing less than accepting parents as equal partners in the educational process. Educators need to develop a positive view of parent participation, an understanding of the diverse cultures within the community, and an appreciation of family needs and potential contributions. Communication is a key for successful school-parent collaboration. For effective communication, teachers need to make themselves accessible to parents, and communicate in language that parents understand (i.e., jargon free). Open, honest, and supportive communication can lead to more positive relationships. School-parent collaboration also requires a school environment that is more inviting to parents. The school should not be seen as educators' turf, but rather as the center of the community. Parents need to be invited not just to visit schools and classrooms, but to participate in school governance, curriculum development, restructuring, instructional improvement, and student assessment.

The most powerful professional development for improved school-parent collaboration involves educators and parents learning together. One example of a mutual activity is the family visit. Family visits typically consist of teachers visiting parents in their homes or some other nonschool location and interviewing them about family make-up and routines, parent values and goals, and student interests, needs, and learning styles. Collaborative professional development also can take the form of teacher-parent action research. Teachers and parents define a problem they want to investigate and solve, discuss jargon-free readings on the topic, gather data on the problem, and design action plans aimed at solving the problem.

An umbrella structure for supporting school-parent collaboration is the parent center, housed in a specific location on the school campus. Lawson and Briar-Lawson (1997) note that when a parent center is established, "parents and other adult community residents are no longer tourists; they have identifiable, permanent responsibilities" (p. 17). Parent centers should be planned, developed, and managed by parents with assistance from educators. Centers can train parent liaisons to provide outreach to parents and the community. They can set up task forces that include parents and educators to address school-family or school-community problems. Centers can provide training on parenting skills, seminars, and support groups. They can be locations for community and cultural celebrations. Parent centers can send parents into the school to assist with teaching and learning, or they can host student programs and projects. In short, parent centers can become the hub of school-parent collaboration.

This chapter closes with Inset 11.1, a needs assessment for professional development to improve teaching and learning.

INSET 11.1 • *Improvement of Teaching and Learning Needs Assessment*

Directions: For each item select the response that most nearly reflects the need for professional development in the designated area. Possible responses are

A. No need for assistance in this area

B. Little need for assistance in this area

C. Moderate need for assistance in this area

D. Great need for assistance in this area

E. Very great need for assistance in this area

Developing a curriculum that addresses . . .

1. Students' intrapersonal development
2. Students' higher-level cognitive development
3. Students' social development
4. Students' moral development
5. Students' physical development
6. Students' artistic development
7. Multicultural education
8. Student inclusion
9. The need for student-centered content
10. The need for integrated content

Restructuring . . .

11. How students and teachers are grouped
12. How the school as a whole is organized
13. The school schedule

Instruction that . . .

14. Is student-centered
15. Is constructivist
16. Is collaborative
17. Uses a variety of instructional strategies
18. Addresses different student learning styles
19. Is adapted for special needs students

20. Provides opportunities for students to engage in service for others and the community
21. Makes effective use of technology

Student assessment in the area of . . .

22. Using the standardized achievement test results to improve teaching and learning
23. Improving teacher-made tests
24. Creating authentic performance tasks
25. Creating rubrics for assessing authentic performance tasks
26. Developing student portfolios

Improving school-parent collaboration through . . .

27. Parenting programs
28. Improved school-parent communication
29. Parent volunteer programs
30. Parent assistance with home learning activities
31. Involving parents in decision-making
32. Creating a parent center at school

Summary

This chapter discussed five interrelated aspects of the improvement of teaching and learning: curriculum development, restructuring, instructional development, improvement of student assessment, and improvement of school-parent collaboration. Professional development should assist educators in developing a curriculum that is holistic, multicultural, inclusive, student centered, and integrated. Examples of "small *r*" restructuring include multiage classes, subschools, and block schedules. Professional development can assist teachers in providing instruction that is student centered, constructivist, collaborative, varied, differentiated, inclusive, service oriented, and technology enhanced. Assessment of student learning can be enhanced by the improvement of traditional tests; however, authentic assessment seems to hold much more promise for improving teaching and learning. Professional development can assist teachers with the improvement of either traditional or authentic assessment. Finally, professional development can improve school-parent collaboration through developing knowledge, skills, and dispositions of educators and parents, and by providing educators and parents opportunities for dialog and joint action.

Assignments

1. Reflect on a curriculum with which you are familiar. On a scale of 1 to 10 (with 1 low and 10 high), to what extent is the curriculum (a) holistic, (b) multicultural, (c) inclusive, (d) student centered, and (e) integrated? Write a paper discussing your five ratings. In your paper, provide specific examples in the curriculum that support each rating.
2. Map what you actually teach from week to week in a particular course. Write a paper comparing your map to the school's formal course description. In your paper, discuss the reasons for any differences between the course description and what you actually teach.
3. Read at least three research studies on one of the examples of restructuring discussed in this chapter. Write a paper in which you review and compare the studies. Include in your paper a discussion of implications for professional development.
4. This chapter describes eight characteristics of quality instruction. Design a plan to increase the presence of one of the characteristics in your own teaching. Implement the plan over a period of several days. Write a paper in which you review the improvement plan, describe the plan's implementation, and assess your level of success.
5. Try out a type of authentic assessment that you have not used previously in your teaching. The assessment should include a performance task for students to complete as well as a rubric for measuring student performance. Write a paper in which you describe the purpose of the authentic assessment, the performance task, and how effective you believe your assessment worked. Attach a copy of the rubric to your paper.
6. Visit a parent center located within a school. Discuss the center's purpose, organization, and activities with staff, teachers, the principal, and students. Write a paper in which you describe the center and its effects on school-parent collaboration.

References

Alvarado, V. (1997). *Service-learning, an effective teaching strategy for Texas middle schools*. (ERIC ED 409 593).

Andrade, H. G. (2000). Using rubrics to promote thinking and learning. *Educational Leadership, 57*(5), 13–18.

Arguelles, M. E., Hughes, M. T., & Schumm, J. S. (2000). Co-teaching: A different approach to inclusion. *Principal, 79*(4), 48–51.

Ark, T. V. (2002). The case for small high schools. *Educational Leadership, 59*(5), 55–59.

Armstrong, T. (1994). *Multiple intelligences in the classroom*. Alexandria, VA: Association for Supervision and Curriculum Development.

Aschbacher, P. (1996). A flare for the arts. *Educational Leadership, 53*(8), 40–43.

Baker, A. J. (2000). Making the promise of parent involvement a reality. *High School Magazine, 7*(5), 14–17.

Black, S. (1993). The parent factor. *Executive Educator, 15*(4), 29–31.

Braio, A., Beasley, T. M., Dunn, R., Quinn, P., & Buchanan, K. (1997). Incremental implementation for learning style strategies among urban low achievers. *Journal of Educational Research, 91*(1), 15–25.

Burke, K. (1998). *How to assess authentic learning* (3rd ed.). Arlington Heights, IL: IRI/Skylight.

Burton, L. D., & Prest, S. (1997, March). *Connecting effective instruction and technology. Intel-elebration. Safari.* Paper presented at the annual conference of the Association for Supervision and Curriculum Development, Baltimore.

Caine, R. N., & Caine, G. (1997). *Education on the edge of possibility.* Alexandria, VA: Association for Supervision and Curriculum Development.

Campbell, D. M., & Harris, L. S. (2001). *Collaborative theme building: How teachers write integrated curriculum.* Boston: Allyn and Bacon.

Clark, D. C., & Clark, S. N. (2000). Appropriate assessment strategies for young adolescents in an era of standards-based reform. *The Clearing House 73*(4), 201–204.

Daniel, T. C., & Terry, K. W. (1995). *Multiage classrooms by design: Beyond the one-room school.* Thousand Oaks, CA: Corwin Press.

Danielson, C., & Abrutyn, L. (1997). *An introduction to using portfolios in the classroom.* Alexandria, VA: Association for Supervision and Curriculum Development.

Dede, C., Salzman, M. C., Loftin, R. B., & Sprague, D. (1997). Multisensory immersion as a modeling environment for learning complex concepts. In N. Roberts, W. Feurzeig, & B. Hunter (Eds.), *Computer modeling and simulation in science education.* New York: Springer-Verlag.

Des Marais, J., Yang, Y., & Farzanehkia, F. (2000). Service-learning leadership development for youth. *Phi Delta Kappan, 81,* 678–680.

Deschenes, C., Ebeling, G. E., & Sprague, J. (1994). *Adapting curriculum and instruction in inclusive classrooms: A teacher's desk reference.* Bloomington, IN: The Center for School and Community Integration, Institute for the Study of Developmental Disabilities.

Dewees, S. (1999). *The school within a school model. ERIC Digest.* (ERIC ED 438 147).

Dorfman, A. (1997, March). *Teachers' understanding of performance assessment.* Paper presented at the annual meeting for the American Educational Research Association, Chicago.

Dounay, J. (2000). High-stakes testing is high-stress, too. *The Education Digest, 65*(9), 9–13.

Dunn, R., Dunn, K., & Price, G. E. (1996). *Learning style inventory.* Lawrence, KS: Price Systems.

Dwyer, D. J., & Hecht, J. B. (1992). Minimal parental involvement. *The School Community Journal, 2*(2), 53–66.

Eggebrecht, J., Dagenais, R., Dosch, D., Merczak, N. J., Park, M. N., Styer, S. C., & Workman, D. (1996). Reconnecting the sciences. *Educational Leadership, 53*(8), 4–8.

English, F. W. (1980). Curriculum mapping. *Educational Leadership, 37*(7), 558–559.

English, F. W. (1983). Contemporary curriculum circumstances. In F. W. English (Ed.), *Fundamental curriculum decisions.* Alexandria, VA: Association for Supervision and Curriculum Development.

Epstein, J. L., Coates, L., Salinas, K. C., Sanders, M. G., & Simon, B. S. (1997). *School, family, and community partnerships: Your handbook for action.* Thousand Oaks, CA: Corwin Press.

Erickson, H. L. (1998). *Concept-based curriculum and instruction.* Thousand Oaks, CA: Corwin Press.

Evans, T. D. (1996). Encouragement: The key to reforming classrooms. *Educational Leadership, 54*(1), 81–85.

Falvey, M. A., Givner, C. C., & Kimm, C. (1995). *Creating an inclusive school.* Alexandria, VA: Association for Supervision and Curriculum Development.

Federico, M. A., Herrold, B., & Venn, J. (2000). Inclusion reaches beyond the classroom. *Kappa Delta Pi Record, 36*(4), 178–180.

Fogarty, R. (1997). *Problem-based learning and other curriculum models for the multiple intelligences classroom.* Arlington Heights, IL: IRI/Skylight.

Forsten, C., Grant. J., & Richardson, I. (1999). Multiage and looping: Borrowing form the past. *Principal, 78*(4), 15–16.

Freeman, C., Maruyama, G., Frederickson, J., & Walkowiak, G. (1997, March). *Block scheduling: A structural change that matters.* Paper presented at the annual meeting of the American Educational Research Association, Chicago.

Gardner, H. (1999). *Intelligences reframed: Multiple intelligences for the 21st century.* New York: Basic Books.

Goodnough, K. (2000, April). *Using multiple intelligences to create a more meaningful science curriculum: An action research approach.* Paper presented at the annual meeting of the American Educational Research Association, New Orleans.

Gordon, S. P., & Reese, M. (1997). High stakes testing: Worth the price? *Journal of School Leadership, 1*(4), 345–368.

Green, R. L., & Etheridge, C. P. (2001). Collaboration to establish standards about accountability: Lessons learned about systemic change. *Education, 121*(4), 821–829.

Gunter, M. A., Thomas, H. E., & Schwab, J. H. (1998). *Instruction: A models approach* (3rd ed.). Boston: Allyn and Bacon.

Hargreaves, A. (2001). Beyond anxiety and nostalgia: Building a social movement for educational change. *Phi Delta Kappan, 82*(5), 373–377.

Harris, R. L. (2000). Batting 1,000: Questioning techniques in student-centered classrooms. *The Clearing House, 74*(1), 25–26.

Heins, E. D., Tichenor, M. S., & Coggins, C. J. (2000). Multiage classrooms: Putting theory into pratice. *Contemporary Education 71*(3), 30–35.

Henry, M. (1996). *Parent-school collaboration: Feminist organizational structures and school leadership.* Albany: State University of New York Press.

Holloway, J. H. (2001). Grouping students for increased achievement. *Educational Leadership, 59*(3), 84–85.

Jacobs, H. H. (1989). *Interdisciplinary curriculum: Design and implementation.* Alexandria, VA: Association for Supervision and Curriculum Development.

Jacobs, H. H. (1997). *Mapping the big picture: Integrating curriculum & assessment K-12.* Alexandria VA: Association for Supervision and Curriculum Development.

Josephsen, S. A. (2000). Design your tests to teach, not just test. *The Education Digest, 66*(3), 65–67.

Joyce, B. R., Weil, M., & Calhoun, E. (1999). *Models of teaching* (6th ed.). Englewood Cliffs, NJ: Prentice Hall.

Keedy, J. L., & Drmacich, D. (1994). The collaborative curriculum at the school without walls: Empowering students for classroom learning. *The Urban Review 26*(2), 121–135.

Kira, N. (1997, March). *Students' participation in a democratic community: A study of high school democracy.* Paper presented at the annual meeting of the American Educational Research Association, Chicago.

Kohn, A. (1996). What to look for in a classroom. *Educational Leadership, 54*(1), 54–55.

Kohn, A. (2001). Fighting the tests: A practical guide to rescuing our schools. *Phi Delta Kappan, 82,* 348–357.

Lambert, L. T. (2000). The new physical education. *Educational Leadership, 57*(6), 34–38.

Landau, B. M., & Gathercoal, P. (2000). Creating peaceful classrooms: Judicious discipline and class meetings. *Phi Delta Kappan, 81*(6), 450–452.

Lawson, H., & Briar-Lawson, K. (1997). *Connecting the dots: Progress toward the integration of school reform, school-linked services, parent involvement and community schools.* Oxford, OH: Institute for Educational Renewal, Miami University.

Lopez, G. R., & Scribner, J. D. (1999, April). *Discourses of involvement: A critical review of parent involvement research.* Paper presented at the annual meeting of the American Educational Research Association, Montreal.

Martin, K. M. (1995, April). *Teachers' collaborative curriculum deliberations.* Paper presented at the annual meeting of the American Educational Research Association, San Francisco. (ERIC ED 388 646).

Marx, E., & Northrop, D. (2000). Partnerships to keep students healthy. *Educational Leadership, 57*(6), 22–24.

Marzano, R. J., Pickering, D., & McTighe, J. (1993). *Assessing student outcomes.* Alexandria, VA: Association for Supervision and Curriculum Development.

Mayer-Smith, J., Pedretti, E., & Woodrow, J. (1997, March). *Learning from teaching with technology: An examination of how teachers' experiences in a culture of collaboration inform technology implementation.* Paper presented at the annual meeting of the American Educational Research Association, Chicago.

McCarthy, B. (1997). A tale of four learners: 4 MAT'S learning styles. *Educational Leadership, 54*(6), 46–51.

McCoy, M. H., & Taylor D. L. (2000, April). *Does block scheduling live up to its promise?* Paper presented at that annual meeting of the American Educational Research Association, New Orleans.

Monroe-Baillargeon, A. P. (1999, April). *Shared work: Collaborative teaching in inclusive classrooms.* Paper presented at the annual meeting of the American Educational Research Association, Montreal.

National Service-Learning Cooperative. (1998). *Essential elements of service learning.* St. Paul, MN: National Youth Leadership Council.

Nichols, J. D. (2000, April). *The impact of block scheduling on various indicators of school success.* Paper presented at the annual meeting of the American Educational Research Association, New Orleans.

Nichols-Solomon, R. (2001). Barriers to serious parent involvement. *Phi Delta Kappan, 66*(5), 33–37.

Olmstead, P. P. (1991). Parent involvement in elementary education: Findings and suggestions from the follow-through program. *The Elementary School Journal, 9*, 221–231.

Palma, L. (2001). Going it together: Mapping the curriculum with autonomous-minded teachers. *Independent School, 6*(1), 26–32.

Palmer, D. J., Stough, L. M., Holbein, J., & Gesek, G. (1997, April). *Special thinking in special settings.* Paper presented at the annual meeting of the Council of Exceptional Children, Salt Lake City.

Paris, C., & Combs, B. (2000, April). *Teachers' perspectives on what it means to be learner-centered.* Paper presented at the annual meeting of the American Educational Research Association, New Orleans.

Pate, P. E., Homestead, E., & McGinnis, K. (1993). Designing rubrics for authentic assessment. *Middle School Journal, 25*(2), 25–27.

Pisapia, J. (1994). *Lessons learned from technology intensive schools. Research Brief # 9.* Richmond, VA: Metropolitan Educational Research Consortium.

Popham, W. J. (2001). *The truth about testing: An educator's call to action.* Alexandria, VA: Association for Supervision and Curriculum Development.

Pugach, M. C., & Wesson, C. L. (1995). Teachers' and students' views of team teaching of general education and learning-disabled students in two fifth-grade classes. *The Elementary School Journal, 95*, 279–295.

Raywid, M. A. (1995). *The sub schools/small schools movement—Taking stock.* (ERIC ED 397 490).

Reese, M., & Gordon, S. P. (1999, October). *Using the high stakes test for school reform: A contradiction in terms.* Paper presented at the annual convention of the University Council of Educational Administration, Minneapolis.

Rothman, R. (1996). Linking standards and instruction: HELPS is on the way. *Educational Leadership, 53*(8), 44–46.

Sandholtz, J. H., Ringstaff, C., & Dwyer, D. C. (1997). *Teaching with technology: Creating student-centered classrooms.* New York: Teachers College.

Schneider, E. (1996). Giving students a voice in the classroom. *Educational Leadership, 54*(1), 22–26.

Seline, A. M. (2001). Reading the media: Media literacy courses show students how to watch with eyes wide open. *Middle Ground, 5*(3), 2–5.

Smith, S. (2001). Technology 101: Integration beyond a technology foundations course. *Journal of Special Education Technology, 16*(1), 43–45.

Standford, P., & Siders, J. A. (2001). Authentic assessment for intervention. *Intervention in School and Clinic, 36*(3), 163–167.

Stix, A. (2000). Bridging standards across the curriculum with portfolios. *Educational Leadership, 59*(5), 7–10.

Stokes, L. C., & Wilson, J. W. (2000). A longitudinal study of teachers' perceptions of the effectiveness of block versus traditional scheduling. *NASSP Bulletin, 85*(619), 90–99.

Stone, S. J. (1998). Creating contexts for mixed-age learning. *Childhood Education, 74*, 234–236.

Thompson, S. (2001). The authentic standards movement and its evil twin. *Phi Delta Kappan, 82*, 358–362.

Thompson, S. C. (2000). Overcoming obstacles to creating responsive curriculum. *Middle School Journal, 32*(1), 47–55.

Toole, J. (2000, April). *Implementing service-learning in K–8 schools: Challenging the learning grammar and the organizational grammar of "real school."* Paper presented at the annual meeting of the American Educational Research, New Orleans.

Veal, W. R., & Flinders, D. J. (2001). How block scheduling reform effects classroom practice. *The High School Journal, 84*(4), 21–31.

Villa, R. A., & Thousand, J. S. (Eds.). (1995). *Creating an inclusive school.* Alexandria, VA: Association for Supervision and Curriculum Development.

Wasley, P. A. (2002). Small classes, small schools: The time is now. *Educational Leadership, 59*(5), 7–10.

Whitbread, K. (1999). Inclusion: Making it work for students and teachers. *Middle Ground, 2*(4), 10–12.

Wooster, J. S. (1993). Authentic assessment: A strategy for preparing teachers to respond to curricular mandates in global education. *Theory into Practice, 32*(1), 47–51.

Yeh, S. S. (2001). Tests worth teaching to: Constructing state-mandated tests that emphasize critical thinking. *Educational Researcher, 30*(9), 12–17.

Resources

Beane, J. A. (1997). *Curriculum integration: Designing the core of democratic education.* New York: Teachers College Press.

Burke, K. (1998). *How to assess authentic learning* (3rd ed.). Arlington Heights, IL: IRI/Skylight.

Campbell, D. M., & Harris, L. S. (2001). *Collaborative theme building: How teachers write integrated curriculum.* Boston: Allyn and Bacon.

Clark, D. C., & Clark, S. N. (2000). Appropriate assessment strategies for young adolescents in an era of standards-based reform. *The Clearing House, 73*(4), 201–204.

Danielson, C., & Abrutyn, L. (1997). *An introduction to using portfolios in the classroom.* Alexandria, VA: Association for Supervision and Curriculum Development.

Jacobs, H. H. (1997). *Mapping the big picture: Integrating curriculum and assessment, K–12.* Alexandria, VA: Association for Supervision and Curriculum Development.

Post, T. R., Ellis, A. K., Humphreys, A. H., & Buggey, L. J. (1997). *Interdisciplinary approaches to curriculum: Themes for teaching.* Upper Saddle River, NJ: Merrill/Prentice Hall.

Weinstein, M. (2000). A framework for critical thinking. *The High School Magazine,* 7(8), 40–43.

Wineburg, S., & Grossman, P. (Eds.). *Interdisciplinary curriculum: Challenges to implementation.* New York: Teachers College Press.

Yeh, S. S. (2001). Tests worth teaching to: Constructing state-mandated tests that emphasize critical thinking. *Educational Researcher, 30*(9), 12–17.

12 Program Development

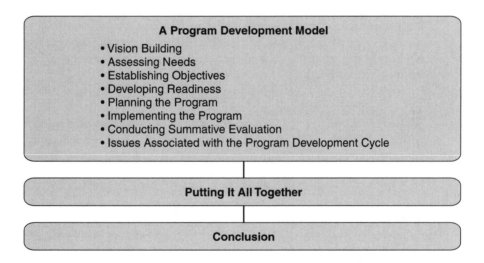

A Program Development Model

- Vision Building
- Assessing Needs
- Establishing Objectives
- Developing Readiness
- Planning the Program
- Implementing the Program
- Conducting Summative Evaluation
- Issues Associated with the Program Development Cycle

Putting It All Together

Conclusion

This chapter will discuss guiding principles for developing professional development and school improvement programs as well as the program development process. One guiding principle is that *a democratic governance process for program development needs to be in place before planning begins.* This process can begin with the establishment of small study groups, with each professional assigned randomly to one of the groups. One representative from each group can be elected as a delegate to a school council charged with facilitating both school improvement and professional development. The school council should include a majority of teachers, specialists, administrators, parents, and other members of the community that the school serves. The study groups and school council make up the primary infrastructure for communication and decision making. Communication between the council and study groups is two-way. Study groups thus contribute to decisions made by the council. Major decisions about the direction of school and professional development can be decided by schoolwide votes, and day-to-day governance can be carried out by the school council with input from study groups.

A second guiding principle is that *the school community should establish a set of ground rules for program development.* One ground rule might be that all teachers actively participate in the program development process. Another possible rule is that the growth and development of all students be the primary criterion for decision making. Ground rules will vary from school to school. The important thing is that consensus be reached on each rule.

A third guiding principle is to *commit to long-term program development.* Even the most effective professional development programs do not lead to school improvement overnight. Expect a total transformation of school culture, teaching, and learning to take at least five years. Change, if it is to be effective and lasting, will be incremental. The functions of professional development and school improvement will never be completed. In successful schools, they have become a continuous journey—a way of life.

A fourth guiding principle is to *seek outside assistance.* Initially, this might mean enlisting the support of critical friends with expertise in school improvement and professional development (Bambino, 2002). The support of parents and the community served by the school is critical. Although the school may be the most promising unit of change, support from the district's central office nonetheless is essential (Pierce, 2001). It is important that the school develop formal partnerships with business, education and other human service agencies, and a nearby college or university. Finally, the World Wide Web allows any school to become part of national and international networks that will provide information and assistance.

A fifth guiding principle, one that cuts across all components of the program development process, is to *base development on collaborative, critical inquiry* (Garet, Porter, Desimone, Birman, & Yoon, 2001; Sparks, 2001). The gathering of data and critical analysis of those data should be the basis for planning, evaluating, and improving programs. Data gathering and analysis should be collegial, accompanied by extensive dialogue about the meaning of the data (Routman, 2002) and how best to proceed with data-based improvement.

Having considered guiding principles, let us now examine a model for program development.

A Program Development Model

Professional development and school improvement can be integrated in the program development model illustrated in Figure 12.1. The model calls for three different types of continuous improvement. First, each of the seven phases of the model (represented by the seven outer circles) includes an internal cycle of formative evaluation and program revision. Formative evaluation is intended to improve a program rather than judge its value (summative evaluation performs the latter function). For example, after stakeholders have developed a tentative vision (Phase 1), they complete a formative evaluation of their vision statement. Based on the evaluation, program developers may wish to revise the vision statement before moving on to the next phase of the model, "assessing needs." Similarly, the needs assessment is evaluated and revised, if necessary,

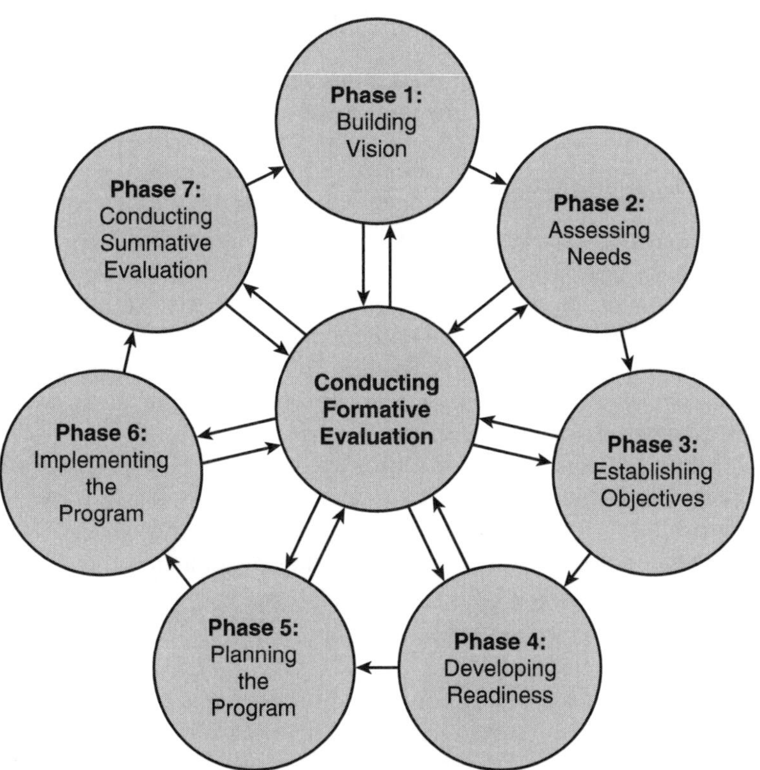

FIGURE 12.1 Program Development Model

before moving on to the "establishing objectives" phase, and so on. As I present the seven phases of the model, I'll include some possible formative evaluation questions for each phase. Each school, however, should develop its own formative evaluation questions, as well as a plan for gathering and assessing data to help answer those questions.

A second means for continuous improvement within the professional development model consists of the "continuation" of each phase, once it is initiated. Using vision building as an example, there will come a point in the program development process when stakeholders are ready to move on to the second phase, "assessing needs." However, vision building does not end when needs assessment begins, but rather continues through each of the remaining phases of program development. As vision building continues, more experience, better information, and deeper reflection will enable the vision to become more complete. The same holds true for each of the phases of program development. As each new phase begins, all of the phases previously initiated continue.

The third means of continuous improvement is the fact that one program development cycle leads to another. Eventually, the seven-phase model ends with a summative evaluation, but the end of one cycle simply initiates the beginning of a new cycle, as stakeholders reexamine their vision and other program components in the light of evaluation data. The next cycle may lead to minor or major program revisions, or an entirely new program.

Having discussed the continuous improvement aspects of the program development model in Figure 12.1, it's time to describe each of the model's seven phases.

Phase 1: Vision Building

Building vision goes far beyond a small group of teachers sitting down at an after-school meeting with the principal to write a vision statement that the rest of the school community may or may not be asked to endorse (Pierce, 2001). Authentic vision building involves all members of the school community engaged in extensive reflection and dialogue concerning the *desired future* (Bassett, 2002). This reflection and dialogue can take place in study groups throughout the school as well as the school council, with liaisons assisting two-way communication.

Stakeholders considering the school's vision can focus on two critical questions about the future:

1. How can we describe our district's ideal future graduate?
2. Given the description generated by consideration of question 1, how can we describe our ideal future school?

Eventually, the school community will agree on a formal but tentative vision statement. The statement should be student centered and general enough to have relevance for all stakeholders. On the other hand, the statement should not be so general that it is too vague to guide program development. One way to provide clarity is to include in the statement four to six broad student learning goals. An example of a vision statement (one that admittedly reveals my bias) follows:

> Lakeside School creates an environment, fosters relationships, and provides learning opportunities that lead to holistic, life-long learning. Learning at Lakeside includes students' intrapersonal, cognitive, physical, moral, social, and aesthetic development.

The first sentence of the vision statement provides a single, coherent focus. The six types of development in the second sentence are broad student learning goals that expand on the first sentence.

The sample vision statement took me only a few minutes to write, because I did not have to include teachers, staff, students, parents, or community members in its development, or attain schoolwide participation and consensus. The vision statement I wrote sounds good enough, but if a principal adopted it as a school's mission statement, it would have little or no effect on the school. This is because it would lack the collective thought, meaning, and commitment of a vision developed by the school community. It would be a vision statement without the consensus that gives a true vision its power.

After drafting its vision statement, the school community can ask the following questions during a formative evaluation of the statement:

1. Did all members of the school community, as well as parent and community representatives, participate in vision building?
2. Were adequate schoolwide study, reflection, and dialogue included in the vision-building process?
3. Was the vision statement agreed on by consensus?
4. Is the vision statement broad enough to be relevant to all members of the school community, yet clear enough to guide program development?
5. Does the vision statement include a few broad student learning goals?
6. Are broad student learning goals consistent with each other?
7. Is the vision statement consistent with the district's vision?

Phase 2: Assessing Needs

The purpose of needs assessment is to (1) examine the gap between the school's vision and its current reality and (2) determine changes necessary to bridge the gap. To consider the first purpose, let us reexamine the example of a vision statement from the previous section. The statement visualizes students as "holistic, life-long learners" and lists six broad student learning goals (intrapersonal, cognitive, physical, moral, social, and aesthetic development). To examine the gap between vision and reality, a needs assessment would ask, How well are we doing at helping our students to become holistic, life-long learners? More specifically, a needs assessment would ask to what extent each of the six broad student learning goals were being met.

The second purpose of needs assessment is to identify school changes that need to be made to bridge identified gaps between vision and reality. Although there are different ways to do this, one way is to identify key school processes, then to examine key changes that need to be made in those processes relative to each broad student learning goal. Along the vertical axis of Figure 12.2 are listed nine school processes which, not coincidently, mirror the functions of professional development discussed in Parts II and III of this text. A comprehensive needs assessment would examine the relationship of each of the nine processes to each of the broad student learning goals listed along the horizontal axis of Figure 12.2. Thus, school process needs might be identified for any of the cells in Figure 12.2.

FIGURE 12.2 Goals and Processes

	Broad Student Learning Goals					
Key School Processes	*Students' Intrapersonal Development*	*Students' Cognitive Development*	*Students' Physical Development*	*Students' Moral Development*	*Students' Social Development*	*Students' Aesthetic Development*
School Leader Development						
Cultural Development						
Team Development						
Teacher Development						
Curriculum Development						
Developing School Structures						
Instruction						
Student Assessment						
School-Parent Collaboration						

A wide variety of data sources can be tapped to assess schoolwide student learning and school process needs: teachers, specialists, administrators, parents, community members, student work, student achievement data, school and community demographics, and other types of archival data (Conderman, 2001). A variety of data gathering methods can be used as well, including questionnaires, interviews, classroom and school observations, traditional testing and authentic assessment, mining of classroom and school documents, and so on (Dubrovich, 2002; Penta, 2002). Stakeholders can divide into teams, with each team assigned to gather and analyze outcome and process data relative to one of the broad student learning goals. The school council can coordinate the needs assessment teams and integrate findings.

Questions to assist in the formative evaluation of a school-based needs assessment include the following:

1. Did all members of the school community, as well as parent and community representatives, participate in the needs assessment?
2. Were data gathered on the extent to which the school's vision (including broad student learning goals) is being met?
3. Were data gathered on needed changes in key school processes intended to assist attainment of broad student learning goals?
4. Was a variety of data sources and data gathering methods used?
5. Were data gathering and analysis methods valid and reliable?
6. Are the identified needs consistent with the needs assessment data?
7. Were the results of the needs assessment presented in a clear and concise manner to all stakeholders?

Phase 3: Establishing Objectives

Establishing objectives involves first deciding which identified needs the school will address, then converting those needs to broad, written objectives. At the most general level, there are two types of school improvement objectives: schoolwide student learning objectives and school process objectives. Learning and process objectives correspond to learning and process needs.

Like the broad student learning goals to which they lead, schoolwide student learning objectives are broad, visionary, and transdisciplinary. They are more general than curriculum objectives, but invariably lead to changes in the written curriculum. Schoolwide student learning objectives are written to address identified needs which, in turn, must be met in order to meet broad student learning goals. The example of a vision statement provided earlier in this chapter included six broad student learning goals. Schoolwide student learning objectives for the first of these goals, *students' intrapersonal development*, would be based on identified student needs relative to that goal, and might include the following:

- Students will develop positive self-concepts.
- Students will develop self-efficacy.

- Students will connect their lives at school to their lives outside of school.
- Students will become self-directed learners.
- Students will develop habits of life-long learning.

Student learning objectives are developed for each broad student learning goal.

School process objectives address needs identified across key school processes like these listed on the vertical axis of Figure 12.2. Each process objective is focused on one or more broad student learning goals, thus, process objectives could be identified for any of the cells in Figure 12.2. To provide some examples of process objectives, again we will focus on the first broad student learning goal listed in Figure 12.2, *students' intrapersonal development.* The first school process listed in Figure 12.2 is *school leader development.* Process objectives for leader development linked to students' intrapersonal development might include:

- School leaders will develop awareness of the knowledge base on students' intrapersonal development.
- School leaders will model successful intrapersonal development.
- School leaders will develop the skills necessary to facilitate the intrapersonal development of students, teachers, and staff.

The second school process in Figure 12.2 is *cultural development.* Cultural development objectives connected to students' intrapersonal development include:

- Attention to and support for intrapersonal development will become a school norm.
- The school environment will be characterized by open communication, trust, and empathy.
- The school culture will foster self-expression.

Some cells in Figure 12.2 might not be assigned process objectives, because either no needs had been identified for those cells, or the school community had decided not to focus on meeting some needs in the current program development cycle.

A team approach is recommended for establishing schoolwide student learning objectives and school process objectives. A different team is assigned to each broad student learning goal. Each team writes tentative learning and process objectives for the broad student learning goal it has been assigned, and the school council works with the teams to establish a consistent and coherent set of objectives for consideration by the school community at large. Even after they are approved by a predominant majority of the school community, objectives should not be set in stone. Rather, a process should be kept in place for revising, adding, and deleting learning and process objectives throughout the remainder of the program development cycle.

Questions to be answered during a formative evaluation of schoolwide student learning objectives and school process objectives include:

1. Were all members of the school community, as well as parent and community representatives, involved in establishing objectives?
2. Are the schoolwide student learning objectives consistent with the school's vision (including its broad student learning goals) and with each other?
3. Are the school process objectives consistent with the school's vision (including its broad student learning goals), the schoolwide student learning objectives, and each other?
4. Were the objectives approved by a predominant majority of the school community?
5. Are the objectives clear enough to guide future program planning and evaluation?
6. Have the objectives been disseminated to all stakeholders?

Phase 4: Developing Readiness

Readiness means that the school community is prepared and committed for detailed planning and implementation of a professional development and school improvement program. There are five types of readiness (Gordon, 1999):

1. *Cultural readiness* means that, based on sufficient communication, trust building, collegiality, and collaboration, the school has reached a capacity for planning and implementing a program aimed at meeting the school's vision, goals, and objectives.
2. *Conceptual readiness* means that the school has developed a broad concept of how the program will look, including the best matches of objectives, professional development frameworks, and school personnel.
3. *Personal readiness* means that individual concerns about the program have been addressed, including concerns about responsibilities, commitment of time and energy, support, and rewards associated with the individual's involvement in the program.
4. *Political readiness* includes securing program support form the central office, parents, and community.
5. *Resource readiness* involves estimating what human and material resources will be necessary for the program, and determining how those resources will be procured. To reach resource readiness, it may be necessary to downsize or eliminate existing school programs that have outlived their usefulness.

To achieve the five types of readiness, the school community may consult with critical friends, partners, and networks; dialogue within study groups; visit other schools with effective programs; invite visiting teams from other schools to discuss their programs; assign teams to help develop each type of readiness; hold schoolwide forums; and conduct awareness sessions for parents and other community members. Exemplar 12.1 tells the story of readiness for school improvement at Wallenpaupack High School.

EXEMPLAR 12.1 • *Readiness at Wallenpaupack High School*

The teachers and administrators at Wallenpaupack (PA) High School already had agreed on the need for school improvement. An influx of families from metropolitan areas of New York into the rural community served by the high school had altered the student population. It was now more diverse in terms of ethnicity, learning needs, and learning styles. In order to meet the needs of the changing community, the school was committed to placing more emphasis on student inquiry, high-level thinking, problem solving, creativity, and communication skills. To meet these broad student learning goals, Wallenpaupack's teachers decided to implement a variety of new processes, including interdisciplinary curriculum, writing across the curriculum, team teaching, teaching to student learning styles, cooperative learning, and authentic assessment. Student portfolios and a senior graduation project were on the drawing board. Administration and teachers, however, believed that the traditional high school schedule would make it difficult to implement many of the aforementioned innovations. The school community agreed that the class schedule needed to change.

Early on, the school community decided on three things: First, teachers would be involved in any decisions about the schedule; second, a readiness phase would precede any significant change; and third, the readiness phase would focus not simply on preparing for changes in the schedule, but on using a restructured schedule as the integrating vehicle for other components of school improvement.

Initial readiness activities involved readings and dialogue on alternative schedules. Eventually, teachers began visiting other schools that had initiated alternative schedules. Experts were brought in to make presentations on alternative scheduling and related reforms. Visiting teams from schools with alternative schedules also were brought in to discuss the benefits and concerns associated with alternative schedules, and the process of implementing a new schedule as part of a broader school improvement process. Teachers from the high school traveled to conferences, clinics, and seminars on alternative scheduling. Wallenpaupack developed a partnership with two schools in Maine that had successfully made the transition to block scheduling. Educators from these schools became critical friends, and consulted Wallenpuapack throughout the readiness phase.

After considerable exploration and dialogue, most members of the faculty were inclined to move toward a 4 × 4 block schedule, but they were not yet ready to make the transition. The next stage of readiness began with the formation of schoolwide readiness teams for scheduling, communications, graduation requirements, and student assessment. Each teacher and specialist was assigned to one of the four teams. An executive committee was established, composed of representatives from each of the four teams and school administrators. All of the readiness teams were provided released time to meet weekly during the instructional day.

The scheduling team focused on how to adapt a block schedule to the particular needs of the school. The communications team addressed awareness and involvement of the school community, parents, the school board, and the public at large. The graduation requirements teams dealt with improving academic standards across the curriculum, the conceptualization of a senior project, and connections between academic requirements and the block schedule. The assessment committee was charged with exploring alternative ways of assessing student learning consistent with new instructional strategies and the increased class time to be made available by the block schedule. The executive committee focused on review of recommendations by the four readiness teams, integrating recommendations into the professional development and school improvement program, and identifying resources necessary to implement recommendations.

After one year of readiness activities, the overwhelming majority of educators at Wallenpaupack voted to engage in one year of detailed planning, then adopt block scheduling as a vehicle for implementing innovations in curriculum, instruction, and student assessment. When asked for suggestions for other schools beginning the readiness stage, teachers suggested that readiness focus on student needs, be teacher driven, and attend to teachers' developmental levels and individual concerns. The school administration suggested that the readiness process be incremental, focusing on a few key issues at a time. One administrator noted that a school would never reach a stage of readiness that assures program success. Rather, the school community must at some point be willing to risk failure, and put its heart and soul into the change process.

The following questions should be answered in formative assessment of the readiness phase:

1. Were all members of the school community, as well as parent and community representatives, involved in the readiness phase?
2. Was the readiness phase focused on the school's vision (including its broad student learning goals), schoolwide student learning objectives, and school process objectives?
3. Did the readiness phase address each type of readiness: cultural, conceptual, personal, political, and resource?
4. Is the school community ready to proceed with detailed planning and implementation of a professional development and school improvement program?

Phase 5: Planning the Program

One aspect of planning a long-range program is the selection of professional development frameworks that will assist the school in meeting program objectives (Willis, 2002). Comprehensive programs usually incorporate multiple frameworks. The planning grid in Figure 12.3 indicates potential connections between professional development frameworks and objectives. If multiple frameworks are to be used, they must be integrated into a coherent program. In addition to professional development frameworks, events, processes, and services need to be included in the long-range plan. Coordination of the overall program as well as each of its major components must be arranged. An infrastructure needs to be planned for ongoing schoolwide and school-community communication about the program. A system of support and rewards for program participants should be designed. Periodic schoolwide forums to reflect on the program's progress might be arranged, and a celebration of school improvement might be planned for the end of the program's first year. All major elements of the program's first year should be described in the written plan.

The design of the summative program evaluation is another aspect of the planning phase. It is not a good idea to wait until the program has been in operation for a year or two before deciding how it should be evaluated formally. It is during the program planning phase when the school needs to decide on pre-measures and other evaluation data that the school will begin gathering in the early stages of program implementation. Program developers need to determine summative evaluation questions, data sources, data gathering methods, and data analysis methods during the planning phase. It is a good idea to create a flowchart or diagram that includes all professional development and evaluation activities, designates beginning and ending dates for each activity, and identifies individuals or teams that will coordinate each activity. Additionally, a one-page overview should illustrate major program components and the relationship of components to each other and to the school vision.

Finally, specific resources needed for all program activities need to be listed. Available resources and resources to be procured should be identified. Although district requirements for program budgets vary, a general guideline is to prepare a detailed budget for the first year of the program and general, tentative budgets for the following three to four years.

Formative evaluation questions for the planning phase are these:

1. Did all members of the school community, as well as parent and community representatives, participate in the planning phase?
2. Is the plan consistent with the school's vision (including its broad student learning goals)?
3. Does the plan address each schoolwide student learning objective and each school process objective?
4. Does the plan effectively integrate relevant professional development frameworks with each other and with other program components?
5. Does the plan include a design for summative program evaluation?
6. Does the plan include a flowchart or diagram depicting all major program and evaluation activities, the relationship between activities, who is responsible for coordinating each activity, and a time line for implementation?
7. Does the plan include a list of needed resources and a budget? Are needed resources available and affordable?
8. Is a system in place for revising the plan when necessary?

FIGURE 12.3 **Relationship of Program Objectives and Professional Development Frameworks**

Professional Development Frameworks	*Schoolwide Student Learning Objectives*														*School Process Objectives*												
Training																											
Peer Coaching																											
Collaborative Work Teams																											
Co-Teaching																											
Study Groups																											
Action Research																											
Teacher Writing																											
Teacher Leadership																											
Partnerships																											
Networks																											
Centers																											

9. Has the plan been approved by the predominant majority of the school community?
10. Has the plan been disseminated to all stakeholders?

Phase 6: Implementing the Program

Perhaps the two most important factors in successful implementation are communication and flexibility. Having a plan is essential, but you should assume from the outset that unforeseen circumstances and problems will arise. The key is to have a communications system in place that will make everyone aware of emerging situations, and to have the capacity to respond accordingly. Feedback and problem solving—not rigid adherence to the written plan—make for successful programs. It should be assumed that the program will have different meaning for different participants, and that individuals will adapt the plan for themselves and their students. The leader's job is to facilitate that adaptation. Program leaders and participants need to meet on a regular basis throughout the implementation phase for program monitoring and continuous program improvement. All stakeholders need to be aware of the program's progress and revisions made necessary by evolving conditions.

Questions for formative evaluation of program implementation are the following:

1. Have all members of the school community, as well as parent and community representatives, participated in program implementation?
2. Thus far, has the program been implemented essentially as planned? If not, what are the major differences between the plan and implementation? Why have these differences developed?
3. Thus far, what are the participants' perceptions of the program quality? What are participant suggestions for improving the program?
4. Thus far, does formative evaluation data indicate that the program is moving satisfactorily toward its objectives? If not, what changes can be made to improve the program?
5. What, if any, changing conditions in the school, district, community, or state indicate a need for program revisions? What revisions are indicated?
6. Is the progress of program implementation being disseminated to all stakeholders?

Phase 7: Conducting Summative Evaluation

At some point, the school must go beyond formative evaluation and complete a comprehensive summative evaluation as basis for judging the overall value of the program and making definitive decisions about the program's future. Based on a summative evaluation at the end of one year of implementation, for example, the school might decide to continue the program with minor revisions, continue the program with major revisions, or discontinue the program and design an entirely new one for the following year. Summative evaluations are used for purposes additional to decisions about the program's future. The evaluation might be used as the basis for a report to the school community, to fulfill a district requirement, to justify external funding, or to disseminate information about the program to educators outside the school district.

One focus of a summative evaluation is the extent to which schoolwide student learning objectives are being met. Additionally, the school will wish to determine the extent to which school process objectives are being met (Ackley, 2001). The effectiveness of school processes such as leadership development, cultural development, and so on, directly affect progress toward meeting student learning objectives, thus the quality of these processes should be examined. As with needs assessment and formative evaluation, summative evaluation should use a variety of data sources and data gathering methods. Multiple sources and methods will provide a more complete picture of program effectiveness. Figure 12.4 illustrates relationships between various evaluation methods and program objectives.

Summative program evaluation is designed during the planning phase of program development. Data gathering for summative evaluation actually may begin prior to program implementation (for example, with pre-measurements), and continue throughout program implementation. Formative and summative evaluation data are not always discrete. For example, formative data gathered periodically as a basis for ongoing program improvement may also be used in summative evaluation. Summative program evaluation usually results in the writing of a formal report that reviews the evaluation's objectives, data sources, data gathering, and data analysis; draws conclusions; and makes recommendations for the program's future. Since different audiences (the school board, teachers, the community) may be interested in varying levels of detail, different versions of the report often are distributed.

All members of the school community can participate in summative program evaluation, with different teams assigned to different evaluation foci, data sources, or data gathering methods. Participation in program evaluation can be a professional growth activity in its own right, as participants engage in collaborative planning, inquiry, reflection, and dialogue.

The summative evaluation process itself can be the focus of formative evaluation, as the stakeholders address the following questions:

1. Were all members of the school community, as well as parent and community representatives, involved in the summative evaluation?
2. Did the summative evaluation examine the extent to which both schoolwide student learning objectives and school process objectives were being met?
3. Were a variety of data sources and data gathering methods used?
4. Were data gathering and analysis methods valid and reliable?
5. Are evaluation results, conclusions, and recommendations consistent with one another?
6. Were appropriate versions of the evaluation report disseminated to different groups of stakeholders?
7. Is a process in place to consider and implement recommendations?

FIGURE 12.4 Relationship of Program Objectives and Evaluation Methods

Evaluation Methods	*Schoolwide Student Learning Objectives*														*School Process Objectives*												
Pre- and Post-measurements																											
Review of Existing Data																											
Running Records																											
Video- and Audiotaping																											
Observations																											
Questionnaires																											
Interviews																											
Case Studies																											
Keeping Logs																											
Journaling																											

Issues Associated with the Program Development Cycle

How long should it take to complete the program development cycle shown in Figure 12.1? During the school's first cycle, it might take an entire year to develop a vision, assess needs, and establish objectives. Readiness and detailed program planning might take another year. This means that program implementation would begin in the third year, with the first summative evaluation at the end of that year. The second and succeeding cycles could be much briefer, completed in one-year periods.

A second issue is whether a new needs assessment is necessary at the beginning of the second cycle, since a summative evaluation at the end of the first cycle gathers data that serves as a basis for program revisions. The answer is that a new, abbreviated, needs assessment should be conducted for the second cycle. This is because the evaluation at the end of the first cycle gathers data only on the current program, not on new student learning needs that may have emerged since the initial needs assessment. Findings from the evaluation for the first cycle and the needs assessment for the second cycle can be integrated and used as a basis for program revision.

How long should a multicycle professional development and school improvement program last? Since we know that it takes from four to five years for schoolwide reforms to succeed, it seems that a comprehensive improvement program should be in place for at least that long, provided the program is moving toward its objectives. Depending on program effects and changing student needs, a rule of thumb is that a school considers designing a new professional development program every five years.

Putting It All Together

The model just described works best when all the components in Figure 12.5 are considered during program development. Throughout the text we've been moving from the outer band of Figure 12.5 toward its center: student growth and development. Now, to review, let us reverse directions, moving from the center toward the outer band. School improvement is the primary vehicle for student growth and development. The focus of school improvement is the improvement of teaching and learning, and the five dimensions of improved teaching and learning—curriculum development, restructuring, instructional development, improvement of student assessment, and improvement of school-parent collaboration—are the core functions of professional development. The extent to which professional development is needed to assist the school leadership, the school culture, teams, and individual teachers depends on their current capacity to support the improvement of teaching and learning. The professional development frameworks—training, collegial support, reflective inquiry, teacher leadership, and external support—all are structures for carrying out capacity building and core functions. They are options to be considered, selected, mixed, and matched with schoolwide student learning objectives and school process objectives.

Exemplar 12.2 is a textbook example of a school-based program that connects all the pieces of professional development and school improvement for improved student learning.

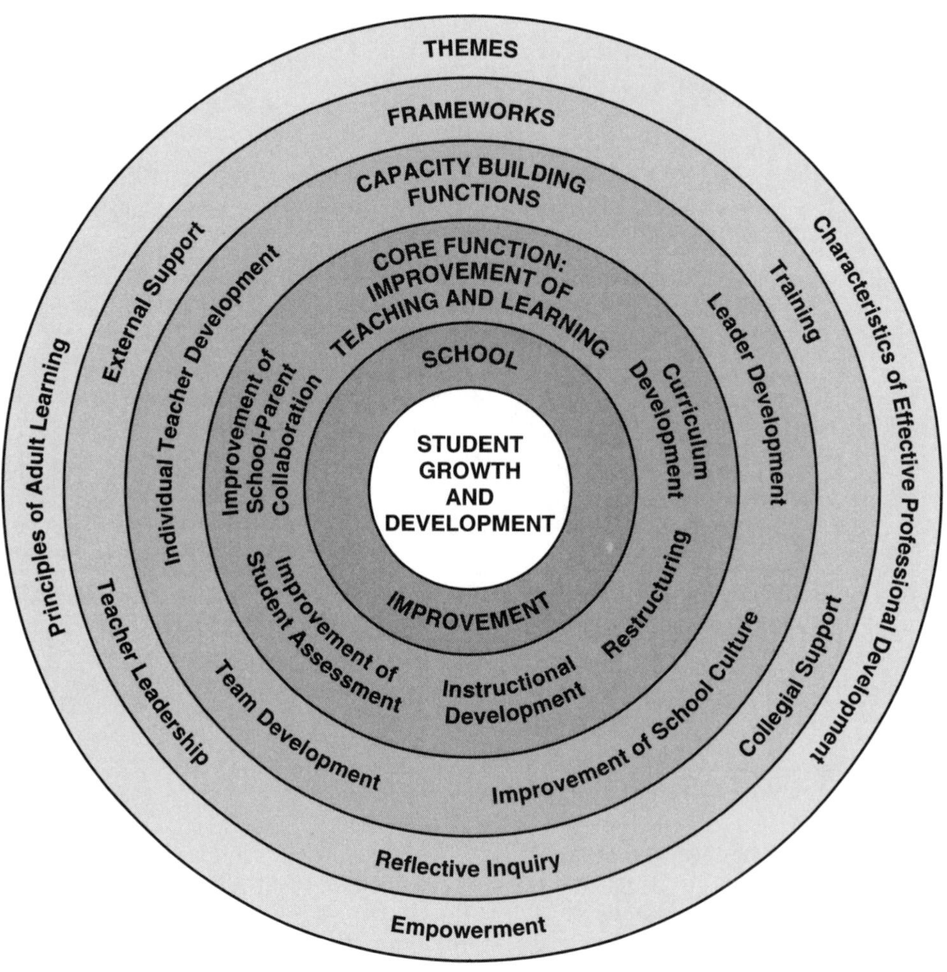

FIGURE 12.5 Comprehensive Model: Professional Development for School Improvement

EXEMPLAR 12.2 • *Professional Development at Mason Elementary*

Samuel Mason Elementary is located in a lower socioeconomic area of Boston, near one of the city's large housing projects. Nearly 80 percent of Mason's students are eligible for free or reduced lunch. A few years ago, Mason's reading scores were in the city's bottom quartile, and it was the least frequently chosen school in the district's school choice plan. The school was in a state of disrepair and scheduled to be closed.

Enter new principal Mary Russo (originally assigned to phase the school out of existence) and her commitment to collaboration, professional development, and school improvement. Russo began the improvement process at Mason Elementary with a commitment to shared governance. A steering committee for professional development and school improvement was formed. Its membership includes the principal, teachers, parents, other community members, and a facilitator from the state department of education. The steering committee formed teams to assist with program development, including academic achievement, school climate, parent involvement, professional development, and marketing teams. Parents serve with teachers on each of the teams. Through these governance teams, the school created a school vision, carried out a needs assessment, and identified improvement objectives. The vision statement includes the broad goals of students developing their "personal best, academically, socially, and physically." Schoolwide learning objectives include developing thinking skills, honoring diversity, and improving literacy in reading, writing, mathematics, and technology. School improvement process objectives include developing curriculum that challenges each child and emphasizes active learning, developing positive school climate, providing opportunities for parent participation, inclusion of children with special needs, broadening the scope of special services, restructuring the school budgeting process, improving professional development opportunities, and improving teamwork and collaboration. Improvement objectives became the basis of a five-year plan for professional development and school improvement.

One aspect of Mason's development program is focused on capacity building. Principal Russo has led the way through her own professional development activities. She designs and implements her own professional development plan each year, belongs to a national principals' network, and spends three weeks each year in training programs focused on instruction, instructional leadership, and professional development leadership.

Cultural development is another type of capacity building at Mason. The school is a member of the Accelerated Schools Network and has adopted the network's process for cultural improvement. Mason also has adopted principles of total quality management, and integrated them with the Accelerated Schools process. School improvement efforts rely heavily on teams, and team development has been a priority. Team learning first focused on simple things, like how to conduct a meeting, but has progressed to deeper topics, like how to engage in reflective dialogue and collaborative problem solving.

Part of Mason's philosophy of professional development is "every teacher a learner." The goal of individual teacher development is threefold: to foster teacher empowerment, competence, and responsibility. Teacher development begins with new teachers participating in a beginning teacher assistance program with mentoring by experienced colleagues. Every teacher plans and implements an individual professional development plan. Principal Russo explained the school's "expectation of teachers' continuous progress": "People are at different places along the learning continuum. Some people are fast learners, some will take longer, but the key is making sure that everybody is learning, everybody is making progress."

(continued)

EXEMPLAR 12.2 • Continued

The professional development frameworks and activities at Mason Elementary are multilayered and multidimensional. A sampling of frameworks follows:

- Each week, visiting experts from local universities provide in-class demonstrations and assist teachers in implementing new strategies. Master teachers provide daily demonstrations of effective teaching in "model classrooms."
- Teachers are partnered to help each other develop skills and to coach each other. The principal provides expert coaching to teachers on a regular basis.
- Study groups choose teaching and learning strategies to focus on for the year, research and discuss the strategies, and reflect together on classroom implementation.
- Grade-level teams plan and implement year-long action research projects. As part of their projects, the teams gather student performance data at the beginning, middle, and end of the school year.
- Lead teachers at each grade level provide training, teach demonstrations lessons, assist in lesson planning and student assessment, co-teach, and provide expert coaching.
- A partnership with a local university provides interns who become co-teachers and, in return, are mentored by their experienced partners.
- School-business partnerships make available training programs, mentors for students, externships for teachers, and grants for teacher-designed improvement projects.
- A school-community partnership has provided the school with services such as an on-site counseling program for at-risk students, delivered by the local community health center.

The focus of professional development and school improvement at Mason has been the improvement of teaching and learning. To that end, reading, writing, thinking skills, and technology have been integrated across the curriculum. The school has restructured its reading program, moving toward a literature-based approach, and adding before-school and after-school reading programs. Teachers have earned a second certification in special education, and interns and aides have been placed in classrooms to help the school achieve its goal of 100 percent inclusion. Instruction at Mason includes a combination of whole group, small group, and one-on-one instruction. Teaching styles are matched with students' learning styles, and active learning can be observed in all classrooms.

Mason places a heavy emphasis on data-based improvement. At the classroom level, teachers make regular use of student observation, analysis of student work, inventories, checklists, and running records. Students develop portfolios that are shared with parents three times a year in parent-teacher conferences. Grade-level and schoolwide assessment of student achievement, including formal testing, takes place at the beginning, middle, and end of the school year. Revisions in school improvement and professional development plans are based on these assessments.

Another hallmark of Mason's improvement efforts is school-parent collaboration. The school's family literacy program provides training to parents on at-home strategies to improve their children's reading. Parents and teachers together attend professional development programs on inclusion and improving students' writing skills. On any school day, parents can be observed throughout the school serving as monitors, tutors, and teacher aides. In addition to service on the school's steering committee and associated teams, parents make up the majority of the Family Involvement Cadre, which promotes parent involvement and coordinates after-school and summer programs.

The results of Mason Elementary's school improvement and professional development programs are impressive. Parent involvement, student attendance, math and reading achievement, and passing rates have increased dramatically. Enrollment has more than doubled, and there is now a waiting list of students. The school has received a variety of city, state, and national awards recognizing its development and student achievement.

Conclusion

My assumption is that most of you who read this book are either preparing for, or are already in, educational leadership roles that include some level of responsibility for facilitating professional development and school improvement. Some closing advice is: Always remember that in professional development and school improvement there are no quick fixes, no complete models, and no magic bullets. Schools are too complex, local context too important, and change too constant for there ever to be a surefire blueprint for the improvement of schools. This warning applies to this book as well as to all the other improvement theories and models found in the literature. Practitioners interested in facilitating school improvement and professional development must be willing to base improvement efforts on local student learning needs; to collaborate with local teachers, parents, and community members in establishing a vision for the future; and to mix and match models and strategies in ways that will bridge the gap between current reality and future vision.

Summary

This chapter provided guidelines for developing professional development programs and a seven-phase development cycle, including building vision, assessing needs, setting objectives, developing readiness, planning the program, implementing the program, and conducting summative evaluation. The cycle allows continuous improvement through formative evaluation of each phase, continuation of each new phase through the remainder of a cycle, and the initiation of a new cycle following summative evaluation of the previous cycle.

Assignments

1. Participate in a school vision-building process. Write a report on the activities that took place during the process, the resulting vision statement, and your perceptions of the quality of the vision-building process.
2. Participate in a school improvement and/or professional development needs assessment. Write a report on the needs assessment, including a review of data sources, data gathering methods, and the identified needs.
3. Participate in the planning of a long-term school improvement and/or professional development program. Write a report, including a review of the program's general purpose, objectives, planned activities, and program evaluation plan.
4. Participate in the evaluation of a professional development program. Write a report including a review of the evaluation's purpose, data sources, data gathering methods, data analysis methods, results, and recommendations.
5. Review a model (different from the model presented in this chapter) for developing a school improvement and/or professional development program. Write a paper comparing and contrasting the model you have reviewed to the model presented in this chapter.

References

Ackley, D. (2001). Data analysis demystified. *Leadership 31*(2), 28–29, 37–38.

Bambino, D. (2002). Critical friends. *Educational Leadership, 59*(6), 25–27.

Bassett, P. F. (2002). Creating a vision for 21st century schools. *Independent School, 61*(2), 7–10.

Conderman, G. (2001). Program evaluation: Using multiple assessment methods to promote authentic student learning and curricular change. *Teacher Education and Special Education, 24*(4), 391–392.

Dubrovich, M. A. (2002). Student achievement data: Holding teachers accountable. *Principal, 81*(4), 30–34.

Garet, M. S., Porter, A. C., Desimone, L., Birman, B. F., & Yoon, K. S. (2001). What makes professional development effective? *American Educational Research Journal, 38*(4), 915–945.

Gordon, S. P. (1999). Ready? How effective schools know it's time to take the plunge. *Journal of Staff Development, 20*(1), 48–53.

Penta, M. Q. (2002). Student portfolios in a standardized world. *Kappa Delta Pi Record, 38*(2), 77–81.

Pierce, M. (2001). Support systems for instructional leaders. *Leadership, 30*(5), 16–18.

Routman, R. (2002). Teacher talk. *Educational Leadership, 59*(6), 32–35.

Sparks, D. (2001). Why change is so challenging for schools. *Journal of Staff Development, 22*(3), 42–47.

Willis, S. (2002). Creating a knowledge base for teaching: A conversation with James Stigler. *Educational Leadership, 59*(6), 6–11.

Resources

Gordon, S. P. (1999). Ready? How effective schools know it's time to take the plunge. *Journal of Staff Development, 20*(1), 48–53.

Guskey, T. R. (2002). Does it make a difference? Evaluating professional development. *Educational Leadership, 59*(6), 45–51.

Pierce, M. (2001). Support systems for instructional leaders. *Leadership, 30*(5), 16–18.

Sparks, D. (2001). Why change is so challenging for schools. *Journal of Staff Development, 22*(3), 42–47.

Willis, S. (2002). Creating a knowledge base for teaching: A conversation with James Stigler. *Educational Leadership, 59*(6), 6–11.

Name Index

Subject Index